MW00639686

# Combat Leader's Field Guide

0 11557 01448 8

# Code of Conduct

**FOR MEMBERS OF THE ARMED FORCES
OF THE UNITED STATES**

1. I am an American, fighting in the forces which guard my country and our way of life. I am prepared to give my life in their defense.
2. I will never surrender of my own free will. If in command, I will never surrender the members of my command while they still have means to resist.
3. If I am captured, I will continue to resist by all means available. I will make every effort to escape and aid others to escape. I will accept neither parole nor special favors from the enemy.
4. If I become a prisoner of war, I will keep faith with my fellow prisoners. I will give no information or take part in any action which might be harmful to my comrades. If I am senior, I will take command. If not, I will obey the lawful order of those appointed over me and will back them up in every way.
5. When questioned, should I become a prisoner of war, I am required to give name, rank, service number, and date of birth. I will evade answering further questions to the utmost of my ability. I will make no oral or written statements disloyal to my country and its allies or harmful to their cause.
6. I will never forget that I am an American, fighting for freedom, responsible for my actions, and dedicated to the principles which made my country free. I will trust in my God and in the United States of America.

**FOR THE GOVERNMENT OF THE UNITED STATES**

The US government also has responsibilities under the code. The Nation has pledged itself:

- To keep faith with you and stand by you as you fight for its defense;
- To care for your family and dependents; and should you be captured,
- To use every practical means to contact, support, and gain release for you and all other prisoners of war.

# Combat Leader's Field Guide

## 14th Edition

MSG Jeff Kirkham,
US Army Special Forces

STACKPOLE
BOOKS

Published by
STACKPOLE BOOKS
5067 Ritter Road
Mechanicsburg, PA 17055
www.stackpolebooks.com

Printed in the United States of America

10 9 8 7 6 5 4 3 2 1

FOURTEENTH EDITION

This book is not an official publication of the Department of Defense or Department of the Army, nor does its publication in any way imply its endorsement by these agencies. The views presented are those of the author and do not necessarily represent the views of the Department of Defense or its Components.

*Cover design by Tessa J. Sweigert*
*Cover photo by Gary Stevens*

**Library of Congress Cataloging-in-Publication Data**

Kirkham, Jeff.
    Combat leader's field guide / MSG Jeff Kirkham, US Army Special Forces. — 14th edition.
        pages cm
    Includes bibliographical references and index.
    ISBN 978-0-8117-1448-8
    1. United States. Army—Field service—Handbooks, manuals, etc. I. Title.
    UD443.J8 2015
    355.4—dc23
                                                    2014040826

# Contents

# Preface

This guide is designed to assist leaders or prospective leaders of combat infantry units or other groups that, in an emergency, must fight as infantry. The content is tactical and logistical, with administrative matter mostly omitted. When in the field, especially under stress of combat or simulated combat, the combat leader cannot instantly recall everything he has been taught. Rapid changes in the situation may cause him to assume a position for which he has not yet been trained. He will then appreciate some brief reference material to guide him. He cannot carry a "5-foot shelf" of field manuals and, unlike the staff officer or higher commander, he does not have ready access to organizational files or a library when in the field. What he needs he must carry in his pocket, condensed yet in a form approximating at-a-glance capability. This field guide has been compiled from current doctrine and field manuals with those requirements in mind. Much of the reference material is in fact a comprehensive checklist to ensure that important considerations of troop leading are not overlooked.

As with the prior edition, the material in this edition is in two parts: unit combat operations and soldier combat skills. The material in Part I focuses on dismounted infantry operations at the platoon and squad levels, including battle drills—those collective actions rapidly executed without applying a deliberate decision-making process. Indeed, a small unit's ability to accomplish its mission often depends on soldiers and leaders executing key actions quickly. Part II focuses on critical individual soldier skills necessary for battlefield effectiveness and survival.

This guide also includes the considerations applicable to how US Army doctrine addresses the range of "full-spectrum operations" across the range of conflict. When conducting full-spectrum operations, commanders combine and sequence offensive, defensive, stability, and support operations to accomplish the mission.

# Acknowledgments

Hidden between the lines of any good piece of work is the idea and source for that work. *Combat Leader's Field Guide* was originally published as the *Junior Leader's Field Notebook* in 1956; since that time, it has gone through twelve revisions, and this one will be the thirteenth, making it the fourteenth edition.

This book is a compilation of "lessons learned" from many great soldiers operating on a myriad of battlefields across the entire spectrum of military operations. It is these soldiers who deserve the credit for this book. You know who you are. Thank you for watching my back for the last two decades.

Military doctrine is evolutionary. It is rooted in scholastic research, tested in training, and then formalized by professional soldiers during real-world experiences. The complexities of modern infantry operations are truly staggering. Never in history have so many skill sets been required by so small a group as the modern infantry. Infantrymen are no longer expected to just understand ground tactics. Now they must also operate high-tech equipment, advanced weaponry, and space-age communications while combating unconventional and conventional forces in asymmetric combat. Instantaneous life-and-death decisions must be made in the blink of an eye, only to be later judged by others in air-conditioned rooms with 20/20 hindsight.

However, one thing hasn't changed—the single most important aspect of surviving in combat is constant improvement through realistic training. Train as you fight.

I would like to thank my comrades in arms, both in and out of uniform, whom I have had the pleasure of working with for the past twenty-eight years. Since 9/11, our way of thinking about military tactics has evolved by leaps and bounds, leaving us with a simple, common-sense methodology that will serve us well in future conflicts.

It is my sincere hope that some of the lessons learned in blood and incorporated into this book will help one of my future comrades.

*Jeff Kirkham*
MSG, US Army Special Forces

# PART ONE

# Unit Combat Operations

# 1

# The Battlefield

## ARMY DOCTRINE

Small-unit leaders must understand the concepts and fundamentals of Army doctrine to effectively lead in combat. The US Army's current operational doctrine holds warfighting as the Army's primary mission. It recognizes the ability of Army forces to dominate land warfare across the full spectrum of conflict, from large-scale operations to military operations other than war (MOOTW). Full-spectrum operations include offensive, defensive, stability, and support operations. Army commanders may combine these different types either simultaneously or sequentially to accomplish the missions of war. For each mission, the joint force commander and Army component commander determine the emphasis Army forces place on each type of operation. Offensive and defensive operations normally dominate.

The foundations of full-spectrum operations are *fundamentals*, *battle command*, and *conduct*.

## FUNDAMENTALS

The fundamentals of full-spectrum operations are the *elements of combat power*, the *principles of war*, the *tenets of Army operations*, and the *operational framework*.

### The Elements of Combat Power

The elements of combat power are building blocks that underlie the Army's ability to dominate land warfare. Commanders combine and apply the elements of combat power to produce overwhelming effects.

*Maneuver.* Maneuver is the employment of forces, through movement combined with fire or fire potential, to achieve a position of advantage with respect to the enemy. It is the means by which commanders concentrate combat power to achieve surprise, shock, momentum, and dominance.

*Firepower.* Firepower provides the destructive force essential to overcoming the enemy's ability and will to fight. Firepower and maneuver complement each other. Firepower magnifies the effects of maneuver by destroying enemy forces and restricting their ability to counter friendly actions; maneuver creates the conditions for the effective use of firepower. The threat of one in the presence of the other magnifies the impact of both. One without the other makes neither decisive.

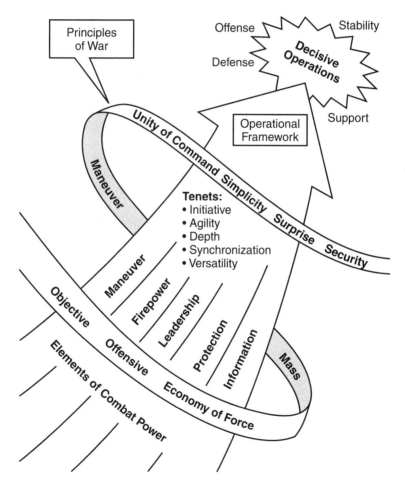

**Fundamentals of Full-Spectrum Operations**

*Leadership.* Because it deals directly with soldiers, leadership is the most dynamic element of combat power. Confident, audacious, and competent leadership focuses available combat power and creates the conditions for success. Leaders who embody the warrior ethos inspire soldiers to succeed. They provide purpose, direction, and motivation in all operations, especially in small units.

*Protection.* Protection is the preservation of the fighting capacity of a force so that the commander can apply it at the decisive time and place. It consists of force protection, field discipline, safety, and avoidance of fratricide.

*Information.* Information enhances leadership and magnifies the effects of maneuver, firepower, and protection. Today, Army leaders use information collected by manned and unmanned systems to increase their understanding of the common operational picture (COP) before engaging the enemy.

## The Principles of War
The nine principles of war provide general guidance for conducting war and military operations other than war at the strategic, operational, and tactical levels. They do not apply in the same way to every situation. Rather, they summarize the characteristics of successful Army operations.

*Objective.* Direct every military operation toward a clearly defined, decisive, and attainable objective. The ultimate military purpose of war is the destruction of the enemy's armed forces and its will to fight. In operations other than war, the ultimate objective might be more difficult to define, but it must be clear from the beginning.

*Offensive.* Seize, retain, and exploit the initiative. Offensive action is the most effective and decisive way to attain a clearly defined common objective.

*Mass.* Mass is the act of bringing overwhelming combat power to bear at the decisive place and time. To achieve mass, you must synchronize all the elements of combat power where they will have decisive effect on an enemy force in a short time.

*Economy of Force.* Economy of force is the judicious employment and distribution of forces in order to achieve mass elsewhere. Allocate minimum essential combat power to secondary efforts.

*Maneuver.* Place the enemy in a position of disadvantage through the flexible application of combat power. Maneuver is the movement of forces in relation to the enemy to secure or retain positional advantage.

*Unity of Command.* For every objective, seek unity of effort under one responsible commander. At all levels of war, employment of forces in a manner that masses combat power toward a common objective requires unity of command and unity of effort.

*Security.* Never permit the enemy to acquire unexpected advantage. Security results from the measures taken by a commander to protect his forces.

*Surprise.* Strike the enemy at a time or place or in a manner for which he is unprepared. The element of surprise can allow forces to achieve success well out of proportion to the effort expended.

*Simplicity.* Prepare clear, uncomplicated plans and concise orders to ensure thorough understanding. Other factors being equal, the simplest plan is preferable.

## The Tenets of Army Operations

The fundamental tenets of Army operations describe characteristics of successful operations, which build on the principles of war. The US Army asserts that the five basic tenets are the keys to victory. In and of themselves, they do not guarantee victory, but their absence makes victory difficult and costly to achieve.

*Initiative.* Initiative means setting or changing the terms of battle by action. Infantry forces attempt to maintain their freedom of action while limiting the enemy's. This requires an offensive spirit in all operations. Decentralized operations in which small units aggressively fight through enemy resistance with the immediately available resources support the seizure or retention of the initiative. Individuals act independently within the framework of their commander's concept. Leaders and soldiers must understand the intent of commanders two echelons above. Commanders use mission-type orders and clear, concise instructions to ensure that subordinates understand the concept and how they fit within it.

*Agility.* Infantry forces seize or retain the initiative by acting and/or reacting faster than the enemy. This begins with the commander, who must have the mental agility to rapidly analyze tactical situations, think through many possible courses of action and the enemy's likely reaction to them, and determine the most effective and least costly course. Standing operating procedures (SOPs) and drills enable the unit to rapidly execute assigned missions without long, detailed orders.

*Depth.* Depth is the extension of operations in time, space, and resources. A commander seeks to fight the enemy throughout the depth of the enemy's formations by properly positioning his forces or by skillfully maneuvering his unit. This allows the unit to seek out and concentrate against enemy weaknesses. By swiftly concentrating against first one, then another enemy weakness, a skilled commander can begin to seize the initiative on a local level, allowing a higher commander to then exploit the opportunity.

*Synchronization.* Synchronization is the arrangement of battlefield activities in time, space, and purpose to produce maximum combat power at the decisive point. A commander synchronizes his subordinates' actions on the battlefield by assigning clear missions, making understood the timing required in the operation, and focusing all actions toward achieving overwhelming combat power at a decisive point. Issuing orders, identifying the main effort, and assigning clear tasks and purposes to each subordinate element are the best means of maintaining synchronization in a fast-paced, fluid environment.

*Versatility.* Versatility is the ability of tactical units to adapt to different missions and tasks. In a force-projection army, the demands for versatility increase. Forces must be prepared to move rapidly from one region to another, one type of warfare to another, and one form of combat to another. This was admirably displayed in the war with Iraq, when US forces switched from a conventional combat mode to a counterinsurgency mode in a matter of days.

## The Operational Framework

The operational framework consists of the arrangement of friendly forces and resources in time, space, and purpose with respect to each other and the enemy or situation. It consists of the *area of operation, battlespace,* and the *battlefield organization.* The framework establishes an area of geographic and operational responsibility and provides a way for commanders to visualize how to employ forces against the enemy. Commanders design an operational framework to accomplish their mission by identifying and arranging its three components. They use the operational framework to focus combat power.

## BATTLE COMMAND

*Battle command is the leadership element of combat power.* It is principally an art that employs skills developed by professional study, constant practice, and considered judgment. Commanders, assisted by the staff, visualize and describe the operation in terms of intent and guidance, and direct the actions of subordinates within their intent. Commanders direct operations in terms of the battlefield operating systems (BOS). They directly influence operations by their personal presence, supported by their command and control ($C^2$) system.

Full-spectrum operations generally follow a cycle of *planning, preparation, execution,* and *continuous assessment.* Battle command, however, is what drives the operations process. Army forces design and conduct operations to win on the offensive; dictate the terms of combat and avoid fighting the enemy on his terms; seize and retain the initiative; and build momentum quickly to win decisively. For more information on full-spectrum operations and battle command, review Army Field Manual (FM) 3-0, Operations.

## BASIC RULES OF COMBAT
These rules appeared in Army doctrine for a short time but are no longer included in recent publications. At the small-unit level, however, they encompass the essence of the above fundamentals.

### Secure
Use cover and concealment
Establish local security and conduct reconnaissance
Protect the unit

### Move
Establish a moving element
Get in the best position to shoot
Gain and maintain the initiative
Move fast, strike hard, and finish rapidly

### Shoot
Establish a base of fire
Maintain mutual support
Kill or suppress the enemy

### Communicate
Keep everybody informed
Tell soldiers what is expected

### Sustain
Keep the fight going
Take care of soldiers

# 2

# Command and Control

Command and control ($C^2$) refers to the process of directing, coordinating, and controlling a unit to accomplish a mission. $C^2$ implements the commander's will in pursuit of the unit's mission. The two components of $C^2$ are the commander and the system. The command and control system includes all collective tasks associated with supporting the exercise of authority and direction by a properly designated commander over assigned and available forces in the accomplishment of the mission. Leadership is what gets these tasks done effectively.

## THE PRINCIPLES OF LEADERSHIP
There are nine basic principles of leadership:
- Be technically and tactically proficient (have a solid working knowledge of your unit's weapons and tactics).
- Know your unit, your soldiers, and your capabilities (build this knowledge base to ensure success on the battlefield and limit casualties).
- Seek responsibility (perpetuate the constant improvement of soldiers, weapons, and equipment).
- Make sound and timely decisions (complete complex problem-solving exercises in preparation for combat).
- Set the example (be the leader that you would want to follow).
- Keep subordinates informed (all soldiers must know the plan).
- Develop a sense of responsibility in subordinates (give the commander's intent with left and right limits).
- Build the team (realistic training is the best way to accomplish this).
- Employ your unit in accordance with (IAW) its capabilities (set your soldiers up for success by working within your unit's strengths).

## INFANTRY LEADERS
The infantry leader must be able to make complex decisions in order to preserve his force and accomplish the mission. The infantry leader is closest to

the fight and must be resourceful, tenacious, and decisive as well as a tactician. Leaders in other branches must also on occasion act as infantry leaders. The leader must understand and use initiative in accomplishing a mission; he cannot rely on a book to solve tactical problems. He is expected to lead by example, be at the point of decision to maintain control, understand the situation, and issue orders when required. This means that he must know how to quickly analyze a situation and make decisions in light of the commander's intent. He must be prepared to take independent action if necessary. The art of making quick, sound decisions lies in the knowledge of tactics, the military estimate process, and platoon and squad (small-unit) techniques and procedures. Infantry leaders are physically tough, technically knowledgeable, and mentally agile, and have a firm grasp of how to motivate soldiers to fight in the face of adversity.

Understanding the complexities of the battlefield means that infantry units must fight as coordinated, cohesive units or suffer the inevitable consequences of defeat. Key to this understanding is the knowledge of the duties and responsibilities of each member of the unit.

The following are the duties and responsibilities of each member of the platoon during the planning process. This does not include all duties, but is a base to work from.

### Platoon/Patrol Leader

Post the time schedule (backwards plan)
Develop the course of action (COA)
Write paragraphs 1 (Situation), 2 (Mission), and 3 (Execution)
Request/assign additional support if needed
Follow the coordination checklist:
     Intelligence; Operations; Adjacent units; Fires; Air
Supervise the soldiers as they prepare, rehearse, and complete the plan
Give the priority of rehearsals:
     Actions on the objective; Actions at linkup; Actions on contact;
       Actions during contact
Know where your unit's elements are at all times
Plan routes and create overlays

### Platoon Sergeant/Assistant Patrol Leader

Help the platoon leader
Write paragraph 4 (Service Support)
Supervise paragraph 5 (Command and Signal)
Coordinate with medics and identify aid and litter teams
Identify the casualty collection point (CCP)

Task organize the support element
Reorganize men, weapons, and equipment as needed in support of
   operation
Provide status reports to commander (keep all informed)
Identify the objective rally point (ORP)
Identify en route rally points
Participate in route planning and creation of overlays
Determine actions at halts as per S-2 (intelligence) brief
Plan for supporting security elements
Know where your unit's elements are at all times
Enforce the six priorities of work in the patrol base (PB) or forward
   operations base (FOB):
   Security plan; Maintenance plan; Hygiene plan; Water plan; Mess
   plan; Rest plan
Maintain the sensitive items list (three copies)

**Squad Leader**
Control the squad
Rotate heavy loads
Prepare for assault, support, and security
Help with paragraphs 1 (Situation), 3 (Execution), and 5 (Command
   and Signal)
Help with the entire planning process (squad mission responsibilities)
Assist with route planning and overlays

**Weapons Squad Leader**
Rotate heavy loads
Determine the tactical employment of crew-served weapons
Assist with paragraphs 1 (Situation) and 3 (Execution)

**Team Leader**
Lead by example
Identify and request supplies for the team
Inspect supplies for deficiencies
Prepare the terrain model and SOP sketches
Post maps, photos, and any visual reference materials
Ready the briefing area for the operations order (OPORD)
Request and coordinate for the rehearsal area
Start rehearsals with the squad leader's guidance
Assist with route planning and overlays

## Medic

Control the aid and litter teams
Organize and ID the casualty collection point (CCP)
Triage and treat the wounded
Determine evacuation (ground or air)
Ensure the hygiene and health of soldiers
Supervise first aid training
Inspect individual first aid kits (IFAK)
Inspect vehicle first aid kits, including trucks and casualty evacuation
(CASEVAC) helicopter if possible
Determine procedure to move wounded and killed in action (KIA)
from target
Assist with paragraphs 3 (Execution) and 4 (Service Support)
Be prepared to brief medical portion of operations order (OPORD)

## Radio Operator

All communication issues (crypto, hop sets, frequencies, timing,
program radios, etc.)
Maintain a frequency card to communicate with all friendlies (ground
and air)
Ensure unit knows all passwords and checkpoint procedures
Maintain patrol log and en route recorder
Prepare the size, activity, location, uniform, time, and equipment
(SALUTE) report
Prepare any situation reports (SITREP)
Prepare sketches and grid reference graphic (GRG)
Assist with overlays (determine any communication blackout areas)
Assist with paragraph 5 (Command and Signal)

## Forward Observer

Plan for all fires
Coordinate all fire support
Be prepared to follow theater SOP for call for fire
Create overlays—determine target reference points (TRP)
Assist with paragraphs 3 (Execution) and 5 (Command and Signal)

## Mobility Element Leader

Ensure all vehicles are in a state of readiness
Check and confirm vehicle load plan
Coordinate with gunners
Handle all aspects of route planning
Prepare overlays (routes and checkpoints)

Coordinate for security, blocking positions, ambulance, and route
  reconnaissance
Provide helicopter landing zone (HLZ) security
Determine actions at halts

**Breachers/EOD**
Identify primary/alternate breach point (door, window, wall, etc.)
Prepare for breach (surreptitious, ladder, mechanical, ballistic,
  thermal, explosive)
Plan for destruction of captured equipment using blow in place
  (BIP) kit
Assist with paragraph 3 (Execution)
Prepare room for operations order (OPORD)

**Reserve Element Leader**
Prepare for sensitive site exploitation (SSE)
Take control of/secure enemy prisoners of war (EPW)
Ensure interpreters (TERP) are standing by for rehearsals/operations
  order (OPORD)
Organize battlefield interrogation team (BIT)
Reinforce mail element if/when necessary
Plan for helicopter landing zone (HLZ)
Assist with paragraphs 1 (Situation) and 3 (Execution)

**Reconnaissance/Sniper Section**
Perform route reconnaissance
Perform close-target reconnaissance (CTR)
Plan for objective reconnaissance (leader's recon)
Prepare overlays (fields of fire and known danger areas along route)
Determine sniper employment and primary/alternate positions
Be prepared for overwatch security where needed
Assist with paragraphs 3 (Execution), 4 (Service Support), and 5
  (Command and Signal)

The listed duties and responsibilities of unit members enable unit success. For example:
- The *assault element* seizes the objective and protects special teams
  during post assault.
- The *security element* isolates and supports withdrawal from the
  objective.

- The *support element* handles direct- and indirect-fire support for the unit and cordons off the target area.
- *Command and control* handles conflicts with internal elements, friendly units, and follow-on objectives or targets, and coordinates fire support.

## MISSION-ORIENTED COMMAND AND CONTROL

The mission-oriented $C^2$ (or mission control) both encourages and helps subordinates to act within the intent and concept of both the battalion and company commanders. Mission-oriented $C^2$ requires that subordinate elements clearly understand the purpose and intent of their commanders two levels up. This allows them the freedom to respond, with disciplined initiative, to the changing situation without further guidance. With mission-oriented $C^2$, the combat leader must:

**Expect Uncertainty.** Understand that the impact of combat and dynamic battle conditions may challenge the leader's ability to know what is happening, even in his immediate area of operation (AO).

**Reduce Leader Intervention.** Adopt the principle that trained subordinates with a clear understanding of the mission will accomplish the task when subordinates must act without leader guidance or intervention.

**Optimize Planning Time for Subordinates.** Ensure that the timelines developed for mission planning and preparation allow adequate troop leading time for the subordinate leaders.

**Allow Maximum Freedom of Action for Subordinates.** Given the expected battlefield conditions, avoid unnecessary limits on soldiers' freedom of action. Soldiers win battles; place them where they can seize the opportunity to do so.

**Encourage Cross Talk.** In some instances, because of their position on the battlefield, two or more subordinates working together may have on-site information that enhances the leader's understanding of the situation, thus providing a clearer view of what is happening. Encourage the sharing of this information.

**Lead Well Forward.** The leader positions himself where he can best employ his unit and make critical decisions to influence the outcome of the fight. This is normally a position with the main effort.

**Battlefield Environment.** The framework of the battlefield can vary, ranging from one extreme of front and rear (linear) to a dispersed, decentralized (noncontiguous) structure with few secure areas and unit boundaries. To visualize the battlefield accurately, the leader must know the friendly situation at least one level higher. The leader must also know the enemy situation and continuously analyze and reform his strategy based on how he sees the operational picture.

When a unit member assumes command of the unit at any point in the operation, he should execute the following duties:

Inform subordinate leaders and higher headquarters (HHQ)
Check security
Check crew-served weapons
Pinpoint unit location
Coordinate as needed with other units/headquarters (HQ)
Check all soldiers, weapons, and equipment and update status
    report/card
Issue a fragmentary order (FRAGO) if needed
Reorganize as needed and maintain unit integrity
Enforce noise and light discipline
Conduct patrol base activities (six priorities of work)
Conduct reconnaissance if needed
Finalize the plan
Execute mission

## EIGHT TROOP-LEADING PROCEDURES

Troop-leading procedures (TLPs) begin when the unit leader receives the first indication of an upcoming mission and continue throughout the operations process (plan, prepare, execute, and assess). They comprise a sequence of actions that help leaders use available time effectively and efficiently to issue and execute tactical operations.

Planning in a field environment will likely reduce the amount of time leaders have for in-depth mission planning. If followed, the TLPs will provide leaders with a framework for mission planning in a time-constrained environment.

---

**THE EIGHT TLPS**
1. Receive the mission from higher command.
2. Issue the warning order (WARNORD) to your unit.
3. Make a tentative plan.
4. Start movement.
5. Conduct reconnaissance.
6. Complete the plan.
7. Issue the complete order.
8. Supervise and refine.

### Step 1. Receive the Mission

The leader may receive the mission in a warning order (WARNORD), an operation order (OPORD), a fragmentary order (FRAGO), or verbally. He immediately begins to analyze it using the factors of METT-TC:

- What is the *mission*?
- What is known about the *enemy*?
- How will *terrain* and *weather* affect the operation?
- What *troops* are available?
- How much *time* is available?
- Are there *civilian* considerations?

### Troop-Leading Procedures

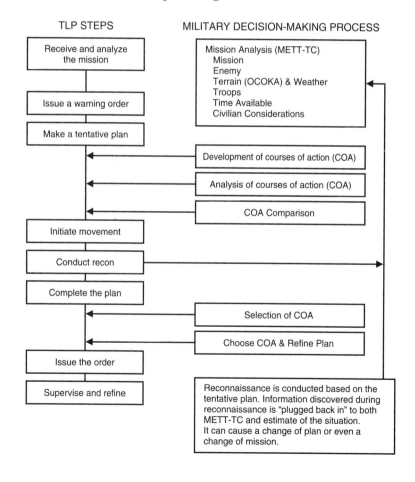

The leader should use no more than one-third of the available time for planning and for issuing his OPORD. The remaining two-thirds should be for subordinates to plan, prepare, and rehearse for the operation, with the majority spent on rehearsal.

A leader should backwards plan, all the while taking into consideration other factors such as available daylight and travel time to and from orders or rehearsals. This is reverse planning; he must allow enough time for the completion of each task. The leader should not become involved in a detailed METT-TC analysis—this will occur after he issues the initial WARNORD.

**Step 2. Issue a Warning Order**
The warning order (WARNORD) should identify the following:
- Number/code name.
- All visual references (maps, imagery, sand tables, etc.).
- Time zone used throughout the order.
- Task organization (list obvious persons/teams that will be involved).

*1. Situation*
Enemy forces:
Special considerations needed for the planning process; Known courses of action; Tactics, techniques, and procedures (TTP)
Friendly forces:
Higher commander's mission and Higher commander's intent
Attachments/detachments:
Who and what job or skill is needed for mission
*2. Mission*
Who; What (task); Where; Why (purpose); When
*3. Execution*
Chain of command
Concept of the operation
Maneuver units:
Reconnaissance; Assault; Security; Support; Command and control; Special teams; Combat support units
General instructions:
Uniforms and equipment common to all persons and vehicles
Weapons, ammo, and equipment needed in addition to SOP
Special equipment
Time schedule
Commander's critical intelligence requirements (CCIR)
Risk guidance
Deception guidance
Specific priorities in order of completion
Time, place, and uniform for receiving the OPORD

Time and place for inspections and rehearsals
Earliest movement time and notice time
Special instructions to all subordinate leaders:
Drawing, checking, and distributing (weapons, ammo,
equipment, rations, and water)
Special equipment
Attachments and detachments
Transportation (ID requirements, pre-positioning, familiarization)
Inspections, rehearsals, and preparing soldiers for the mission
Reconnaissance
Persons assisting with OPORD preparation

**4. Service Support**
Coordination for the transfer of equipment and supplies to or from
other units
Coordination for transport to or from the HLZ, rehearsal area,
briefing, etc.

**5. Command and Signal**
Chain of command
Identify current signal requirements
Determine what fire support assets are available
Begin mission-supporting direct- or indirect-fire (FIRES)
coordination

| Who | Frequency | Call Sign |
|---|---|---|
| Battalion (Bn) Command | | |
| Fire Support | | |
| MEDEVAC | | |
| Company | | |
| Platoon | | |
| Platoon Sergeant | | |
| 1st Squad Leader | | |
| 2nd Squad Leader | | |
| 3rd Squad Leader | | |
| Weapons Squad | | |

## Step 3. Make a Tentative Plan
There are five key steps to making a tentative plan:
1. Understand the commander's intent.
2. Identify the unit's specific and implied tasks:
Specific tasks are written/directed in the OPORD
Implied tasks become apparent during mission analysis

3. Identify limitations: equipment shortages, time, phase lines, etc.
4. List mission-essential tasks that ensure mission success.
5. Review mission statement to clarify mission-essential tasks and purpose: Who (unit); What (tasks); When (critical times); Where (grid location and target description); Why (purpose the unit must achieve).

The leader should overall ensure that the plan is feasible, reasonable, and distinguishable.

The leader must also consider the factors of METT-TC:

*(M) Mission.* The leader considers the mission given to him by his commander and analyzes it in light of the *commander's intent* two command levels higher. He derives the specified task, essential tasks, implied tasks, and limitations and/or constraints of the mission.

*(E) Enemy.* The leader considers the type, size, organization, tactics, and equipment of the enemy he expects to encounter. He identifies the greatest threat to his mission and the enemy's greatest vulnerability.

*(T) Terrain and Weather.* The leader considers the effect of terrain and weather on enemy and friendly forces using the guidelines below (OCOKA):

- *(O) Observation and fields of fire.* The leader considers ground that allows him observation of the enemy throughout his area of operation. He considers fields of fire in terms of the characteristics of the weapons available to him, for example maximum effective range, the requirement for grazing fire, and the arming range and time of flight for antiarmor weapons.
- *(C) Cover and concealment.* The leader looks for terrain that will protect him from direct and indirect fires (cover) and from aerial and ground observation (concealment).
- *(O) Obstacles.* In the attack, the leader considers the effect of restrictive terrain on his ability to maneuver. In the defense, he considers how he will tie in his obstacles to the terrain to disrupt, turn, fix, or block an enemy force and protect his own forces from enemy assault.
- *(K) Key terrain.* Key terrain is any locality or area whose seizure or retention affords a marked advantage to either combatant. The leader considers key terrain in his selection of objectives, support positions, and routes in the offense and in the positioning of his unit in the defense.
- *(A) Avenues of approach.* An avenue of approach is an air or ground route of an attacking force leading to its objective or key terrain in its path. In the offense, the leader identifies the avenue of approach that affords him the greatest protection and places him at the enemy's most

vulnerable spot. In the defense, the leader positions his key weapons along the avenue of approach most likely to be used by the enemy. In considering the effects of weather, the leader is most interested in visibility and trafficability.

*(T) Troops Available.* The leader considers the strength of subordinate units, the characteristics of his weapon systems, and the capabilities of attached elements as he assigns tasks to subordinate units.

*(T) Time Available.* The leader refines his allocation of time based on the tentative plan and any changes in the situation.

*(C) Civilian Considerations.* The leader identifies any civilian considerations that may affect the mission. These factors may include refugees, humanitarian assistance requirements, or specific considerations related to the applicable rules of engagement (ROE) or rules of interaction (ROI).

## Step 4. Initiate Movement
The unit may need to begin moving soldiers, weapons, or equipment in preparation for the upcoming mission. Initiation of movement can include additional troops, reconnaissance, troop movers, and consolidation on the staging area.

## Step 5. Reconnoiter
Reconnaissance will come in many forms. On today's modern battlefield there are multiple options at the disposal of the combat leader. These include low-visibility operations for route screening, close-target reconnaissance, and intelligence surveillance reconnaissance (ISR) aircraft. Leaders can also review all available imagery, maps, and human intelligence (HUMINT) reports. A good combat leader will use as many assets as possible to gain the knowledge he needs to make sound decisions that will enable the unit to make it successfully to the objective and back to a secure area.

## Step 6. Complete the Plan
Completion of the plan includes several actions that transform the commander's intent and concept and the platoon's concept into a fully developed platoon OPORD. These actions include preparing overlays, refining the indirect-fires list, completing combat service support (CSS) and $C^2$ requirements, and updating the tentative plan as a result of the reconnaissance or information updates. Completing the plan allows the platoon leader to make final coordination (coordination checklist) with other units or the commander before issuing the OPORD to his subordinates. It also enables him to prepare his briefing site and materials.

**Step 7. Issue the Complete Order**
Platoon and squad leaders normally issue oral OPORDs. The best way to brief an OPORD is for each sub-unit leader to brief his own portion of the mission. This provides confirmation to senior leaders that each portion of the mission is fully understood by the sub-unit performing that task. For example, the assault commander should brief the "actions on the objective" portion and the medic should brief the medical portion. To aid in the understanding of the concept of the operation, leaders should use a sand table, sketches, and maps. It is essential that all persons conducting the mission understand the objective, the commander's intent, the concept of the operation, and their assigned tasks. Rehearsals are the time for leaders to watch and ask questions about the mission to ensure they and their soldiers understand what is required of them.

**Step 8. Supervise and Refine**
Leaders supervise the preparation for combat by conducting confirmation briefs to ensure subordinates know the mission, the commander's intent, the concept of the operation, and their assigned tasks. Rehearsals confirm to the leader that soldiers understand the mission and what is expected of the unit.

*Rehearsals.* Rehearsals are the single most effective means to ensure mission success. They will show where and how a plan needs to be refined. The closer to the actual mission a rehearsal is, the better. Emergency plans, reporting, wounded, and fire support are among the tasks that should be exercised.

Rehearsals will help infantry leaders discover and identify the unknowns. They should accomplish the following:
- Practice essential tasks (improve performance).
- Reveal weaknesses or problems in the plan.
- Coordinate the actions of subordinate elements.
- Improve soldier understanding of the concept of the operation (foster confidence in soldiers).

The leader should conduct rehearsals on terrain that resembles the actual ground and in similar light conditions. The platoon may begin rehearsals of battle drills and other SOP items before the receipt of the OPORD. Once the order has been issued, the platoon can rehearse mission-specific tasks.

Some important tasks to rehearse include:
- Action on the objective.
- Assaulting a trench, bunker, or building.

- Actions at the assault position.
- Breaching obstacles (mine or wire).
- Using specific weapons or demolitions.
- Actions on unexpected enemy contact.

***Pre-combat Inspection.*** Squad leaders should conduct initial inspections shortly after receipt of the warning order. The platoon sergeant spot-checks the unit's preparation for combat. The platoon leader and platoon sergeant make a final inspection of the following:

- Weapons and ammunition.
- Uniforms and equipment.
- Mission-essential equipment.
- Soldiers' understanding of mission and their specific responsibilities.
- Communications.
- Rations and water.
- Camouflage.
- Deficiencies noted during earlier inspections.

*Note:* Pre-combat inspections do not take the place of final combat inspections.

## COMBAT ORDERS
### Operation Order
An operation order (OPORD) is a directive issued by the leader to his subordinate leaders to effect the coordinated execution of a specific operation. The leader and sub-unit leaders brief the OPORD using briefing aids while following the five-paragraph format below.

Copy number ___ of ___ copies
Issuing HQ
Place of issue
Date/time group
Message reference number
Operation order number/code name
References used (maps, imagery, sketches, sand table, etc.)
Time zone (local or Zulu)
Rules of engagement
Task organization (essential elements for mission):
    Orient the unit to the maps with friendly and enemy locations
    If the task organization is long or complicated, use an annex
Effects of weather, light, and general forecast on friendly and enemy
    forces

| High Temp | Moonrise | Sunrise |
|---|---|---|
| Low Temp | Moonset | Sunset |
| Wind Speed | Moon Phase | EENT (ending evening nautical twilight) |
| Wind Direction | % Illumination | BMNT (begin morning nautical twilight) |
| Prayer Times | Wake Times | Sleep Times |

*Note*: Activity levels vary with the season. For example, persons may sleep on the roof in the summer, retire early in the winter, and sleep in the fields during the planting season. During Ramadan, the population lives on a reverse schedule, sleeping during the day and staying up late at night.

Terrain and effects on friendly and enemy forces
OAKOC + water:
> Obstacles; Avenues of approach; Key terrain; Observation and fields of fire; Cover and concealment; Water sources

## 1. Situation
Enemy forces:
> Composition; Identification (clothing, weapons, tactics); Location (known and suspected); Activity (recent or past that apply); Strength; Morale; Capabilities (tactics, equipment); Reaction time for reinforcements; Probable locations and ingress routes of reinforcements; Civilians on the battlefield; Most dangerous course of action; Most probable course of action

*Note*: The rules of engagement are derived from this information, and it is vital in case of a critical incident.

Friendly forces:
> Commander's intent one and two levels up (overall picture); Locations of units to the left, right, front, and rear; Location of checkpoints and the procedure to pass; Other forces' operations in the objective, task, and purpose; Effect on the operation

Units providing fire support:
> Close-air support; Emergency close-air support; Indirect-fire support; Direct-fire support; Intelligence, surveillance, and reconnaissance (ISR); Quick reaction force (QRF)

Attachments (state at what point persons will become attached):
> Liaison officer for joint-unit operations; Interpreters; Explosive ordnance disposal (EOD); Medical; Battlefield interrogation team (BIT); Civil affairs (CA); Psychological operations; Host

nation government representatives; Host nation troops; Host
nation females (for women and children on target)
Detachments (state at what point persons will become detached):
    Cross-loading of personnel; Liaison officer (L/O) for joint-unit
    operations; Unit members in support of host nation troops; Any
    changes to unit manning SOP

## 2. Mission

Who; What (task); Where; When; Why (purpose)
*Note*: State the mission twice.

## 3. Execution

*Concept of the Operation.* This is a brief snapshot explanation of the mission, based on the COA. Use all available maps, imagery, sketches, and terrain models and include the following:

Describe the operation without in-depth details:
    Main effort; Major maneuver units; Special teams; Intelligence;
    Reconnaissance; Infiltration; Security; Actions on the
    objective; Exfiltration
Determine the fire support plan:
    How is it going to support the maneuver? What fire support assets
    are available?
Prepare for follow on missions

*Maneuver.* This section describes in detail what is going to happen on the mission. If possible, it should be briefed by the element leader in charge of the portion. This section should include:

Detailed responsibilities and mechanics for subordinate unit leaders
Routes (primary/alternate)
Travel time to the target
Main assault effort
Supporting assault, breaching, and snipers
Outside target security, command and control, and casualties
Cordon security
Special teams
Attachments (task and purpose)
Engagement and disengagement criteria
Alternate plan:
    Compromise; Unplanned movement of the enemy
Withdrawal plan
Travel time back to friendly lines
GOTWA 5-point contingency plan, issued any time an element leaves
    the main body:

Going (location the parting element is going to); Others (all personnel that are going); Time (estimated time of return); What (what should be done if unit does not return); Actions (if enemy contact, what both parties will do)

Fires:

Identify the forward observer (FO)
Identify the controller (CAS)
Identify supporting unit(s)
CAS availability:
Dedicated? ECAS (Emergency)?
Scheme of fire to support overall mission
Purpose of fires
Types of available fire support
How much time to receive fire support?
Types of available ammunition
Special equipment needed (laser designator, strobe light, VS-17 panel, etc.)
Priority of fire (main effort)
Allocations of fire
Target list/worksheet/overlay—target reference points (TRP) and known position

Control measures:

Checkpoints; Boundaries; Phase lines; Coordination measures; Restrictions of fire; No-fire areas
Specific targets, if any (before, during, and after the operation)—pre-assault and post-assault fires

Precoordinated authentication
Communication frequencies (primary and alternate)

***Coordinating Instructions.*** This section should describe the following five key phases:

*Phase 1: Infiltration*

Start time (occupy the assembly area)
Order of movement (OOM)
Movement technique/means/formation
Departure of friendly lines time and method
Routes (primary and alternate)
Grid to the initial rally point (IRP)
Actions at halts
Actions on enemy contact
Bump plan
Vehicle recovery technique (SOP)
Actions at danger areas

CASEVAC technique
Success criteria
Abort criteria (minimum personnel/equipment essential)
*Phase 2: Actions on the Objective*
Times (H-hour)
Vehicle drop-off (VDO)
Objective rally point (ORP)
Leader reconnaissance/AFO
Order of movement (OOM)
Movement technique/means/formation
Last covered and concealed position (LCC)
Security positions (five-point contingency plan)
Support positions (five-point contingency plan)
Fratricide reduction measures (phase lines, friendly ID, etc.)
Rules of engagement (ROE)
Assault
C4 (command, control, commo, casualties):
     Location; Activities
Approach target
Entry
Compromised assault
Actions on enemy contact
Casualty collection point (CCP)
Persons under control (PUC) handling
Success criteria
Abort criteria
*Phase 3: Consolidate on the Target*
Secure the target
Limit of advance (LOA)
Status reports (all elements check in)
Ammo, casualties, equipment (ACE) report
PUCs, EPWs, KIAs, CCPs
*Phase 4: Sensitive Site Exploitation (SSE)*
Search techniques
Sensitive material description and marking procedures
Primary intelligence requirement (PIR)
Battlefield interrogation team (BIT)
Cataloging process for persons on target (photos, fingerprints)
Time on target (TOT) and time constraints
Success criteria
Abort criteria

*Phase 5: Withdrawal Plan*
    Predetermined time to withdraw
    Exiting procedures
    Order of movement (OOM)
    Movement technique/means/formation
    Movement of EPWs, KIAs, WIAs:
        Accountability of men, weapons, and equipment; Routes
        (primary and alternate); Actions at halts; Enemy contact
        action plan; Actions at danger areas; Re-entry of friendly
        lines (SOP to pass through lines); Anticipated time of
        return; Linkup procedures (passing checkpoints,
        convoys, etc.)
    Fratricide reduction measures (phase lines, friendly force ID)
    Escape and evade (E&E), go-to-hell plan (safe haven location)
    Detailed time schedule posted:
        Inspections; Rehearsals; Time of rehearsals and of departure;
        Time of operation; Time of return

**4. Service Support**
    Rations, ammo, weapons, medical supply, repair parts, etc.
    Location of additional supplies
    Destruction plan (own equipment and enemy equipment)
    Point of contact (POC) for supply requirements (S-4)
    Locations of helicopter landing zones (HLZ)
    Transportation to assembly area (AA), airfields, etc.
    MWR support (showers, chow hall, gym, laundry, PX)
    Maintenance/storage facilities for vehicles and sensitive items
    ***Medical.*** This section describes in detail the responsibilities of all medical personnel on the mission. It should include:
    Identification of medics
    Medic location throughout operation
    Health and hygiene of unit
    Casualty collection point (CCP) location and markings
    SOP for moving and marking wounded
    Priorities for medical treatment and movement
    SOP for individual first aid kit (IFAK) contents and location
    SOP for tourniquets location
    Medical evacuation (land, air, or combination)
    Grid locations for CASEVAC HLZs (primary/alternate)
    Location of hospitals (grid and route)
    Call sign, frequency, and phone number of hospital
    Precoordinated POC in hospital and phone number

Grid of hospital HLZ
Call sign and frequency of CASEVAC
CASEVAC SOP for medical equipment
CASEVAC theater SOP:
> Alerting CASEVAC; HLZ set-up and far and near recognition
> signals; Loading of wounded; Additional considerations

Precoordination with medical facility:
> Facility on standby; Ready to receive; Special equipment/skill
> sets on standby

**5. *Command and Signal***
Chain of command:
> Location of higher commander, C2/C4, and key
> Location of key personnel (see task organization):
>> During each phase of operation; During actions on the
>> objective; During movement
>
> Succession of command/assumption of command
> Adjustments to unit SOP

Signal:
> Current signal operating instructions in effect/will remain
> throughout the operation; Methods of communication—PACE
> (primary, alternate, contingency, emergency); Electronic;
> Visual (laser, lights, hand and arm, pyrotechnic, etc.)

| Who | Frequency | Call Sign |
|---|---|---|
| B Command | | |
| Fire Support | | |
| MEDEVAC | | |
| Company | | |
| Platoon | | |
| Platoon Sergeant | | |
| 1st Squad Leader | | |
| 2nd Squad Leader | | |
| 3rd Squad Leader | | |
| Weapons Squad | | |

Verbal:

Challenge password (number/code) _____

Running password _____

Pro-words (initiate action) _____

Code words (conceal activity) _____

Brevity code (conceal/shorten SITREP) _____

Identify friendly forces (IFF):
    Uniform/equipment; Glint tape/flag; IR chemlight; IR strobe
      light; Other
    Special instructions to communications soldier
    Unit SOP for five-point contingency plan (GOTWA)

The OPORD should conclude with a space for questions, annexes (see next section), and time hack (common time from the GPS).

## ANNEXES

Operation order annexes are *necessary* to facilitate understanding of complex or critical tasks by the main effort and supporting units.
Information issued in annex form can include:

• Fire support.
• Air assault.
• Aerial resupply.
• Truck movement.
• Patrol base.
• Linkup.
• Any other complex part of the overall mission.

Annexes are prepared for supporting units whose portion of the mission is not addressed thoroughly enough in the OPORD, or when a supporting unit sends a representative for the OPORD and not the whole supporting unit. For example, an entire artillery unit will not attend the OPORD briefing but will need clear concise information on the best way to support the mission. Annexes are always issued after the operations order. Some examples are below.

### Fire Support Annex

Reference: map, fire support overlay
*1. Situation*
    Enemy forces (reference the base document)
    Friendly forces:
        Location of units that are/may provide fire support; Fire support
          plans of supporting units (if known); Additional fire support
          resources that may become available (air, naval gunfire,
          artillery, mortars, etc.)
*2. Mission*
    Who; What (fire support tasks); Where; When; Why (purpose)

*3. Execution*

    Concept of the operation:

        What is the mission; Major groupings of fire means/needs;

            Priority of fires; Targets (how many/grids)

    Air support:

        Task(s); Priorities to ground units; Specific control arrangements;

            Control measures

    Field artillery/naval gunfire (NGF) support:

        General concept; Phasing; Duration; Indirect; Trajectory

            limitations

    Frequency allocations:

        Method of engagement; Control

    Coordinating instruction:

        Fire support coordination measures to be used; Effective times

            and the time for operations to begin; Coordinating instructions

            on target engagement; High payoff target list, if developed

*4. Service Support*

    At a minimum, include what communications/signaling equipment

        the team will deploy with

*5. Command and Signal*

    Command:

        Chain of command; Location of fire support officer throughout

            the operation

    Signal:

        Give means/method of requesting fire support

        What radios and frequencies will the team use to control:

            Close-air support (CAS); Emergency close-air support

            (ECAS); Naval gunfire (NGF); Field artillery (FA)

        Frequencies (primary/alternate/plain text)

        Communications schedule

        Authentication (verbal/visual)

**Air Assault Annex**

*1. Situation*

    Enemy situation:

        Enemy air capability; Enemy air defense artillery (ADA)

            capability; Weather, % illumination, illumination angle, NVG

            window, ceiling, and visibility

    Friendly Situation:

        Units supporting operation; Friendly ADA status

*2. Mission*

    Who; What (task); Where; When; Why (purpose)

**3.** *Execution*
    Concept of the operation
    Sub-unit missions
    Coordinating instructions:
        Pickup zone (PZ):
            Name/number; Coordinates/grid; Load time; Take-off time;
            Markings; Control; Landing formation; Approach and
            departure directions; Alternate PZ (name, number, grid);
            Penetration points; Extraction points
        Landing zone (LZ):
            Name/number; Coordinates; H-hour; Markings; Control;
            Landing formation/direction; Alternate LZ (name, number,
            grid); Deception plan (Extraction plan, Extraction LZ);
            Laager site (area—cardinal direction/distance/azimuth—
            communications, and security force); Flight routes and
            alternates; Abort criteria; Down aircraft/crew; Designated
            area of recovery (DAR); Special instructions; Cross-load
            considerations; Aircraft speed; Aircraft altitude; Aircraft
            crank time; Rehearsal schedule/plan; Actions on enemy
            contact (en route and on ground)
**4.** *Service Support*
    Forward area refuel/rearm point (FARP)
    Class I, III, V (specific)
**5.** *Command and Signal*
    Chain of command
    Signal:
        Air/ground call signs and frequencies; Air/ground emergency
        code; Passwords/number combinations; Code words; Fire
        net/quick fire net; Time zone/time hack

## Aerial Resupply Annex

**1.** *Situation*
    Enemy forces (include weather)
    Friendly forces
    Attachments and detachments
**2.** *Mission*
    Who; What (task); Where; When; Why (purpose)
**3.** *Execution*
    Concept of the operation:
        Maneuver; Fires
    Tasks to combat units:
        Command and control; Security; Marking; Recovery/transport

Tasks to combat support units
Coordinating instructions:
    Flight route:
        General; Checkpoints; Communication checkpoint (grid);
           Marking of communication checkpoint; Report time
    Landing/drop zone:
        Location (grid); Primary/alternate; Marking (near/far)
    Drop information:
        Date/time of resupply and alternatives; Code letter on
           DZ/LZ; Length of DZ; Dimensions of LZ; Procedures for
           turning off DZ/LZ; Formation, altitude, and air speed (En
           route and at DZ/LZ); Actions on enemy contact during
           resupply; Abort criteria at DZ/LZ; Actions at DZ/LZ
           (rehearsals and contingencies)

*4. Service Support*

*5. Command and Signal*
    Command:
        Location of patrol leader; Location of assistant patrol leader;
           Locations of members not involved in resupply
    Signal:
        Air to ground call signs and frequencies (primary/alternate/plain);
           Long-range visual signals; Short-range visual signals;
           Emergency procedures and signals; Air drop communication
           procedures; Code words

**Truck Annex**

*1. Situation*
    Enemy forces
    Friendly forces
    Attachments and detachments

*2. Mission*
    Who; What (task); Where; When; Why (purpose)

*3. Execution*
    Concept of the operation:
        Maneuver; Fires
    Tasks to combat units
    Tasks to combat support units
    Coordinating instructions:
        Time of departure/return; Loading plan and duties; Order of
           movement; Route (primary/alternate); Air support (route
           clearing, fire support, etc.); Actions on enemy contact during
           loading, unloading, and movement; Actions at the de-trucking

point (vehicle drop-off—VDO); Rehearsals; Vehicle speed,
separation, and recovery plan; Down vehicle (mechanical or
otherwise) plan; Bump plan
*4. Service Support*
*5. Command and Signal*
Command location (PL and PSG)
Signal:
Radio call signs and frequencies; Code words; Visual signals

**Patrol Base Annex**
*1. Situation*
Enemy forces
Friendly forces
Attachments and detachments
*2. Mission*
Who; What (task); Where; When; Why (purpose)
*3. Execution*
Concept of the operation:
Maneuver; Fires
Tasks to combat units:
Teams (squads)
Security
Reconnaissance
Listening post (LP)
Observation post (OP)
Individuals (six priorities of work):
Security (situational awareness at all times); Maintenance
(weapons and equipment clean and working); Water;
Hygiene (hands and body clean, adherence to latrine plan);
Mess (food is energy); Rest (fatigue clouds judgment; rest
when appropriate)
Tasks to combat support units
Coordinating instructions:
Occupation plan (based off terrain to gain advantage)
Operations plan (patrol base needs to support operations)
Security plan (100 percent, 50 percent, or less?)
Alert plan (early warning devices, radio, and verbal)
Priorities of work (enforced by team leaders)
Evacuation plan (predesignated rally point that is defendable)
Alternate patrol base (primary, unsuitable, or compromised)

*4. Service Support*
Water plan (resupply)
Maintenance plan (ongoing with inspections)
Hygiene plan (medic supervises slit trench trash, checks soldiers)
Chow plan (security not compromised)
Rest plan (where, when, and how long)
*5. Command and Signal*
Command:
Location of patrol command post (CP); Location of patrol leader
(PL); Location of assistant patrol leader (APL); Location of
radio operator (RTO)
Signal:
Call signs and frequencies; Code words and passwords;
Emergency signals

**Linkup Annex**
*1. Situation*
Enemy forces (recent activity in the vicinity of linkup)
Friendly forces
Attachments and detachments
*2. Mission*
Who; What (task); Where; When; Why (purpose)
*3. Execution*
Concept of the operation:
Maneuver; Fires
Tasks to combat units:
Security teams; Surveillance teams (AFO/low vis); Linkup
element
Tasks to combat support units
Coordinating instructions:
Time of linkup; Location of linkup site (primary and alternate);
Rally points; Actions upon enemy contact; Actions at the
linkup site; Actions following linkup; Rehearsals; Restrictive
fire lines; Time schedule
*4. Service Support*
Liaison officer to facilitate passage of lines
Emergency resupply if needed
*5. Command and Signal*
Command:
Location of patrol leader (PL) and assistant patrol leader (APL);
Location of patrol headquarters

Signal:
>    Call signs and frequencies; Spares and code words (Far
>        recognition signal, Near recognition signal, Linkup complete
>        signal)
> Posting authentication (verbal)
> Brevity code
> Identification of friendly forces (IFF)
> Emergency signals
> Abort criteria

## OVERLAYS

An operation overlay is a tracing of graphic control measures on a map. It shows boundaries, phase lines, unit positions, routes, objectives, and other control measures and helps to clarify and control the battlespace. Higher headquarters use the overlay to de-conflict battlespace during ongoing operations. It is a fratricide reduction measure that must take place and is an essential part of the coordination checklist.

## FRAGMENTARY ORDERS

A fragmentary order (FRAGO) is a short operations order that can be issued to update the existing OPORD, thus saving time by not having to brief the entire order.

The field FRAGO is issued after an OPORD to change, modify, or refocus that order or to execute a branch or sequel, such as "Follow on targets." It should take no longer than forty minutes to issue, with the focus (approximately thirty minutes) of actions on the objective.

Below is a general planning guide to follow:

Paragraph 1 (Situation) and 2 (Mission)—five minutes
Paragraph 3 (Execution)—twenty–thirty minutes (focus of the
    FRAGO)
Paragraph 4 (Service Support) and Paragraph 5 (Command and
    Signal)—five minutes

The FRAGO should focus on the actions on the objective. The platoon leader should use subordinate leaders to prepare Paragraphs 1, 4, and 5 in addition to the routes and the fire support coordination plan. Subordinates should brief the portions of the FRAGO that they were responsible for in order to cut down on preparation time and to clarify any specific issues that arise.

It is critical that leaders use maps, imagery, sketches, and a terrain model to allow for rapid understanding of the operation or FRAGO.

The key to success of any operation is rehearsal, particularly with the constrained planning model of the field FRAGO. Rehearsals used in conjunction with the FRAGO reduce preparation time and allow the platoon leaders more time for movement and reconnaissance.

**Fragmentary Orders Format (FRAGO)**
The elements of a FRAGO are listed in the following order:
Number/code name
Time zone used
Task organization

| High Temp | Moonrise | Sunrise |
|---|---|---|
| Low Temp | Moonset | Sunset |
| Wind Speed | Moon Phase | EENT (ending evening nautical twilight) |
| Wind Direction | % Illumination | BMNT (begin morning nautical twilight) |
| Prayer Times | Wake Times | Sleep Times |

Terrain (effect on the new operation)
OAKOC + water:
    Obstacles; Avenues of approach; Key terrain; Observation/fields
        of fire; Cover/concealment; Water (sources)
*1. Situation*
Include any changes from that base order or prudent factors to restate.
    Enemy situation:
        Composition, disposition, strength, morale; Capabilities/weapons;
            Recent activities; Most likely course of action; Most dangerous
            course of action
    Friendly situation:
        Higher unit's mission; Adjacent patrols (task/purpose); Adjacent
            unit objectives and routes
*2. Mission*
    Who (unit performing mission); What (task); Where (description,
        location, and grid); When (NLT date/time); Why (purpose)
*3. Execution*
    Concept of the operation:
        General scheme of maneuver
        Mission-essential task
        Main effort and focus

Supporting efforts
Maneuver:
    Task/purpose for squads/elements; Actions on the objective
      in detail from ORP-OBJ-ORP; Use a terrain model and all
      available imagery or sketches
Fires:
    Time/how it will support the mission (type); What purpose
    fires will perform; Allocation; Restrictions; Fires planned
    during movement; Fires planned on objective
Tasks to maneuver units:
    List all tasks that apply to each squad
Coordinating instructions:
Timeline (backwards plan):
    Hit time; ORP time; Movement from patrol base; Final
    inspection; Platoon rehearsal; Squad rehearsal; FRAGO
    brief complete
Movement plan (use sketch, maps, and imagery to brief):
    Route (primary/alternate); Order of movement (OOM);
    Formations; Movement technique/means
Priority intelligence requirements (PIR) specific to mission
Rehearsal plan (sand table, rock drill, map, diagrams, etc.)
Patrol base plan (if not in accordance with SOP):
    Teams; Occupation plan; Operations plan (security plan or
    alert plan); Priorities of work
Air assault plan:
    Number of aircraft; Type; Weight/size of cargo limit; PZ
    grid; PZ posture time; Load time; Lift time; Flight time
    and number of lifts and composition; Air checkpoints en
    route (time hacks); HLZ grid; HLZ time; Actions at HLZ
    (dismounted posture); Actions if contact at HLZ
Linkup plan (if applicable):
    Time of linkup; Location of linkup site (grid/description);
    Stationary element (checkpoint, overwatch, LP/OP, etc.);
    Moving element (patrol, convoy, leader recon, etc.); Rally
    points; Actions at linkup point; Near and far recognition
    signals (day/night)

*4. Service Support*
Material and services:
    Changes in supply classes; Resupply plan; Water resupply; Aerial
    resupply; Truck plan; Maintenance issues specific to plan

Medical evacuation plan specific to mission:
> Casualty collection point (CCP) location and markings; Location
> of medics; Aid and litter team/duties (if not SOP); Movement
> plan for wounded; CASEVAC coordination; Special equipment

## 5. Command and Signal

Command:
> Location/markings of company CP; Location of platoon leader
> (PL); Location of all key leaders; Succession of command

Signal:
> Location of radio operator (RTO)
> Location of radios:
>> During movement; During actions on the objective
> Signal operation instructions (SOI) in effect

| Who | Frequency | Call Sign |
|-----|-----------|-----------|
| Bn Command | | |
| Fire Support | | |
| MEDEVAC | | |
| Company | | |
| Platoon | | |
| Platoon Sergeant | | |
| 1st Squad Leader | | |
| 2nd Squad Leader | | |
| 3rd Squad Leader | | |
| Weapons Squad | | |

Pyrotechnic signals in use
Identification of friendly forces (IFF)
Running password/number combination

## COORDINATION CHECKLISTS

The following checklists are for the platoon leader and squad leaders when planning a combat mission. The company commander or platoon leader should provide this information or the location where it can be found. Checklists are used to keep leaders from overlooking anything that could be vital to the success of the mission.

## INTELLIGENCE (S-2) CHECKLIST

This coordination informs the leader of any known changes in the situation as given in the OPORD. Constant updating is essential to ensure the operation plan is sound.

**DATE**

| | |
|---|---|
| _____ | Identification of the enemy unit |
| _____ | Weather and light data |
| _____ | Terrain update |
| _____ | Imagery (satellite if possible) |
| _____ | Trails, roads, buildings, obstacles not previously known |
| _____ | Close target reconnaissance (CTR) |
| _____ | Known or suspected enemy locations |
| _____ | New enemy tactics, techniques, and procedures (TTPs) |
| _____ | Weapons |
| _____ | Probable course of action |
| _____ | Recent enemy activities |
| _____ | Reaction time of enemy reinforcements |
| _____ | Civilians on the battlefield |
| _____ | Update to commander's critical intelligence requirements (CCIR) |

## OPERATIONS CHECKLIST

The company commander coordinates this checklist with the platoon leader, who in turn communicates it to the squad leader, to confirm the mission and the operational plan. Any last-minute changes are discussed. Subordinates are updated, and a FRAGO is issued if necessary.

**DATE**

| | |
|---|---|
| _____ | Mission back brief |
| _____ | Identification of supporting unit(s) |
| _____ | Mission and objective |
| _____ | Route to and from the objective (primary/alternate) |
| _____ | Time of departure and expected time of return |
| _____ | Unit target list (derived from fires plan) |
| _____ | Type of fires (artillery, mortar, naval gunfire, aerial) |
| _____ |     Army, Navy, Air Force, or Marine |
| _____ |     Location |

## OPERATIONS CHECKLIST *continued*

| | |
|---|---|
| _____ | Call sign/frequency |
| _____ | Ammunition available (including fuses) |
| _____ | Priority of fires |
| _____ | Control measures |
| _____ | Checkpoints |
| _____ | Boundaries |
| _____ | Phase lines |
| _____ | Fire support coordination measures |
| _____ | Priority targets (target list) |
| _____ | Restricted fires area (RFA) |
| _____ | Restricted fires lines (RFL) |
| _____ | No-fire areas |
| _____ | Precoordinated authentication |
| _____ | Communication |
| _____ | Primary/alternate |
| _____ | Emergency signals |
| _____ | Code words |

---

## COORDINATION WITH FORWARD UNIT CHECKLIST

A platoon or squad that plans movement through a friendly forward unit *must* coordinate with that unit for safe passage. If no time or place has been designated for the coordination, the platoon or squad leader *must* coordinate with the S-3 (Operations), who in turn *must* coordinate with the forward unit's commander.

### DATE

| | |
|---|---|
| _____ | Information to be exchanged |
| _____ | Identification of unit |
| _____ | Size of element (platoon/squad) |
| _____ | Time(s) and place(s) of departure |
| _____ | Initial rally point (IRP) |
| _____ | Dismounting points if applicable |
| _____ | Return time(s) and place(s) |
| _____ | General area of operation |
| _____ | Information on terrain and vegetation |
| _____ | Known or suspected enemy positions |
| _____ | Possible enemy ambush sites (S-2 update) |
| _____ | Latest enemy activity |

**COORDINATION WITH FORWARD UNIT CHECKLIST** *continued*

_____ Details on friendly positions (crew-served weapons, final protective fire, etc.)
_____ Fire and barrier plan
_____ Support that forward unit can provide (duration, capabilities)
_____ Fire support
_____ Litter teams
_____ Medical facilities
_____ HLZ
_____ Navigational aids/signals
_____ Guides
_____ Communications
_____ Reaction force (QRF)
_____ Other assets available
_____ Call signs and frequencies
_____ Pyrotechnic plan
_____ Challenge and password/running password
_____ Identification of friendly forces (IFF)
_____ Recognition signals
_____ Emergency signals and code words
_____ Dissemination of coordination information if unit changes

---

## ADJACENT UNIT COORDINATION CHECKLIST

Upon completion of the operations order, the platoon or squad leader should coordinate with the other platoon or squad leaders working in the same areas. If unknown, the S-3 (Operations) can help arrange the needed coordination between elements. The leaders should exchange the following information with adjacent units in the area.

**DATE**

_____ Identification and type of unit (foreign/coalition)
_____ Mission and size of unit
_____ Planned times and points of entry; departure from battlespace
_____ Routes
_____ Fire support and control measures
_____ Frequencies and call signs
_____ Challenge and password, running password, number combination

## ADJACENT UNIT COORDINATION CHECKLIST *continued*

_____ IFF of other units
_____ Pyrotechnic plan
_____ Any up-to-date information on the enemy
_____ Recognition signals

---

## REHEARSAL AREA COORDINATION CHECKLIST

This coordination is conducted with the platoon leader, company commander, and/or S-3 (Operations) to facilitate the time and detailed effective use of assets as they apply to the tactical mission.

**DATE**

_____ Identification and type of unit (foreign/coalition)
_____ Mission
_____ Terrain similar to objective
_____ Buildings similar to objective
_____ Security of area (extra persons needed to secure area?)
_____ Availability of aggressors/role players
_____ Use of Simunitions, blanks, pyrotechnics, live fire
_____ Mock-ups available
_____ Day/night rehearsal time's availability
_____ Transportation to and from site
_____ Coordination with other units using site

---

## ARMY AVIATION COORDINATION CHECKLIST—SITUATION

**DATE**

| | | | |
|---|---|---|---|
| _____ | Enemy situation | | |
| _____ | Enemy air | % illumination | Window |
| _____ | Enemy ADA | Illumination angle | Ceiling |
| _____ | Weather | NVG | Visibility |
| _____ | Friendly situation | | |
| _____ | Unit(s) supporting operation | | |
| _____ | Axis of movement | | |
| _____ | Corridor | | |
| _____ | Routes | | |
| _____ | Friendly ADA status | | |

**ARMY AVIATION COORDINATION CHECKLIST—MISSION**

**DATE**                                    **DATE**

_____  Who                _____  Where
_____  What               _____  Why
_____  When

**ARMY AVIATION COORDINATION CHECKLIST—EXECUTION**

Concept of the operation to explain what the requesting unit wants to accomplish with the air assault/air movement.

**DATE**

_____  Tasks to combat units
_____    Infantry
_____    Attack aviation
_____  Tasks to combat support units
_____    Artillery
_____    Aviation (lift)
_____  Coordinating instructions
_____  PZ operations
_____    Direction/azimuth of landing
_____    Time of landing
_____    Flight direction
_____    Location of PZ/Alt. PZ
_____    Name of PZ/Alt. PZ
_____    Loading procedures
_____    Marking of PZ (panel, smoke, mirror, strobe, buzz saw, etc.)
_____    Flight route planned (SP, ACP, RP)
_____    Formations
_____    En route LZ (staging point or deception plan)
_____    Code words
_____      PZ secure (prior to landing)
_____      PZ clear (lead bird and last bird)
_____      Alternate PZ
_____    TAC air/artillery
_____    Number of passengers per bird for entire lift
_____    Equipment carried by individuals
_____      Marking of key leaders
_____      Abort criteria (PZ, en route, LZ)
_____  LZ operations
_____    Direction of landing

## ARMY AVIATION COORDINATION CHECKLIST—
## EXECUTION *continued*

| | |
|---|---|
| _____ | False insertion plans |
| _____ | Time of landing (LZ time) |
| _____ | Marking of LZ (panel, smoke, laser, strobe, etc.) |
| _____ | Formation at landing |
| _____ | Code words, LZ name, alternate LZ name |
| _____ | TAC air/artillery prep fires |
| _____ | Fire support coordination |
| _____ | LZ secure |

## ARMY AVIATION COORDINATION CHECKLIST—
## SERVICE SUPPORT

**DATE**

| | |
|---|---|
| _____ | Number of aircraft per lift |
| _____ | Number of lifts |
| _____ | Refuel/rearm during mission |
| _____ | Time aircraft will be off station |
| _____ | Special aircraft equipment or configuration to support unit's equipment |
| _____ | Bump plan |

## ARMY AVIATION COORDINATION CHECKLIST—
## COMMAND AND SIGNAL

**DATE**

| | |
|---|---|
| _____ | Location of air mission commander |
| _____ | Location of air assault force commander |
| _____ | Location of ground tactical commander |
| _____ | Frequencies and call signs for all aircraft |
| _____ | Non-electric signals (day/night) |

*Note*: The minimal separation between aircraft/obstacles is as follows:

| | |
|---|---|
| Observation helicopters | 25 meters |
| UH-1 | 35 meters |
| UH-60/AH-64 | 50 meters |
| Cargo helicopters | 80 meters |

Ground slope considerations:

| | |
|---|---|
| 0–6 percent | upslope landing |
| 7–15 percent | side slope landing |
| Over 15 percent | no touchdown (hover) |

## ARMY AVIATION COORDINATION CHECKLIST—
## VEHICLE MOVEMENT COORDINATION

Coordinate with the supporting unit through the COC to facilitate the effective, detailed, and efficient use of vehicular support and assets.

**DATE**

_____ Identification of the unit
_____ Support unit identification
_____ Number and type of vehicles and tactical preparation
_____ In-trucking point
_____ Load time
_____ Departure time
_____ Preparation of vehicles for movement
_____    Driver tasks and responsibilities
_____    Platoon/squad responsibilities
_____    Special supplies/equipment required
_____ Availability of vehicles for preparation/rehearsals/inspection
_____ Time and location for preparation/rehearsals/inspection
_____ Routes
_____    Primary/alternate
_____    Checkpoints
_____ De-trucking points (VDO)
_____    Primary/alternate
_____ Distance/spacing between vehicles
_____ Movement speed
_____ Dismounted troops speed with vehicles
_____ Communications (call signs/frequencies/codes)
_____ Emergency procedures and signal

## VEHICLE CHECKLIST

| | |
|---|---|
| ❏ Ammunition | ❏ MRE |
| ❏ Strobe | ❏ Spare tires |
| ❏ Crew-served weapons | ❏ 5-gallon fuel cans |
| ❏ IR tape | ❏ Shovel/pick |
| ❏ Radios/batteries | ❏ Fuel spout |
| ❏ First aid pack IAW SOP | ❏ Sand bags |
| ❏ Gun mounts | ❏ Tow bar |
| ❏ Camo net | ❏ Spare batteries |
| ❏ Transmission fluid | ❏ Tow strap |
| ❏ Extra air filter | ❏ IR chemlights |
| ❏ Oil | ❏ PZ marking kit |
| ❏ Drinking hose x 2 | ❏ Spare coms handsets |
| ❏ Antifreeze/coolant | ❏ GPS |
| ❏ Tire chains | ❏ Weapons tie downs |
| ❏ 5-gallon water cans | ❏ High-lift jack |
| ❏ Lug wrench | ❏ Bino/range finder |

**POST-MISSION**
After any mission, it is essential that units conduct After Action Reports (AAR). This is the only way to identify strengths and weakness, thereby learning from actions taken while on missions.
    Below is an example of how to perform an AAR.

**After Action Review (AAR) Format**
Discuss only the "good and bad" that pertain to the mission. The object of the AAR is to *learn* and *improve*, not to celebrate or complain.
*Pre-Mission Preparation*
    Command:
        Time schedule; Develop COA; Paragraph 1 (Situation);
        Paragraph 2 (Mission); Paragraph 3 (Execution); Paragraph 4
        (Service Support); Paragraph 5 (Command and Signal);
        Coordination checklist; Communication
    Assault:
        Route planning; Infiltration; Actions on the objective; Exfiltration
    Security:
        Breach; Actions on the objective; Follow on targets; Exfiltration
    Support:
        Cordon/blocking positions; Actions on the objective; Sensitive
        site exploitation (SSE)

Command and control:
     Infiltration; Actions on the objective; Status reports;
     Dissemination of information; Exiting procedures; Exfiltration
*Mission—C4*
Control of movement to assembly area:
     Assembly area to initial rally point; Initial rally point to objective
     rally point; Objective rally point to objective; Control on
     objective; Casualty collection point; Objective to objective rally
     point; Objective rally point to assembly area
Assault/security/support:
     Control of movement to assembly area; Assembly area to initial
     rally point; Initial rally point to objective rally point; Objective
     rally point to objective; Actions on objective; Consolidation
     activities; Exfiltration; Objective to objective rally point;
     Objective rally point to assembly area
Post-mission clean up (supervised by squad leaders):
     Account for all personnel, weapons, and equipment; Perform
     priorities of work; Replenish water, ammo, chow, and batteries;
     Maintenance of vehicles; Refill all fluids
*Post-Mission Debrief*
The following are examples of possible questions from higher headquarters:
     Size and composition of unit conducting patrol
     Mission of the unit and the type of patrol
     Location/area of the patrol
     Purpose of the patrol
     Departure and return times
     Routes (new information on roads, checkpoints, etc.)
     Terrain description (vegetation, water, ditches, etc.)
     Enemy contact results and TTPs
     Unit status at mission end
     Any other pertinent information
     Recommendations

**MEDICAL ASPECTS OF MISSION PLANNING AND EXECUTION**
Medical mission planning is an integral part of overall operations planning
and greatly affects the leader's decision-making process during all phases.
As a combat leader, it is imperative to have a complete understanding of
your medical resources, responsibilities, and capabilities.
     There are seven key aspects of medical mission planning:
     • Intelligence.
     • Training.

- Supply.
- Readiness.
- Preventive medicine measures.
- Casualty evacuation measures.
- AAR information.

Coordinate with the battalion S-1, battalion surgeon, physician's assistant, and medical platoon leader, as they are responsible for planning and executing medical functions within the battalion.

### Duties and Responsibilities

Following are some of the duties and responsibilities of medical leaders:

Perform required duties to support unit mission (a shooter, first and always)

Treat team members and indigenous personnel

Advise commander on all medical matters

Collect, analyze, and disseminate medical intelligence (assess medical threat)

Provide medical training to military and civilian indigenous personnel

### Treat and Support

Team/platoon/company

Attachments

Indigenous military or civilians

Other units in area

Extended time periods (forty-eight to seventy-two hours without CASEVAC or resupply)

Think equipment

Think drugs

Existing facilities and indigenous medical personnel

### Assess Medical Threats

It is crucial to properly assess all potential medical threats. Leaders should ensure they have the most up-to-date area study and make use of all available resources. Assess vulnerabilities immediately and institute proper countermeasures.

### Training

Training applies not only to the leader but also to the members of the unit. In addition, work with the host nation's military and local civilians to ensure proper assistance in a medical situation.

### Pre-Mission Activities

Before a mission, check that all medical information and supplies are in order:

Perform records maintenance—know your team (allergies, illnesses, injuries, family history)

Perform physicals and immunizations
Ensure accurate blood types for all personnel
Maintain equipment and supplies
Inventory every six months
Know every piece of equipment and its use, function, and
    maintenance
Replace or add supplies or equipment
Replace soon-to-expire medications
Train all team members in basic first responder medicine
Identify team members who can be trained to a minimum of combat
    lifesaver level
Prepare for mass casualty situations

*Isolation/Planning Phase*
Prepare a medical area study that includes prevalent diseases, an evacuation net, and a list of medical equipment needed. Be sure to factor in mission requirements. Initiate vaccinations and administer prophylactic drugs based on the results of the area study.

*Exfiltration Phase*
Coordinate evacuation of sick, wounded, and dead as required, stressing *safety* above all. Also account for all medical supplies used during the mission.

*Post-Mission Phase*
Complete the following post-mission:
    Turn in controlled drugs
    Complete a medical area assessment/AAR
    File SF600s in medical records
    Follow up with treatments and consults
    Continue drug prophylaxis
    Complete labs (PPD, HIV)
    Inventory and restock medical supplies
    Perform equipment maintenance and repair

## OPERATIONS SECURITY

All measures taken to maintain security and achieve tactical surprise constitute operations security (OPSEC). These measures include counter surveillance, physical security, signal security, and information security. OPSEC also involves the elimination or control of tactical indicators that can be exploited by the enemy. To provide the most effective OPSEC, you must see the enemy before it sees you. The following measures can be used to provide OPSEC:

- Use hide and defilade positions habitually.
- Position observation posts to observe enemy avenues of approach.
- Camouflage positions, vehicles, and equipment against both visual and infrared detection. Break up silhouettes, reduce glare, and reduce vehicle signatures caused by dust, exhaust smoke, and tracks.
- Reduce infrared and thermal signatures by parking in shadows, turning off engines and heaters, and using terrain masking.
- Maintain noise and light discipline.
- Patrol aggressively to prevent enemy surveillance and to gather information about the enemy.
- Use smoke to screen movement.
- Enforce proper radio operating procedures: authentication, encoding, limiting transmission time, using low power, and tying down antennas.
- Use radio operators trained in antijam, interference, and deception procedures.
- Overwatch friendly barriers and obstacles.
- Maintain contact with adjacent units.

## FRATRICIDE PREVENTION (IFF)

The underlying principle of fratricide prevention is simple: Leaders who know where their soldiers are, and where they want them to fire, can keep those soldiers alive to kill the enemy. At the same time, leaders must avoid becoming tentative out of fear of fratricide; rather, they must strive to eliminate the risk through tough, realistic combined arms training in which each soldier and unit achieves the set standard.

### Causes

Leaders must identify any factors that may affect their units and then strive to eliminate or correct them. These can include:

- Failure in the direct-fire control plan, especially in designation of target engagement areas.
- Land navigation failures.
- Combat identification failures.
- Inadequate maneuver control measures.
- Reporting and communications failures.
- Weapons errors.
- Battlefield hazards such as unexploded ordnance and unmarked or unrecorded minefields.
- Reliance on instruments and failure to balance technology and basic soldier skills.

**Prevention**
There are five key principles to fratricide reduction and prevention:
- Identify and assess potential risks.
- Maintain situational understanding.
- Ensure positive target identification.
- Maintain effective fire control.
- Establish a command climate that emphasizes prevention.

## FINAL COMBAT INSPECTIONS
Inspections allow leaders to check the unit's operational readiness. The key goal is to ensure that soldiers, equipment, weapons, and vehicles are fully prepared to execute the upcoming mission. Inspections also contribute to improved unit confidence. Below is a checklist of items to inspect:

---

### FINAL COMBAT INSPECTION CHECKLIST

|                                        | GO | NO GO |
|----------------------------------------|----|-------|
| **SHOOT**                              |    |       |
| Rifle                                  |    |       |
| Pistol                                 |    |       |
| Crew-served weapons and mounts         |    |       |
| Lights                                 |    |       |
| Sights                                 |    |       |
| Night vision goggles (NVG)             |    |       |
| Lasers                                 |    |       |
| Ammo/grenades                          |    |       |
| Maintenance/cleaning                   |    |       |
| Demo/breaching                         |    |       |
| **MOVE**                               |    |       |
| All SOP/IAD movement techniques        |    |       |
| SOP for moving wounded                 |    |       |
| SOP for moving enemy prisoners of war (EPWs) |    |       |
| Vehicle driver training (day/night)    |    |       |
| Vehicle battle drills                  |    |       |
| Firing weapons from vehicles           |    |       |
| Helicopter training (load and offload rehearsals) |    |       |
| Convoy/drivers training                |    |       |

## FINAL COMBAT INSPECTION CHECKLIST *continued*

| | GO | NO GO |
|---|---|---|
| Another mode of infiltration/exfiltration | | |
| Batteries, water, fuel, etc. | | |
| SOP for all weapons and equipment | | |
| GPS/compass | | |
| Vehicle weights | | |

**COMMUNICATE**

| | GO | NO GO |
|---|---|---|
| Radios checked and working | | |
| Batteries fully charged | | |
| Crypto up to date | | |
| Frequency and hop sets accurate and working | | |
| All personnel trained in the use of all communication equipment | | |
| ABCs of communication, antennas, batteries, and crypto verified | | |
| Maintenance performed and firmware up to date | | |
| Communication plan complete (cheat sheets available) | | |
| Primary alternate contingency emergency (PACE) understood | | |
| Electric and nonelectric communication SOP rehearsed | | |

**MEDICATE**

| | GO | NO GO |
|---|---|---|
| Individual first aid kits (IFAK) | | |
|    Contents/packing list | | |
|    SOP location on body | | |
|    Extra tourniquets | | |
| Vehicle medical kits inspected and in SOP location | | |
| Medic bags contents inspected in accordance with (IAW) SOP | | |
| Water filtration/purification/ location verified | | |
| All extraction equipment in vehicles and soldiers trained in use | | |

## FINAL COMBAT INSPECTION CHECKLIST *continued*

|  | GO | NO GO |
|---|---|---|
| Combat lifesavers (CLS) and equipment up to date | _____ | _____ |
| Medical persons training and credentials up to date | _____ | _____ |

**PERSONAL**

| | | |
|---|---|---|
| Confirm physicals, allergies, blood type, and ID tags on all soldiers | _____ | _____ |
| Confirm shots and immunizations | _____ | _____ |
| Verify personal medications (bee sting kit, malaria pills, antibiotics, etc.) | _____ | _____ |
| Personal info on all soldiers is secure (team leader) | _____ | _____ |
| Inspect deployment equipment (SOP and serviceable) | _____ | _____ |
| Ensure that all soldiers are mission ready and capable | _____ | _____ |

# 3

# Movement

Infantry's key strength is its ability to cross almost any terrain during all weather conditions. Infantry soldiers moving undetected gain an advantage over the enemy. Movement fundamentals, formations, and techniques provide the leader with security and maneuver advantages during engagements.

## FUNDAMENTALS
- Ensure that movement supports a rapid transition to maneuver.
- Conduct reconnaissance of the terrain and the enemy to the extent possible.
- Move on covered and concealed routes and, if the situation permits, during limited visibility.
- Select routes that avoid natural lines of drift, likely ambush sites, and other danger areas.
- Establish security during movement and halts. Avoid moving directly forward from covered positions. All weapons should be prepared to engage targets.
- Enforce camouflage, noise, and light discipline.
- Designate air guards.
- Make enemy contact with the smallest element possible.

## FORMATIONS
Formations are arrangements of elements and soldiers in relation to one another. Squads use formations for control, flexibility, and security. Leaders choose formations based on the geometry of the battlefield (METT-TC). Leaders are located where they can best command and control forces.

---

**PLATOON AND SQUAD FORMATION ABBREVIATIONS**

| | |
|---|---|
| PLT LDR | Platoon leader |
| PSG | Platoon sergeant |
| SL | Squad leader |
| TL | Team leader |
| RATELO | Radiotelephone operator |
| FO | Forward observer |
| R and RFLM | Rifleman |
| AR | Automatic rifleman/SAW gunner |
| GRN | Grenadier |
| MG | Machine gun |
| MEDIC | Medic/corpsman |

---

**Fire Team Formations**

*Wedge.* The wedge is the basic formation for the fire team. The interval between soldiers in the wedge formation is normally 10 meters. The wedge expands and contracts depending on the terrain. When rough terrain, poor visibility, or other factors make it difficult to control the wedge, the normal interval is reduced so that all team members can still see their team leader and the team leaders can still see their squad leader. The sides of the wedge can contract to resemble a single file. When moving in less rugged terrain, where control is easier, soldiers expand the wedge or resume their original positions.

*File.* When the terrain precludes use of the wedge, fire teams use the file formation.

**Fire Team Wedge**                 **Fire Team File**

| MOVEMENT FORMATION | WHEN NORMALLY USED | CHARACTERISTICS | | | |
|---|---|---|---|---|---|
| | | CONTROL | FLEXIBILITY | FIRE CAPABILITIES/ RESTRICTIONS | SECURITY |
| FIRE TEAM WEDGE | BASIC FIRE TEAM FORMATION | EASY | GOOD | ALLOWS IMMEDIATE FIRES IN ALL DIRECTIONS | ALL-ROUND |
| FIRE TEAM FILE | CLOSE TERRAIN, DENSE VEGETATION, LIMITED VISIBILITY CONDITIONS | EASIEST | LESS FLEXIBLE THAN WEDGE | ALLOWS IMMEDIATE FIRES TO THE FLANKS, MASKS MOST FIRES TO THE REAR | LEAST |

**Comparison of Fire Team Formations**

| MOVEMENT FORMATION | WHEN NORMALLY USED | CHARACTERISTICS | | | |
|---|---|---|---|---|---|
| | | CONTROL | FLEXIBILITY | FIRE CAPABILITIES/ RESTRICTIONS | SECURITY |
| SQUAD COLUMN | SQUAD PRIMARY FORMATION | GOOD | FACILITATES MANEUVER, GOOD DISPERSION LATERALLY AND IN DEPTH | ALLOWS LARGE VOLUME OF FIRE TO THE FLANK— LIMITED VOLUME TO THE RIGHT | ALL-ROUND |
| SQUAD LINE | WHEN MAXIMUM FIREPOWER IS REQUIRED TO THE FRONT | NOT AS GOOD AS SQUAD COLUMN | LIMITED MANEUVER CAPABILITY (BOTH FIRE TEAMS COMMITTED) | ALLOWS MAXIMUM IMMEDIATE FIRE TO THE FRONT | GOOD TO THE FRONT, LITTLE TO THE FLANKS AND REAR |
| SQUAD FILE | CLOSE TERRAIN VEGETATION, LIMITED VISIBILITY CONDITIONS | EASIEST | MOST DIFFICULT FORMATION FROM WHICH TO MANEUVER | ALLOWS IMMEDIATE FIRE TO THE FLANK, MASKS MOST FIRE TO THE FRONT AND REAR | LEAST |

**Comparison of Squad Formations**

### Squad Formations

Squad formations describe the relationships between fire teams in the squad.

*Squad Column.* The squad column is the most common formation. It provides good lateral and deep dispersion without sacrificing control and it facilitates maneuver. The lead fire team is the base fire team. When the squad moves independently or as the rear element of the platoon, the rifleman in

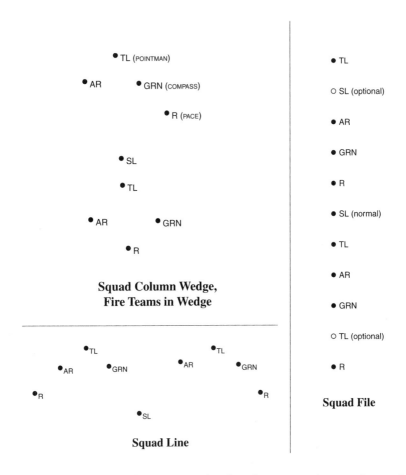

Squad Column Wedge,
Fire Teams in Wedge

Squad File

Squad Line

the trail fire team provides rear security. Squads can move in normal or modified columns as terrain dictates.

*Squad Line.* The squad line provides maximum firepower to the front. When a squad is acting as the base squad, the fire team on the right is the base fire team.

*Squad File.* When not traveling in a column or line, squads travel in file. The squad file has the same characteristics as the fire team file. If the squad leader wants to increase his control over the formation, enhance morale by leading from the front, and be immediately available to make key decisions, he moves forward to the first or second position. Additional control over the rear of the formation can be provided by moving a team leader to the last position.

## Platoon Formations

*Platoon Column.* The platoon column is the primary movement formation. It provides good lateral and deep dispersion and simplifies control. The lead squad is the base squad. (*Note*: METT-TC will determine where crew-served weapons move in the formation. They normally move with the platoon leader so he can quickly establish a base of fire.)

*Platoon Line, Squads on Line.* This formation allows the delivery of maximum fire to the front but little fire to the flanks. It is hard to control and does not lend itself well to rapid movement. When two or more platoons are attacking, the company commander chooses one as the base platoon. The base platoon's center squad is its base squad. When the platoon is not acting as the base platoon, its base squad is its flank squad nearest the base platoon. The machine guns can move with the platoon, or they can assume a support position. This is the basic platoon assault formation.

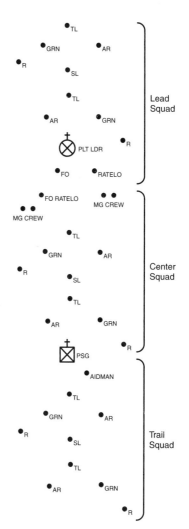

**Platoon Column**

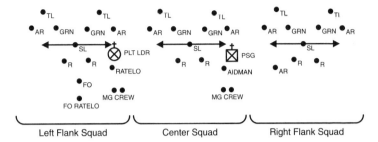

Left Flank Squad        Center Squad        Right Flank Squad

NOTE: The platoon leader (PLT LDR), forward observer (FO), radio-telephone operator
(RATELO), platoon sergeant (PSG), and the squad leaders (SL) position
themselves where they can best control the squad.

### Platoon Line, Squads on Line

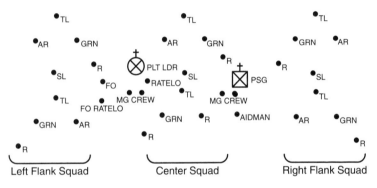

Left Flank Squad        Center Squad        Right Flank Squad

### Platoon Line, Squads in Column

*Platoon Line, Squads in Column.* The platoon leader uses this formation when he does not want to deploy all personnel on line and when he
wants the squads to react to unexpected contact. This formation is easier to
control and lends itself better to rapid movement than the platoon line or
squads on line formation; however, it is harder to control than a platoon column and does not facilitate rapid movement as well. When two or more platoons are moving, the company commander chooses one as the base platoon.
The base platoon's center squad is its base squad. When the platoon is not
the base platoon, its base squad is its flank squad nearest the base platoon.

***Platoon Vee.*** This formation has two squads up front to provide a heavy volume of fire on contact. It also has one squad in the rear that can either overwatch or trail the other squads. This formation is hard to control, and movement is slow. The platoon leader designates one of the front squads as the platoon's base squad.

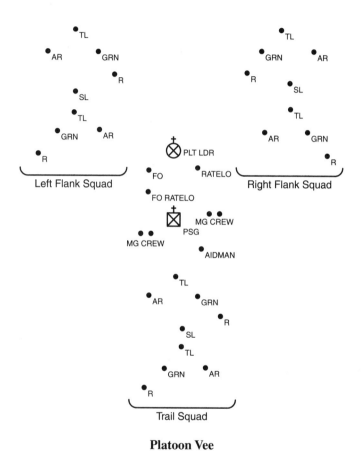

**Platoon Vee**

*Platoon Wedge.* This formation has two squads in the rear that can overwatch or trail the lead squad. It provides a large volume of fire to the front or flanks. It also allows the platoon leader to make contact with a squad and still have one or two squads to maneuver. The lead squad is the base squad.

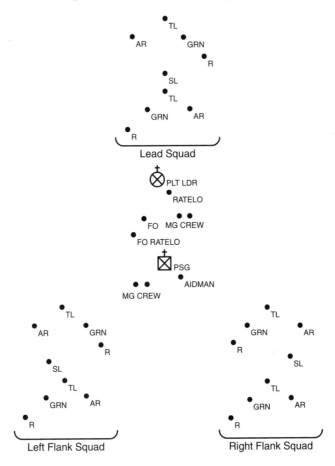

**Platoon Wedge**

*Platoon File.* This formation can be set up in several ways. One method is to have three-squad files follow one another using one of the movement techniques. Another method is to have a single platoon file with a front security element (point) and flank security elements. This formation is used when visibility is poor because of terrain, vegetation, or light conditions. The distance between soldiers is less than normal to allow communication by passing messages up and down the file. The platoon file has the same characteristics as the fire team and squad files.

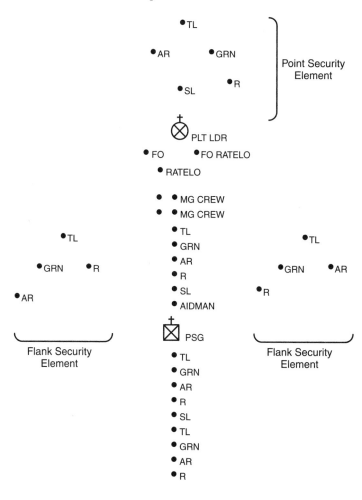

**Platoon File**

## MOVEMENT TECHNIQUES

A movement technique is the manner used to traverse terrain. There are three movement techniques: *traveling*, *traveling overwatch*, and *bounding overwatch*. The selection of a movement technique is based on the likelihood of enemy contact and the need for speed. Factors to consider for each technique are control, dispersion, speed, and security. Movement techniques are not fixed formations. They refer to the distances between soldiers, teams, and squads, which vary based on mission, enemy, terrain, visibility, and other factors that affect control. Soldiers and squad leaders must be able to see their fire team leaders. The platoon leader should be able to see his lead squad leader. Leaders control movement with arm and hand signals, using radios only when needed. Any of the three movement techniques can be used with any formation.

| MOVEMENT TECHNIQUES | WHEN NORMALLY USED | CHARACTERISTICS | | | |
|---|---|---|---|---|---|
| | | CONTROL | DISPERSION | SPEED | SECURITY |
| TRAVELING | CONTACT NOT LIKELY | MORE | LESS | FASTEST | LEAST |
| TRAVELING OVERWATCH | CONTACT POSSIBLE | LESS | MORE | SLOWER | MORE |
| BOUNDING OVERWATCH | CONTACT EXPECTED | MOST | MOST | SLOWEST | MOST |

**Movement Techniques**

### Techniques of Squad Movement

The squad or platoon leader determines and directs which movement technique the squad will use.

*Traveling.* Traveling is used when contact with the enemy is not likely and speed is needed.

*Traveling Overwatch.* Traveling overwatch is used when contact is possible. Attached weapons move near the squad leader and are under his control so that he can employ them quickly.

*Bounding Overwatch.* Bounding overwatch is used when contact is expected; when the squad leader believes that the enemy is near (based on movement, noise, reflection, trash, fresh tracks, or even a hunch); or when a large, open danger area must be crossed.

The lead fire team overwatches first. Soldiers scan for enemy positions. The squad leader usually stays with the overwatch team.

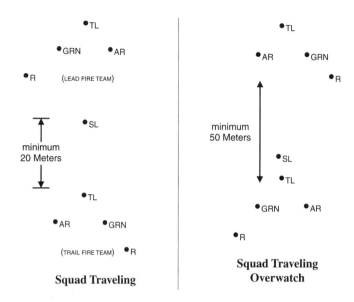

The trail fire team bounds and signals the squad leader when his team completes its bound and is prepared to overwatch the movement of the other team. Both team leaders must know whether successive or alternate bounds will be used and with which team the squad leader will be. The overwatching team leader must know the route and destination of the bounding team. The bounding team leader must know his team's destination and route, possible enemy locations, and actions to take when he arrives. He must also know where the overwatching team will be and how he will receive his instructions.

The cover and concealment on the bounding team's route dictate how its soldiers move. Teams can bound successively or alternately. Successive bounds are easier to control; alternate bounds can be faster.

*Alternate Bounds.* Covered by the rear element, the lead element moves forward, halts, and assumes overwatch positions. The rear element advances past the lead element and takes up overwatch positions. The sequence continues as necessary, with only one element moving at a time.

*Successive Bounds.* The lead element, covered by the rear element, advances and takes up overwatch positions. The rear element advances to an overwatch position roughly abreast of the lead element and halts. This sequence continues as necessary. The rear element never advances forward of the lead element.

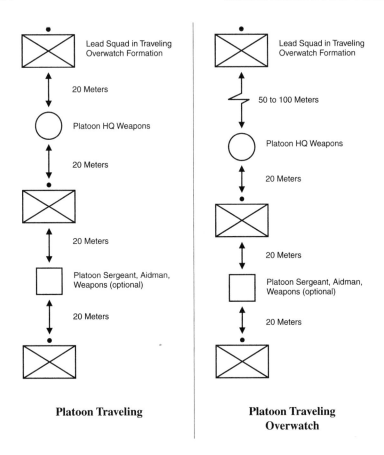

**Techniques of Platoon Movement**

The platoon leader determines and directs which movement technique the platoon will use.

*Traveling.* Traveling is used when enemy contact is not likely and speed is needed.

*Traveling Overwatch.* Traveling overwatch is used when contact is possible but speed is needed. The platoon leader moves where he can best control the platoon. The platoon sergeant travels with the trailing squad, although he is free to move throughout the formation to enforce security, noise and light discipline, and distances between squads. The lead squad uses traveling overwatch, and the trailing squads use traveling.

*Bounding Overwatch.* Bounding overwatch is used when enemy contact is expected. Platoons conduct bounding overwatch using successive or alternate bounds. One squad bounds forward to a chosen position; it then

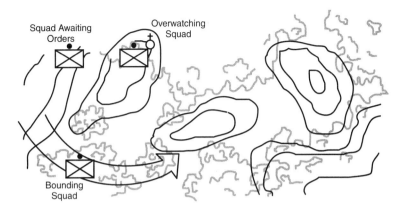

**Platoon Bounding Overwatch**

becomes the overwatching element unless contact is made en route. The bounding squad can use traveling overwatch, bounding overwatch, or individual movement techniques (low and high crawl, and short rushes by fire teams or pairs). One squad overwatches the bounding squad from covered positions where it can see and suppress likely enemy positions and view the squad's assigned sector. The platoon leader remains with the overwatching squad. Normally, the platoon's machine guns are located with the overwatching squad. One squad is uncommitted and ready for employment as directed by the platoon leader. The platoon sergeant and the leader of the squad awaiting orders position themselves close to the platoon leader.

*Considerations.* When deciding where to have his bounding squad go, a platoon leader considers the following:

- The requirements of the mission.
- Where the enemy is likely to be.
- The routes to the next overwatch position.
- The ability of an overwatching element's weapons to cover the bound.
- The responsiveness of the rest of the platoon.
- The fields of fire at the next overwatch position.

*Instructions.* Before a bound, the platoon leader gives an order to his squad leaders from the overwatch position. He tells and shows them the following:

- The direction or location of the enemy (if known).
- The positions of the overwatching squad.
- The next overwatch position.
- The route of the bounding squad.

- What to do after the bounding squad reaches the next position.
- What signal the bounding squad will use to announce that it is prepared to overwatch.
- How the squad will receive its next orders.

## DANGER AREAS

A danger area is any place on the movement route where the unit might be exposed to enemy observation, fire, or both. Units try to avoid danger areas. If a danger area must be crossed, it should be done with great caution and as quickly as possible. Before crossing a danger area, leaders should designate near- and far-side rally points, secure the near side (both flanks and rear), and reconnoiter and secure the far side.

The unit halts when the lead elements signal "danger area." The leader confirms the danger area, then selects and informs subordinate leaders of near- and far-side rally points. Near-side security is posted to overwatch the crossing. The far-side security team crosses the danger area and clears the far side. Once the far side is cleared, the main body moves quickly and quietly across the danger area. A small unit may cross all at once, in pairs, or one soldier at a time. A large unit normally crosses its elements one at a time. As each element crosses, it moves to an overwatch position or to the far-side rally point. The near-side security element then crosses and resumes its place in the formation as the unit continues its mission.

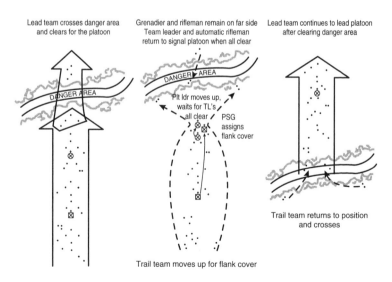

**Crossing a Danger Area**

## Crossing Techniques

*Open Areas.* When crossing an open area, stay concealed and observe carefully from the near side. Post security to give early warning, and send an element across to clear the far side. When cleared, quickly cross the rest of the unit at the shortest exposed distance.

To cross large open areas, use a combination of traveling overwatch and bounding overwatch. Bounding overwatch is used at any point in the open area where enemy contact may be expected or when the element comes within small-arms range (250 meters) of the far side.

Small open areas may be bypassed by either using the detour bypass method or contouring around the open area. In the detour bypass method, the force moves around the open area using 90-degree turns to the right or left until the far side is reached. To contour around the open area, the unit uses the wood line and vegetation for cover and concealment until it reaches the far-side rally point.

*Roads and Trails.* Cross a road or trail at or near a bend, at a narrow spot, or on low ground to reduce enemy observation and minimize the unit's exposure.

*Villages.* Pass on the downwind side and well away from a village. Avoid animals, especially dogs, that might reveal your presence.

*Enemy Positions.* Pass enemy positions on the downwind side (the enemy might have scout dogs). Be alert for trip wires or other warning devices.

*Minefields.* Bypass a minefield, even if it means changing your route by a great distance. If you must pass through a minefield, the lead elements should clear a lane for the rest of the unit. Soldiers use their hands to detect trip wires and sharpened sticks to probe for mines.

*Streams.* When crossing a stream, select a narrow spot that offers concealment on both banks. Observe the far side carefully and place security out for early warning. Clear the far side, then cross quickly but quietly.

*Wire Obstacles.* Avoid crossing wire obstacles if possible, as they are normally under observation. If wire must be breached during daytime, use the method that exposes the unit for the shortest amount of time. Check the wire for mines, booby traps, and warning devices. To breach wire at night, either cross over or go under the wire using the following procedures.

To cross *over* the wire, grasp the first strand lightly and cautiously lift one leg over. Lower your foot slowly to the ground, feeling carefully for sure footing, then lift the other foot over the wire. Quietly release this wire and feel for the next strand. Cross it in the same way.

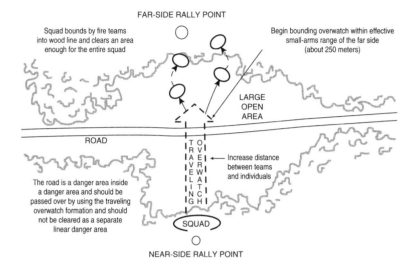

**Crossing a Large Open Area**

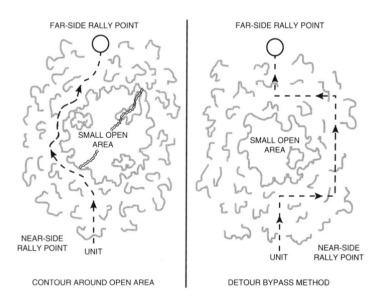

**Crossing a Small Open Area**

To go *under* the wire, move headfirst. Lie on your back and slide under the bottom strands, pushing forward with your heels. Carry your weapon lengthwise on your body, steadying it with either hand. To prevent the wire from catching on clothing or equipment, let it slide along the weapon. Inch along, holding the wire up with one hand. Do not jerk or pull on the wire. Feel ahead with your free hand for low strands or trip wires.

If you must *cut* the wire, cut only the lower strands to minimize discovery of the gap. Soldiers should work in a team if possible. Wrap the wire with a cloth near a picket, cut partway through, and then bend it back and forth until it breaks. Carefully roll the loose end back to clear the lane. Concertina is hard to control after cutting and can snap back. If you must cut it, stake down two loops far enough apart that a soldier can crawl between them. Then cut partway through and break it as previously described.

### Enemy Contact at Danger Areas

If the unit makes contact in or around a danger area, the leader determines whether to assault the enemy or break contact, depending on the situation and mission. If the unit becomes disorganized, the near- and far-side rally points are used to link up and reorganize. Ideally, using movement fundamentals, the unit will see the enemy first, remain undetected, and ambush it.

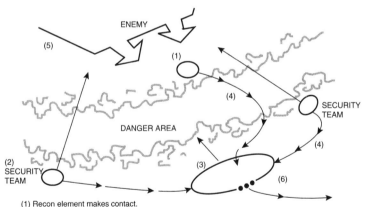

(1) Recon element makes contact.
(2) Flank security fires on enemy.
(3) Main body takes overwatch position and fires on enemy.
(4) Security and recon return to main body.
(5) Smoke and indirect fire used to break contact.
(6) The platoon moves to different place to cross danger area; or
(7) Reorganizes and assaults enemy.

**Crossing Danger Area—Enemy Contact on Far Side**

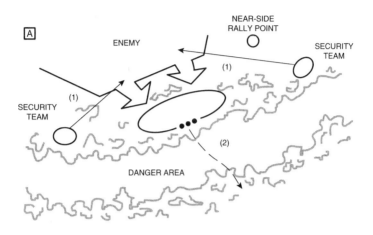

(1) Flank security teams fire in the direction of the enemy.
(2) The platoon moves quickly across danger area.

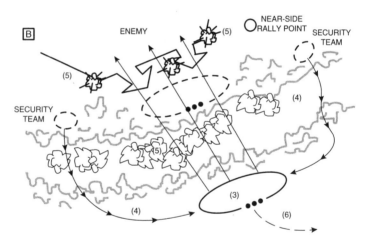

(3) The platoon sets up overwatch position.
(4) Security teams cross danger area and rejoin platoon.
(5) Smoke or artillery used.
(6) The platoon moves out of area; or
(7) Platoon reorganizes and assaults enemy.

## Crossing Danger Area—Enemy Contact on Near Side

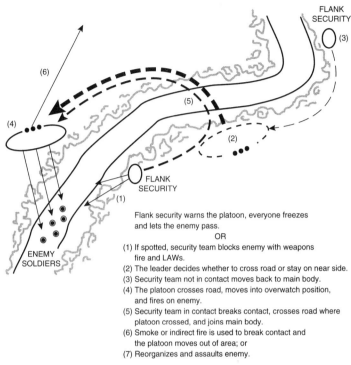

Flank security warns the platoon, everyone freezes
and lets the enemy pass.
OR
(1) If spotted, security team blocks enemy with weapons
    fire and LAWs.
(2) The leader decides whether to cross road or stay on near side.
(3) Security team not in contact moves back to main body.
(4) The platoon crosses road, moves into overwatch position,
    and fires on enemy.
(5) Security team in contact breaks contact, crosses road where
    platoon crossed, and joins main body.
(6) Smoke or indirect fire is used to break contact and
    the platoon moves out of area; or
(7) Reorganizes and assaults enemy.

**Crossing Danger Area—Enemy Contact on Road or Trail**

## SECURITY DURING MOVEMENT
Security during movement includes whatever the platoon or squads do to
secure the unit or the larger force, such as the following tactics.

### Terrain
When planning movements, consider how terrain affects security.

### Formations and Movement Techniques
When choosing a movement formation or technique, consider the most recent
situation update and the level of $C^2$ needed for the mission. Choose the option
that will provide the greatest security and is most likely to result in mission
accomplishment. During individual platoon movement, place the smallest
element forward. This gives the rest of the platoon freedom to maneuver.

### Positioning of the Machine-Gun Teams or Weapons Squad
The maneuvering of the crew-served weapons system is key to successful
light infantry tactics. The platoon leader positions his crew-served weapons

such as machine guns and Javelins where they can best provide security to the platoon. METT-TC will determine the placement. He may task-organize some of the weapons to the rifle squads or keep them together under the weapons squad leader (if he has a weapons squad) and close to the command post. Keeping the weapons squad close allows the platoon leader to quickly deploy the guns into an overwatch position or to provide a base of fire against a threat.

**Light Discipline**
If soldiers need more illumination than an image intensifier can provide in infrared mode during movement, they should use additional infrared light sources to provide the light needed with the least risk of enemy detection. When using infrared light, leaders must consider the enemy's night vision and infrared capabilities. For instance, an enemy with night vision capability can send infrared light signals and can concentrate direct and indirect fire on a platoon that is using infrared light.

**SOLDIER'S LOAD**
The soldier's load greatly affects movement and is of crucial concern to leaders. Research has shown that a soldier can carry up to 30 percent of his body weight and still retain a high percentage of his agility, stamina, alertness, and mobility. For the average soldier weighing 160 pounds, that would be a 48-pound load. The soldier loses a proportional amount of his functional ability for each pound over 30 percent.

**Load Management**
Use the following techniques for load management:
- Distribute loads evenly over the body and load-bearing equipment (LBE), load-bearing vest (LBV), or modular lightweight load-carrying equipment (MOLLE).
- Don't carry anything on the front of the body that would prevent the soldier from taking well-aimed shots.
- Distribute loads throughout the unit. If it is necessary to man-pack bulk ammunition, water, rations, or demolitions, divide them into small loads.
- Rotate heavy loads (radios, machine guns, mortars, and antitank weapons) among several soldiers.
- Always consider transportation assets to carry loads.
- Upon enemy contact, drop rucksacks or leave them in an objective rally point (ORP), an assault position, or the assembly area.

- Share or consolidate items. Carry only enough sleeping bags for those who will sleep at the same time. In the same manner, two or three soldiers can share a rucksack and take turns carrying it.
- Consider carrying fewer rations for short operations.
- While carrying rucksacks, use water and rations carried in them first. Then rucksacks can be dropped and soldiers will still have a full supply on their LBE, LBV, or MOLLE.

A recent combat load study called "Soldier Loads in Combat" was conducted on dismounted infantry serving in combat in Afghanistan and Iraq. A cover letter summarized conditions as such: "Despite the best efforts made by military leaders, today's dismounted infantry soldier continues to carry excessive loads even during the conduct of short duration missions. This harsh reality is not due to these soldiers carrying unnecessary equipment, but due to the facts that the essential items that they must carry simply weigh too much and that we have few to no means today for offloading the dismounted soldier while keeping his gear near at hand." Leaders should always attempt to keep the combat load of the soldier as light as possible without sacrificing protection and mission-essential equipment. Until we can find better ways to lighten the soldier's load and get him into battle, the following doctrine still applies.

*Combat Load.* The combat load consists of the minimum mission-essential equipment—as determined by the commander responsible for carrying out the mission—required for soldiers to fight and survive immediate combat operations. It is the essential load carried by soldiers in forward subunits, or the load that accompanies soldiers other than fighting loads.

*Fighting Load.* The fighting load includes a soldier's armor, bayonet, weapon, clothing, helmet, IFAK, water and LBE, and a reduced amount of ammunition. Keep fighting loads under 48 pounds when cross-loading small-unit equipment.

*Approach March Load.* The approach march load consists of only mission-essential gear: clothing, weapon, the basic load of ammunition, armor, water, and special equipment. Enforce a limit of 72 pounds.

*Emergency Approach March Loads.* Circumstances such as approach marches through terrain impassable to vehicles or areas where ground or air transportation resources are not available could require soldiers to carry loads heavier than 72 pounds in larger rucksacks. These emergency approach march loads can be carried easily by well-conditioned soldiers. When the mission demands that soldiers be employed as porters, loads of up to 120 pounds can be carried for several days over distances of 20 kilometers a day. Although loads of up to 150 pounds are feasible, soldiers could become fatigued or even injured. If possible, avoid contact with the enemy since march speeds will be slow.

## FOOT MARCH

Foot marches are the movement of troops and equipment mainly by foot, with limited support by vehicles. They are characterized by combat readiness, ease of control, adaptability to terrain, slow rate of movement, and increased personnel fatigue. Foot marches do not depend on the existence of roads.

A dismounted company moves in a column of twos, with a file on each side of the road. Distances are: day, 2 to 5 meters between men, 50 meters between platoons; night, 1 to 3 meters between men, 25 meters between platoons. Rates are: day, 4 kmph; night, 3.2 kmph. Cross-country rates are: day, 2.4 kmph; night, 1.6 kmph. Halts are: 15 minutes after the first 45 minutes, 10 minutes out of every hour thereafter.

NOTE: 3rd squad can be on either side of the road.

**Road March Formation**

### Road Space, Foot Column

The road space (RS) of a company foot column, used in determining time length (TL) of the column, consists of two parts: the space occupied by the men alone (including the distance between them) and the sum of distances between elements of the foot column. Total RS = RS men + RS platoon distances.

The RS of the men alone is determined by multiplying the number of men by the appropriate factor selected from the table below:

| Formation | 2 meters per man | 5 meters per man |
|---|---|---|
| Single file | 2.4 | 5.4 |
| Column of twos | 1.2 | 2.7 |

The total RS between platoons is obtained by multiplying the number of platoons (minus one) by the platoon distances.

## TIME LENGTH (TL), FOOT COLUMN

| Rate | Formula |
|------|---------|
| 4.0 kmph | TL (min.) = RS (meters) $\times$ .0150 |
| 3.2 kmph | TL (min.) = RS (meters) $\times$ .0187 |
| 2.4 kmph | TL (min.) = RS (meters) $\times$ .0250 |
| 1.6 kmph | TL (min.) = RS (meters) $\times$ .0375 |

**Completion Time**

The completion time of a foot march is determined by using this formula:
Completion time = SP (start point) time + TL + scheduled halts.

# 4

# Offense

The four types of offensive operations are *movement to contact (MTC)*, *attack, exploitation*, and *pursuit*. Companies can execute MTCs and attacks. Platoons generally conduct these forms of the offense as part of a company. Companies and platoons participate in an exploitation or pursuit as part of a larger force. The nature of these operations depends largely on the amount of time and enemy information available during the planning and preparation for the operational phases. This chapter will focus on the first two types of offense: attacks and movements to contact.

The MTC is a type of offensive operation designed to develop the situation and establish or regain contact. The platoon will likely conduct an MTC as part of a company when the enemy situation is vague or not specific enough to conduct an attack.

An attack is an offensive operation that destroys enemy forces or seizes or secures terrain. Movement supported by fires characterizes an attack. The platoon will likely participate in a synchronized company attack; however, it may conduct a special purpose attack as part of or separate from a company offensive or defensive operation. Special purpose attacks consist of ambushes, spoiling attacks, counterattacks, raids, feints, and demonstrations.

## FORMS OF MANEUVER
In typical offensive operations, the platoon maneuvers against the enemy in an area of operation (AO). Maneuver places the enemy at a disadvantage through the application of friendly fires and movement. The five forms of maneuver are *envelopment, turning movement, infiltration, penetration*, and *frontal attack*.

## SEQUENCE OF OFFENSIVE OPERATION
As the platoon leader plans for an offensive mission, he generally considers the actions the unit must accomplish in the following phases of an offensive operation.

## Assembly Area

To prepare the platoon for the upcoming battle, the platoon leader plans, directs, and supervises mission preparations in the assembly area (AA). This time allows the platoon to conduct pre-combat checks and inspections, rehearsals, and combat service support (CSS) activities. The platoon will typically conduct these preparations within a company AA.

## Reconnaissance

Leaders should aggressively seek information about the terrain and the enemy. The enemy situation and available planning time may limit a unit's reconnaissance. In this circumstance, the platoon will likely conduct reconnaissance to answer the company commander's priority of intelligence requirement (PIR). An example may be to reconnoiter and time routes from the AA to the objective rally point (ORP).

## Movement to the Objective Rally Point

The platoon will typically move from the AA to the ORP as part of the company movement plan. The ORP is the final position that an element occupies before moving to the target. At the ORP, leaders make final preparations, receive and disseminate intelligence updates, and tweak the plan accordingly. From the ORP, elements separate and move into pre-rehearsed attack positions. The ORP can be occupied for a period of time long enough to allow other units or assets to pre-stage at their individual ORPs. The ORP is typically an easily identified area that can be defended and is the first rally point to which unit members egress post-assault.

## Maneuver

The company commander will plan the approach of all platoons to the objective to ensure synchronization, security, speed, and flexibility. He will select the routes, movement techniques, formations, and methods of movement to best support his intended actions on the objective. The platoon leader must recognize this portion of the battle as a *fight*, not as a movement. He must be prepared to make contact with the enemy and plan accordingly to obtain the objective.

## Deployment

The platoon deploys and moves from the ORP toward the assault position with minimum delay and confusion and begins the final positioning of the squads as directed by the company commander. The last covered and concealed position (LCC) is the final position where rehearsed, simple

preparations can take place, such as breachers priming explosives, medics
extending stretchers, etc. Movement should be as rapid as the terrain, unit
mobility, and enemy situation permit.

**Assault**
During an offensive operation, the platoon's objective may be terrain-oriented or force-oriented. Terrain-oriented objectives require the platoon to
seize or retain a designated area and often require fighting through enemy
forces. If the objective is force-oriented, the platoon's efforts are focused on
the enemy's actual location. Actions on the objective begin when the company or platoon begins placing direct and indirect fires on the objective.

**Consolidation and Reorganization**
The platoon consolidates and reorganizes as required by the situation and
mission. Consolidation is the process of organizing and strengthening a
newly captured position so that it can be defended. Reorganization is the
actions taken to shift internal resources within a degraded unit to increase its
level of combat effectiveness.

**BATTLEFIELD OPERATING SYSTEMS**
**PLANNING CONSIDERATIONS**
The battlefield operating systems (BOS) are a list of seven critical tactical
activities that provides a means of reviewing preparation and execution. Synchronization and coordination among the BOS are critical for success.
   1. *Maneuver.* The purpose of maneuver is to close with and destroy the
      defending enemy. Maneuver requires a base-of-fire element to sup-
      press and/or destroy enemy forces with accurate direct fires and
      bounding elements to gain positional advantage over the enemy.
   2. *Fire support.* The platoon may be able to employ indirect fires from
      field artillery or company and/or battalion mortars to isolate part of
      the enemy defense or to suppress the enemy on the objective.
   3. *Mobility, countermobility, and survivability.* The platoon will likely
      focus on mobility during offensive operations and may be required
      to breach obstacles as part of an offensive operation. These obstacles
      may be protective (employed to assist units in their close-in protec-
      tion), which the platoon is expected to breach without additional
      assets. However, tactical obstacles that disrupt, turn, or fix unit for-
      mations require engineer assets to breach.
   4. *Air defense.* The platoon leader should address how to react to
      enemy air attacks if no air defense assets are available or operating
      within his AO. Unit SOPs should stipulate internal air security meas-
      ures and active air defense measures.

5. *Combat service support.* The primary purpose of CSS in the offense is to assist the platoon and company in maintaining momentum during the attack. Key CSS planning considerations for the platoon leader during the offense include a high expenditure of ammunition, an increase in casualties, and how to evacuate the casualties.

6. *Intelligence.* The generation of knowledge about the enemy is crucial. The platoon leader should be given as much information on the enemy as can be gotten in the time available.

7. *Command and control.* Command and control refers to the process of directing, coordinating, and controlling a unit to accomplish a mission.

## ATTACKS

Platoons and squads conduct an attack as part of the infantry rifle company. An attack requires detailed planning, synchronization, and rehearsals to be successful. The company commander designates and explains platoon objectives with tasks and milestones for his assault, support, and breach elements. To ensure synchronization, all leaders must know the location of their subordinates and adjacent units during the attack. Attacks are characterized as *hasty* or *deliberate.* The primary difference between the two is the extent of planning and preparation conducted by the attacking force. Attacks may take the forms of attacks against a stationary enemy force, attacks against a moving enemy force, or terrain-oriented attacks.

### Organization for an Attack

In a company attack, the commander usually structures his force into assault, support, and breach elements. Platoon attacks may be similarly structured.

The *assault element* closes with and captures or destroys the enemy.

The *support element* provides a base of fire that supports the assault element and breach element when one is used.

The *breach element*'s usual task is to break the enemy's line, position, or fortification to facilitate the success of the assault element.

### DELIBERATE ATTACK

Platoons and squads conduct deliberate attacks as part of a larger force. The commander may designate separate platoon objectives for his assault, support, and breach elements, resulting in decentralized execution at all levels. The five phases of the deliberate attack are *reconnaissance, movement to the objective, isolate the objective, seize a foothold,* and *exploit.*

## Reconnaissance

Before a deliberate attack, the platoon and company should gain enemy and friendly information from the battalion reconnaissance platoon; however, this may not always occur. The platoon and company should be prepared to conduct a reconnaissance of the objective to confirm, modify, or deny their tentative plan. If possible, the company should determine the enemy's size, location, disposition, most vulnerable point, and most probable course of action (COA). The tentative plan may change as a result of the reconnaissance if the platoon or squad discovers that terrain or enemy dispositions are different than determined earlier in the troop-leading procedure, requiring a modification of the attack plan.

## Movement to the Objective

The attacking force advances to within assault distance of the enemy position under supporting fires, using a combination of traveling, traveling overwatch, and/or bounding overwatch. Platoons advance to successive positions using available cover and concealment. The company commander may designate SBF positions to protect friendly forces with suppressive direct fires. As the company maneuvers in zone, it employs fires to suppress, neutralize, and obscure the enemy positions.

*Assembly Area to the Objective Rally Point.* The ORP is where elements of the assault force transition to secure movement techniques in preparation for contact with the enemy. Platoons may maneuver from the ORP to designated SBF positions, assault positions, or breach or bypass sites. Before leaving the AA, the platoon leader should receive an update of the location of forward and adjacent friendly elements. He should also receive updated enemy locations. The platoon moves forward from the AA to the ORP, usually as part of a company formation, along a planned route. The platoon leader should have reconnoitered the route to the ORP (with either a map, scouts, or aircraft).

*Objective Rally Point to Assault Position.* The platoon's assault element moves from the ORP to the assault position. If necessary, the platoon leader plots waypoints to coincide with checkpoints along the route. During movement, he ensures the platoon navigates from checkpoint to checkpoint or phase line by using basic land navigation skills supplemented with precision navigation.

*Assault Position to the Objective.* The assault position is the last covered and concealed (LCC) position before reaching the objective. Ideally, the platoon's assault element occupies the assault position without the enemy detecting any of the platoon's elements. Preparations in the assault position may include preparing Bangalores, other breaching equipment, or demolitions; fixing bayonets; lifting or shifting fires; or preparing smoke pots. The platoon may halt in the assault position if necessary to ensure synchronization of friendly forces. Once the assault element moves forward of the assault position, the assault must continue.

Supporting fire from the heavy weapons must continue to suppress the enemy and must be closely controlled to prevent fratricide.

When the assault element moves to the breach point, the base-of-fire leader verifies the assault element is at the right location. The base-of-fire leader is responsible for tracking the assault element as it assaults the objective. The company commander shifts or lifts indirect fire when it endangers the advancing soldiers and coordinates this with the platoons' assaults. As the fire of the platoons' support is masked, the platoon leader shifts or lifts it or displaces the weapons squad to a position where continuous fire can be maintained.

### Isolate the Objective
The goals of isolation are to prevent the enemy from reinforcing the objective and to prevent enemy forces on the objective from leaving. Infantry platoons will likely be an isolating force within a company.

### Actions on the Objective: Seize a Foothold and Exploit the Penetration
The platoon leader often designates assault, support, and breach elements within his platoon to conduct a deliberate attack. One technique is to designate the machine-gun teams (or weapons squad) as the support element, an infantry squad as the breach element, and the remaining platoon as the assault element. The supporting elements support the breach element's initial breach with suppressive fires; as the breach is being established, the support element should shift fires to allow the breach element to penetrate the objective and to avoid committing fratricide. The support element positions itself to provide continual close-in suppressive fire to aid the actions of the assault squad (or squads) as it moves across the objective. Once the breach element has seized the initial foothold on the objective, the assault element may then move through the breach lane to assault the objective. All communication from the support element to the breach, assault, and weapons squads is by FM radio or signals. Problems and status updates are continuously communicated or observed, and changes are made as necessary.

## Consolidation and Reorganization

Once enemy resistance on the objective has ceased, the platoon must quickly take steps to consolidate and prepare to defend against a counterattack. There are two main consolidation techniques:

*Clock Technique.* In this method, the platoon leader designates either a compass direction or the direction of attack as 12 o'clock. He then uses clock positions to identify the left and right boundaries for squads. The platoon leader positions key weapons along the most likely avenue of approach based on his assessment of the terrain.

*Terrain Feature Technique.* In a similar manner, the platoon leader identifies obvious terrain features as the left and right limits for squads. Terrain can also be used to identify where defensive positions can be established.

In both techniques, the platoon leader ensures that squad sectors of fire overlap each other and provide mutual support for adjacent units.

Once platoons have consolidated on the objective, they begin to reorganize to continue the attack. Reorganization involves:

• Reestablishing command and control.
• Re-manning key weapons and redistributing ammunition and equipment.
• Clearing the objective of casualties and EPWs.
• Assessing and reporting the platoon status of personnel, ammunition, supplies, and essential equipment (ACE report to higher).

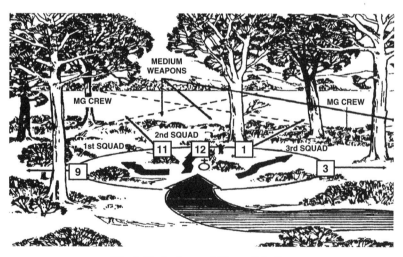

**Clock Technique of Consolidation**

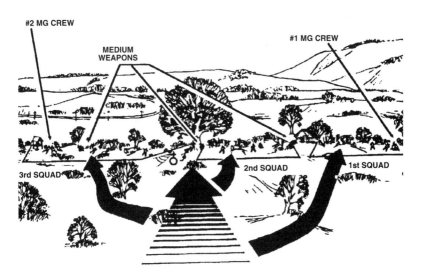

**Terrain Technique of Consolidation**

## HASTY ATTACK

Platoons and squads normally participate in a hasty attack as part of a larger unit, during an MTC, as part of a defense, or whenever the commander determines that the enemy is in a vulnerable position and can be quickly defeated by immediate offensive action. Hasty attacks are used to exploit a tactical opportunity, maintain the momentum, regain the initiative, prevent the enemy from regaining organization or balance, and gain a favorable position that may be lost with time. Because its primary purpose is to maintain momentum or take advantage of the enemy situation, the hasty attack is normally conducted with only the resources that are immediately available. The key to hasty attacks is maintaining unrelenting pressure on the enemy and attacking before the enemy can act. Synchronization in the hasty attack can be degraded a bit, so commanders should minimize risk by maximizing the use of standard formations, SOPs, and well-rehearsed, thoroughly understood battle drills. The hasty attack is often the preferred option during continuous operations and frequently results from an MTC, successful defense, or continuation of a previous attack.

### Task Organization

The hasty attack is conducted using the principles of fire and movement. The controlling headquarters normally designates a base-of-fire force and a maneuver force.

**Conduct of the Hasty Attack**

The platoon must first conduct actions on contact, allowing the commander to gather the information he needs to make an informed decision. The term "hasty" refers to limits on planning and preparation time, not to any acceleration in the conduct of actions on contact. Because the intelligence picture is vague, the commander normally needs more time, rather than less, during this process to gain adequate information about the enemy force. Execution begins with the establishment of a base of fire, which then suppresses the enemy force. The maneuver force uses a combination of tactical techniques and combat multipliers (such as indirect fire) to maintain its security as it advances in contact to a position of advantage. Understanding the geometry of the battlefield is key to successful attacks by allowing the infantry commander to effectively occupy and take advantage of superior positions.

Once the maneuver force has gained the positional advantage, it can execute a tactical task, such as an assault to destroy the remaining enemy.

**MOVEMENT TO CONTACT**

Platoons and squads participate in an MTC as part of a company, using the movement formations and techniques explained in Chapter 3. A company generally conducts an MTC when it must gain or maintain contact with the enemy or when it lacks sufficient time to gain intelligence or make extensive plans to defeat the enemy.

**Planning an MTC**

Firsthand enemy information provides the intelligence necessary to respond to the enemy, so reconnaissance is a critical aspect to planning. However, if the enemy situation remains vague, the platoon must be prepared to act in any situation. This is accomplished through proper planning, appropriate movement formations and techniques, fire control measures, platoon SOPs, engagement criteria, and studying the terrain before and during movement to anticipate likely enemy locations. While moving, all leaders study the terrain (geometry) and anticipate enemy contact by noting positions that would facilitate enemy attack. Based on these terrain studies, leaders should avoid likely areas of enemy ambush or exposing their platoon to long-range observation and fires.

**Techniques**

Infantry units will participate in two techniques for conducting an MTC: approach march or search and attack (see page 86). The approach march technique is used when the enemy is expected to deploy using relatively fixed offensive or defensive formations but the situation remains vague. The search and attack technique is used when the enemy is dispersed, or expected to avoid contact or quickly disengage and withdraw, or when the higher unit needs to deny the enemy movement in an AO.

## Command and Control

The company commander will dictate a number of $C^2$ techniques for the unit to employ. The platoon leader may modify these to better control his squads based on the commander's intent and guidance and METT-TC. Some examples of $C^2$ follow.

*Phase Lines and Checkpoints.* The company commander will normally assign phase lines and checkpoints to control the forward movement of the platoons. The platoon does not stop at a phase line unless told to do so. If necessary, the platoon leader designates additional phase lines or checkpoints for use within the platoon to reduce the number and length of radio transmissions used to control movement.

*Fire Control and Distribution.* The platoon uses boundaries, direct-fire plans, pyrotechnics, signals, and FRAGOs for direct-fire control and distribution. This is important because of the scarcity of information about the enemy and is crucial in avoiding fratricide.

*Indirect-Fire Plan.* The platoon leader must have a good indirect-fire plan for his route in order to cover anticipated places of contact. Precoordinated target reference points (TRPs) are the basis of a fire plan; the leader can quickly use them for immediate fire suppression. They can be points that are easy to recognize to adjust fire from or points where enemy activity is suspected.

## Developing the Situation

Once the platoon makes contact with the enemy, it maintains contact until the commander orders otherwise. The platoon leader develops the situation based on the effectiveness of enemy fire, friendly casualties, size of the enemy force, and freedom to maneuver. A good MTC plan will provide the infantry leader with the knowledge needed to take advantage of the terrain. It will also facilitate reporting critical information about the enemy in order to recommend a COA. The platoon can bypass the enemy with permission from the commander, conduct an attack, fix the enemy so another platoon can conduct the assault, conduct a defense, establish an ambush, or break contact.

## Defensive Considerations

In some situations, a platoon conducting an MTC makes contact with a much larger and more powerful enemy force. If the platoon encounters a larger enemy force where the terrain gives the platoon an advantage, it should attempt to fix the enemy force. This allows the rest of the company to maneuver against the force. If the platoon cannot fix the enemy, it may have to assume a defensive posture or break contact to more advantageous terrain, but it should do so only if it is in danger of being overwhelmed.

## Approach March Technique

The approach march technique may be used when the enemy is expected to deploy using relatively fixed offensive or defensive formations. The concept behind the approach march is to make contact with the smallest element, allowing the commander the flexibility of maneuvering or bypassing the enemy force. As part of a larger unit using the approach march technique, platoons may act as the advance, flank, or rear guard. They may also receive on-order missions as part of the main body.

*Advance Guard.* As the advance guard (probe), the platoon finds the enemy and locates gaps, flanks, and weaknesses in its defense. The advance guard attempts to make contact on ground of its own choosing, to gain the advantage of surprise, and to develop the situation (either fight through or support the assault of all or part of the main body).

The advance guard operates within the range of the main body's indirect-fire support weapons. One rifle squad leads the advance guard. The platoon uses appropriate formations and movement techniques, and the leader rotates the lead squad as necessary to keep soldiers fresh.

*Flank or Rear Guard.* The entire platoon may use the approach march technique to act as the flank or rear guard for a battalion conducting a movement to contact. The platoon moves using the appropriate formation and movement technique; provides early warning; destroys enemy reconnaissance units; and prevents direct fires or observation of the main body.

*Main Body.* When moving as part of the main body, platoons may be tasked to assault, bypass, or fix an enemy force or to seize, secure, or clear an assigned area. The platoon may also be detailed to provide squads as flank guards, stay-behind ambushes, rear security, or additional security to the front. These squads may come under the direct control of the company commander. Platoons and squads use appropriate formations and movement techniques, assault techniques, and ambush techniques.

## Search and Attack Technique

Search and attack is used when the enemy is dispersed or is expected to avoid contact or quickly disengage and withdraw, or to deny the enemy movement in an area. The search and attack technique involves the use of multiple squads and fire teams in coordinated actions to make contact with the enemy. Platoons attempt to find the enemy and then fix and finish it. They combine patrolling techniques with the requirement to conduct hasty or deliberate attacks once the enemy has been found.

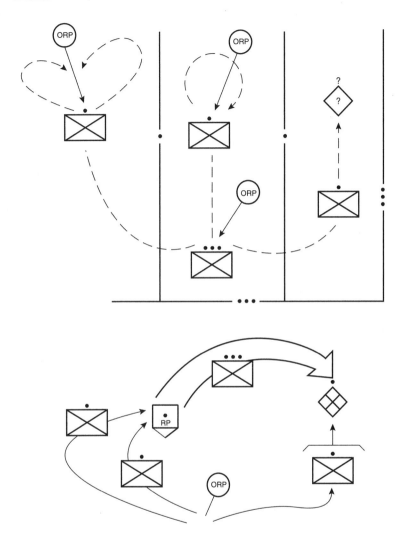

**Search and Attack Technique**

## LIMITED-VISIBILITY ATTACKS

Effective use of night vision devices (NVGs) during limited-visibility attacks enhances squad and platoon ability to achieve surprise and cause panic in a lesser-equipped enemy. NVGs allow soldiers to see farther and with greater clarity, and provide a marked advantage over the enemy. Leaders also have an increased ability to control fires during limited visibility.

The well-equipped platoon has multiple types of enhancements for use, including laser target designators; aiming lights; and target illuminators consisting of infrared parachute flares, infrared trip flares, infrared 40mm rounds, infrared mortar rounds, infrared bike lights, and remote black lights. These assets greatly aid in target acquisition and fire control. The platoon leader and squad leaders follow tactical SOPs to synchronize the employment of infrared illumination devices, target designators, and aiming lights during their assault on the objective.

Leaders use strobe lights, luminous tape, or chemical lights to mark assault personnel to prevent fratricide. The enemy must not be able to see the markings. Two techniques are to place tape on the back of the helmet or to use small infrared chemical lights (if the enemy has no NVGs).

The supporting elements must know the location of the lead assault element. To reduce the risk to the assault element, the platoon leader may assign weapons control restrictions. For example, the squad on the right in the assault might be assigned weapons free to the right flank because no friendly soldiers are there. The squad on the left may be assigned weapons tight or weapons hold, which means that another friendly unit is located there.

The platoon leader may use the following techniques to increase control during the assault:

- Prohibit use of flares, grenades, or smoke on the objective.
- Allow only certain personnel with NVGs to engage targets on the objective.
- Use a magnetic azimuth for maintaining direction.
- Use mortar or artillery rounds to orient attacking units.
- Assign a base squad or fire team to pace and guide others.
- Reduce intervals between soldiers and squads.

Mortar, artillery, and antiarmor fires are planned as in a daylight attack. However, they are not fired unless the platoon is detected or is ready to assault. Some weapons may fire before the attack and maintain a pattern to deceive the enemy or to help cover noise made by the platoon's movement. This is not done if it will disclose the attack.

Indirect fire is hard to adjust when visibility is poor. If the exact location of friendly units is not clearly known, indirect fire is directed first at enemy positions beyond the objective and then moved (creeping fire) back onto the objective.

Illuminating rounds that are fired to burn on the ground can be used to mark objectives. This helps the platoon orient on the objective but may adversely affect NVGs.

Smoke is planned to further reduce the enemy's visibility, particularly if he has NVGs. The smoke is laid close to or on enemy positions so that it does not restrict friendly movement or hinder the breaching of obstacles. Employing smoke on the objective during the assault may make it hard for assaulting soldiers to find enemy fighting positions. However, if enough thermal sights are available, smoke on the objective may provide a decisive advantage for a well-trained platoon.

Illumination is always planned for limited-visibility attacks, giving leaders the option of calling for it. Battalion commanders normally control the use of conventional illumination but may authorize the company commander to do so. If the commander decides to use conventional illumination, he should not call for it until the assault is initiated or the attack is detected. It should be placed on several locations over a wide area to confuse the enemy as to the exact place of the attack. Also, it should be placed beyond the objective to help assaulting soldiers see and fire at withdrawing or counterattacking enemy soldiers.

*Note*: If the enemy is equipped with NVGs, leaders must evaluate the risk of using each technique and ensure the mission is not compromised because the enemy can detect infrared light sources.

## SPECIAL PURPOSE ATTACKS

When the company commander directs it, the platoon conducts a special attack. The commander bases his decision on the METT-TC. Special purpose attacks are subordinate forms of an attack and include the ambush, raid, counterattack, spoiling attack, feint, and demonstration. As forms of the attack, they share many of the same planning, preparation, and execution considerations of the offense. Feints and demonstrations are also associated with military deception operations.

*Note*: To eliminate confusion, this guide will cover the ambush and raid in Chapter 7 (Patrolling) until current doctrine agrees on category. These techniques are actually a member of both offensive operations as much as they are a member of patrolling. See Chapter 7 for their explanation.

### Counterattack

The counterattack is a form of attack by part or all of a defending force against an enemy attacking force, with the general objective of denying the enemy's goal of attacking. This attack by defensive forces regains the initiative or denies the enemy a successful attack. The platoon may conduct a counterattack as a lightly committed force within a company or as the battalion reserve. The platoon counterattacks after the enemy begins his attack, reveals his main effort, or creates an assailable flank. As part of a higher headquarters, the platoon conducts the counterattack much like other attacks. However, the platoon leader must synchronize the execution of his counterattack within the overall defensive effort. Counterattacks afford the defender the opportunity to create favorable conditions for the commitment of combat power. The platoon should rehearse the counterattack battle drill and prepare the ground to be traversed. Counterattacks are more useful to the higher headquarters when the platoon anticipates employment; plans and prepares for employment; and executes with the other defending, delaying, or attacking forces in conjunction with the higher commander's plan.

## Spoiling Attack

A spoiling attack is a form of attack that preempts or seriously impairs an enemy attack while the enemy is in the process of planning or preparing to attack. The purpose of a spoiling attack is to disrupt the enemy's offensive capabilities and timelines while destroying his personnel and equipment. The purpose is not to secure terrain or other physical objectives. A commander (company or battalion) may direct a platoon to conduct a spoiling attack during friendly defensive preparations to strike the enemy while he is in assembly areas or attack positions preparing for his own offensive operation. The platoon leader plans for a spoiling attack as he does for other attacks.

## Feint

A feint is a form of attack used to deceive the enemy as to the location and time of the actual operation. Feints attempt to induce the enemy to move reserves and shift his fire support to locations where they cannot immediately impact the actual operation. When directed to conduct a feint, the platoon seeks direct fire or physical contact with the enemy, but avoids decisive engagement. The commander (company or battalion) will assign the platoon an objective limited in size or scope. The planning, preparation, and execution considerations are the same as for the other forms of attack. The enemy must be convinced that the feint is the actual attack.

## Demonstration

A demonstration is a form of attack designed to deceive the enemy as to the location or time of the actual operation by a display of force. Demonstrations attempt to deceive the enemy and induce him to move reserves and shift his fire support to locations where they cannot immediately impact the actual operation. When directed to conduct a demonstration, the platoon does not seek physical contact with the enemy. The planning, preparation, and execution considerations are the same as for the other forms of attack. It must appear to be an actual impending attack.

## BATTLE DRILLS

Infantry battle drills or immediate action drills (IAD) describe how platoons and squads apply fire and maneuver to commonly encountered situations. The battle drill is not intended to replace the estimate of the situation but to *reduce* the estimate of the situation and the decision-making process to the essential elements. (Experience at the Army's combat training centers revealed a deficiency in the action and reaction of small units.) The emphasis on drills is intended to instill an immediate, aggressive response. Battle drills must be performed immediately in order to gain the full benefit. This type of rapid response can only be accomplished by sustained rehearsal. Soldiers must react without hesitation in order to take advantage of gaps in the attack.

### React to Contact Drill

The react to contact drill takes place when a squad or a platoon is receiving fire from enemy riflemen or an automatic weapon.

**Step 1.** Soldiers take cover and return fire.

**Step 2.** Leaders locate known or suspected enemy positions and engage with well-aimed fire. Leaders control fire using the following standard fire commands: alert, direction, description of target, range, method of fire, and command to commence firing.

**Step 3.** Soldiers maintain contact to left and right, as well as with leaders, and report enemy locations.

**Step 4.** Leaders check the status of their men.

**Step 5.** The platoon leader moves to the squad in contact. He brings with him his communications NCO, forward observer (FO), the leader of the nearest squad, and a machine-gun crew. The platoon sergeant moves forward with the second machine gun-crew and links up with the platoon leader, ready to assume control of the base-of-fire element.

**Step 6.** The platoon leader determines whether he must move out of an enemy engagement area. If he is not in an engagement area, he determines whether he can gain and maintain suppressive fire with his element in contact, based on the volume and accuracy of the enemy fire.

**Step 7.** The platoon leader makes an assessment of the situation, identifying the following:

1. Location of the enemy position and obstacles.
2. Size of the enemy force (the number of automatic weapons, the presence of vehicles, and the employment of indirect fires are indicators of enemy strength).
3. Vulnerable flanks.
4. Covered and concealed flanking routes to the enemy position.

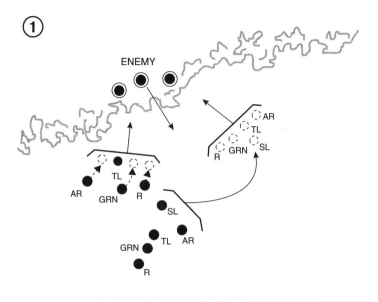

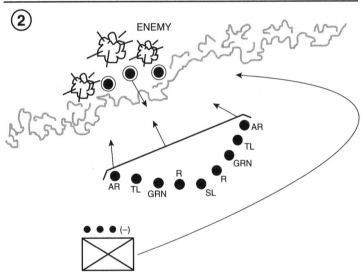

**React to Contact Drill**

**Step 8.** The platoon leader then determines his next course of action, such as fire and movement, assault, breach, knock-out bunker, or enter and clear a building or trench.

**Step 9.** The platoon leader reports the situation to the company commander and begins to maneuver, calling for an adjusting artillery or mortar fire.

### Break Contact Drill

The break contact drill takes place when the squad or platoon is under enemy fire and must break contact.

**Step 1.** The platoon leader directs one squad in contact to support the disengagement of the remainder of the platoon.

**Step 2.** The platoon leader orders the first squad to move a certain distance and direction or to a terrain feature or the last ORP. Meanwhile, the base-of-fire (supporting) squad continues to suppress the enemy.

**Step 3.** The moving element uses smoke grenades to mask its movement until it takes up its designated position and engages the enemy position.

**Step 4.** The platoon leader then directs the base-of-fire squad to move to its next location.

**Step 5.** While continuing to suppress the enemy, the platoon bounds away from the enemy until it either breaks contact or passes through a high-level support-by-fire position.

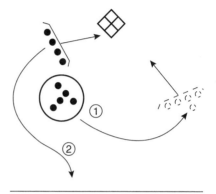

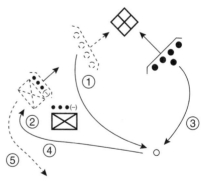

**Break Contact Drills**

**Step 6.** Once contact is broken, the platoon should change direction, if possible, to avoid indirect enemy fire.

**Step 7.** Leaders account for soldiers, report (ACE), reorganize as necessary, and continue the mission.

## React to Ambush Drill

In a near ambush (within hand-grenade range), use the following procedures:

**Step 1.** Immediately return fire.

**Step 2.** Take up covered positions.

**Step 3.** Throw fragmentation, concussion, and smoke grenades.

**Step 4.** Immediately after the grenades detonate, the soldiers in the kill zone assault through the ambush using fire and movement, while soldiers not in the kill zone identify enemy positions, initiate suppressive fire, take up covered positions, and shift fires as soldiers in the kill zone assault through the ambush.

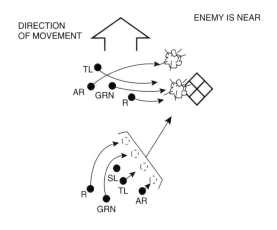

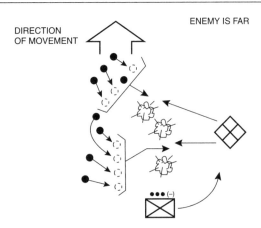

**React to Ambush Drills**

In a far ambush (beyond hand-grenade range), use the following procedures:

**Step 1.** Soldiers receiving fire immediately return fire, take up covered positions, and suppress the enemy by destroying or suppressing enemy crew-served weapons first, obscuring the enemy position with smoke, and sustaining suppressive fires.

**Step 2.** Soldiers not receiving fires move by a covered and concealed route to a vulnerable flank of the enemy position and assault using fire and movement.

**Step 3.** Soldiers in the kill zone continue suppressive fires and shift fires as the assaulting element fights through the enemy position.

In both near and far ambushes, the platoon leader then calls for mortar or artillery fire to isolate the enemy or to attack as the enemy retreats. Leaders account for soldiers, report (ACE), reorganize as necessary, and continue the mission.

### Knock-out Bunker Drill

The knock-out bunker drill is used when the platoon identifies enemy in bunkers.

**Step 1.** The platoon initiates contact.
1. The squad in contact establishes a base of fire.
2. The platoon leader, communications operator (COMMO), FO, and one machine-gun team move to the squad in contact.
3. The platoon sergeant moves the second machine-gun team forward and takes charge of the base of fire.

**Step 2.** The base-of-fire element destroys or suppresses enemy crew-served weapons first and uses smoke to obscure the enemy position. The FO calls for and adjusts indirect fire.

**Step 3.** The platoon leader determines whether he can maneuver by identifying the following:
1. The enemy bunkers, other supporting positions, and any obstacles.
2. The size of the enemy force engaging the platoon.
3. A vulnerable flank of at least one bunker.
4. A covered and concealed flanking route to the bunker.

**Step 4.** The platoon leader determines which bunker to knock out and directs a squad not in contact to assault it.

**Step 5.** If necessary, the platoon sergeant repositions base-of-fire elements to isolate the enemy bunker.

**Step 6.** The assault squad, along with the platoon leader and FO, moves along the covered and concealed route.
1. The squad leader moves with the assaulting fire team.
2. The assaulting fire team approaches the bunker from its blind side.

3. Soldiers constantly watch for other bunkers or enemy positions in support of the known bunker.
4. Upon reaching the last covered and concealed position, the fire team leader and automatic rifleman remain in place and add their fires to suppressing the bunker, while the squad leader positions himself where he can best control his teams.
5. On the squad leader's signal, the base-of-fire element lifts or shifts fires to the opposite side of the bunker from the assaulting team's approach.
6. A rifleman and grenadier continue forward to the blind side of the bunker. One soldier takes up a covered position near the exit while the other cooks off (two seconds maximum) a grenade, shouts "Frag out!" and throws it through an aperture.
7. After the grenade detonates, the soldier covering the exit enters the bunker, firing short bursts to destroy the enemy.
8. The squad leader inspects the bunker to ensure that it has been destroyed.

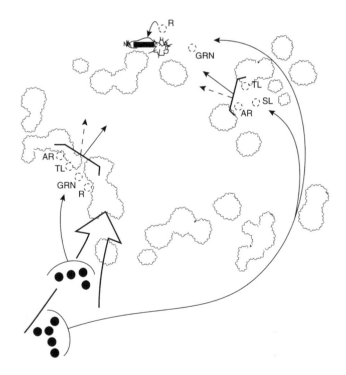

**Knock-out Bunker Drill—Squad**

9. The squad leader then reports, reorganizes as needed, and continues the mission.

**Step 7.** The platoon leader repositions the base-of-fire element as necessary to continue to isolate and suppress the remaining bunkers as squads are maneuvered to knock them out.

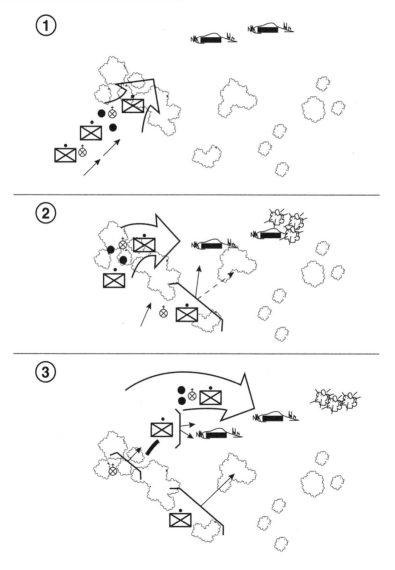

**Knock-out Bunker Drill—Platoon**

### Enter and Clear a Trench Drill

The enter and clear a trench drill is used when the platoon is moving and identifies enemy in a trench line, and the platoon leader determines that he can maneuver and assault the trench line.

**Step 1.** The platoon leader directs one squad to enter the trench and secure a foothold.

**Step 2.** The platoon leader designates the entry point of the trench line and the direction of movement once the platoon begins clearing.

**Step 3.** The platoon sergeant positions soldiers and machine guns to suppress the trench and isolate the entry point.

**Step 4.** The platoon leader directs the platoon FO to initiate a fire mission, if necessary, in support of the assault. The platoon FO maintains accurate battle tracking of all friendly elements to facilitate quick clearance of fires. He lifts or shifts fires to isolate the objective as the assault team advances.

**Step 5.** The assaulting squad executes actions to enter the trench and establish a foothold. The squad leader signals to the platoon leader that the foothold is secure and the follow-on elements can move into the trench. The squad leader remains at the entry point and marks it. The platoon follows the success of the seizure of the foothold with the remainder of the platoon as part of the platoon actions to clear a trench line.

**Step 6.** The platoon leader moves into the trench with the assaulting squad.

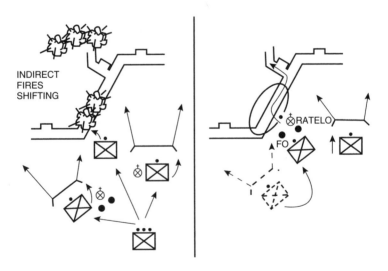

**Clearing a Trench—Platoon**

**Step 7.** The platoon leader directs one of the base-of-fire squads to move into the trench and begin clearing it in the direction of movement from the foothold.

**Step 8.** The base-of-fire element repositions as necessary to continue suppressive fires.

**Step 9.** The assaulting squad passes the squad that has secured the foothold and executes actions to take the lead and clear the trench.

- The squad leader designates a lead fire team and a trail fire team.
- The lead fire team and the squad leader move to the forward most secure corner or intersection. The squad leader tells the team securing that corner or intersection that his squad is ready to continue clearing the trench. The trail fire team follows, maintaining visual contact with the last soldier of the lead team.

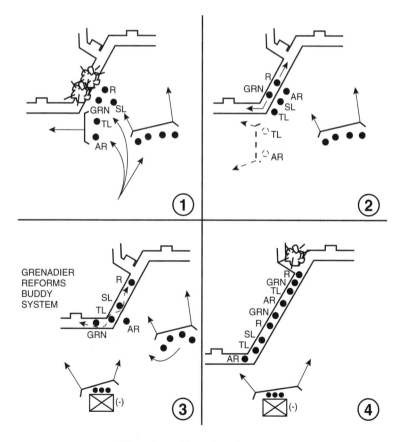

**Entering a Trench—Squad**

- *Note*: The fire support element must be able to identify the location of the lead fire team in the trench at all times.
- *Note*: Throughout this battle drill, the team leader positions himself at the rear of the fire team to have direct control (physically, if necessary) of his soldiers. Other soldiers in the fire team rotate the lead to change magazines and prepare grenades. Rotating the lead provides constant suppressive fires down the trench and maintains the momentum of the attack as the squad clears the trench.
- The lead fire team passes the element securing the foothold. The following then occurs:
  —The lead soldier of the fire team moves abreast of the soldier securing the corner or intersection, taps him, and announces, "Taking the lead."
  —The soldier securing the corner or intersection acknowledges that he is handing over the lead by shouting, "Okay!" He allows the fire team to pass him.
- The lead fire team starts clearing in the direction of movement. They arrive at a corner or intersection. The following then occurs:
  —Allowing for cook off (two seconds maximum) and shouting, "Frag out," the second soldier prepares and throws a grenade around the corner.
  —Upon detonation of the grenade, the lead soldier moves around the corner, firing three-round bursts and advancing as he fires. The entire fire team follows him to the next corner or intersection.
- The squad leader:
  —Follows behind the team.
  —Ensures that the trailing fire team moves up and is ready to pass the lead at his direction.
  —Rotates fire teams as necessary to keep his soldiers fresh and to maintain the momentum of the attack.
  —Requests indirect fires, if required, through the platoon leader. The squad leader also directs the employment of the M203 to provide immediate suppression against positions along the trench line.
  —Ensures fire teams maintain sufficient interval to prevent them from being engaged by the same enemy fires.
- At each corner or intersection, the lead fire team performs the same actions previously described.

- If the lead soldier finds that he is nearly out of ammunition before reaching a corner or intersection, he announces, "Ammo!" The following then occurs:
    —The lead soldier stops and moves against one side of the trench, ready to let the rest of the team pass. He continues to aim his weapon down the trench in the direction of movement.
    —The next soldier ensures that he has a full magazine, moves abreast of the lead soldier, taps him, and announces, "Taking the lead."
    —The lead soldier acknowledges that he is handing over the lead by shouting, "Okay." Positions rotate and the squad continues forward.
- The trailing fire team secures intersections and marks the route within the trench as the squad moves forward. The trailing fire team leader ensures that follow-on squads relieve his buddy teams to maintain security.
- The squad leader reports the progress of the clearing operation. The base-of-fire element must be able to identify the location of the lead fire team in the trench at all times.

**Step 10.** The platoon leader rotates squads to keep the soldiers fresh and to maintain the momentum of the assault.

**Step 11.** The platoon sergeant (PSG) calls forward ammunition resupply and organizes teams to move it forward into the trench.

**Step 12.** The base-of-fire element ensures that all friendly forces move into the trench only through the designated entry point to avoid fratricide.

**Step 13.** The platoon leader reports to the company commander that the trench line is secured, or that he is no longer able to continue clearing. If trench line is secured, then the platoon leader directs the platoon FO to develop a fire plan to support the defense of the platoon position.

### Breach an Obstacle Drill

The breach an obstacle drill is used when the lead squad identifies a wire obstacle, reinforced with mines, that cannot be bypassed, and when there are enemy positions on the far side of the obstacle.

**Step 1.** The platoon leader moves forward with his FO and one machine-gun team.

**Step 2.** The platoon leader determines whether he can maneuver.

**Step 3.** The platoon leader directs one squad to be the base-of-fire element, another to be the breach squad, and a third to be the assault squad once the breach has been made.

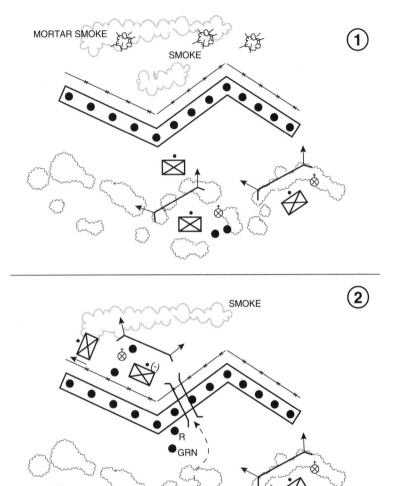

**Initial Breach of a Mined Wire Obstacle—Platoon**

**Step 4.** The base-of-fire squad is joined by the platoon sergeant and the second machine-gun team. Together they begin to suppress the enemy and obscure the enemy positions with smoke.

**Step 5.** The platoon leader leads the breach and assault squads to the breach point.

1. The breach squad leader designates a breach fire team and a support fire team.
2. The breaching fire team moves to the breach point using the covered and concealed route. The squad and fire team leader obscure the breach point, using smoke grenades.
3. The breaching fire team leader and an automatic rifleman are positioned on one flank of the breach point to provide security.
4. The grenadier and rifleman of the breaching fire team probe for and mark mines and cut the wire obstacle, marking their path as they proceed. (If available, Bangalore torpedoes are preferred for clearing a lane through a minefield.)

**Step 6.** Once the obstacle has been breached, the fire team leader and the automatic rifleman move to the far side of the obstacle and take up covered and concealed positions with the rifleman and the grenadier.

**Step 7.** The squad leader signals the supporting fire team to move up and through the breach to the far side, where it takes up covered and concealed positions. The squad leader then moves through the breach and joins the breaching fire team.

**Step 8.** The squad leader reports to the platoon leader and consolidates as needed.

**Step 9.** The platoon leader leads the assault squad through the breach and positions it to support the movement of the remainder of the platoon, or assaults the enemy position covering the obstacle.

**Step 10.** The platoon leader reports to the company commander.

# 5

# Defense

Platoons and squads normally defend as part of a larger force to disrupt, disorganize, delay, or defeat an attacking enemy; deny an area to an enemy; or protect a flank. They may also defend as part of a larger unit in a retrograde operation. The challenge to the defender is to retain the initiative: that is, keep the enemy reacting and unable to execute its own plan. The characteristics of the defense are preparation, security, disruption, mass and concentration, and flexibility. These are also the planning fundamentals for the combat leader.

## CHARACTERISTICS OF DEFENSE
**Preparation.** The defender arrives in the battle area before the attacker. The platoon must take advantage of this by making all possible preparations for combat in the time available. Constant improvement on defensive positions and infrastructure (CCP location) is mandatory.

**Security.** The goals of the platoon's security efforts are normally tied to the company's efforts. Security efforts include providing early warning, destroying enemy reconnaissance units, and impeding and harassing elements of the enemy's main body. Emplacing of listening/observation posts (LP/OP) and early warning devices provide needed alarm to the main body.

**Disruption.** Defensive plans vary with the circumstances, but all defensive concepts of the operation aim at disrupting the attacker's synchronization. Counterattacks, indirect fires, obstacles, and the retention of key terrain prevent the enemy from concentrating his strength against selected portions of the platoon's defense.

**Mass and Concentration.** The platoon masses to concentrate combat power at the decisive place and time if it is to succeed. Offensive action may also be necessary. For concentration, all available combat power should be requested and employed, not just numbers of soldiers and weapons systems.

**Flexibility.** Flexibility is derived from sound preparation and effective command and control ($C^2$). The platoon must be agile enough to counter an attack, withstand the attacker's blows, and then strike back effectively.

## SEQUENCE OF THE DEFENSE

As part of a larger element, the platoon conducts defensive operations in a sequence of integrated and overlapping actions:
1. Reconnaissance, security operations, and enemy preparatory fires.
2. Occupation of a defensive position.
3. Approach of the enemy main attack.
4. Enemy assault.
5. Counterattack or withdrawal.
6. Consolidation and reorganization.

### Reconnaissance, Security Operations, and Enemy Preparatory Fires

Security forces forward of the battle area must protect friendly forces in the main battle area (MBA) and allow them to prepare for the defense. The goals of a forward security force are to provide early warning, destroy enemy reconnaissance elements (within its capability), and disrupt enemy forward detachments or advance guard elements. During this last step, the platoon may be attached to a larger element or remain with the parent company. Additionally, the platoon performs counter-reconnaissance and security operations by conducting patrols or manning LP/OPs to observe named areas of interest (NAIs).

### Occupation of a Defensive Position

The platoon plans, reconnoiters, and occupies the defensive position. This involves moving from one location to the defensive location. A quartering party that will clear the defensive position and prepare it for occupation normally leads this movement. The battalion establishes security forces, and the remaining forces prepare the defense.

Occupation and preparation of the defense site are conducted in accordance with the company commander's plan and the results of the reconnaissance. The quartering party reconnaissance element marks the friendly positions, which are entered onto the operational graphics. Each squad moves in—or is led in by a guide—to its marker. Once in position, each squad leader checks his position location. As the platoon occupies its positions, the platoon leader manages the positioning of each squad to ensure they are located in accordance with the initial plan. The unit leader should personally walk the positions to ensure that everyone understands the plan in terms of the following:

- Weapons orientation.
- Machine-gun or weapons squads' positions.
- Rifle squads' positions.
- CCP location.
- Platoon leader's and the platoon sergeant's locations.

Once the position is occupied, subordinate leaders begin to develop their sector sketches based on the basic fire plan developed during the leader's reconnaissance. Positions are improved continuously. In addition to establishing the platoon's primary positions, the platoon leader and subordinate leaders normally plan for alternate, supplementary, and subsequent positions in accordance with the company order. The following are tactical considerations for these positions:

*Alternate Position.* Covers the same avenue of approach or sector of fire as the primary position. It is located slightly to the front, flank, or rear of the primary position; positioned forward of the primary defensive positions during limited-visibility operations; and normally employed to supplement or support positions with weapons of limited range, such as infantry squad positions.

*Supplementary Position.* Covers an avenue of approach or sector of fire different from those covered by the primary position and is occupied based on specific enemy actions.

*Subsequent Position.* Covers the same avenue of approach and/or sector of fire as the primary position, is located in depth through the defensive sector, and is occupied based on specific enemy actions or conducted as part of the higher headquarters' scheme of maneuver.

### Approach of the Enemy Main Attack
Higher-level units engage the enemy at long range using combat multipliers in an effort to disrupt his synchronization and degrade his combat power. Platoons cease security patrolling and usually bring LP/OPs back into the defense position. Positions may be shifted in response to enemy actions or other tactical factors.

### Enemy Assault
During this step, enemy forces attempt to fix friendly forces and complete their assault. During execution of the defense, friendly forces attempt to mass effects of fires to destroy the assaulting enemy. The platoon leader determines if the platoon can destroy the enemy from its assigned positions; if it can, the platoon continues to fight the defense.

The platoon leader continues to call for indirect fires as the enemy approaches. The platoon begins to engage the enemy at maximum effective range and attempts to mass fires and initiate them simultaneously to achieve maximum weapons effects. Indirect fires and obstacles integrated with direct fires should disrupt the enemy's formations, channel him toward engagement areas (EAs), prevent or severely limit his ability to observe the location of friendly positions, and destroy him as he attempts to breach tactical obstacles.

Leaders control fires using standard commands, pyrotechnics, and other prearranged signals. The platoon increases the intensity of fires as the enemy closes within range of additional weapons. Squad leaders work to achieve a sustained rate of fire from their positions by having buddy teams engage the enemy so that both soldiers are not reloading their weapons at the same time.

The enemy closes on the platoon's protective wire. Crew-served weapons and machine guns fire along interlocking fields of fire or final protective lines (FPLs) as previously planned and designated. These include the platoon's machine guns, while other weapons fire at their designated fields of fire. Grenadiers engage the enemy with M203 grenade launchers in dead space or as the enemy attempts to breach protective wire. The platoon leader requests final protective fire (if assigned in support of his positions).

The platoon continues to defend until it repels the enemy or is ordered to disengage. If the platoon cannot destroy the enemy from its assigned positions, the platoon leader reports the situation to the company commander and continues to engage the enemy. He repositions the platoon (or squads of the platoon) when directed by the commander to continue fires into the platoon sector, occupy supplementary positions, reinforce other parts of the company, counterattack locally to retake lost fighting positions, and/or withdraw from an indefensible position using fire and movement to break contact.

### Counterattack

As the enemy's momentum is slowed or stopped, friendly forces may counterattack. Counterattack can be launched purely for offensive purposes to seize the initiative from the enemy, or it may be mainly defensive—for example, to reestablish the forward edge of the battle area (FEBA) or to restore control of the sector. The company or platoon may participate in the counterattack as a base-of-fire element or as the counterattack force.

### Consolidation and Reorganization

The platoon secures its sector and reestablishes the defense by repositioning forces, occupying advantageous terrain, destroying enemy elements, processing EPWs, and reestablishing obstacles. The platoon conducts all necessary combat service support (CSS) functions as it prepares to continue defending. Consolidation includes organizing and strengthening a position so that it can continue to hold against the enemy, using means such as adjusting other positions to maintain mutual support; reoccupying and repairing prior positions; relocating selected weapons to alternate positions if leaders believe that the enemy may have pinpointed them during the attack; repairing damaged obstacles; replacing mines (Claymores) and booby traps; and reestablishing security and communications.

Reorganization includes shifting internal resources within a degraded unit to increase its level of combat effectiveness, using means such as manning key weapons; providing first aid and preparing injured soldiers for casualty evacuation (CASEVAC); redistributing ammunition and supplies; and processing and evacuating EPWs.

## BATTLEFIELD OPERATING SYSTEMS
## PLANNING CONSIDERATIONS

The Battlefield Operating Systems (BOS) are the seven critical tactical activities whose synchronization and coordination are critical for success. The following BOS pertain to defense operations.

**Maneuver.** Effective weapons positioning enables the platoon to mass fires at critical points on the battlefield and to enhance survivability. The combat leader must maximize the strengths of the platoon's weapons systems while minimizing its exposure to enemy observation and fires.

**Fire Support.** For the indirect-fire plan to be effective in the defense, the unit must plan and execute indirect fires in a manner that achieves the intended task and purpose of each target. Indirect fires slow and disrupt the enemy, prevent enemy breaching operations, destroy or delay enemy forces at obstacles, defeat attacks along dismounted avenues of approach using FPF, and obscure enemy observation, among other effects.

**Mobility, Countermobility, and Survivability.** Mobility in defense means the ability to reposition forces, including unit displacement and the commitment of reserve forces. The company commander's priorities may specify that some routes be improved to support such operations. Countermobility (obstacles) limits the maneuver of enemy forces and enhances the effectiveness of the defender's direct and indirect fires. Survivability focuses on protecting friendly forces from the effect of enemy weapons systems.

**Air Defense.** The focus of an air defense plan is on likely air avenues of approach for enemy fixed-wing aircraft, helicopters, and unmanned aerial vehicles, which may not correspond with the enemy's ground avenues of approach. A platoon leader is not likely to emplace air defense assets; however, he must be aware that higher headquarters may employ air defense assets near his defensive position.

**Combat Service Support.** In addition to the CSS functions required for all, the platoon leader's mission analysis (or guidance) may reveal that the unit's ammunition needs during an operation could exceed its basic load. This requires the platoon to establish ammunition caches. These caches, which may be positioned at alternate or subsequent positions, should be dug in and security provided by active or passive means (such as guarded or observed) or passive measures employed to indicate when and if the cache is tampered with.

**Intelligence.** Gaining information about the enemy is critical in defense. Continuing intelligence updates as well as constant reconnaissance of the area afford the infantry leader the information needed to constantly improve the unit's position.

**Command and Control.** Command and control refers to the process of directing, coordinating, and controlling a unit to accomplish a mission. Having effective communication to higher and supporting units is an essential BOS.

## ENGAGEMENT AREA DEVELOPMENT
The engagement area (EA) is the place where the unit leader intends to destroy an enemy force using the massed fires of all available weapons. The success of any engagement depends on how effectively the leader can integrate the obstacle and indirect-fire plans with his direct-fire plan in the EA to achieve the unit's purpose. Despite its complexity, EA development resembles a drill. The leader and his subordinate leaders use a standardized set of procedures. Beginning with an evaluation of the factors of METT-TC, the development process covers these steps:
1. Identify likely enemy avenues of approach.
2. Identify the enemy scheme of maneuver.
3. Determine where to kill the enemy.
4. Emplace weapons systems.
5. Plan and integrate obstacles.
6. Plan and integrate indirect fires.
7. Conduct an EA rehearsal.

### Identify Likely Enemy Avenues of Approach
The infantry leader conducts an initial reconnaissance of the enemy's probable avenue of approach into the sector or EA. He confirms key terrain identified by the company commander, including locations that afford positional advantage over the enemy and natural obstacles and choke points that restrict forward movement. The platoon leader determines which avenues will afford cover and concealment for the enemy while allowing him to maintain his tempo. The leader also evaluates lateral mobility corridors (routes) that adjoin each avenue of approach.

**Identify the Enemy Scheme of Maneuver**
The leader greatly enhances his planning by gaining information early. He attempts to receive answers (from higher headquarters) about the enemy's purpose, direction, terrain orientation, mission, objectives, attack structure, recon assets, expected rate of movement, and response to friendly actions.
***Determine Where to Kill the Enemy.*** As part of his troop-leading procedures, the infantry leader must determine where he will mass combat power on the enemy to accomplish his purpose. This decision is tied to his assessment of how the enemy will fight into the platoon's EA. Normally this entry point is marked by a prominent reference point (RP) that all platoon elements can engage with their direct-fire weapons. This allows the commander to identify where the platoon will engage enemy forces through the depth of the company EA. In addition, the leader will:
• Select target reference points (TRPs) that match the enemy's scheme of maneuver, allowing the platoon (or company) to identify fire support adjustment points.
• Identify and record the exact location of each TRP.
• Determine how many weapons systems can focus fires on each TRP to achieve the desired purpose.
• Determine which squad(s) can mass fires on each TRP.
• Begin development of a direct-fire plan that focuses at each TRP.
*Note*: In marking TRPs, use thermal sights to ensure visibility at the appropriate range under varying conditions, including daylight and limited visibility.

**Emplace Weapons Systems**
To position weapons effectively, leaders must know the characteristics, capabilities, and limitations of the weapons as well as the effects of terrain and the tactics used by the enemy. Platoon leaders should position weapons where they have protection, where they can avoid detection, and where they can surprise the enemy with accurate, lethal fires. In order to place them, the platoon leader must know where he wants to destroy the enemy and what effect he wants the weapons to achieve. He should also consider:
• Selecting tentative squad defensive positions.
• Conducting a leader's reconnaissance of the tentative defensive positions.
• Walking the EA to confirm that the selected positions are tactically advantageous.
• Confirming and marking the selected defensive positions.
• Developing a direct-fire plan that accomplishes the platoon's purpose.

- Ensuring the defensive positions do not conflict with those of adjacent units and are effectively tied in with adjacent positions.
- Selecting primary, alternate, and supplementary fighting positions to achieve the desired effect for each TRP.
- Ensuring the squad leaders position weapons systems so the required numbers of weapons or squads effectively cover each TRP.
- Inspecting all positions.

*Note*: When possible, select fighting and crew-served weapon positions while moving in the EA. Using the enemy's perspective enables the platoon leader to assess survivability of the positions.

**Plan and Integrate Obstacles**

To be successful in the defense, the platoon leader will integrate tactical obstacles with the direct-fire plan, taking into account the intent of each obstacle. Obstacles disrupt, turn, or fix the enemy. A combat platoon must have a clear task and purpose in order to properly emplace a tactical obstacle. Once the tactical obstacle has been emplaced, the platoon leader must report its location and any gaps in the obstacle to the company commander.

**Abatis**

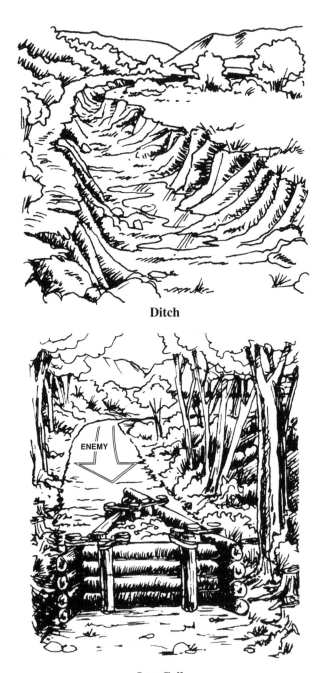

**Ditch**

**Log Crib**

There are two types of obstacles: existing and reinforcing. *Existing obstacles* are those natural or cultural restrictions to movement that are part of the terrain when battle planning begins, such as slopes, gullies, rivers, swamps, trees, or built-up areas. *Reinforcing obstacles* are those specifically constructed, emplaced, or detonated to tie together, strengthen, and extend existing obstacles. Reinforcing obstacles include road craters, abatis, ditches, log hurdles, cribs, rubble, or wire entanglements.

*Wire Obstacles.* Wire is classified by its use and location.

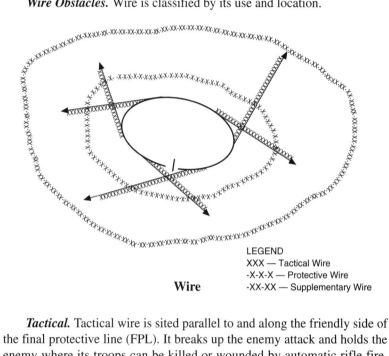

**Wire**

LEGEND
XXX — Tactical Wire
-X-X-X — Protective Wire
-XX-XX — Supplementary Wire

*Tactical.* Tactical wire is sited parallel to and along the friendly side of the final protective line (FPL). It breaks up the enemy attack and holds the enemy where its troops can be killed or wounded by automatic rifle fire, Claymores, hand grenades, and machine-gun fire.

*Protective.* Protective wire is located to prevent surprise assaults from points close to the defense area. It is close enough for day and night observation but far enough away (40 to 100 meters) to keep the enemy from using hand grenades. Protective wire of adjacent platoons is connected by supplementary wire; this encloses the entire defensive position. Gaps must be provided, however, to allow patrols to exit and enter the position.

*Supplementary.* Supplementary wire is used to disguise the exact lines of the tactical wire. It prevents the enemy from locating the unit's perimeter and machine guns by following the wire.

*Minefields.* Mines are one of the most effective tank destroyers and personnel killers on the battlefield. The infantry platoon most commonly emplaces hasty protective, point, and phony minefields (see Appendix C).

### Plan and Integrate Indirect Fires

In planning and integrating indirect fires, the platoon leader must accomplish the following:

- Determine the purpose of fires, if the company commander has not already done so.
- Determine where that purpose will best be achieved, if the company commander has not already done so.
- Establish the observation plan with redundancy for each target. Observers will include the platoon leader as well as members of subordinate elements (such as team leaders) with fire support responsibilities.
- Establish triggers based on enemy movement rates.
- Obtain accurate target locations using survey and navigational equipment.
- Refine target locations to ensure coverage of obstacles.
- Register artillery and mortars and plan final protective fires (FPF).

Also see the "Fires" portion of the coordination checklists on pages 24 and 28–29.

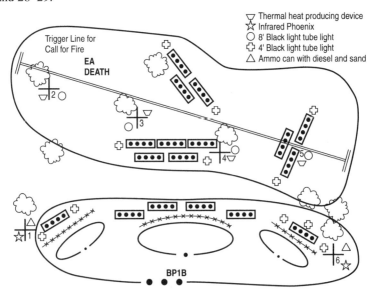

**Integrated Engagement Area Plan—Platoon**

**Conduct an Engagement Area Rehearsal**

The purpose of rehearsal is to ensure that every leader and every soldier understands the plan and is prepared to cover his assigned areas with direct and indirect fires. The platoon will likely participate in a company level EA rehearsal.

The company commander has several options for conducting a rehearsal, but the combined arms rehearsal produces the most detailed understanding of the plan. One rehearsal technique is to have the platoon sergeant and squads conduct a movement through the EA to depict the attacking enemy force, while the platoon leader and squad leaders rehearse the battle from the platoon defensive positions. The rehearsal should cover:

- Rearward passage of security forces (as required).
- Closure of lanes (as required).
- Use of fire commands, triggers, and/or maximum engagement lines (MELs) to initiate direct and indirect fires.
- Shifting of fires to refocus and redistribute fire effects.
- Disengagement criteria.
- Identification of displacement routes and times.
- Preparation and transmission of critical reports.
- Assessment of the effects of enemy weapons systems.
- Displacement to alternate, supplementary, or subsequent defensive positions.
- Cross-leveling or resupply of Class V items.
- Evacuation of casualties.

*Note*: When conducting his rehearsal, the platoon leader should coordinate with the company to ensure other units' rehearsals are not planned for the same time and location and to eliminate the danger of misidentification of friendly forces in the rehearsal area.

**Fire Commands and Engagement Priorities**

Leaders use fire commands to direct the fires of the unit. A fire command has six parts:

1. *Alert*. The leader alerts the soldiers by name or unit designation, by some type of visual or sound signal, by personal contact, or by any other practical method.
2. *Direction*. The leader tells the soldiers the general direction or pinpoint location of the target.
3. *Description*. The leader describes the target briefly but accurately. Always give the formation of enemy soldiers.
4. *Range*. The leader tells the range to the target in meters.

5. *Method of fire.* The leader designates the weapons to fire. He can also tell the type and amount of ammunition to fire and the rate of fire.

6. *Command to fire.* The leader tells soldiers when to fire. He can use an oral command, a sound, or a visual signal. When he wants to control the exact moment, he says, "At my command." When he wants firing to start at the completion of the command, he just says, "Fire."

Targets appear in random order at different times and locations throughout the battlefield. *Engagement priorities* allow the leader to designate which target he wants destroyed first. Engagement priorities are usually done by weapons systems. For example, Dragon gunners would fire first at the most threatening armored vehicle and then at any other armored vehicle in the kill zone or primary sector. Machine guns would fire at groups of five or more in the primary sector and then at automatic weapons. Riflemen would fire in their primary and secondary sectors from nearest to farthest, starting on the flank and working toward the center. Any number of priorities can be assigned to any weapon system.

## OCCUPATION AND PREPARATION OF DEFENSIVE POSITIONS
Occupying and preparing a defensive position is not sequential. One potential problem is the lack of adequate preparation time if the platoon also has several other defensive positions (alternate, supplementary, and subsequent) and EAs to develop.

### Occupation of Defensive Positions
The platoon occupies defensive positions in accordance with the leader's plan, which has been based on prior reconnaissance.

To ensure an effective and efficient occupation, rifle squads move to the locations marked previously by the reconnaissance element. Once in position, each squad leader checks his location on the map to ensure he is complying with the platoon leader's graphics. As the platoon occupies its positions, the platoon leader verifies squad locations and corrects discrepancies.

Once each rifle squad has occupied its position, the platoon leader must walk the positions to verify that weapons orientation, positioning of the rifle squads, and understanding of the plan are in accordance with the pre-established plan. For C² purposes, each squad leader must know the location of the platoon leader and the platoon sergeant.

Night vision equipment enhances the occupation process under limited-visibility conditions. For instance, the platoon leader can mark his position with an infrared light source, and the squad leaders can move to pre-marked positions with infrared light sources showing them where to locate.

The platoon may conduct a hasty occupation in the defense during a counterattack or after disengagement and movement to alternate, supplementary, or subsequent defensive positions.

The platoon conducts deliberate occupation of defensive positions when time is available, when enemy contact is not expected, and when friendly elements are positioned forward in the sector to provide security for forces in the main battle area. Actually establishing defensive positions is accomplished concurrently with the development of the EA. The platoon leader directs the initial reconnaissance from the EA and then tentatively emplaces crew-served weapon systems.

Once the defensive positions are established, subordinate leaders can begin to develop their sector sketches and fire plans based on the basic fire plan developed during the leader's reconnaissance. Fighting positions are improved while the direct-fire plan is finalized and proofed. The platoon leader, with guidance from the company commander, designates the level of preparation for each defensive position based on the time available and other tactical considerations for the mission.

In addition to establishing the platoon's primary defensive positions, the platoon leader and subordinate leaders normally plan for preparation and occupation of alternate, supplementary, and subsequent defensive positions (layered defense) in accordance with the company order.

### Priority of Work

Leaders must ensure that their soldiers prepare for the defense quickly and efficiently. Work must be done in order of priority to accomplish the most in the least amount of time while maintaining security and the ability to respond to enemy action. Below are basic considerations for priorities of work:

- Emplace local security.
- Position and assign sectors of fire for each squad (platoon leader).
- Position and assign sectors of fire for the crew-served weapons and the machine-gun teams (platoon leader).
- Position and assign sectors of fire for SAW, grenadiers, and then riflemen (squad leader).
- Clear fields of fire (remove vegetation if applicable) and prepare range cards.
- Prepare sector sketches (leaders).
- Dig fighting positions (stage 1; see Chapter 13).
- Establish communication/coordination with the company and adjacent units.
- Coordinate with adjacent units and review sector sketches.
- Emplace AT and Claymore mines, then wire and other obstacles.

- Improve primary fighting positions and add overhead cover (stage 2; see Chapter 13).
- Prepare supplementary and then alternate positions (same procedure as the primary position).
- Distribute and stockpile ammunition, food, and water.
- Establish the HQ element with communicator.
- Establish the CCP.

Priorities of work are dictated by unit SOPs and commander's guidance based on METT-TC. Many actions are completed at the same time; thus it is important that leaders are constantly supervising activities.

**Security in the Defense**
Security in the defense includes all active and passive measures taken to avoid detection by the enemy, deceive the enemy, and deny enemy reconnaissance elements accurate information on friendly positions. The two primary tools available to the platoon leader are listening/observation posts (LP/OPs) and patrols. In planning for the security in the defense, the platoon leader considers the terrain and intelligence updates to plan his courses of action.

*Listening/Observation Posts.* An LP/OP gives the platoon its first echelon of security in the defense. It provides early warning of impending enemy contact by reporting direction, distance, and size. It also detects the enemy early and sends accurate reports to the platoon. The platoon leader establishes LP/OPs along the most likely enemy avenues of approach into the position or into the EA. Leaders ensure that LP/OPs have communication with the platoon.

*Patrols.* Platoons actively patrol in the defense. Patrols enhance the platoon's ability to fill gaps in security between LP/OPs. The platoon leader forwards his tentative patrol route to the commander to ensure that it does not conflict with other elements within the company. The commander forwards the entire company's patrol routes to the battalion. This allows the battalion S-3 and S-2 to ensure all routes are coordinated for fratricide prevention and that the company and platoons are conforming to the battalion intelligence, surveillance, and reconnaissance (ISR) plan.

**Establishment of Defensive Positions**
Platoons establish defensive positions in accordance with the platoon leader and commander's plan. They mark EAs using marking techniques prescribed by unit SOP. The platoon physically marks obstacles, TRPs, targets, and trigger lines in the EA. During limited visibility, the platoon can use infrared light sources to mark TRPs for the rifle squads. When possible, platoons should mark TRPs with both a thermal and an infrared source so the rifle squads can use the TRP.

***Range Cards.*** A range card is a sketch of a sector that a direct-fire weapons system is assigned to cover. A range card aids in planning and controlling fires and aids the crew in acquiring targets during limited visibility. It is also an aid for replacement personnel, platoons, or squads to move into the position and to orient on their sector. During good visibility, the gunner should have no problems maintaining orientation in his sector. During poor visibility, he may not be able to detect lateral limits. If the gunner becomes disoriented and cannot find or locate reference points or sector limit markers, he can use the range card to locate the limits. The gunner should make the range card so that he becomes more familiar with the terrain in his sector. Range cards are prepared immediately during stage 1 of defensive fighting positions (see Chapter 13) and are updated as necessary. Two copies of the range card are prepared, one for the position and one for the squad leader to prepare his sketch.

The range card has two sections: a sector sketch section and a data section. The marginal information at the top of the card is listed as follows:

- *SQD, PLT, and CO.* The squad, platoon, and company designations are listed. Units higher than company are not listed.
- *Magnetic north.* The range card is oriented with the terrain, and the direction of magnetic north arrow is drawn.

The gunner's sector of fire is drawn in the sector sketch section. It is not drawn to scale, but the data referring to the targets must be accurate.

- The weapon symbol is drawn in the center of the small circle.
- Left and right limits are drawn from the position. A circled "L" and "R" are placed at the end of the left and right limit lines, respectively.
- The value of each circle is determined by using a terrain feature farthest from the position that is within the weapon's capability. The distance to the terrain is determined and rounded off to the next even hundredth, if necessary. The maximum number of circles that will divide evenly into the distance is determined and divided. The result is the value for each circle. The terrain feature is then drawn on the appropriate circle.
- All TRPs and reference points are drawn in the sector. They are numbered consecutively and circled.
- Dead space is drawn in the sector.
- A maximum engagement line is drawn on range cards for antiarmor weapons.
- The weapon reference point is numbered last. The location is given a six-digit grid coordinate. When there is no terrain feature to be designated, the location is shown as an eight-digit grid coordinate.

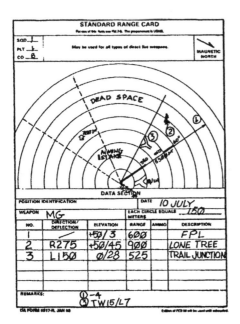

Primary sector with FPL

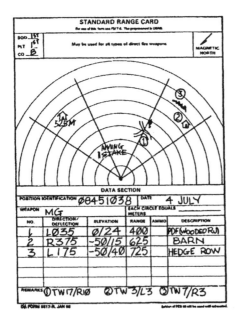

Primary sector with PDF

**Completed Range Card—Machine Gun**

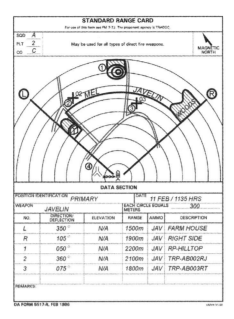

**Completed Range Card—Javelin**

The data section is filled in as follows:

• *Position identification.* Identify the position as primary, alternate, or supplementary.

• *Date.* Enter the date and time the range card was completed.

• *Weapon.* The weapon block indicates the weapons used.

• *Distance.* Each circle equals meters. Write in the distance in meters between circles.

• *No.* Starting with left and right limits, list the TRPs and reference points in numerical order.

• *Direction/deflection.* List the direction in degrees and the deflection in mils.

• *Elevation.* List the elevation in mils.

• *Range.* List the distance in meters from the position to the left and right limits and TRPs and reference points.

• *Ammo.* List the type of ammunition used.

• *Description.* List the name of the object(for example, farmhouse, woodline, hilltop).

• *Remarks.* List the weapon reference point data and any additional information.

*Sector Sketches.* Leaders prepare sector sketches based on their defensive plan. They use the range card for each fighting position (prepared by the soldiers in each position). Detailed sketches aid in the planning, distribution, and control of the platoon fires. Squad leaders prepare squad sector sketches, section leaders prepare section sketches, and the platoon leader prepares the platoon sketch.

*Squad Sector Sketch.* Each squad leader prepares a sector sketch to help him plan his defense and control fire. The squad leader prepares two copies of the sector sketch. He gives one to the platoon leader and keeps the second at his position. The SOP should state how soon after occupying the position the leader must forward the sketch. The sketch shows the following:

- Squad and platoon identification.
- Date/time group.
- Magnetic north.
- The main terrain features in his sector of fire and the ranges to them.
- Each primary fighting position.
- Alternate and supplementary positions.
- The primary and secondary sectors of fire of each position.
- Maximum engagement line.
- Machine-gun FPLs or PDF.
- Dragon positions with sectors of fire.
- The type of weapon in each position.
- Observation posts and the squad leader's position.
- Dead space to include coverage by grenade launchers.
- Location of night vision devices (NVGs).
- Obstacles, mines, and booby traps.

*Platoon Sector Sketch.* The platoon leader checks range cards and squad sector sketches. If he finds gaps or other flaws in his fire plan, he adjusts the weapons or sectors as needed. If he finds any dead space, he takes steps to cover it with mines, grenade-launcher fire, or indirect fire. He then makes two copies of his platoon sector sketch—one for his use and the other for the company commander. His sketch shows the following:

- Squad sectors of fire.
- Machine-gun and antiarmor weapon positions and their sectors of fires, including FPLs and PDFs of the automatic rifles and machine guns and TRPs for the antiarmor weapons.
- MELs for antiarmor weapons.
- Mines (Claymores) and obstacles.
- Indirect fire planned in the platoon's sector of fire (targets and FPF).
- OPs and patrol routes, if any.
- Platoon CP.

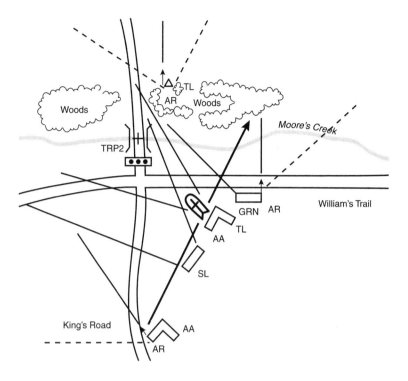

**Squad Sector Sketch**

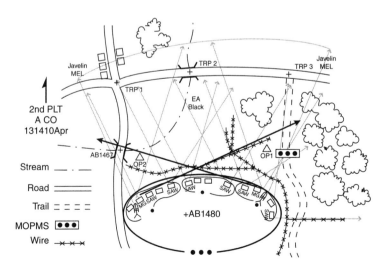

**Platoon Sector Sketch**

- Platoon/company identification.
- Date/time group.
- Magnetic north.
- Location of CCP.
- Location of NVDs/thermal sights that are part of the limited-visibility security plan.
- Adjustments during limited visibility to maintain coverage of assigned TRPs.

## Establishment of Command Post and Wire Communications

The platoon CP is set up where the platoon leader can best see and control his platoon. If he cannot see the entire platoon sector from one place, he sets up where he can see and control the main effort. He then sets up an alternate CP where the platoon sergeant can see and control the rest of the platoon.

In the defense, the platoon CP ties in to the company wire net with a field telephone. Wire is the primary means of communications between the platoon leader and squad leaders. The platoon has its own radio net, and the platoon leader also uses messengers, visual signals, personal contact, or whistles to communicate.

## Weapons and Soldier Placement

To position weapons effectively, leaders must know the characteristics, capabilities, and limitations of the weapons; the effects of terrain; and the tactics used by the enemy. Additionally, the platoon leader must consider whether his primary threat will be vehicles or infantry. His plan should address both mounted and dismounted threats.

*Javelin (Antiarmor) Employment.* The Javelin's (or antiarmor weapon such as the older M-47 Dragon) primary role is to destroy enemy armored vehicles. When there is no such enemy, the Javelin can be employed in a secondary role of providing fire support against point targets such as crew-served weapons positions. In addition, the Javelin's command launch unit (CLU) can be used alone as an aided vision device for reconnaissance, security operations, and surveillance. Reduced or limited visibility will not degrade the effectiveness of the Javelin. This fact allows the antiarmor specialist to continue to cover his sector without having to reposition closer to the avenue of approach.

*M240B and M249 Machine-Gun Employment.* The M240B and M249 machine guns are the platoon's primary crew-served weapons and are positioned first if the enemy is a dismounted force. Once these guns are sited, the leader positions riflemen to protect them. The guns are positioned to place direct fire on locations where the platoon leader wants to concentrate combat power to destroy the enemy. Each gun is usually given a primary and secondary sector of fire. These sectors should overlap each other and those of adjacent platoons (if possible). Additionally, the platoon leader will designate FPLs and/or FPF. Each machine gun's primary sector includes an FPL (if terrain allows) or a principal direction of fire (PDF).

The FPL is a line along which *grazing fire*—no more than 1 meter above the ground—is placed to stop an assault. The FPL is fixed in elevation and direction. A soldier walks the FPL to find dead space. The gunner watches the soldier walking the line and marks spaces that cannot be grazed; this dead space is then covered with obstacles, grenade-launcher fire, or mines.

When the terrain does not lend itself to an FPL, the platoon leader assigns the machine gun a PDF to cover an area that provides good fields of fire or has a likely avenue of approach. The gun is laid on the FPL or the PDF unless engaging other targets. When FPFs are called for, the gunner shifts to and engages on the FPL or PDF.

**Grazing Fire**

FPFs are prearranged barriers of indirect fires used to defeat the assaulting enemy unit as soon as possible after it moves into its assault formation. The FPF can be anywhere between the forward position of the friendly unit and the enemy's assault position, which is normally just out of range of the platoon's organic weapons. The FPF should be used only to stop an enemy assault. On signal, the FPF is fired continuously until the order is given to stop or the mortar or artillery unit runs out of ammunition. All other platoon weapons fire while the FPF is being fired.

***M203 Grenade Launcher Employment.*** The M203 grenade launcher is the squad leader's indirect-fire weapon. He positions it to cover dead space in the squad's sector, especially the dead space for the M240Bs and M249s. The grenadier is also assigned a sector of fire overlapping the riflemen's sectors of fire. The high-explosive, dual-purpose (HEDP) round is effective against lightly armored enemy vehicles.

**Employment of Riflemen**
The platoon and squad leaders assign positions and sectors of fire to each rifleman in the platoon. Normally, they position the riflemen to support and protect the machine guns, SAWs, and antiarmor weapons. Riflemen also are positioned to cover obstacles, provide security, cover gaps between platoons and companies, or provide observation.

**Coordination**
Coordination is important in every operation. In the defense, coordination ensures that units provide mutual support and interlocking fires. In most circumstances, the platoon leader conducts face-to-face coordination to facilitate understanding and to resolve issues. The platoon leader should send and receive the following information prior to conducting face-to-face coordination:
• Location of leaders.
• Location of primary, alternate, and supplementary positions and sectors of fire of machine guns, antiarmor weapons, and sub-units.
• Route to alternate and supplementary positions.
• Location of dead space between platoons and squads and how to cover it.
• Location of OPs and withdrawal routes back to the platoon's or squad's position.
• Location and types of obstacles and how to cover them.
• Patrols to be conducted, including their size, type, times of departure and return, and routes.
• Location, activities, and passage plans for scouts and other units forward of the platoon's position.
• Signals for fire, ceasefire, and any others that may be observed.
• Engagement and disengagement criteria.
Fire team leaders should also coordinate to ensure that each position knows who and what weapons are to the left and right. This ensures that all positions and all units are mutually supportive and that any gaps between units are covered by fire, observation, patrols, or sensors.
***Preparation of Fighting Positions.*** As mentioned earlier, defensive positions are classified as *primary*, *alternate*, *supplementary*, or *subsequent*. All positions should provide observation and fields of fire within the weapon's or platoon's assigned sector of fire. They should take advantage of natural cover and concealment even before soldiers camouflage them. Soldiers prepare their positions in four stages (see Chapter 13).

As a guideline, a squad can physically occupy a front of about 100 meters. From this position, it can defend 200 to 250 meters of frontage. The frontage distance between two-man fighting positions should be about 20 meters (allowing for a "lazy W" configuration on the ground, which would put fighting positions about 25 meters apart physically). Every position should be observed and supported by the fires of at least two other positions. One-man fighting positions may be located closer together to occupy the same platoon frontage. The distance between fighting positions depends on the leader's analysis of the factors of METT-TC. In determining the best distance between fighting positions, the squad leader must consider:

- The requirement to cover the squad's assigned sector by fire.
- The need for security—that is, to prevent infiltrations of the squad position.
- The requirement to prevent the enemy from using hand grenades effectively to assault adjacent positions should it gain a fighting position.

**FIGHTING THE DEFENSE**
Forces defend aggressively, continually seeking opportunities to take advantage of the enemy's errors or failures. Defense includes maneuver and counterattack, as well as keeping key positions secure. The battle begins when the planned signal or event for beginning fire occurs. The platoon leader determines whether the platoon can destroy the enemy from its assigned positions. If the answer is yes, the platoon continues to fight the defense. The platoon leader or FO continues to call for indirect fires as the enemy approaches.

The platoon normally begins engaging the enemy at maximum effective range. It attempts to mass fires and initiate them simultaneously to achieve surprise. Long-range fires tied in with obstacles should disrupt enemy formations, channelize the enemy toward engagement areas, prevent or severely limit his ability to observe the location of friendly positions, and destroy the enemy as he attempts to breach tactical obstacles.

Leaders control fires using standard commands, pyrotechnics, and other prearranged signals. The platoon increases the intensity of fires as the enemy closes within range of additional weapons. Squad leaders work to achieve a sustained rate of fire from their positions by having buddy teams fire their weapons so that both are not reloading at the same time. In controlling and distributing fires, the platoon and squad leaders consider:

- Range to the enemy.
- Priority targets (what to fire at, when to fire, and why).
- Nearest or most dangerous targets.
- Shifting to concentrate fires on their own initiative or as directed by higher headquarters.

- Ability of the platoon to engage dismounted enemy with enfilading, grazing fires.
- Ability of the platoon's antiarmor weapons to achieve flank shots against enemy vehicles.

As the enemy closes on the platoon's protective wire, the platoon leader initiates FPFs:

- Machine guns and automatic weapons fire along interlocking PDFs or FPLs as previously designated and planned. Other weapons fire at designated PDFs. M203 grenade launchers engage the enemy in dead space or against enemy attempts to breach protective wire.
- The platoon continues to fight with Claymores and hand grenades.
- If applicable, the platoon leader requests indirect FPFs if they have been assigned in support of his positions.

The platoon continues to defend until the enemy is repelled or the platoon is ordered to disengage.

If the platoon cannot stop or destroy the enemy from its current position, the platoon leader reports the situation to the company commander and continues to engage the enemy or repositions the platoon (or squads). In this situation—and when directed by the company commander—the platoon leader may:

- Continue fires into the platoon sector (engagement area).
- Occupy supplementary positions.
- Reinforce other parts of the company.
- Counterattack locally to retake lost fighting positions.
- Withdraw from an untenable position using fire and movement to break contact. (The platoon leader will not be ordered to move his platoon out of position if it will destroy the integrity of the company defense.)

*Note:* In any movement out of a defensive position, the platoon must employ all direct and indirect fire means available to suppress the enemy long enough for the unit to move.

## DEFENSIVE TECHNIQUES

The company commander's analysis will determine the most effective manner in which to defend. He will direct the platoons in what defensive techniques to employ. The platoon normally will defend using one of these basic techniques:

1. Defend in sector or area of operation (AO).
2. Defend a battle position (BP).
3. Defend a strongpoint.
4. Defend a perimeter.
5. Defend a reverse slope.

### Defend in Sector/Area of Operation

Defending an area allows a unit to maintain flank contact and security, affords depth in the platoon defense, and facilitates clearance of supporting fires. Area/sector defense is used when flexibility is desired; when retention of specific terrain features is not necessary; or when the unit cannot concentrate fires because of extended frontages, intervening terrain features, and/or multiple avenues of approach. The platoon is assigned an AO defense mission to prevent a specific number of enemy forces from penetrating the rear boundary of the AO. To maintain the integrity of the AO defense, the platoon must remain tied to adjacent units on the flanks. The company commander may direct the platoon to conduct the defense in one of two ways:

1. He may specify a series of subsequent defensive positions within the AO from which the platoon will defend to ensure that the fires of two platoons can be massed.

2. He may assign an AO to the platoon. The platoon leader assumes responsibility for most tactical decisions and controlling maneuvers of his subordinate squads by assigning them a series of subsequent defensive positions in accordance with guidance from the company commander in the form of intent, specified tasks, and the concept of the operation. The company commander normally assigns an AO to a platoon only when it is fighting in isolation.

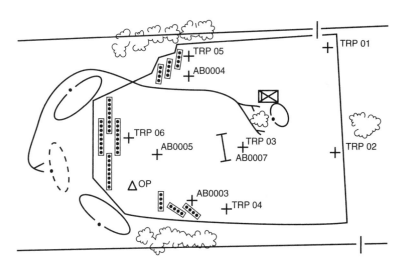

**Concept of the Operation for a Defend in Sector (AO)**

**Defend a Battle Position**

The company commander assigns the defend a battle position defensive technique to his platoons when he wants to mass the fires of two or more platoons in a company EA or to position a platoon to execute a counterattack. A unit defends from a BP to destroy an enemy force in the EA, block an enemy avenue of approach, control key or decisive terrain, and/or fix the enemy force to allow another unit to maneuver. The company commander designates EAs to allow each platoon to concentrate its fires or to place it in an advantageous position for the counterattack.

BPs are developed in such a manner to provide the platoon the ability to place direct fire throughout the EA. The size of the platoon BP can vary, but it should provide enough depth and maneuver space for subordinate squads to maneuver into alternate or supplementary positions and to counterattack. The BP is a general position on the ground. The platoon leader places his squads on the most favorable terrain in the BP, based on the higher unit mission and commander's intent. The platoon then fights to retain the position unless ordered by the company commander to counterattack or displace. The basic methods of employing a platoon in a BP are:

- Same BP, same avenue of approach.
- Same BP, different avenues of approach.
- Different BPs, same avenue of approach.
- Different BPs, different avenues of approach.

***Same Battle Position, Same Avenue of Approach.*** Rifle squads are on the same BP, covering the same avenue of approach. The platoon can defend against mounted and dismounted attacks and move rapidly to another position. All squads are in the same BP when the terrain provides good observation, fields of fire, and cover and concealment.

Employing all the squads of the platoon on the same BP and covering the same avenue of approach is the most conservative use of the platoon. It has two primary advantages: It facilitates $C^2$ functions because of the proximity of squad elements on the same approach, and it provides increased security.

***Same Battle Position, Different Avenues of Approach.*** Rifle squads occupy the same BP but cover different enemy avenues of approach. Try to choose BPs that will cover multiple avenues of approach or require minimum movement.

***Different Battle Positions, Same Avenue of Approach.*** Rifle squads are on different BPs, covering the same avenue of approach. If positioned on separate BPs, rifle squads must fight in relation to each other when covering the same avenues of approach. A weapons squad can provide supporting

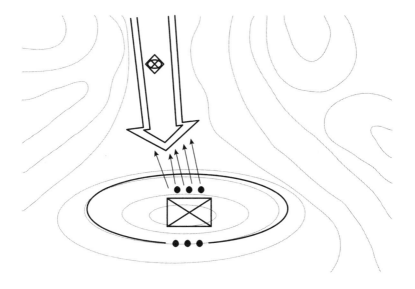

**Same Battle Position, Same Avenue of Approach**

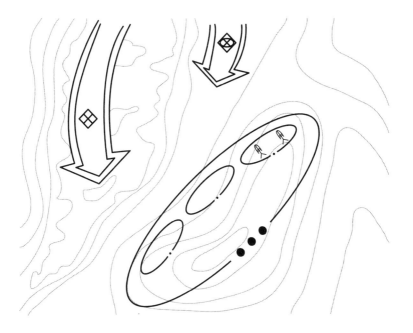

**Same Battle Position, Different Avenues of Approach**

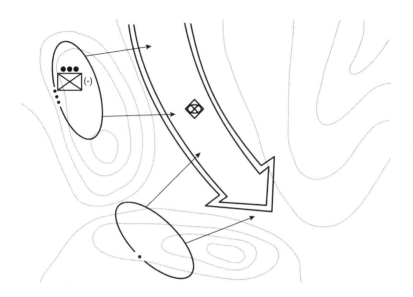

**Different Battle Positions, Same Avenue of Approach**

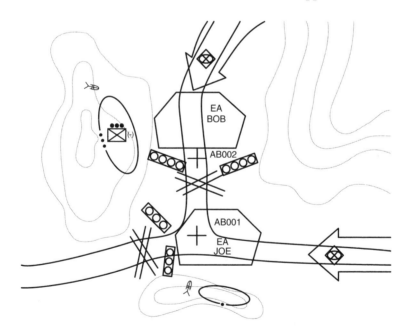

**Different Battle Positions, Different Avenues of Approach**

fires for the rifle squads from their primary, alternate, or supplementary positions. All squads are positioned to engage enemy forces on the same avenue of approach but at different ranges.

*Different Battle Positions, Different Avenues of Approach.* Squads may be employed on different BPs and different avenues of approach. Take caution in planning to ensure that the squad BPs cannot be either fixed or isolated and defeated by the enemy.

### Defend a Strongpoint

Defending a strongpoint is not a common mission for an infantry platoon. A strongpoint defense requires extensive engineer support (in terms of expertise, materials, and equipment) and takes a long time to complete. When the platoon is directed to defend a strongpoint, it must retain the position until ordered to withdraw. The success of the strongpoint defense depends on how well the position is tied into the existing terrain. This defense is most effective when it is employed in terrain that provides cover and concealment to both the strongpoint and its supporting obstacles. Mountainous, forested, or urban terrain can be adapted easily to a strongpoint defense. Strongpoints placed in more open terrain require the use of reverse slopes or extensive camouflage and deception efforts. This defensive mission may require the platoon to perform one or more of the following:

- Hold key or decisive terrain critical to the company or battalion scheme of maneuver.
- Provide a pivot to maneuver friendly forces.
- Block an avenue of approach.
- Canalize the enemy into one or more EAs.

The prime characteristic of an effective strongpoint is that it cannot be easily overrun or bypassed. It must be positioned and constructed so that the enemy knows he can reduce it only at the risk of heavy casualties and significant loss of materiel. Techniques and considerations involved in establishing and executing the strongpoint defense include:

- The projected size of the strongpoint versus available troops and equipment.
- Routes in and out.
- Placement of antiarmor weapons in and outside the defense.
- Availability of 360-degree observation.
- Number of needed EAs.
- Placement and use of platoon reserve.
- Best use of internal squad battle positions.

Engineers support a strongpoint defense by reinforcing the existing obstacles. Priorities of work will vary depending on the factors of METT-TC, especially the enemy situation and time available. For example, the first twelve hours of the strongpoint construction effort may be critical for emplacing countermobility and survivability positions and $C^2$ bunkers. On the other hand, if the focus of engineer support is to make the terrain approaching the strongpoint impassable, the battalion engineer effort must be adjusted accordingly.

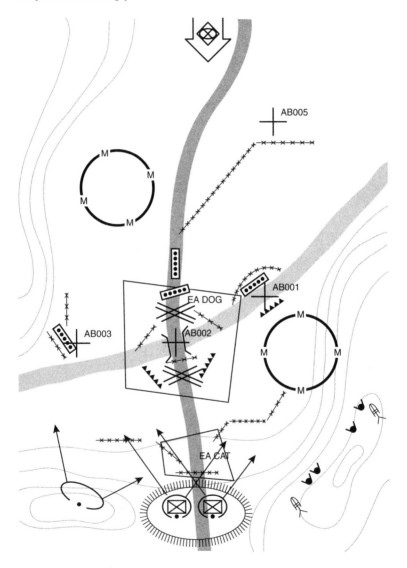

**Defend a Strongpoint**

### Defend a Perimeter

A perimeter defense allows the defending force to orient in all directions. In terms of weapons emplacement, direct- and indirect-fire integration, and reserve employment, a platoon leader conducting a perimeter defense should consider the same factors as a strongpoint operation.

1. The perimeter defense allows only limited maneuver and limited depth. Nonetheless, the platoon may be called on to execute a perimeter defense under a variety of conditions that include:
   - Holding critical terrain in areas where the defense is not tied in with adjacent units.
   - Defending in place when it has been bypassed and isolated by the enemy.
   - Conducting occupation of an independent avenue of approach (AA) or reserve position.
   - Preparing a strongpoint.
   - Concentrating fires in two or more adjacent avenues of approach.
   - Defending CS or CSS assets.
   - Occupying a patrol base.

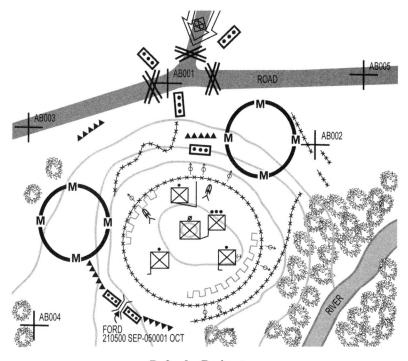

**Defend a Perimeter**

2. The major advantage of the perimeter defense is the platoon's ability to defend against an enemy avenue of approach. A perimeter defense differs from other defenses in that:
   - The trace of the platoon is circular or triangular rather than linear.
   - Unoccupied areas between squads are smaller.
   - Flanks of squads are bent back to conform to the plan.
   - The bulk of combat power is on the perimeter.
   - The reserve is centrally located.

*Note*: A variant of the perimeter defense is the use of the shaped defense, which allows two of the platoon's squads to orient at any particular time on any of three EAs.

**Reverse Slope Defense**

The platoon leader's analysis of the factors of METT-TC often leads him to employ his forces on the reverse slope. If the rifle squads are on a mounted avenue of approach, they must be concealed from enemy direct-fire systems. This means rifle squads should be protected from enemy tanks and observed artillery fire. Some reverse slope defense considerations are:

1. The majority of a rifle squad's weapons are not effective beyond 600 meters. To reduce or preclude destruction from enemy direct and indirect fires beyond that range, a reverse slope defense should be considered. In some cases, it may be necessary for these weapons systems to be deployed forward while the rifle squads remain on the reverse slope (to take advantage of their long ranges). The Javelins withdraw from their forward positions as the battle closes. Their new positions should be selected to take advantage of their long-range fires and to get enfilade shots from the depth and the flanks of the reverse slope.

2. The nature of the enemy may change at night, and the rifle squads may occupy the forward slope or crest to deny it to the enemy. In those circumstances, it is feasible for a rifle squad to have an alternate night position forward. The area forward of the topographical crest must be controlled by friendly forces through aggressive patrolling and both active and passive reconnaissance measures.

3. The company commander normally makes the decision to position platoons on a reverse slope when:
   - He wishes to surprise or deceive the enemy about the location of his defensive position.
   - A forward slope might be made untenable by direct enemy fire.
   - Occupation of the forward slope is not essential to achieve depth and mutual support.

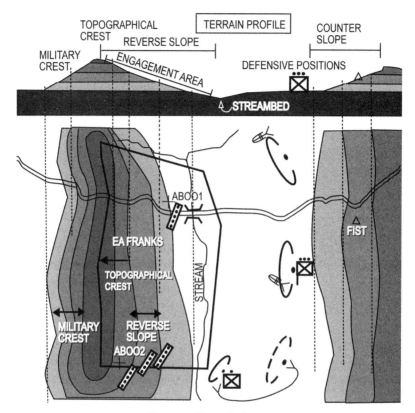

**Reverse Slope Defense**

- Fields of fire on the reverse slope are better or at least sufficient to accomplish the mission.
- Forward slope positions are likely to be the target of concentrated enemy artillery fires.

Obstacles are necessary in a reverse slope defense. Since the enemy will be engaged at close range, obstacles should prevent the enemy from closing too quickly and overrunning the positions. Obstacles on the reverse slope can halt, disrupt, and expose enemy vehicles to flank AT fires. They should also facilitate the platoon's disengagement.

### Reorganization in Combat

Reorganization begins automatically at team and squad levels during the battle to prepare for the next battle. To prepare for the next attack, the platoon should accomplish the following tasks:

*Man Key Weapons.* Replace key soldiers lost during battle. For example, ensure that crew-served weapons are manned and new team leaders are designated.

*Reestablish Security.* If soldiers withdrew from the OPs to their fighting positions, return them to their OPs. If some did not get back to their positions, check their status and replace casualties. As soon as possible, reestablish the sleep-alert system.

*Treat and/or Evacuate Casualties.* Treat casualties as far forward as possible. Return those who can continue to fight to their positions; evacuate the others.

*Redistribute Ammunition and Supplies.* Distribute remaining ammunition and supplies equally among the soldiers, including ammunition from the casualties.

*Relocate Fighting Positions and Weapons Positions.* During the assault, the enemy may have pinpointed some of the fighting and weapons positions. If certain positions are in danger, move soldiers and weapons (especially crew-served weapons) to their alternate positions.

*Reestablish Communications.* If a phone line was cut during the attack, soldiers on each end of the line should try to find and repair the break or lay new wire. If a signal, such as a green star cluster, was used to cease fire, consider changing it since the meaning may now be known by the enemy.

*Repair Fighting Positions.* Each soldier should check and replace the camouflage, overhead cover, and sandbags on existing positions and camouflage new positions.

*Repair and/or Replace Obstacles.* Repair and/or replace damaged or breached obstacles, mines, and booby traps only if enemy soldiers are far enough away that it can be done safely. Otherwise, wait for poor visibility to do so, or use smoke to hinder observation.

# 6

# Tactical Enabling Operations

The infantry platoon may conduct other tasks to complement or support its primary mission. Enabling operations include reconnaissance, retrograde (withdrawal, delay, and retirement), special purpose operations (linkup, stay-behind, relief in place, and passage of lines), air assaults, and security operations (convoy security, checkpoints, roadblocks, and OPs. Squads and platoons conduct these operations on their own or as part of a larger force.

## RECONNAISSANCE
Reconnaissance is any mission undertaken, using visual observation or other methods, to seek out and obtain information regarding the activities and resources of enemy forces or the physical characteristics of a particular area.

### Planning and Types of Reconnaissance
Before an operation, the company commander determines what he must know about the enemy and terrain. The platoon may be called upon or required to conduct reconnaissance before or after an operation in the following situations:
- Reconnaissance by a quartering party of an assembly area (AA) and the associated route to it.
- Leader's reconnaissance from the AA to and in the vicinity of the operations area or area of operation before an offensive operation.
- Reconnaissance by rifle squads to probe enemy positions for gaps open to attack or infiltration.
- Reconnaissance by rifle squads to observe forward positions and to guide elements to key positions, such as support or assault on the battlefield.
- Reconnaissance by rifle squads to locate bypasses around obstacle belts or to determine the best locations and methods for breaching operations.

- Reconnaissance by rifle squads of choke points or other danger areas in advance of the remainder of the company.
- Leader's reconnaissance of defensive positions or engagement areas (EAs) for conducting the defense.
- Reconnaissance rifle squads as part of security operations to secure friendly obstacles, to clear possible enemy OPs, or to cover areas not observable by stationary operations.
- Close target reconnaissance (CTR) typically performed by low visibility teams in preparation for an assault on a building or small area.

See Chapter 7 for more information on reconnaissance patrolling.

## LINKUP OPERATIONS

The most dangerous operation in combat is the linkup, which entails the meeting of two or more friendly units (or their leaders or designated representatives). This can happen on the ground or even in the air. Typically when a linkup goes awry it is because the element that is moving assumes that the static or receiving element knows that a friendly unit is passing. Assumptions like this can kill or wound fellow soldiers. Blue-on-blue engagements are more common when soldiers are on edge, tired, or uninformed. Linkups depend on control, detailed planning, and stealth. Night vision devices (NVGs) enhance the execution of linkup operations and reduce the likelihood of fratricide.

The platoon conducts linkup activities independently or as part of a larger force. The platoon may lead the linkup force. The linkup consists of three steps:

**Step 1. Far Recognition Signal.** The units or elements involved in the linkup establish communication before they reach direct-fire range, using a far recognition signal.

**Step 2. Coordination.** Before initiating movement to the linkup point, the forces coordinate necessary tactical information, including:

- The enemy situation and type and number of friendly elements and vehicles.
- Disposition of stationary forces.
- Routes to the linkup and rally points.
- Fire control measures.
- Near recognition signal(s).
- Communications information.
- Combat support (CS) and combat service support (CSS) coverage.
- Finalized location of the linkup and rally points.
- Special coordination (such as covering maneuver instructions or requests for medical support).
- Visual linkup signals or alternate linkup locations (in case of contact).

**Step 3: Movement to the Linkup Point and Linkup.** All units or elements involved in the linkup must enforce strict fire control measures to prevent fratricide. Linkup points and restrictive fire lines (RFLs) must be recognizable by moving or converging forces. Linkup elements ensure they conduct long-range (far) recognition by FM radio and short-range (near) recognition using the designated signal, complete movement to the linkup point, establish local security at the linkup point, and conduct additional coordination and linkup activities as necessary.

## PASSAGE OF LINES

A passage of lines entails movement of one or more units through another unit. This operation is necessary when the moving unit(s) cannot bypass the stationary unit and must pass through it. The primary purpose of the passage is to maintain the momentum of the moving elements. A passage of lines may be either forward or rearward. The controlling unit is responsible for planning and coordinating a passage of lines involving the platoon. In some situations, the platoon leader must take responsibility for planning and coordinating each phase of the operation. Also, platoons may conduct passages of lines when conducting patrols, ambushes, raids, or other operations that require them to pass through friendly units.

### Planning Considerations

In planning passage of lines, the platoon leader must consider the following tactical factors and procedures:

1. The passage should be large enough to support doctrinal formations for the passing units.
2. Deception techniques (such as the use of smoke) may be employed to enhance security during the passage.
3. The controlling commander must clearly define the battle handover criteria and procedures to be used during the passage. His order should cover the roles of both the passing unit and the stationary unit and the use of direct and indirect fires in both a forward or rearward passage.
4. The passing and stationary units coordinate obstacle information, including the location of enemy and friendly obstacles, existing lanes and bypasses, and guides for the passage.
5. Air defense coverage is imperative during the high-risk passage operation. Normally the stationary unit will be responsible for providing air defense.
6. Responsibility for CSS actions such as vehicle recovery or casualty evacuation in the passage lane must be clearly defined for both passing and stationary units.

7. To enhance $C^2$ during the passage, the platoon will co-locate a $C^2$ element, normally the platoon leader or platoon sergeant, with a similar element from the stationary or moving unit.

## Reconnaissance and Coordination
Detailed reconnaissance and coordination are critical in a passage of lines. The platoon leader or a designated representative coordinates the following items:
- Unit designation and composition, including type and number of passing soldiers and vehicles (if any).
- Passing unit arrival time(s).
- Location of attack positions or AAs (should be confirmed by reconnaissance).
- Current enemy situation.
- Obstacles.
- Stationary unit's mission and plan (including OP, patrol, and obstacle locations).
- Location of movement routes, contact points, and passage points and lanes. (*Note*: The use of GPS waypoints will simplify this process and speed the passage.)
- Guide requirements.
- Order of march.
- Anticipated actions on enemy contact.
- Requirements for supporting direct and indirect fires, including the location.
- NBC conditions.
- Available CS and CSS assets and their locations.
- Radio frequencies and near and far recognition signals.
- Criteria for and location of the battle handover.

In a forward passage, the passing unit first moves to an AA or an attack position behind the stationary unit. Designated liaison personnel move forward to link up with guides and confirm coordination information with the stationary unit. Guides from the stationary unit lead the passing elements through the passage lane. In a rearward passage of lines, the risk of fratricide is increased, so coordination of recognition signals and fire restrictions is critical.

## RELIEF IN PLACE
A relief in place may be needed to maintain combat effectiveness during prolonged combat operations. A relief in place is an operation in which a platoon is replaced in combat by another platoon. The incoming platoon assumes responsibility for the combat mission and assigned sector or zone of action of the outgoing platoon.

## Coordination

Platoon responsibility is usually limited to the detailed coordination between key personnel and their counterparts.

Leaders must reconnoiter different routes into and out of the position; assembly area; logistics points; primary, alternate, and supplementary positions; obstacles; immediate terrain; and, when possible, patrol routes and OP locations. The outgoing leader must provide copies of the platoon sector sketch, fire plan, range cards for all weapons, barrier plan, minefield records, counterattack plans, and plans for any other tasks the platoon may have been ordered to perform.

Both leaders must know which method and sequence of relief has been prescribed in the higher unit order and how they will execute the plan. They are responsible for the following:

- Knowing whether their platoons will execute the relief by squads or as a complete platoon (method). Platoons may also execute the relief by occupying adjacent terrain or terrain in depth (to the rear) rather than by relieving soldiers in position.
- Knowing the order of relief (sequence) for platoons within the company.
- Coordinating the use of guides (outgoing unit provides guides to move incoming unit to positions), signals, challenge and password, and passage of responsibility for the mission and control of the platoon (normally when the majority of the incoming platoon is in place).
- Coordinating the exchange of tripods for crew-served weapons, phones or switchboards, and emplaced munitions. Platoons do not exchange radios.
- Identifying numbers, types, and location of supplies to be left behind, including sensors, construction materiel, wire, and any other items that might slow down the movement of the outgoing platoon.

## Execution

During the execution, both leaders should co-locate at the outgoing platoon leader's command post (CP). The leader of the outgoing platoon remains responsible for the defense of the area until the majority of the incoming platoon is in position. If the enemy attacks during the relief, the leader who has responsibility at the time is in control. The other leader assists with assets under his control as directed.

Squad leaders physically walk soldiers to positions and trade them out on a one-for-one basis. They allow time for outgoing soldiers to brief their reliefs on their position, range cards, and other pertinent information. Both the relieved and relieving platoons must maintain security to deny the enemy knowledge of the relief. The relieved platoon keeps local security elements in place. These elements are the last soldiers to be relieved. Both platoons observe strict communications security and maintain normal movement and activity. All leaders report completion of their portion of the relief as soon as possible.

## WITHDRAWAL
In a withdrawal, all or part of a deployed force voluntarily disengages from the enemy to free itself for a new mission. The mission might be to defend another position or to attack someplace else. Units withdraw either under pressure or not under pressure. Platoons have three basic methods of disengaging from the enemy: They can thin their lines (disengage by individuals) or move out either by fire teams or by squads.

**Thinning the Lines.** To disengage by thinning the lines, also known as disengagement by individuals, squad and team leaders direct soldiers to move rearward in buddy teams, with each soldier covering the other as they move back in turn. Smoke must be used for concealment if the soldiers are moving across open areas.

**Disengagement by Fire Teams.** To disengage by fire teams, one team fires while the other one moves, alternating roles. This method can be used if thinning the lines is not needed because enemy fire is light or teams have already moved back far enough.

**Disengagement by Squads.** To disengage by squads, the platoon leader has each squad move back in turn, covered by the fire of the others. The platoon moves back by squads if thinning the lines or maneuver by fire teams is not needed because enemy fire is light or squads have already moved back sufficiently.

### Withdrawal Not Under Pressure
Withdrawal not under pressure is conducted with speed, secrecy, and deception, and is best performed at night or during periods of reduced visibility. The company disengages and moves to the rear while the enemy is not attacking. The company leaves a detachment left in contact (DLIC) as a security force to cover the withdrawal by deception, fire, or maneuver. A platoon or one squad from each platoon serves as the DLIC. The composite platoon is normally the best method because there is less repositioning involved. As the DLIC, platoons perform the following:

- Reposition squads and weapons to cover the company's withdrawal.
- Reposition a squad in each of the other platoon positions to cover the most dangerous avenue of approach into the area.
- Continue the normal operating pattern of the company.

**Disengagement by Individuals (Thinning the Lines)**

**Disengagement by Fire Teams**

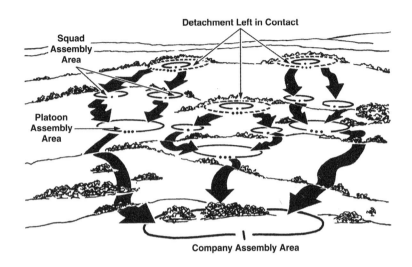

Company Withdrawal / Not Under Pressure

- Cover the company withdrawal by fire if the company is attacked during withdrawal.
- Withdraw once the company is at its next position. If under contact, the DLIC might have to maneuver to the rear until contact is broken, then assemble to move to the company.

**Withdrawal Under Pressure**

The amount of enemy pressure determines how this withdrawal is conducted. If it is not possible to prepare and position the security force, the platoon conducts a fighting withdrawal. The platoon disengages from the enemy by maneuvering to the rear. Soldiers, fire teams, and squads not in contact are withdrawn first so they can provide suppressive fires to allow the soldiers, teams, or squads in contact to withdraw. If enemy pressure is light enough to permit a security force, a platoon (or a composite platoon) repositions itself to fight the enemy as the rest of the company withdraws.

**DELAY**

In a delay, the enemy slows its movement when the platoon forces him to repeatedly deploy for the attack. After causing the enemy to deploy, the delaying force withdraws to new positions. The squads or sections and platoons disengage from the enemy as described in a withdrawal under pressure and move directly to their next position, where they defend again. The squads and platoons slow the advance of the enemy by causing casualties and equipment losses by employing ambushes, snipers, obstacles, minefields (including phony minefields), and artillery and mortar fire.

## STAY-BEHIND OPERATIONS
Stay-behind operations can be used as part of defensive or delay missions. In the defense, once the enemy's combat units have passed, his weakest point (CS and CSS units) can be attacked. The two types of stay-behind operations are unplanned and deliberate.

**Unplanned.** An unplanned stay-behind operation is one in which a unit finds itself cut off from other friendly elements for an indefinite time without specific planning or targets and must rely on its organic assets.

**Deliberate.** A deliberate stay-behind operation is one in which a unit plans to operate in an enemy-controlled area as a separate yet cohesive element for a certain amount of time or until a specified event occurs. A deliberate stay-behind operation requires extensive planning. Squads, sections, and platoons conduct this type of operation as part of larger units.

### Planning
The most important troop-leading procedures (TLP) that apply to stay-behind operations are task organization, reconnaissance, and combat service support.

*Task Organization.* The stay-behind unit includes only the soldiers and equipment needed for the mission. It needs minimal logistics support and can provide its own security. It must be able to hide easily and move through restrictive terrain.

*Reconnaissance.* This is the most important aspect in a stay-behind operation. Reporting tasks and information requirements can include suitable sites for patrol bases, hide positions, OPs, caches, water sources, dismounted and mounted avenues of approach, kill zones, EAs, and covered and concealed approach routes.

*Combat Service Support.* Because the stay-behind unit will not be in physical contact with its supporting unit, supplies of rations, ammunition, radio batteries, water, and medical supplies are cached. Provisions for casualty and enemy prisoner of war (EPW) evacuation depend on the company and battalion plans.

### AIR ASSAULT OPERATIONS
Infantry platoons may be required to participate in air assault operations as part of the tactical plan. The platoon has the ability to be airlifted as part of a larger operation. The battalion is the lowest level with sufficient personnel

to plan, coordinate, and control an air assault. When company-size or smaller unit operations are conducted, the planning takes place at battalion or higher headquarters.

## Ground Tactical Plan
The foundation of a successful air assault operation is the commander's ground tactical plan, around which subsequent planning is based. The ground tactical plan specifies actions that must be performed in the objective area and addresses subsequent operations. The ground tactical plan contains essentially the same elements as any other infantry attack plan but capitalizes on speed and mobility to achieve surprise.

## Landing Plan
The landing plan must support the ground tactical plan. This plan sequences elements into the areas of operations (AOs) to ensure that platoons arrive at designated locations and times prepared to execute the ground tactical plan. The following should be taken into account in the landing plan:
- The availability, location, and size of potential landing zones (LZs) are overriding factors.
- The company is most vulnerable during landing.
- Elements must land with tactical integrity.
- Troops are easily disoriented if the landing direction changes and they are not kept informed.
- The company must be prepared to fight in any direction after landing, since there may be no other friendly troops in the area.
- The landing plan should offer flexibility so that a variety of options is available in developing a scheme of maneuver.
- Supporting fires (artillery, attack helicopters, close air support, and naval gunfire) must be planned in and around each LZ.
- Although the objective may be beyond the range of supporting artillery fire, artillery or mortars can be brought into the LZs early to provide fire support for maneuver troops.
- Resupply and medical evacuation by air must be provided for.

*Selection of Landing Zones.* Each LZ is selected using the following criteria:
- *Location.* It can be located on, near, or away from the objective, depending on METT-TC.
- *Capacity.* The size determines how much combat power can be landed at one time and the need for additional LZs or separation between serials.

- *Alternates.* An alternate LZ should be planned for each primary LZ to ensure flexibility.
- *Enemy disposition and capabilities.* Consider enemy troop concentrations, air defenses, and their capability to react when selecting an LZ.
- *Cover and concealment.* LZs are selected that will deny enemy observation and acquisition of friendly ground and air elements while they are en route to or from (and in) the LZ. Depending on METT-TC, the LZ and approaches should be masked from the enemy by terrain features.
- *Obstacles.* If possible, the company should land on the enemy side of obstacles when attacking, and at other times use the obstacles to protect LZs from the enemy. LZs must be free of obstacles. Engineers must be part of the task organization for contingency breaching of obstacles.
- *Identification from the air.* LZs should be easily identifiable from the air. If pathfinder support or friendly reconnaissance units are present, they should mark the LZ with chemical lights, preferably of the infrared type, if the assault troops wear night vision goggles.
- *Approach and departure routes.* Approach and departure routes should avoid continued flank exposure of aircraft to the enemy.
- *Weather.* Reduced visibility or strong winds may preclude or limit the use of marginal LZs.

**Single Versus Multiple Landing Zones.** In addition to deciding where to land in relation to the objective, consideration is given to the use of a single LZ or multiple LZs. The following are the advantages of using a single LZ:
- Allows concentration of combat power.
- Facilitates control of the operation.
- Concentrates supporting fire.
- Provides better ground security for subsequent lifts.
- Requires fewer attack helicopters for security.
- Makes it more difficult for the enemy to detect the operation by the reduced number of flight routes in the operation area.
- Centralizes any required resupply efforts.
- Concentrates efforts of limited LZ control personnel and engineers on one LZ.
- Requires less planning and rehearsal time.

The following are the advantages of using multiple LZs:
- Avoids grouping assets in one location and creating a lucrative target for enemy fire.

- Allows for rapid dispersal of ground elements to accomplish tasks in separate areas.
- Reduces the enemy's ability to detect and react to the initial lift.
- Forces the enemy to fight in more than one direction.
- Reduces the troop and aircraft congestion that can occur on one LZ.
- Makes it difficult for the enemy to determine the size of the air assault force and the location of supporting weapons.

**Air Movement Plan**

The air movement plan is based on the ground tactical and landing plans. It specifies the schedule and provides the instructions for air movement of soldiers, equipment, and supplies from LZs and pickup zones (PZs).

**Loading Plan**

The loading plan is based on the movement plan. It guarantees that soldiers, equipment, and supplies are loaded on the correct aircraft and that platoon integrity is maintained. Cross-loading of essential personnel and equipment is imperative to ensure survivability of $C^2$ assets and to ensure that the mix of personnel and weapons arriving at the LZ is ready to fight. The platoon leader or squad leader should always check the aircraft is loaded so that dismounting soldiers react promptly. The platoon leader must have a *bump plan*, which ensures essential soldiers and equipment are loaded ahead of less critical loads in case of aircraft breakdown or other problems.

Planning must cover the organization and operation of the PZ, including load positions, day and night markings, and communications. The loading plan is most important when mixing aircraft types. Ground and aviation unit movement to the PZ is scheduled so that only the troops to load and the helicopter to be loaded arrive at the PZ at the same time. To coordinate movement of units to the PZ, assembly areas, holding areas, and routes of movement are selected.

At company and lower levels, each man and major items of equipment or supplies are assigned to specific aircraft by an airloading table. The airloading table is a loading manifest for each aircraft and serves as an accountability tool. When time is limited, the table can be a sheet of paper from the squad leader's notebook. These lists are left with a specified person

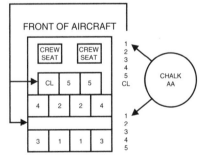

**UH-60 Loading Diagram**

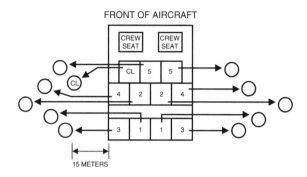

**UH-60 Unloading Diagram**

in the PZ. This procedure ensures that if an aircraft is lost, a list of personnel and equipment on board is available.

During load planning, unit leaders attempt to maintain the following:

• *Tactical integrity of units.* Fire teams and squads are loaded intact on the same aircraft, and platoons in the same serial. This ensures integrity as a fighting unit upon landing.

• *Self-sufficiency of loads.* Each load should be functional by itself whenever possible. Every towed item is accompanied by its prime mover. Crews are loaded with their vehicle or weapon. Ammunition is carried with the weapon. Component parts accompany the major items of equipment. Sufficient personnel are on board to unload the cargo.

• *Tactical cross-loading.* Loads should be planned so that all leaders or all crew-served weapons are not on the same aircraft. Thus, if an aircraft is lost, the mission is not seriously hampered.

*Aircraft Bump Plan.* Each aircraft load has a bump sequence designated on its airloading table. Bump priority ensures that the most essential personnel and equipment arrive at the objective area first. It specifies personnel and equipment that may be bumped and delivered later. If all personnel within the load cannot be lifted, individuals must know whom to off-load and in what sequence. This ensures that key personnel are not bumped arbitrarily.

Bump sequence is also designated for aircraft within each serial or flight. This ensures that key aircraft loads are not left in the PZ. When an aircraft within a serial or flight cannot lift off and key personnel are on board, they off-load and reboard another aircraft that has priority. A PZ bump and straggler collection point is established to account for, regroup, and reschedule these personnel and/or loads for later delivery.

*Lifts, Serials, and Loads.* To maximize operational control, aviation assets are designated as lifts, serials, or loads. A *lift* is one sortie of all utility and cargo aircraft assigned to a mission. Each time all assigned aircraft pick up troops and/or equipment and set them down on the LZ, one lift is completed. The second lift is completed when all lift aircraft place their second loads on the LZ.

When a lift is too large to fly in one formation, it is organized into a number of *serials.* A serial is a tactical grouping of two or more aircraft under the control of a serial commander and separated from other tactical groupings within the lift by time or space. Serials also may be organized when the capacity of available PZs or LZs is limited, or to take advantage of available flight routes.

A *load* is personnel or equipment designated to be moved by a specific aircraft. Each aircraft within the lift is termed a load. For example, within a lift of ten, there are aircraft loads one through ten.

## Staging Plan

The staging plan is based on the loading plan and prescribes the arrival time of ground units (soldiers, equipment, and supplies) at the PZ in the order of movement.

## Helicopters

Several types of helicopters may be used in air assault operations: observation, utility, cargo, and attack.

*Observation Helicopters (OHs).* OHs are used to provide command and control, aerial observation and reconnaissance, and aerial target acquisition.

*Utility Helicopters (UHs).* UHs are the most versatile of all helicopters, performing a variety of tasks. As such, they are available in almost every unit possessing helicopters. UHs are used to conduct combat assaults and provide transportation, command and control, and resupply. When rigged with special equipment, they also can be used to provide aeromedical evacuations, conduct radiological surveys, and dispense scatterable mines.

*Cargo Helicopters (CHs).* These aircraft are organic to corps aviation units. They normally provide transportation, resupply, and recovery of downed aircraft.

*Attack Helicopters (AHs).* AHs are organized in groups varying in size from company to battalion and can also be task organized to meet mission needs. They are used to provide overwatch and security, destroy point targets, and suppress air defense weapons.

*Capabilities.* Under normal conditions, helicopters can ascend and descend at relatively steep angles; this enables them to operate from confined and unimproved areas. Troops and their combat equipment can be unloaded from a helicopter hovering a short distance above the ground with troop ladders and rappelling means, or if the helicopter can hover low enough, the troops may jump to the ground. The troop ladder can also be used to load personnel when the helicopter cannot land. Cargo can be transported as an external load and delivered to areas inaccessible to other types of aircraft or to ground transportation.

Because of their wide speed range and high maneuverability at slow speeds, helicopters can fly safely and efficiently at low altitudes, using terrain and trees for cover and concealment. With their ability to fly at high or low altitudes, decelerate rapidly, maintain slow forward speed, and land nearly vertically, helicopters also can operate under marginal weather conditions. Helicopters can land on the objective area in a tactical formation, LZs permitting. Night and/or limited-visibility landings and liftoffs can be made with a minimum of light. Helicopters flying at low levels are capable of achieving surprise, deceiving the enemy at the LZs, and employing shock effect through the use of suppressive fires. Engine and rotor noise may deceive the enemy as to the direction of approach and intended flight path.

*Limitations.* The high fuel consumption of helicopters imposes limitations on range and allowable cargo load (ACL). Helicopters may reduce fuel loads to permit an increased ACL, but reducing the fuel load also reduces the range and flexibility. The load-carrying capability of helicopters decreases with increases in altitude, humidity, and temperature. This limitation may be compensated for through reduction of fuel load. Weight and balance affect flight control. Loads must be properly distributed to keep the center of gravity within allowable limits.

Hail, sleet, icing, heavy rains, and gusty winds (30 knots or more) limit or preclude the use of helicopters. Crosswind velocities above 15 knots for utility helicopters and 10 knots for cargo helicopters, and downwind velocities above 5 knots for either type affect the selection of the direction of landing and liftoff.

Engine and rotor noise may compromise secrecy. Aviator fatigue requires greater consideration in the operation of rotary-wing aircraft than in the operation of fixed-wing aircraft.

## Loads

The *type-load method* is the most efficient method used in the conduct of air assault operations and in operational planning. Army aviation units are frequently required to support numerous major units operating over expansive tactical zones. Standardization of type loads within the theater of operations ensures responsive and effective air mobility with a minimum of time required for planning.

The use of type loads does not limit the flexibility of a ground tactical unit to be airlifted. The type-load method is very useful at battalion and company levels to plan and conduct air assault operations. Your supporting aviation unit will supply you with necessary load and type-load planning information.

## Seats-Out Operation

With the UH-60, if the troop seats are removed, twenty-two combat-loaded soldiers and their rucksacks can be loaded (this is contingent on area-specific equipment such as armor, water, etc). Conducting combat operations with seats out reduces the number of aircraft needed for each mission. The aircraft can be loaded from either or both sides. Loading is quicker if both sides are used. Before the soldiers enter the aircraft, each soldier's rucksack is placed on the floor of the aircraft where the soldier will sit. Once all rucksacks are in, the soldiers are loaded from rear to front. Soldiers in the aircraft help by pulling the others in tightly until they are all on board and the doors are closed. The aircraft doors should be opened as the helicopter approaches the LZ. Soldiers hold on to each other until time to unload. They should unload from both sides if the ground slope permits. (*Caution*: The seats-out technique is used in combat only—never in training.)

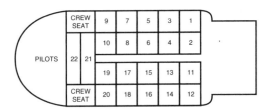

**UH-60 Seats-out Loading Diagram**

## AREA SECURITY OPERATIONS

Area security operations protect specific critical and vulnerable assets or terrain from enemy observation and direct fire. These operations can consist of escorting friendly convoys (with an augmentation of vehicles); protecting critical points such as bridges, $C^2$ installations, or other key and vulnerable sites; or participating in protection of large areas such as airfields. During stability or support operations, the platoon may be required to establish OPs, roadblocks, or checkpoints. The platoon normally performs an area security operation when conventional security or combat operations would not work, and does so independently or as part of a larger force. Infantry platoons normally conduct area security missions to protect high-value points, areas, or assets. Whether these need protection, how much protection they require, and the defensive technique chosen to protect them depends on the factors of METT-TC. The platoon leader must integrate his elements into the overall security plan for the area he must protect. Area security operations rely on various techniques, which may include reconnaissance, security, defensive tasks, and offensive tasks.

## CONVOY AND ROUTE SECURITY

Company and larger organizations usually perform convoy or route security missions. Convoy security provides protection for a specific convoy. Route security aims at securing a specific route for a designated period of time, during which multiple convoys may use the route. These missions include tasks such as escorting, reconnaissance, and establishing a combat reaction force. These tasks become missions for subordinate units. The size of the unit performing a convoy or route security operation depends on many factors, including the size of the convoy, the terrain, and the length of the route.

### Vehicles

In order for an infantry platoon to conduct convoy or route security, it must be augmented with vehicles. Vehicles should include up-armored vehicles. There are numerous types of armored vehicles in the inventory. What is most important is that drivers are knowledgeable and well trained for combat operations. Second, the vehicles used in combat need to be the same vehicles used in rehearsals. This will ensure that combat drills are executed swiftly and correctly.

*Route Reconnaissance.* In this mission, the platoon leader focuses on the route's trafficability and on enemy forces that might influence the route. Below is an example of a movement route survey.

---

### MOVEMENT ROUTE SURVEY—PRIMARY, ALTERNATE, VARIANT, AND EMERGENCY

Code name _____

Primary/alternate _____

Maps/charts: area _____

Maps/imagery: neighborhood _____

Road surface: condition, construction _____

## MOVEMENT ROUTE SURVEY—PRIMARY, ALTERNATE, VARIANT, AND EMERGENCY *continued*

Weather concerns: difficult, impassable   _____
Chokepoints/danger areas: (i.e. checkpoint survey)   _____
Dead-end/one-way streets: location, markings   _____
Major turns: _____
Landmarks: local name, code name, grid   _____
Possible attack points along route: demeanor of persons in area   _____
Historic attack points   _____
Enemy TTP in the area: IED, gunfire   _____
Evasion possibilities   _____
Cameras along route: police, military   _____
Location of hospitals: level of care, hours of operation   _____
Location of hard points/Alamo: along route, close to route   _____
Location of safe haven: friendlies (military, police, UN, NGO)   _____
Distance _____
Traffic conditions: time of day, day of week   _____
Travel time: time of day dependent, rush hour   _____
Natural flow of traffic: rush hour   _____
Local customs: right- or left-side drive, horn   _____
Conflicting events or holidays that will impact the movement   _____
Pedestrian traffic: time of day, day of week   _____
Timeline _____

*Checkpoint/Chokepoint/Roadblock Reconnaissance.* The leader needs to know certain pieces of information so that checkpoints, chokepoints, and roadblocks can be navigated with as little disruption to the mission as possible. Below is an example of a checkpoint survey.

## CHOKEPOINT/CHECKPOINT/ROADBLOCK SURVEY

Code name _____
Location: grid/map _____
GRG: series/number and pictures/imagery   _____
Barrier type: construction/materials   _____
Barrier layout _____
Historical: attack point/riot point/demonstration point (intelligence)   \_\_\_\_
What elements/unit guarding   _____
Number: military/police/militia   _____
Uniform or civilian clothes   _____

## CHOKEPOINT/CHECKPOINT/ROAD BLOCKSURVEY *continued*

Disposition of guards (alert, trained, bored, etc.) _____
Guards known for corruption? _____
What are the procedures to pass (ID, placards, pre-coordination, etc.) \_\_\_\_

TTP used to pass chokepoint (bounding, speed, etc.) _____
Nearest safe haven (near and far side) _____
Nearest friendly unit (near and far side) _____


### Convoy Escort

The platoon may perform a convoy escort mission either independently or as part of a larger unit's convoy security mission. The convoy escort mission requires that the platoon provide the convoy with limited close-in protection from direct small-arms fire. Vehicles include military CSS and $C^2$ vehicles and civilian trucks and buses. Leaders must carefully evaluate the enemy before assigning a convoy escort mission to platoon-size elements.

### Command and Control

Because of the task organization of the convoy escort mission, $C^2$ is especially critical. The relationship between the platoon and the convoy commander must provide unity of command and effort if combat operations are required during the course of the mission. In most cases, the platoon will execute the escort mission under the control of the security force commander, who is usually under the operational control (OPCON) of—or attached to—the convoy commander. It is vital that the convoy commander issues a complete operation order (OPORD) to all convoy vehicle commanders before executing the mission because the convoy may itself be task-organized from a variety of units and some vehicles may not have tactical radios. Ensure all immediate action drills are covered and rehearsed.

### Convoy Security Operations

*Tactical Disposition.* During all escort missions, the convoy security commander and platoon leader must establish and maintain security in every direction. Several factors, including convoy size, affect this disposition. The key consideration is whether the platoon is operating as part of a larger escort force or is executing the escort mission independently. Additional METT-TC considerations include the employment of rifle squads during the mission and whether fire teams ride in escorted vehicles.

*Actions on Contact.* As the convoy moves to its new location, the enemy may attempt to harass or destroy it. This contact usually will occur in the form of an ambush, often with the use of a hastily prepared obstacle. The safety of the convoy rests on the speed and effectiveness with which escort elements can execute appropriate actions on contact. Based on the factors of METT-TC, portions of the convoy security force such as the platoon may be designated as a reaction force. The reaction force performs its escort duties, conducts tactical movement, or occupies an AA (as required) until enemy contact occurs and the convoy commander gives it a reaction mission.

*Actions at an Ambush.* An ambush is one of the more effective ways to interdict a convoy. Reaction to an ambush must be immediate, overwhelming, and decisive. Actions on contact must be planned for and rehearsed so they can be executed quickly.

*Actions at an Obstacle.* Obstacles are a major impediment to convoys. The purpose of reconnaissance ahead of a convoy is to identify obstacles and either breach them or find bypasses. In some cases the enemy or its obstacles may avoid detection by the reconnaissance element.

*Actions during Halts.* During a short halt, the convoy escort remains alert for possible enemy activity. If the halt is for any reason other than an obstacle, the convoy will be halted for an extended period of time. If this is the case, the element must move into a security formation such as a herringbone (be aware of mines on the edges of the road), and tactical support and security vehicles will move into a security and ready posture. This activity needs to be rehearsed prior to the convoy's departure.

## CHECKPOINTS, ROADBLOCKS, AND OBSERVATION POSTS
Construction and manning of checkpoints, roadblocks, and observation posts (OPs) are high-frequency tasks for an infantry company and subordinate elements when they must establish area security during stability operations.

**Checkpoint.** A checkpoint is a predetermined point used as a means of controlling movement, such as a place where military police check vehicular or pedestrian traffic to enforce circulation control measures and other laws, orders, and regulations.

**Roadblock.** A roadblock is used to limit the movement of vehicles along a route or to close access to certain areas or roads. Checkpoints and roadblocks can be either deliberate or hasty, the primary difference being the extent of planning and preparation conducted by the establishing force.

**Observation Post.** An observation post is a position from which military observations are made or fire is directed and adjusted, and which has appropriate communications. OPs are both overt (conspicuously visible, unlike their tactical counterparts) and deliberately constructed. They are similar in construction to bunkers and are supported by fighting positions, barriers, and patrols.

The platoon may be directed to establish a checkpoint, roadblock, or OP for the following reasons:

- Show a military presence to all parties and to the population in the area.
- Survey all activity in the terrain, along roads, and in inhabited areas.
- Check and/or inspect and register all personnel and vehicles in and out of the controlled area.
- Survey airspace, coastal areas, airfields, ceasefire lines, and borders.
- Deter illegal movement.
- Create an instant roadblock.
- Control movement into the AOs or on a specific route.
- Prevent smuggling of contraband.
- Enforce the terms of peace agreements.
- Ensure proper use of routes by both civilian and military vehicles.

**Planning and Establishing**
The layout, construction, and manning of checkpoints, roadblocks, and OPs should reflect the factors of METT-TC, especially the time available for emplacing them. The layout of deliberate checkpoints can be found in various battle books. The following procedures and considerations may apply:

1. Position the checkpoint or roadblock where it is visible and where traffic cannot turn back, get off the road, or bypass without being observed.
2. Position a combat vehicle (up-armored HUMVEE with a mounted machine gun or MK19) off the road, but within sight, to deter resistance to soldiers manning the checkpoint. The vehicle should be in a defensive position and protected by local security. It must be able to engage vehicles attempting to break through or bypass the checkpoint.
3. If combat vehicles are not available, place M240B machine-gun defensive positions in locations to cover and engage vehicles attempting to break through or bypass the checkpoint.
4. Place obstacles in the road to slow or canalize traffic into the search area.
5. Establish a reserve.
6. Establish wire communications in the checkpoint area to connect the checkpoint bunker, the combat vehicle, the search area, security forces, the rest area, and any other elements involved in the operation.
7. Designate the search area. If possible, it should be below ground to provide protection against such incidents as the explosion of a booby-trapped vehicle. Establish a parking area adjacent to the search area.

8. If applicable, checkpoint personnel should include linguists and women soldiers in case indigenous women need to be searched.
9. Establish an early warning system around the perimeter of the OP (trip flares, empty cans, dry branches, etc.).
10. Prepare shelters and defensive positions.

**Manning Observation Posts and Checkpoints**

When manning OPs and checkpoints, proper order and a systematic approach must be emphasized. Personnel must behave so that no misunderstanding occurs. The personnel manning the checkpoint must be in complete control of the surrounding terrain.

1. Although the OP is usually manned on a twenty-four-hour basis, it may also be manned only by day or night. During darkness, at least two persons must be in the OP; one observes while the other is resting. In remote areas, or if the situation in the area is tense, more personnel man the OP for security and observation.
2. A minimum of two soldiers should man the checkpoint, depending on traffic and the general situation. One soldier examines people and vehicles; the other soldier covers the area where people and vehicles are checked. The soldier covering the other area is armed and has easy access to radio and telephone. If more soldiers are manning the checkpoint, one of them should be ready to set up obstacles to stop vehicles trying to force their way through the checkpoint.

**Communication**

All OPs and checkpoints are connected to their unit or directly to the battalion operations center by radio and/or telephone. A spare radio and batteries should be supplied to the OP and checkpoint, especially to remote OPs located in dangerous areas. Radio and telephone checks are carried out at least twice every twenty-four hours; three times is recommended. Special code words are prepared for use in certain situations. Conversation must be coded. Reserve frequencies must be available. OPs and checkpoints of great operational value may be connected by direct landline to ensure rapid coordination in urgent situations.

**Equipment**

Many items are used to reinforce a roadblock, checkpoint, or OP. Recommended equipment includes:

• Barrels filled with sand, water, or heavy concrete blocks (emplaced to slow and canalize vehicles).
• Concertina wire (emplaced to control movement around the checkpoint).

- Secure facilities for radio and wire communications with the controlling headquarters.
- First aid kit or a medic if available.
- Sandbags for defensive positions.
- Bunker construction material.
- Binoculars, NVGs, and flashlights.
- Long-handled mirrors (used to inspect vehicle undercarriages).
- Signs stating the speed limit into and out of the checkpoint. The text of these signs must be written in both English and the local language.
- Floodlights.
- Duty log.
- Flag and unit sign.
- Barrier pole that can be raised and lowered.
- Generators with electric wire.

**Control**

During periods in which the civilian administration is not functioning, refugees will be traveling routinely throughout the area. All soldiers participating in these operations must fully understand the procedures for identifying and controlling personnel and vehicles moving through their AO.

***Personnel Identification.*** People who have permission to enter a sector are regulated by special instructions to the patrol conducting the operation. Often local and civilian employees, mayors, and chiefs of tribes in villages in the AO are given special identification (ID) cards and may pass without being checked. These ID cards must be registered. Other personnel must identify themselves with an ID card, passport, and so on. Such ID cards are written in the local language. Examples of different ID cards must be kept in the checkpoint. A US translator on site is helpful, if available.

***Personnel Control.*** Personnel control is conducted in different ways. Soldiers manning the checkpoint should watch for people acting strangely or with bulging clothing. If there is a danger of car bombs, special attention should be paid to cars containing only one person. When conducting body searches, soldiers should feel along clothes, not just pat them. Special attention must be paid to the lower parts of the back and from the shoes up to the knees. Armpits also must be checked. The wide trousers used by some cultures should be carefully examined. Soldiers also should check boots and hats. Extreme caution should be taken when suicide vehicle or human bombers are a threat.

***Checking Women and Clerical Personnel.*** Making a body search of women and clerical personnel is often difficult in Muslim countries and may lead to strong reactions. The commander must thoroughly discuss this with mayors and other leaders, and the procedure used must be consistent with agreements and treaties. Women usually are only checked with a metal detector or by another woman, such as a female police officer. One technique used in Afghanistan to search women was to search the husband with the metal detector wand and then have him wand his wife and any other female family members.

Elderly women often remain in the vehicle during inspection of a car. If there is a suspicion that the "rules" are being misused, then other, better checks must be made. Host nation females or female soldiers can help solve this issue. The battalion commander makes these decisions.

# 7

# Patrolling

Patrols are missions to gather information, to conduct combat operations, or to establish a presence in an area of operation (AO) as part of a stability operation. Infantry platoons and squads conduct four types of patrols: combat (ambush and raid), recon, tracking, and presence.

There are five principles of patrolling:
1. Planning.
2. Reconnaissance.
3. Security.
4. Control.
5. Common sense.

This chapter describes the planning considerations used in preparation for patrols, conduct of patrols, and establishment of and actions taken in a patrol base.

## ORGANIZATION AND PLANNING

To accomplish its mission, a patrol must perform specific tasks—for example, secure itself; cross danger areas; establish rally points; reconnoiter the patrol objective; and breach, support, or assault. When possible, in assigning tasks the leader should maintain squad and fire team integrity. The chain of command continues to lead its elements during a patrol. Some squads and fire teams may perform more than one task in an assigned sequence; others may perform only one task. The leader must plan carefully to ensure that he has identified and assigned all required tasks in the most efficient way. Elements and teams for platoons conducting patrols include the common and specific elements for each type of patrol. The following elements are common to all patrols:

**Headquarters Element (C2/4).** The headquarters consists of the platoon leader, communications operator, platoon sergeant, forward observer

(FO), and medical. It may consist of other attachments that the platoon leader or the platoon sergeant must control directly (for example, the medic).

**Surveillance Team.** A surveillance team keeps watch on the objective from the time the leader's reconnaissance ends until the unit deploys for actions on the objective. It then joins its element.

**En Route Recorder (SSE).** The en route recorder records all information collected during the mission. In recent years, this individual has turned into the sensitive site exploitation (SSE) team. As the military performs more low-intensity conflict operations, SSE has become an integral part of successful operations.

**Navigation.** The navigation soldier assists in navigation by ensuring that the lead fire team leader remains on course at all times. In modern warfare, GPS is extensively used and redundancy in the unit is a must. In some units, all personnel carry a GPS for their own personal awareness as well as to assist with deconfliction of maneuvering units. The GPS provides the real-time exact location of the bearer, which is essential information for combat leaders.

**Aid and Litter Team.** Aid and litter teams are responsible for treating and evacuating casualties.

**Enemy Prisoner of War Team.** EPW teams are responsible for controlling enemy prisoners in accordance with the five Ss (search, silence, segregate, safeguard, and speed to the rear) and the leader's guidance.

**Initial Planning and Coordination**

Leaders plan and prepare for patrols using troop-leading procedures (TLPs) and the estimate of the situation. Leaders identify required actions on the objective, then plan backward to the departure from friendly lines and forward to the reentry of friendly lines. They normally receive the OPORD in the battalion or company command post (CP), where communications are good and key personnel are available.

Because patrols act independently, move beyond the direct-fire support of the parent unit, and operate forward of friendly units, coordination must be thorough and detailed. Leaders normally coordinate directly with three different elements: higher headquarters (usually battalion staff or the company commander); the unit through which the platoon or squad will conduct its forward and rearward passage of lines; and the leaders of other units that will be patrolling in adjacent areas at the same time.

Patrol leaders use checklists to preclude the omission of any items vital to the accomplishment of the mission. For an example, see the coordination checklists on pages 39–41.

*Higher Headquarters Coordination.* Items coordinated between the leader and the battalion staff or company commander include:
- Changes or updates in the enemy situation.
- Best use of terrain for routes, rally points, and patrol bases.
- Light and weather data.
- Changes in the friendly situation.
- The attachment of soldiers with special skills or equipment (for example, engineers, sniper teams, scout dog teams, FOs, or interpreters).
- Use and location of LZs.
- Departure and reentry of friendly lines.
- Fire support on the objective and along the planned routes, including alternate routes.
- Rehearsal areas and times.
- Special equipment requirements.
- Transportation support, including transportation to and from the rehearsal site.
- Signal plan (call sign frequencies, code words, pyrotechnics, and challenge and password).

*Forward Unit Coordination.* The departure from friendly lines must be thoroughly planned and coordinated. The leader should consider the following sequence of actions:
1. Make contact with friendly guides at the contact point.
2. Move to the coordinated initial rally point.
3. Complete final coordination.
4. Move to and through the passage point.
5. Establish a security-listening halt beyond the friendly unit's final protective fires.

The coordination includes signal operation instructions (SOI) information, signal plan, fire plan, running password, procedures for departure and reentry lines, dismount points, initial rally points, departure and reentry points, and information about the enemy. The platoon leader provides the forward unit leader with the unit identification, size of the patrol, departure and return times, and AO. The forward unit leader provides the patrol leader with the following:
- Additional information on terrain.
- Known or suspected enemy positions.
- Likely enemy ambush sites.
- Latest enemy activity.
- Detailed information on friendly positions and obstacle locations, including the location of OPs.

- Friendly unit fire plan.
- Support that the unit can provide (for example, fire support, litter teams, guides, communications, and reaction force).

## Completion of the Plan

As the platoon leader completes his plan, he considers the following:

*Essential and Supporting Tasks.* The leader ensures that he has assigned all essential tasks to be performed on the objective, at rally points, at danger areas, at security or surveillance locations, along the route(s), and at passage lanes.

*Key Travel and Execution Times.* The leader estimates time requirements for movement to the objective, the leader's reconnaissance of the objective, the establishment of security and surveillance, the completion of all assigned tasks on the objective, the movement to an ORP to debrief the platoon, and the return to and through friendly lines.

*Primary and Alternate Routes.* The leader selects primary and alternate routes to and from the objective. The return routes should differ from the routes to the objective.

*Signals.* The leader should consider the use of special signals, such as arm and hand signals, flares, voice, whistles, radios, and infrared equipment. All signals must be rehearsed so that all soldiers know what they mean.

*Challenge and Password Forward of Friendly Lines.* The challenge and password from the SOI must not be used beyond the forward edge of the battle area (FEBA). In the odd-number system, the leader specifies an odd number. The challenge can be any number less than the specified number. The password is the number that must be added to it to equal the specified number.

The platoon leader can also designate a running password. This code word alerts a unit that friendly soldiers are approaching in a less than organized manner and possibly under pressure. This may be used to get soldiers quickly through a compromised passage of friendly lines. The running password is followed by the number of soldiers approaching (for example, "Moosebreath five"). This prevents the enemy from joining a group in an attempt to penetrate a friendly unit.

*Location of Leaders.* The leader considers where he and the platoon sergeant and other key leaders should be located for each phase of the patrol mission. The platoon sergeant is normally with the following elements for each type of patrol:

- On a raid or ambush, he normally controls the support element.
- On an area reconnaissance, he normally stays in the ORP.
- On a zone reconnaissance, he normally moves with the reconnaissance element that sets up the linkup point.

*Actions on Enemy Contact.* Unless required by the mission, the platoon avoids enemy contact. The leader's plan must address actions on chance contact at each phase of the patrol mission. The platoon's ability to continue the mission will depend on how early contact is made, whether the platoon is able to break contact successfully (so that its subsequent direction of movement is undetected), and whether the platoon receives any casualties as a result of the contact.

The plan must also address the handling of seriously wounded soldiers and those killed in action (KIAs), as well as the handling of prisoners who are captured as a result of chance contact and are not part of the planned mission.

*Contingency Plans.* The leader leaves for many reasons throughout the planning, coordination, preparation, and execution of his patrol mission. Each time any element departs or separates from the main body, a five-point contingency plan, abbreviated as GOTWA, should be given:

1. *Going* (where the element is heading).
2. *Others* who are going with them.
3. *Time* that the element will depart and return.
4. *What* to do if the element does not return.
5. *Actions* on contact (the departing unit and the main body).

## Abort Criteria
Every operation should have pre-established abort criteria. This is the critical analysis of the mission and what the mission-essential elements and equipment are. If elements or equipment are lost during the mission, it may have to be aborted. Determining the abort criteria in the planning phase keeps emotions out of the decisions leaders will have to make under stress.

## RALLY POINTS
The leader considers the use and locations of rally points. A rally point is a place designated by the leader where the platoon moves to reassemble and reorganize if it becomes dispersed.

## Selection of Rally Points
The leader physically reconnoiters routes to select rally points whenever possible. He selects tentative points if he can conduct only a map reconnaissance. He confirms them by actual inspection as the platoon moves through them. Rally points must:
- Be easy to find.
- Have cover and concealment.
- Be away from natural lines of drift.
- Be defendable for short periods.

**Types of Rally Points**

The most common types of rally points are initial, en route, objective, reentry, and near- and far-side rally points. Soldiers must know which rally point to move to at each phase of the patrol mission. They should know what actions are required there and how long they are to wait at each rally point before moving to another.

*Initial Rally Point.* An initial rally point (IRP) is a place inside friendly lines where a unit may assemble and reorganize if it makes enemy contact during the departure of friendly lines or before reaching the first en route rally point.

*En Route Rally Point.* The leader designates en route rally points (ERPs) every 100 to 400 meters (based on the terrain, vegetation, and visibility). When the leader designates a new ERP, the previously designated one goes into effect. This precludes uncertainty over which one soldiers should move to if contact is made immediately after the leader designates a new rally point. There are three ways to designate a rally point:

1. Physically occupy it for a short period (preferred method).
2. Pass by at a distance and designate using arm and hand signals.
3. Walk through and designate using arm and hand signals.

*Objective Rally Point.* The ORP is a point out of sight, sound, and small-arms range of the objective area. It is normally located in the direction that the platoon plans to move after completing its actions on the objective. The ORP is tentative until the objective is pinpointed. Actions at or from the ORP include:

- Reconnoitering the objective.
- Issuing a fragmentary order (FRAGO).
- Disseminating information from reconnaissance if contact was not made.
- Making final preparations before continuing operations (for example, re-camouflaging; preparing demolitions; lining up rucksacks for quick recovery; preparing enemy prisoner of war (EPW) bindings; first aid kits and litters; and inspecting weapons).
- Accounting for soldiers and equipment after actions at the objective are complete.
- Reestablishing the chain of command after actions at the objective are complete.

*Occupation of an ORP by a Squad.* In planning the occupation of an ORP, the squad leader follows this sequence:

- Halt beyond sight, sound, and small-arms weapons range of the tentative ORP (200 to 400 meters in good visibility, 100 to 200 meters in limited visibility).

- Position security.
- Move forward with a compass man and one member of each fire team to confirm the location of the ORP and determine its suitability. Issue a five-point contingency plan before departure.
- Position the Team A soldier at 12 o'clock and the Team B soldier at 6 o'clock in the ORP. Issue them a contingency plan and return with the compass man.
- Lead the squad into the ORP; position Team A from 9 to 3 o'clock and Team B from 3 to 9 o'clock.

The squad may also occupy the ORP by force. This requires more precise navigation but eliminates separating the squad.

*Occupation of an ORP by a Platoon.* The platoon leader should consider the same sequence in planning the occupation of an ORP. He brings a soldier from each squad on his reconnaissance of the ORP and positions them at the 10, 2, and 6 o'clock positions. The first squad in the order of march establishes the base leg (10 to 2 o'clock). The trailing squads occupy from 2 to 6 o'clock and from 6 to 10 o'clock positions, respectively.

### Reentry Rally Point
The reentry rally point (RRP) is located out of sight, sound, and small-arms weapons range of the friendly unit through which the platoon will return. This also means that the RRP should be outside the final protective fires of the friendly unit. The platoon occupies the RRP as a security perimeter.

### Near- and Far-Side Rally Points
These rally points are on the near and far sides of danger areas. If the platoon makes contact while crossing the danger area and control is lost, soldiers on either side move to the rally point nearest them. They establish security; reestablish the chain of command; determine their personnel and equipment status; and continue the patrol mission, link up at the ORP, or complete their last instructions.

## LEADER'S RECONNAISSANCE OF THE OBJECTIVE
The plan must include the leader's reconnaissance of the objective once the platoon or squad establishes the ORP. During his reconnaissance, the leader pinpoints the objective; selects security, support, and assault positions for his squads and fire teams; and adjusts his plan based on his observation of the objective. Each type of patrol requires different tasks during the leader's reconnaissance. The platoon leader takes different elements with him. The leader must plan time to return to the ORP, complete his plan, disseminate information, issue orders and instructions, and allow his squads to make any additional preparations.

## REENTRY OF FRIENDLY LINES

The platoon leader's initial planning and coordination must include the reentry of friendly lines and should follow this sequence:

• The platoon halts in the RRP and establishes security.
• The platoon leader radios the code word, advising the friendly unit of the platoon's location and that it is ready to return. The friendly unit must acknowledge the message and confirm that guides are waiting before the platoon moves from the RRP.
• If radio communications are not possible, the platoon leader, RATELO, and a two-man (buddy team) security element move forward and attempt to contact an OP using the challenge and password. The OP notifies the friendly unit that the platoon is ready to return and requests a guide.
• If the platoon leader cannot find an OP, he moves with the RATELO and security element to locate the coordinated reentry point. He must move straight toward (and away from) friendly lines, never parallel to them. All lateral movement should be outside of small-arms weapons range. (*Note*: The platoon leader should attempt this procedure only during daylight. At night, he should use other backup signals to make contact with friendly units. The preferred method is to wait until daylight if contact with the friendly unit cannot be made as planned.)
• Once the friendly unit acknowledges the return of the platoon, the platoon leader issues a five-point contingency plan and moves with his RATELO and a two-man (buddy team) security element on a determined azimuth and pace to the reentry point.
• The platoon leader uses far and near recognition signals to establish contact with the guide.
• The platoon leader signals the platoon forward (radio) or returns and leads it to the reentry point. He may post the security element with the guide at the enemy side of the reentry point.
• The platoon sergeant counts and identifies each soldier as he passes through the reentry point.
• The guide leads the platoon to the assembly area.
• The platoon leader reports to the command post of the friendly unit. He tells the commander everything of tactical value concerning the friendly unit's area of responsibility.

## RECONNAISSANCE PATROLS

The three types of reconnaissance patrols are area, zone, and route. Reconnaissance patrols provide timely and accurate information on the enemy and terrain. The commander must inform the patrol leader of the specific information requirements for each mission.

## Organization
Besides the common elements, reconnaissance patrols use a reconnaissance team and/or a reconnaissance and security (R&S) team. Reconnaissance teams reconnoiter the objective area once the security teams are in position. Normally these are two-man (buddy) teams to reduce the possibility of detection. R&S teams are normally used in a zone reconnaissance but may be useful in any situation when it is impractical to separate the responsibilities for reconnaissance and security.

## Area Reconnaissance
An area reconnaissance is conducted to obtain information about a specified location and the area around it. The location may be given as a grid coordinate or as an objective on an overlay. In an area reconnaissance, the platoon or squad uses surveillance or vantage points around the objective to observe it and the surrounding area. After observing the objective for a specified time, all elements return to the ORP and report their observations to the leader or the recorder. Once all information is collected, it is disseminated to every soldier.

## Zone Reconnaissance
A zone reconnaissance is conducted to obtain information on enemy, terrain, and routes within a specified zone. Zone reconnaissance techniques include the use of moving elements, stationary teams, or a series of area reconnaissance actions.

### Moving Elements
The leader plans the use of squads or fire teams moving along multiple routes to cover the entire zone. Methods for planning the movement of multiple elements through a zone include the fan, the box, converging routes, and successive sectors.

*Fan Method.* The leader first selects a series of ORPs throughout the zone. The platoon establishes security at the first ORP. Each R&S team moves from the ORP along a different fan-shaped route that overlaps with others to ensure reconnaissance of the entire area. The leader maintains a reserve at the ORP. When all R&S teams have returned to the ORP, the platoon collects the information and disseminates it to every soldier before moving on to the next ORP.

*Box Method.* The leader sends his R&S teams from the ORP along routes that form a boxed-in area. He sends other teams along routes through the area within the box. All teams meet at a linkup point at the far side of the box from the ORP.

*Converging Routes Method.* The leader selects routes from the ORP through the zone to a linkup point at the far side of the zone from the ORP.

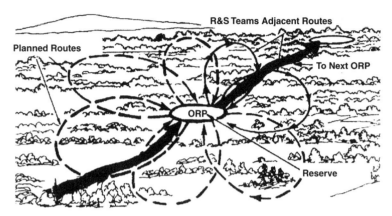

**Fan Method**

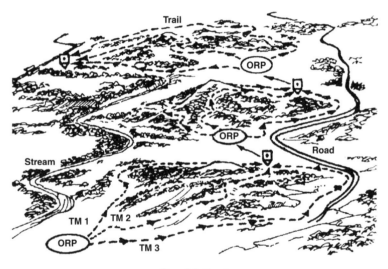

**Box Method**

Each R&S team moves along a specified route and uses the fan method to reconnoiter the area between routes. The leader designates a time for all teams to linkup.

*Successive Sector Method.* The leader divides the zone into a series of sectors. Within each sector, the platoon uses the converging routes method to reconnoiter to an intermediate linkup point, where it collects and disseminates the information gathered so far before reconnoitering the next sector.

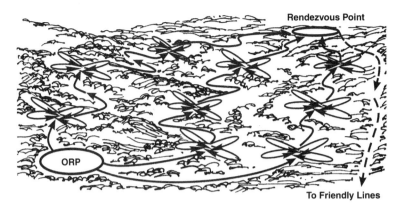

**Converging Routes Method**
Using Fans Enroute

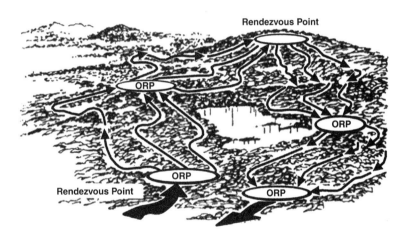

**Successive Sector Method**

*Stationary Teams*
Using this technique, the leader positions surveillance teams in locations where they can collectively observe the entire zone for long-term, continuous information gathering. He must consider sustainment requirements when developing his soldiers' load plan.

*Multiple Area Reconnaissance*
The leader tasks each of his squads to conduct a series of area reconnaissance actions along a specified route.

## Route Reconnaissance

A route reconnaissance is conducted to obtain detailed information about one route and all the adjacent terrain or to locate sites for emplacing obstacles. A route reconnaissance is oriented on a road, a narrow axis such as an infiltration lane, or a general direction of attack. Normally, engineers are attached to the infantry unit for a complete route reconnaissance. Infantry can conduct a hasty route reconnaissance without engineer support. A route reconnaissance results in detailed information about trafficability, enemy activity, NBC contamination, and aspects of adjacent terrain from both the enemy and the friendly viewpoint. In planning a route reconnaissance, the leader considers the following:

- The preferred method for conducting a route reconnaissance is the fan method described above. The leader must ensure that the fans are extensive enough to reconnoiter intersecting routes beyond direct-fire range of the main route.
- If all or part of the proposed route is a road, the leader must treat the road as a danger area. The platoon moves parallel to the road using a covered and concealed route. When required, R&S teams move close to the road to reconnoiter key areas.

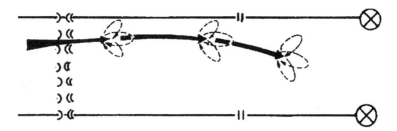

**Route Reconnaissance Using Fans**

## COMBAT PATROL

Combat patrols are conducted to destroy or capture enemy soldiers or equipment; destroy installations, facilities, or key points; or harass enemy forces. They also provide security for larger units. The two types of combat patrol missions are ambush and raid.

## Organization

Besides the common elements, combat patrols also have the following elements and teams:

*Assault Element.* The assault element seizes and secures the objective and protects special teams as they complete their assigned actions on the objective.

*Security Element.* The security element provides security at danger areas, secures the ORP, isolates the objective, and supports the withdrawal of the rest of the platoon once it completes its assigned actions on the objective.

*Support Element.* The support element provides direct-fire support and may control indirect fires for the platoon.

*Breach Element.* The breach element breaches the enemy's obstacles when required.

*Demolition Team/EOD.* Demolition teams are responsible for preparing and exploding the charges to destroy equipment, vehicles, or facilities on the objective. They will also take control of any possible explosives on target.

*Search Team/SSE.* Sensitive site exploitation (SSE) teams can be made up from the assault element and may comprise two-man (buddy) teams or four-man search teams to investigate bunkers, buildings, or tunnels on the objective. These teams may search the objective or kill zone for casualties, documents, or equipment.

## Leader's Reconnaissance of the Objective

In a combat patrol, the leader has additional considerations when conducting his reconnaissance of the objective from the ORP. He is normally the assault element leader, and should also take the support element leader, the security element leader, and a surveillance team (a two-man team from the assault element) with him. The leader designates a release point halfway between the ORP and the objective. Squads and fire teams separate at the release point and move to their assigned positions. The platoon leader confirms the location of the objective and determines that it is suitable for the assault or ambush. He notes the terrain and identifies where he can place mines or Claymores to cover dead space. He notes any other features of the objective that may cause him to alter his plan.

If the objective is the kill zone for an ambush, the leader's reconnaissance party should not cross the objective—doing so would leave tracks that might compromise the mission. The platoon leader confirms the suitability of the assault and support positions and routes from them back to the ORP. The platoon leader posts the surveillance team and issues a five-point contingency plan before returning to the ORP.

## AMBUSH

An ambush is a surprise attack from a concealed position on a moving or temporarily halted target. Antiarmor ambushes are established when the mission is to destroy enemy armored or mechanized forces. Ambushes are classified by category (hasty or deliberate), type (point or area), and formation (linear or L-shaped). The leader uses a combination of all three classifications in developing his ambush plan. The key planning considerations include:

- Covering the entire kill zone by fire.
- Using existing or reinforcing obstacles (Claymores and other mines) to keep the enemy in the kill zone.
- Protecting the assault and support elements with mines, Claymores, or explosives.
- Using security elements or teams to isolate the kill zone.
- Assaulting into the kill zone to search dead and wounded, assemble prisoners, and collect equipment (the assault element must be able to move quickly through its own protective obstacles).
- Timing the actions of all elements of the platoon to preclude loss of surprise.
- Using only one squad to conduct the entire ambush and rotating squads over time from the ORP (this technique is useful when the ambush must be manned for a long time).

### Hasty Ambush

A platoon or squad conducts a hasty ambush when it makes visual contact with an enemy force and has time to establish an ambush without being detected. The actions for a hasty ambush must be well rehearsed so that soldiers know what to do on the leader's signal. They must also know what action to take if detected before they are ready to initiate the ambush.

### Deliberate Ambush

A deliberate ambush is conducted against a specific target at a predetermined location. The leader requires detailed information in planning a deliberate ambush, including:
- Size and composition of the targeted enemy unit.
- Weapons and equipment available to the enemy.
- The enemy's route and direction of movement.
- Times that the targeted unit will reach or pass specified points along the route.

### Point Ambush

In a point ambush, soldiers deploy to attack an enemy in a single kill zone. The security or surveillance teams should be positioned first, and the support element should be in position before the assault element moves forward of the release point. The support element must overwatch the movement of the assault element into position.

The platoon leader is the leader of the assault element. He must check each soldier once the assault position has been established. He signals the surveillance team to rejoin the assault element.

Actions of the *assault element* include:
* Identifying individual sectors of fire as assigned by the platoon leader.
* Emplacing aiming stakes.
* Emplacing Claymores and other protective devices.
* Emplacing Claymores, mines, or other explosives in dead space within the kill zone.
* Camouflaging positions.

Actions of the *support element* include:
* Identifying sectors of fire for all weapons, especially machine guns.
* Emplacing limiting stakes to prevent friendly fires from hitting the assault element in an L-shaped ambush.
* Emplacing Claymores and other protective devices.

Instructions to security teams must include how to notify the platoon leader of the enemy's approach into the kill zone (SALUTE report—size, activity, location, unit, time, and equipment). The security element must also keep the platoon leader informed if any enemy forces are following the lead force.

The platoon leader must determine how large an element his ambush can engage successfully. He must be prepared to let units pass that are too large and report to higher headquarters any units that pass his ambush unengaged.

The platoon leader also initiates the ambush. The ambush should be initiated by the most casualty producing weapon the unit has, which may be a command-detonated Claymore. There should be a plan for a backup method for initiating the ambush should the primary means fail. This should also be a heavy casualty-producing device, such as a machine gun. This information must be passed out to all soldiers and practiced during rehearsals.

Soldiers must have a means of engaging the enemy in the kill zone during periods of limited visibility if it becomes necessary to initiate the ambush then. Use of tracers must be weighed against how it might help the enemy identify friendly positions. The platoon leader may use handheld or indirect illumination flares.

The platoon leader should include indirect-fire support as part of his plan. Indirect fires can cover the flanks of the kill zone to help isolate it. They can also help the platoon disengage if the ambush is compromised or if the platoon must depart the ambush site under pressure.

The platoon leader must have a good plan to signal the advance of the assault element into the kill zone to begin its search and collection activities. Smoke may not be visible to the support element. All soldiers must know and practice relaying this signal during rehearsals.

The assault element must be prepared to move across the kill zone using individual movement techniques if there is any return fire once they begin to search. Otherwise, the assault element moves across by bounding fire teams. Other actions in the kill zone include the following:

- Collect and secure all EPWs and move them out of the kill zone before searching bodies. Establish a location for EPWs and enemy wounded who will not be taken back that provides them cover yet allows them to be found easily by their units.
- Search from one side to the other and mark bodies that have been searched to ensure that the area is thoroughly covered.
- Use the two-man search technique. As the search team approaches a dead enemy soldier, one man guards while the other man searches.
- Identify and collect equipment to be carried back and prepare it for transport. (Clear all weapons and place them on "safe.")
- Identify and collect remaining equipment for destruction. The demolition team prepares dual-primed explosives (C4 with two M60 fuse lighters and time fuse) and awaits the signal to initiate. This is normally the last action performed before departing the objective and may signal the security elements to return to the ORP.

The platoon leader must plan the withdrawal from the ambush site:

- Elements normally withdraw in the reverse order that they established their positions.
- The elements may return first to the release point, then to the ORP, depending on the distance between elements.
- The security element at the ORP must be alert to assist the platoon's return to the ORP. It maintains security for the ORP while the rest of the platoon prepares to leave.

**Area Ambush**

In an area ambush, soldiers deploy in two or more related point ambushes. A platoon is the smallest unit to conduct an area ambush. Platoons conduct area ambushes where enemy movement is largely restricted to trails or streams.

The platoon leader selects one principal ambush site around which he organizes outlying ambushes. These secondary sites are located along the enemy's most likely approach to and escape from the principal ambush site. Squad-size elements are normally responsible for each ambush site. They establish an area ambush as described above.

The platoon leader must determine the best employment of his machine guns. He normally positions them both with the support element of the principal site.

Squads responsible for outlying ambushes do not initiate their ambushes until after the principal one is initiated. They then engage to prevent enemy forces from escaping or reinforcing.

### Linear Ambush

In an ambush using a linear formation, the assault and support elements deploy parallel to the enemy's route. This positions both elements on the long axis of the kill zone and subjects the enemy to flanking fire. This formation can be used in close terrain that restricts the enemy's ability to maneuver against the platoon or in open terrain, provided a means of keeping the enemy in the kill zone can be effected.

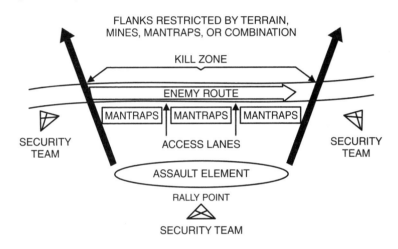

**Linear Ambush Formation**

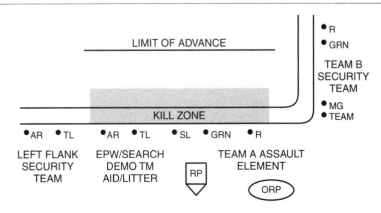

**L-shaped Ambush Formation**

## L-Shaped Ambush

In an L-shaped ambush, the assault element forms the long leg parallel to the enemy's direction of movement along the kill zone. The support element forms the short leg at one end of and at a right angle to the assault element. This provides both flanking (long leg) and enfilading (short leg) fires against the enemy. The L-shaped ambush can be used at a sharp bend in a trail, road, or stream. It should not be used where the short leg would have to cross a straight road or trail.

## Antiarmor Ambush

The purpose of an antiarmor ambush is to destroy armored vehicles. A squad can conduct a dismounted antiarmor ambush, organizing into an armor-killer team and a support-and-security team. The armor-killer team fires into the kill zone. Normally, the Dragon is the main weapon of this team. Where fields of fire are less than 100 meters, light antitank weapons (LAWs) may be the main antiarmor weapon. In that case, the armor-killer team must mass LAW fires into the kill zone to make sure the enemy vehicle is destroyed. The support-and-security team provides security and should be positioned where it can cover the withdrawal of the armor-killer team.

ARMOR-KILLER TEAM

LAW
SAW

DRAGON
M16

SQUAD LEADER
LAW
M16

SUPPORT/SECURITY TEAM

LAW
M203

M60

LAW
SAW

R/S
M16

ASST SQUAD LEADER
M203

**Squad Antiarmor Ambush**

*At the Ambush Site.* When the squad arrives at the ambush site, the leader reconnoiters and picks the kill zone. Good positions have the following attributes:

• Good fields of fire.
• Cover and concealment.
• An obstacle between the teams and the kill zone.
• Covered and concealed withdrawal routes.

*Establishing an Antiarmor Ambush.* Position a support-and-security team first, and provide security on both flanks. Position the Dragon and then the machine gun so they can cover the kill zone.

The leader initiates the ambush when the enemy enters the kill zone. A command-detonated antiarmor mine is an excellent means of initiating the ambush. The Dragon may be used to initiate the ambush, but it has a slow rate of fire, gives off a signature, and may not hit the target. When possible, the first and last vehicles of a column should be destroyed to keep other vehicles from escaping.

The rest of the squad opens fire when the ambush is initiated. Indirect fires should fall into the kill zone as soon as possible. If the kill zone is in range, squad members fire a LAW.

If enemy dismounted troops precede the armored vehicles, the squad leader must decide whether they pose a threat to the ambush. If they can out-flank his squad before the enemy armor can be hit, he may decide to withdraw and set up another ambush somewhere else.

## RAID
A raid is a combat operation to attack a position or installation followed by a planned withdrawal. Squads do not execute raids. The sequence of platoon actions for a raid is similar to that for an ambush. Additionally, the assault element of the platoon may have to conduct a breach of an obstacle. It may have additional tasks to perform on the objective: for example, demolition of fixed facilities.

## TRACKING PATROL
Platoons and squads may receive the mission to follow the trail of an enemy unit. Even while tracking, they still gather information about the enemy, the route, and surrounding terrain.

## Training
Soldiers must be taught to move stealthily and well trained in tracking techniques. Once soldiers are deployed into an area of operation, training continues so that the platoon can learn about local soil, climate, vegetation, animals, vehicles, footwear, and other factors.

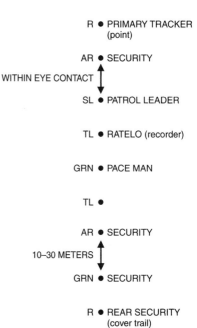

**Tracking Patrol**

## Organization

When the platoon receives the mission to conduct a tracking patrol, it assigns the task of tracking to only one squad. The remaining squads and attachments provide security.

## Trail Signs

Men, machines, and animals leave signs of their presence as they move through an area. These signs can be as subtle as an odor or as obvious as a well-worn path. All soldiers can read obvious signs such as roads, worn trails, or tracks in sand and snow. However, attention to detail, common sense, alertness, logic, and knowledge of the environment and enemy habits enable soldiers to obtain better information from signs they find in the battle area.

*Trail and Sign Analysis.* Once the first sign is discovered, it must not be disturbed or covered and should be analyzed carefully before the patrol follows the enemy. If the sign is found at the site of enemy activity, the exact occurrence can often be reconstructed. If a trail is the first sign found, the tracker can still determine such facts as the size and composition of the groups being tracked, their direction, and their general condition. The tracker must determine as much as possible about the enemy before following it. His knowledge of the enemy continues to grow as he finds additional signs.

*Finding the Trail.* Finding the trail is the first task. The tracking team can reconnoiter around a known location of enemy activity when the trail cannot be found in the immediate area. There are two ways to hunt for a trail:

1. The tracking team can locate and follow the enemy's trail from a specific area or location where the enemy has been seen. This can be a camp or base or the site of an enemy attack or enemy contact.
2. The route of a friendly unit may cross a trail left by an enemy group. This can be by chance, or the team can deliberately take a route it believes will cut across one or more probable enemy routes.

*Regaining a Lost Trail.* If the tracker loses the trail, he immediately stops. The tracking team then retraces its path to the last enemy sign and marks this point. The team studies the sign and the area around it for any clue as to where the enemy went. It looks for signs that the enemy scattered, backtracked, doglegged, or used any other countertracking method. If the trail still cannot be found, the team establishes security in a spot that avoids destroying any sign. Then the tracker and an assistant look for the trail by "boxing" the area around the last sign. The tracking team always returns to the same path, away from the last sign, to create as few trails as possible.

## PRESENCE PATROL

US forces are deployed increasingly in support of stability and support operations (SASO) missions all around the world. The infantry platoon plans and conducts a presence patrol much the same as a combat patrol. The primary difference is that the patrol wants to both be seen as a show of force and to lend confidence and stability to the local population of the host nation. As its name implies, this patrol is constituted to achieve a presence. It can be used only if a peace agreement has been negotiated between belligerents. The presence patrol is armed, and it conducts the planning and preparation necessary for combat operations at all times. The patrol can be used as a component of a larger force conducting stability and/or support operations.

The platoon could be tasked to conduct mounted (if augmented with vehicles) or dismounted patrols planned by the higher headquarters to accomplish one or more of the following:

- Confirm or supervise an agreed ceasefire.
- Gain information.
- Cover gaps between OPs or checkpoints.
- Show a stability force presence.
- Reassure isolated communities.
- Inspect existing or vacated positions of former belligerents.
- Escort former belligerents or local populations through trouble spots.

## PATROL BASES

A patrol base is a position set up when a squad or platoon conducting a patrol halts for an extended period. When the unit must halt for a long time in a place not protected by friendly troops, it takes both active and passive security measures. Patrol bases should be occupied no longer than twenty-four hours and the same one is never used twice. Patrol bases are used for the following purposes:

- To avoid detection by stopping all movement.
- For hiding during a long, detailed reconnaissance of an objective area.
- To eat, clean weapons and equipment, and rest.
- To plan and issue orders.
- To reorganize after infiltrating an enemy area.
- As a base from which to conduct several consecutive or concurrent operations such as ambush, raid, reconnaissance, or security.

Once in the patrol base, there are six priorities of work: security, maintenance, hygiene, water (resupply), mess, and rest.

## Site Selection

A tentative site is normally selected from a map or by aerial reconnaissance. Its suitability must be confirmed before occupation. An alternate site is selected in the event the first site is unsuitable or must be evacuated unexpectedly. The site should be on terrain of little tactical value to the enemy, off natural lines of drift, difficult for foot movement, and near a source of water; offer cover and concealment; and be defensible for a short period of time.

## Occupation of the Patrol Base

The area is reconnoitered, and when it is determined to be secure, the patrol enters from a 90-degree turn. The platoon sergeant and the last fire team get rid of any tracks from the turn. A two-man OP is left at the turn. The platoon moves into the position, with squad leaders moving to the left flank of their squad sector. The platoon leader checks the position, starting at 6 o'clock and moving in a clockwise direction. He meets each squad leader at the squad's left flank, adjusts the perimeter as needed, and repositions machine guns if he finds better locations.

When the perimeter is secure, the platoon leader directs each squad to conduct a reconnaissance to the front of its sector. Each squad sends out a team from the left flank of the squad sector, which moves a distance away from the position as directed by the platoon leader (200 to 400 meters, depending on terrain and vegetation). It then moves clockwise and reenters

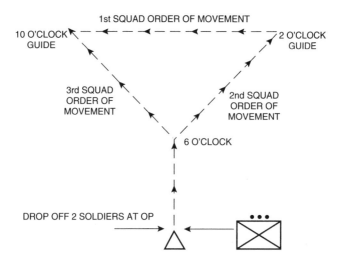

**Occupation of a Patrol Base**

the patrol base at the right flank of the squad sector. The team looks for enemy, water, built-up areas, human habitat, roads, or trails. The platoon leader gathers information from the reconnaissance teams and determines the suitability of the area as a patrol base.

### Patrol Base Activities

The considerations for a perimeter defense apply to establishing a patrol base. The leader assigns a priority of work, including the following.

*Security.* Each squad establishes an OP, and the soldiers quietly dig hasty fighting positions. Priorities of work can be accomplished by two-man positions, with one soldier on guard while the other soldier digs, conducts personal hygiene and maintenance, and eats. Noise and light discipline is enforced. Claymores are put out. Sector sketches and range cards are prepared. Soldiers should use only one point of entry and exit.

*Alert Plan.* The platoon leader states the alert posture (for example, 50 percent or 33 percent awake) and stand-to time for day and night. He prepares a roster for periodic checks of fighting positions and OPs, and ensures that OPs are relieved periodically and that at least one leader is awake at all times. No more than half of the platoon eats at one time.

*Withdrawal Plan.* The platoon leader prepares a contingency plan for enemy contact, including a signal (for example, star cluster) to withdraw, order of withdrawal (squads not in contact move out first), and rendezvous point.

*Maintenance.* Leaders ensure that weapons and equipment are cleaned and maintained. Machine guns, radios, and night vision devices are not broken down at the same time. Weapons are not disassembled at night.

*Field Sanitation and Personal Hygiene.* Latrines are dug and trash points designated. Soldiers shave, wash, and brush teeth daily. A water party is organized to fill all canteens. No trash is left behind, and the position is sterilized upon departure.

# 8

# Urban Operations

This chapter describes the basic techniques, procedures, and special considerations that platoons and squads will use throughout the planning and execution of operations in an urban environment, along with some lessons learned during Operations Enduring Freedom and Iraqi Freedom. Remember, however, that in urban combat the principles and fundamentals of combat remain basically the same as in other combat operations.[*]

According to the US Army Center for Lessons Learned, only 5 percent of the casualties sustained during the 3 October 1993 raid by Task Force Ranger in Mogadishu, Somalia, occurred during the conduct of close quarter battle (CQB) inside buildings. The remaining 95 percent were sustained in the streets. Because of global urbanization, combat in built-up areas has become an important mission for the US forces and thus, this type of combat cannot be avoided.

## PRINCIPLES OF URBAN MOVEMENT
The principles of urban movement include security, coordinated fires and movement, communications, cover and concealment, speed, momentum, and violence of action.

**Security.** As with any combat operation, a 360-degree area of security is maintained at all times. In an urban environment the dimension of height must be considered because of the numerous multilevel buildings. This added dimension provides the enemy with more area in which to operate. In larger urban areas, security considerations become truly three-dimensional—subways, sewers, water mains, and other underground structures should be considered.

**Coordinated Fires and Movement.** Individuals and fire teams coordinate their fire and movements to maintain security. When moving down a

---

[*]Information on CQB and infantry tactics provided by Evan Hafer.

street, overwatching fire teams provide suppressive fire for their fellow fire teams. This process is continuous, as in the need for 360-degree, three-dimensional situational awareness.

During actual operations it is recommended that one to two light anti-tank weapons or antitank-4s (LAWs or AT-4s) be assigned per fire team to take out vehicles, fortified positions, or other obstacles. Remember that the fire team (four to five assaulters) is the smallest maneuver element. It must move quickly and together in order to handle all contingencies that can't be dealt with by one soldier.

**Communications.** Radio communications are maintained with the overwatching teams. Use of verbal and nonverbal (day and night) communications should be a part of the unit's SOP and *must* be rehearsed. Emphasis is placed on keeping radio traffic to a minimum during the operation, and radio communication needs to be planned prior to the operation.

**Cover and Concealment.** Cover is the use of objects that can stop bullets, such as thick concrete walls or the engine of a vehicle. Concealment is the use of shadows, vegetation, or light structures such as wooden walls to limit the enemy's observation of your position. Do not silhouette yourself in interior doorways. When smoke is used to mask your patrols, remember that while the enemy cannot see you, you cannot see the enemy either. Smoke is more effective when an overwatch or sniper team in a higher position can see past the smoke and engage targets on the other side of the street. However, don't sacrifice speed to employ snipers. Smoke also identifies your position or that your element is active.

**Speed.** Speed is critical and also a form of security. Individual actions must be practiced until muscle memory has been developed through the use of battle drill rehearsals and other unit collective training. When moving outside, stay approximately 1 meter away from the walls of buildings or other structures because bullets that strike walls travel down or along them.

**Momentum.** Continual movement of the assault force is a key to mission success. When an assault element stops, it gives the enemy time to go on the offensive and puts friendly forces in a reactive/defensive posture. Assault elements should continue to move and take ground in order to keep the enemy off balance. Offensive movements are better than defensive ones. When possible, fight from the top (vertical) down.

**Violence of Action.** Violence of action comes from a "never quit" attitude and from knowing you are better trained and equipped than your enemy. It also keeps the enemy off guard and unsure of his ability to defeat you.

## OFFENSIVE OPERATIONS IN URBAN AREAS

While operating in urban areas, the major offensive collective tasks of a platoon and squad are attacking and clearing buildings. This involves isolating the objective, suppressing the enemy, advancing the assault element, assaulting the building, clearing the building, and consolidating and reorganizing the force. Regardless of the type of urban area or its structural characteristics, there are six interrelated requirements for attacking a defended building:

- Isolation of objective.
- Supporting fires.
- Tactical movement.
- Conducting the breach.
- Conducting the assault.
- Consolidation and reorganization.

Proper application and integration of these requirements reduces casualties and hastens accomplishment of the mission. The type of building to be assaulted, the rules of engagement (ROE), and the nature of the surrounding urban area will determine the method of execution. Platoon and squad leaders consider the assigned task, its purpose, and the method they will use to achieve the desired results.

You do not always have to commit your troops to an assigned building, area, or sector. An unmotivated enemy with low morale may surrender before you have to commit troops, while simple negotiations or use of psychological operations (PSYOPS) may give the desired results. On the other hand, a motivated and well-trained enemy may require you to commit direct- and indirect-fire assets into the area (ROE allowing); this alone may cause a surrender, again keeping you from committing your troops.

### Task Organization (Platoon Attack of a Building)

The platoon normally operates as part of a company force in urban operations. However, this chapter will focus on the platoon as if it is acting alone or has become isolated from the rest of the company. The platoon leader normally will organize his platoon into at least two elements: an *assault* element and a *support* element. If engineers are available, they are normally attached to the assault element and they will usually perform breaching tasks. If engineers are not available, the platoon leader may designate a breaching team from within either the assault or the support element, or he may task organize a separate breach element. The size of these elements is METT-TC dependent.

*Assault Element.* The purpose of the assault element is to kill, capture, or force the withdrawal of the enemy from any urban objective and to seize key terrain. The assault element of a platoon may consist of one, two, or

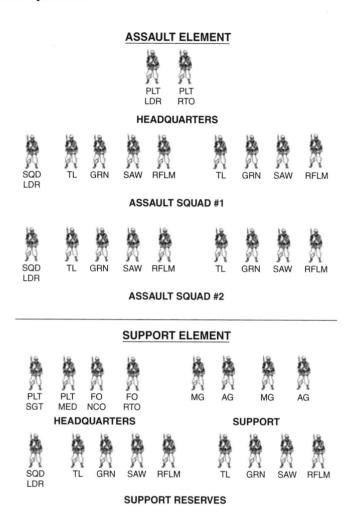

**ASSAULT ELEMENT**

PLT
LDR

PLT
RTO

**HEADQUARTERS**

SQD
LDR

TL GRN SAW RFLM TL GRN SAW RFLM

**ASSAULT SQUAD #1**

SQD
LDR

TL GRN SAW RFLM TL GRN SAW RFLM

**ASSAULT SQUAD #2**

**SUPPORT ELEMENT**

PLT
SGT

PLT
MED

FO
NCO

FO
RTO

MG AG MG AG

**HEADQUARTERS** **SUPPORT**

SQD
LDR

TL GRN SAW RFLM TL GRN SAW RFLM

**SUPPORT RESERVES**

**Task Organization—Platoon Attack of a Building**

three squads. Squad leaders normally organize their two fire teams into two clearing teams or, in special circumstances, the squad may be kept as a single assault squad. The assault force could be divided into two clearing teams with a breaching element designated from within one or both teams. As the breaching element and one clearing team move into position at the initial entry point, the remaining clearing team provides additional fire support. Once the lead clearing team has gained a foothold in the building, the remaining clearing team enters and secures the foothold.

*Support Element.* The support element's purpose is to provide immediate suppressive fire support to enable the assault element to close with the enemy and to assist in the isolation of the building. The support element at platoon level may consist of the weapons squad (or machine-gun teams and antiarmor gunners) and any personnel not designated as part of the assault element. This assistance includes, but is not limited to:

- Suppressing enemy weapons systems and obscuring the enemy's observation within the objective building(s) and adjacent structures.
- Isolating the objective building(s) with direct fires to prevent enemy withdrawal, reinforcement, or counterattack.
- Obscuring enemy observation of obstacles en route and at the entry point to the objective during breaching operations.
- Using ladder teams for accessing the tops of buildings and structures.
- Destroying or suppressing enemy positions with direct-fire weapons.
- Engaging enemy armor with antitank (AT) weapons.
- Securing cleared portions of the objective.
- Providing replacements for the assault element.
- Providing the resupply of ammunition and pyrotechnics.
- Bringing up specific equipment that the assault element could not carry in the initial assault.
- Evacuating casualties, prisoners, and civilians.

*Note*: The platoon sergeant must be prepared to rapidly evacuate the wounded from the objective area to the company CCP. Barricades, rubble in the streets, and demolition of roads may impede ground ambulances; therefore, litter teams may be needed.

*Breach Team.* The purpose of the breach team is to clear and mark lanes through obstacles during movement and to provide the assault element with access to an urban objective. The platoon leader organizes the force to ensure that breaching teams are identified.

## Tactical Movement

When moving in an urban area, squads and platoons use modified variations of the traveling, traveling overwatch, and bounding overwatch movement techniques (see pages 62–66). Leaders must be aware of the three-dimensional aspect of urban terrain such as streets, buildings, subsurface, and airspace. Because of sniper vulnerability, countersniper techniques must be well rehearsed and implemented. Elements move in a manner that prevents the entire force from becoming decisively engaged at one time.

The assault force minimizes the effects of the enemy's defensive fires during movement by using covered and concealed routes; moving only after enemy fires have been suppressed or enemy observation obscured; moving at night or during periods of reduced visibility; selecting routes that will not

Street

Cutaway Views

Subways

Sewers and
Utility Tunnels

Cellars

**Three-Dimensional Urban Terrain**

mask friendly suppressive fires; crossing open areas quickly under the concealment of smoke and suppression provided by the support element; and moving on rooftops not covered by enemy fires. To avoid exposure on the street or to provide mutual support, if possible, the infantry squads may attempt moving through the buildings. The platoon moves along streets and alleys with two squads leading (one on either side of the street) and the third squad in the overwatch. The squads should move using bounding overwatch to quickly locate, identify, engage, and eliminate all enemy weapons systems.

### Isolate the Objective or Building
When planning the isolation, leaders determine a three-dimensional and in-depth isolation of the objective (front, flanks, rear, upper stories, and rooftops). They should employ all available direct- and indirect-fire weapons allowed by the ROE, including attack helicopters and close air support. Isolating the objective also involves seizing terrain that dominates the area so that the enemy cannot supply, reinforce, or withdraw its defenders. It also includes selecting terrain that provides the ability to place suppressive fire

on the objective. (This step may be taken at the same time as securing a foothold.) If isolating the objective is the first step, speed is necessary so that the defender has no time to react.

The brevity code for the four sides of a building is as follows:

The *white* side is the side of the breach point

The *black* side is the side opposite of the breach point

The *red* side is the right side of the building (using the breach point as reference)

The *green* side is the left side of the building (using the breach point as reference)

This brevity code is used to avoid the possibility of confusion when deep in an urban setting and establishes the breach point as the reference point for that particular assault.

### Assault a Building

The assault element must quickly and violently execute the assault and subsequent clearing operations. The momentum is maintained to deny the enemy time to organize a more determined resistance on other floors or in other rooms.

*Approaches.* All routes to the breach and/or entry point are planned in advance. The best route is confirmed and selected during the leaders' reconnaissance. The route should allow the assault element to approach the breach (entry) point from the blind side, if possible.

*Order of March.* The method of breach usually determines the order of march. Establishing an order of march aids the team leader with command and control ($C^2$) and minimizes exposure time in open areas and at the entry point. If the breach has been conducted prior to its arrival, the assault team quickly moves through the breach (entry) point. If a breach has not been made prior to its arrival at the breach point, and depending on the type of entry point to be made, the team leader conducts the breach himself or signals forward the breacher or element.

*Conduct of the Breach.* Soldiers may be fighting just to get to the breach point; therefore, proper fire and movement will be required all the way there. All members not conducting the breach will provide internal support and suppressive fires onto enemy targets and probable enemy positions using direct fire and grenades (ROE dependent). Additionally, the rest of the squad or platoon will provide support to secure (left, right, up, and down) the assault element in the three-dimensional environment.

Until an entry point into the building is established, all possible enemy positions and entryways are watched and suppressed as necessary for potential enemy and booby traps. If possible, the breach is conducted in such a manner as to allow the assault element to continue movement without having to wait at the breach (entry) point. Deception (by use of fragmentation grenades, concussion grenades, or stun grenades in an area other than the actual breach or entry point) should be used to confuse the enemy as to the location of the primary entry point.

**Breaching Methods.** There are six breaching methods:

1. *Explosive breach.* This method requires the use of an explosive composition such as C4, deta sheet explosives, or a manufactured shape charge directed against the target.
2. *Ballistic breach.* This method requires the use of a weapon firing a projectile at the breach point (shotgun).
3. *Mechanical breach.* This method uses machines such as quickie saws, chainsaws, hydraulic separators, or even the front of a vehicle.
4. *Thermal breach.* This method uses torches when steel bars or doors are encountered on the target.
5. *Manual breach.* This is the use of brute force, such as by means of a sledgehammer, ram, crowbar, etc.
6. *Surreptitious breach.* This method is the act of picking locks, scaling walls to gain access through windows, unlocking doors from the inside, etc.

**Breach Locations.** The success of the assault element often depends on the speed with which they gain access into the building. It is important that the breach location provides the assault element with covered or concealed access, fluid entry, and the ability to be overwatched by the support element. An example of this would be using a ladder on a wall with a rifleman who is responsible for covering the entry of the assault element from behind cover and on the high ground.

**Security.** Because of the three-dimensional enemy associated with urban terrain, the assault element must maintain 360-degree security during movement to the breach (entry) point. If the assault element is to stop in the vicinity of the breach (entry) point to wait for the breach element to complete its task, the support element must maintain suppressive fire to protect the assault element.

**Assault Location.** The assault may begin from the top or bottom of the building. Entering at the top and fighting downward is the preferred method of clearing a building. This method is only feasible, however, when the platoon can gain access to an upper floor or rooftop by ladder; from the windows or roofs of adjoining, secured buildings; or by helicopter. Entry at the bottom is common and may be the only option available. When entering from the bottom, breaching a wall is the preferred method because doors and windows may be booby-trapped and covered by fire from inside the structure. If the assault element must enter through a door or window, it should enter from a rear or flank position.

*Suppressive Fires during the Assault.* The blocking position (BP) provides suppressive fire while the assault force systematically clears the building. It also provides suppressive fire on adjacent buildings to prevent enemy reinforcements or withdrawal. The BP destroys or captures any enemy personnel trying to exit the building. It also must deal with civilians displaced by the assault.

*Clearing Rooms.* The platoon leader must ensure that the clearing squads carry enough room-marking equipment and plainly mark cleared rooms from the friendly side in accordance with unit SOPs. Markings must be visible to friendly units even if the operation occurs during limited visibility. The support force must understand which markings will be used and ensure that suppressive fires do not engage cleared rooms and floors. Maintaining awareness of where the assault teams are and of which rooms and floors have been cleared is imperative and a key C$^2$ function for the platoon leader. (See the Enter Building and Clear Room battle drill on page 197 as an example.)

***Direction of Assault Technique of Direct-Fire Planning and Control.*** In this technique, building numbers are assigned in a consistent pattern in relation to the direction of assault. In the example shown below, the buildings are numbered consecutively in a clockwise manner. Additionally, the

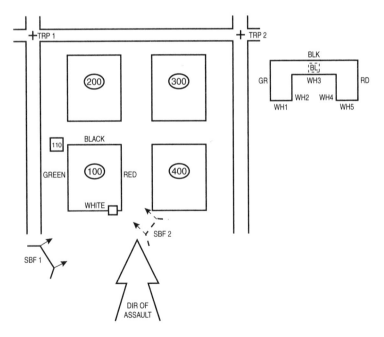

**Direction of Assault Technique of Fire Control**

sides of the buildings are color-coded consistently throughout the objective area (WHITE = breach side/direction of assault side, GREEN = left side, BLACK = rear side or opposite the breach point, RED = right side, BLUE = CCP). An odd-shaped building is also shown. Note that a "four-sided" concept was retained to minimize confusion.

The grid reference graphic (GRG) is a picture of the target area with structures labeled with a number so that the ground force commander can keep track of his force. This GRG is also given to close air support to aid in the precision needed for urban air support. All designations are labeled in relation to the direction of assault.

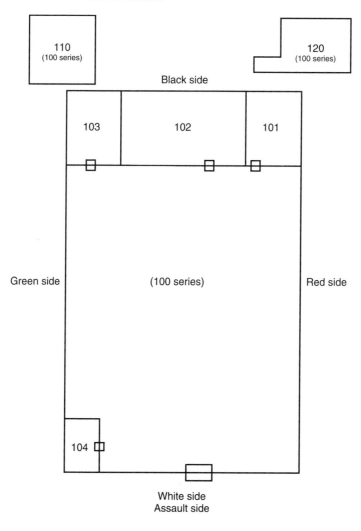

**Enter and Clear a Building**
Success or failure in urban terrain is often determined by actions taken instinctively by individual soldiers and fire teams as they encounter complex situations (such as the intermixing of combatants and civilians). Instinct in combat is a learned behavior that is only possible after realistic tough training. Training must make soldiers unconsciously competent in the skills sets needed to be successful in combat; this is especially true in the case of urban combat.

*Principles.* The principles of urban combat are surprise, speed, and controlled violence of action. These principles do not change, regardless of ROE. The three principles of urban combat are each relative to one another; i.e., successful surprise allows increased speed, and controlled violence coupled with speed increases surprise.

- *Surprise* is one of the elements necessary for a successful assault at close range. The assault team achieves surprise by attacking at a time and location unexpected by the defender, using everything from surreptitious entry to hand grenades, silent ropes, and ladders to explosive or ballistic breaching intended to stun the occupants of a room.
- *Speed* can provide a measure of security to the clearing unit by allowing soldiers to use the first few seconds provided by surprise to their advantage. In urban combat, speed cannot be careless—it must be careful and deliberate. The only way to develop speed with the care and deliberateness that this type of combat requires is through realistic training.
- *Controlled violence of action* eliminates or neutralizes the enemy and decreases his chances of inflicting friendly casualties. It also maintains coordination and control of friendlies, thereby avoiding the fratricide issues that can be prevalent in a chaotic urban fight.

**Fundamentals of Clearing Operations**
The actions soldiers take while moving through and clearing a building include:
- *Dominate the space.* When moving down hallways and corridors, it is essential that the team covers all potential danger areas and spaces. Soldiers should constantly be looking for work.
- *Dominate the room.* Soldiers should occupy the points of domination that are within their area of responsibility and that will overwhelm the enemy and provide interlocking fields of fire in order to cover potential threats.
- *Eliminate the threat.* As quickly as possible, the team should eliminate the threat in the room. This can be accomplished by using verbal

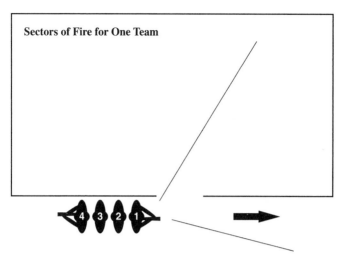

Sectors of Fire for One Team

signals, hand signals, or lethal force. Positively identify the threat IAW ROE and look at the hands to properly identify the immediate threat—threatening actions identify potential threats.

- *Control the situation.* Obtain control of the situation in the initial few moments. Loss of control or lack of control will result in a lack of momentum and an increase in the likelihood of confrontation.

### Clearing Techniques

Methods of movement, firing techniques, weapon positioning, and reflexive shooting are fundamentals used in urban combat. Special clearing techniques may be required when highly restrictive ROE are in effect. The enemy situation may require that the units clear only a few selected buildings methodically to accomplish their mission rather than using firepower to suppress and neutralize buildings in the objective area. On the other hand, a robust ROE may favor the use of overwhelming firepower, in which case units should employ direct and indirect fires, demolitions, and fragmentation or concussion grenades as necessary to assist in clearing an objective defended by an alert and determined force without noncombatants.

### Enter Building and Clear Room Drill

The fundamentals of surprise, speed and violence of action are of particular importance in CQB. Leaders must take care that fratricide or "blue on blue" incidents do not happen. Friendly fire incidents are avoided only through constant coordination and knowledge of where assets are in the battlespace. Avoid splitting up forces inside buildings and observe vigilant security in order to not fall victim to the complex geometry of rooms and hallways.

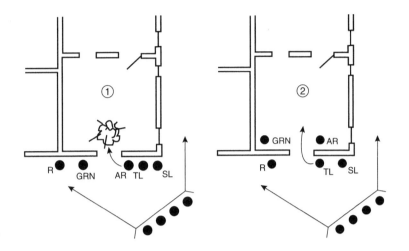

**Entering a Building—Squad**

**Step 1.** The fire team initiating contact establishes a base of fire and suppresses the enemy in and around the building.

**Step 2.** The squad leader determines whether he can maneuver by identifying the building and any obstacles, the size of the enemy force engaging the squad, an entry point, and a covered and concealed route to the entry point.

**Step 3.** The squad leader directs the fire team in contact to support the entry of the other fire team. He also designates the entry point. The platoon and squad shift direct fires and continue to suppress the enemy in adjacent positions and to isolate the building. Indirect fires are lifted or shifted, as necessary.

**Step 4.** The squad leader and assaulting fire team approach the building and position themselves at either side of the entry point. (Doors and windows should be avoided because they will normally be covered by enemy soldiers inside the building.)

**Step 5.** The lead soldier of the assaulting fire team cooks off the grenade(s) (two seconds maximum); shouts, "Frag out" if element of surprise is lost; and then throws the grenade(s) into the building or room. The type of grenade used is dependent on the rules of engagement (ROE):

- METT-TC factors and types of construction materials used in the objective building influence whether *flash bang*, *concussion*, or *fragmentation* grenades can be used in assaulting an urban objective.
- Soldiers should engage upper-level openings with grenades (by hand or launcher) before entering to eliminate enemy who might be near the entrance.

**Step 6.** After the grenade detonates, an element of up to four soldiers moves to the entrance. Clearing begins as soon as the first soldier can see into the building (the soldier does not have to be physically in the room to engage the enemy within). The team enters the building, each in opposite directions from the soldier in front of him. Clearing of the room should be taking place the moment a soldier can see into the room and up to the point the unit reaches its point of domination. Each soldier will position himself to the left or right of the entrance, up against the wall. The entry team engages all identified enemy positions with rapid, well-aimed fire and then scans the room.

*Note:* It is important to understand that the securing of the room takes place as the soldiers are moving and does not wait for them to reach points of domination.

The rest of the team provides immediate security outside the building. The size, shape, adjacent space, and angles of the room cause the entry team soldiers to adjust their positions after the initial engagement.

Speaking is kept to a minimum to limit confusion.

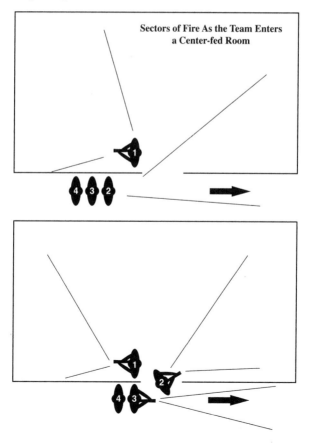

Sectors of Fire As the Team Enters a Center-fed Room

Sectors of Fire As the Team Enters a Center-fed Room *(continued)*

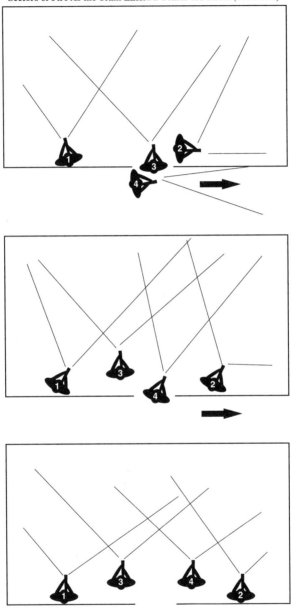

**Sectors of Fire As the Team Enters a Corner-fed Room**

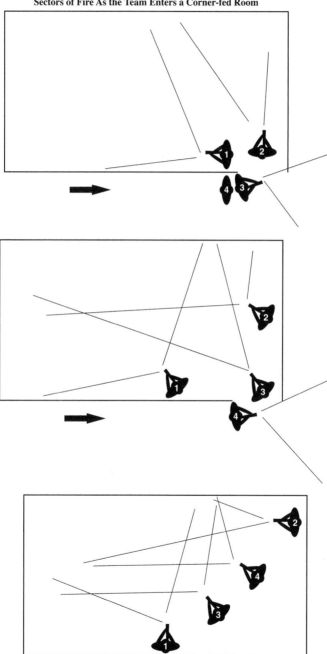

**Step 7.** The second team then moves into the room and falls in with the initial team or flows through the initial team to the immediate adjoining threat in the room (adjacent rooms, hallways, intersections, etc.) The clearing procedures continue on in the same manner.

Take care that the teams do not get out of the range or ability of the support by fire element. Also be careful that the team does not get separated in the building, which can lead to confusion and fratricide.

**Step 8.** Upon a slowdown in the action, the squad leader will radio back to higher headquarters (HHQ) to inform them of the situation. He should convey the following:

- Report to the platoon leader that the squad has entered the building and seized a foothold.
- Ammo, casualties, and equipment (ACE) report to HHQ and report if medical support or resupply is needed.
- Inform HHQ of the unit's exact location and what identify friendly forces (IFF) markings are being used to limit fratricide.
- Determine location of the CCP and continue to direct the assault.

**Step 9.** The squad leader directs the team in where to clear next if momentum starts to slow down. The squad leader also constantly confirms that all areas are cleared and secure IAW the unit SOP.

**Step 10.** The squad consolidates its position in the building and then reorganizes as necessary. All sub-unit leaders pass on ACE reports. *Note*: Normally the squad or platoons will use large-caliber weapons (if available) to suppress enemy in adjacent buildings.

### Consolidation and Reorganization

The squad and platoon will conduct consolidation and reorganization immediately after each action in which soldiers are engaged and ammunition is expended. Consolidation in an urban environment must be quick in order to repel enemy counterattacks and to prevent the enemy from infiltrating back into cleared areas. Immediate tactical reloads by any soldiers that expended any amount of rounds should take place, and ACE reports should be passed up the chain of command.

Reorganization occurs after consolidation. These actions prepare the unit to continue the mission by ensuring key leadership positions are filled and important weapon systems are manned. Many reorganization actions occur simultaneously during the consolidation of the objective. For more information on consolidation and reorganization, see Chapters 4 and 5.

## DEFENSIVE OPERATIONS IN URBAN AREAS

This section covers the basic planning considerations, weapons selection, preparations, and the construction of a platoon defensive position on urbanized terrain.

### Planning the Defense

Leaders plan an urban defense that uses terrain wisely, designates a point of main effort, uses defensive positions that force the enemy to make costly attacks or conduct time-consuming maneuvers to avoid them, and achieves surprise. They must consider civilians, ROE, limited collateral damage, and coordination with adjacent units to eliminate the probability of fratricide.

The squad's and platoon's focus for defending in an urban area is the retention of terrain. The platoon will be given either an AO to defend or a battle position to occupy. By using the terrain and fighting from well-prepared and mutually supporting positions, a defending force can delay, block, fix, or inflict heavy losses on a much larger attacking force.

In urban operations, the platoon is often a strongpoint defense of a building, part of a building, or a group of small buildings that is normally integrated into the company's mission. Weapon systems and personnel are positioned to maximize their capabilities. Supporting fires are incorporated into the overall defensive plan to provide depth to the engagement area (EA). The platoon leader organizes the defense into a series of individual, team, and squad fighting positions located to cover avenues of approach and obstacles and to provide mutual support to repel the enemy advance.

The platoon and squad leader have only two choices in an urban defense—*hasty* or *deliberate*. Having time to plan and prepare and knowledge of the enemy is really the only difference between a hasty and deliberate defense. All of the troop-leading procedures (TLPs) are the same, as well as many of the priorities of work, and the two types may even take place concurrently. Units are deployed, key weapons emplaced, and fighting positions prepared in accordance with the amount of time available to the unit.

### Occupation and Preparation of Positions

Normally, when occupying defensive positions, the platoon takes advantage of the cover and concealment already present and continues to make improvements to the positions given more time and materials.

The platoon first positions crew-served weapons. Normal defensive priorities of work apply (see Chapter 5). Fighting positions in buildings are constructed in the shadows of the room, away from windows and other openings, using appliances, furniture, and other convenient items and materials. Some

Firing Around Cover | Firing From Window
Firing From Loophole | Firing From Peak of Roof

**Initial Firing Positions**

of the more common fighting positions in an urban area are corners of buildings, behind walls, windows, unprepared loopholes, and the peak of a roof.

*Urban Priorities of Work.* In addition to general defensive priorities of work, special attention is to be given the following in the urban environment:

1. Select key weapons positions for Javelins, AT-4s (Gustavs), and M240B MGs to cover likely mounted and dismounted avenues of approach. Position the Javelins where flank engagements will occur inside buildings with adequate space and ventilation for backblast (on upper floors, if possible, for long-range shots). Position squad automatic weapons (SAWs) and machine guns (MGs) near ground level to increase grazing fires or on upper levels if ground rubble obscures grazing fire.
2. Ensure the positions are free of noncombatants. Remove them from the AOs before occupation of the position.
3. Clear fields of fire by using loopholes, aiming stakes, sector stakes, and TRP markings. Construct positions with overhead cover and camouflage (inside and outside).

4. Identify and secure subterranean avenues of approach (sewers and basements) as well as stairwells and rooftops.
5. Stockpile ammunition, food, fire-fighting equipment, and drinking water throughout the depth of your defense.
6. Construct barriers and emplace obstacles to deny the enemy access to streets, underground passages, and buildings, and to slow his movement. Erect the obstacles in an irregular pattern to hinder enemy movement. Employ the obstacles in depth (if possible). Tie the obstacles in with existing ones and cover all of them with fire and observation.
7. Improve and mark movement routes between positions and to alternate and supplementary positions. An escape route to fallback positions is essential to an adequate defense. This is accomplished by digging trenches, using sewers and tunnels, creating mouseholes, and emplacing ropes for climbing and rappelling and ladders for ascent and descent.

Additional defensive preparation tasks may be required in basements, on ground floors, and on upper floors.

**Obstacles Blocking Street**

*Basements and Ground Floors.* Basements and ground floors require similar preparation. Any underground system not used by the defender that could provide enemy access to the position must be blocked. Unused doors should be locked or nailed shut, as well as blocked and reinforced with furniture, sandbags, or other field expedients. If not required for the defender's movement, hallways should be blocked with furniture and tactical wire. Unused stairs should be blocked with furniture and tactical wire or removed. If possible, all stairs should be blocked and ladders should be used to move from floor to floor and then removed. Remove all window glass and block unused windows with boards or sandbags to prevent observation and access. Make fighting positions in the floors. If there is no basement, fighting positions can give additional protection from heavy direct-fire weapons. Erect support for ceilings that cannot withstand the weight of rubble from upper floors. Block rooms not required for defense with tactical wire.

*Upper Floors.* Upper floors require the same preparation as ground floors. Windows need not be blocked but should be covered with wire mesh, canvas, ponchos, or other heavy material to prevent grenades from being thrown in from the outside. The covering should be loose at the bottom to permit the defender to drop grenades.

*Interior Routes.* Routes that permit defending forces to move within the building to engage enemy forces from any direction are required. Plan and construct escape routes to permit rapid evacuation of a room or a building. Mouseholes should be easily identified and marked and made through interior walls to permit movement between rooms.

*Fire Prevention.* Buildings that have wooden floors and rafter ceilings require extensive fire prevention measures. Cover the attic floor and other wooden floors with about 1 to 2 inches of sand or dirt and position buckets of water for immediate use. Place fire-fighting materials (dirt, sand, fire extinguishers, and blankets) on each floor. Fill water basins and bathtubs as a reserve for fire fighting. Turn off all electricity and gas.

*Communications.* Be aware that structures and a high concentration of electrical power lines may degrade radio communication in built-up areas. Visual signals are often not effective because of the screening effects of buildings and walls and can signal location and intent to the enemy. Signals must be planned, widely disseminated, and understood by all assigned and attached units. Increased noise makes the effective use of sound signals difficult. Messengers and wire can be used as other means of communication.

*Rubbling.* Destroying or damaging parts of the building may provide additional cover and concealment for weapons emplacements or serve as an obstacle against the enemy. Ensure you know what you are doing and get permission from higher headquarters.

*Rooftops.* Platoons must position obstacles on the roofs of flat-topped buildings to prevent helicopters from landing and to deny troops access to the building and adjacent buildings from the roof.

*Obstacles.* Position obstacles adjacent to buildings to stop or delay vehicles and infantry. Save time and resources by using available materials such as cars. The principles of mining are the same, except the ground is much harder to deal with and may require special equipment.

*Fields of Fire.* Selectively clear fields of fire in accordance with the weapon capabilities. Designate primary and alternate sectors of fire.

*Antitank Weapons Positions.* Employ AT weapons in areas that maximize their capabilities. Position AT weapons in upper stories and in pairs (if possible) to allow the same target to be engaged at the same time by pair firing. Ensure the AT systems are secured by additional positions and personnel.

## Conduct of the Defense
The conduct of the defense in an urban area is similar to the conduct of the defense in any other area. The process of consolidation and reorganization in an urban area is also similar to the process in any other area. Both are discussed in Chapter 5.

## COMBAT MULTIPLIERS
An important lesson learned from recent urban operations is the need for a fully integrated combined arms team. The nature of urban operations makes it mostly an infantry operation; however, the more additional combat multipliers the better. The integration of armor (for information on armored vehicles, see Chapter 9) and engineers increases lethality, and these additional assets must be supported by integrated aviation, field artillery, communications, and logistical elements.

## Engineers
Normally an engineer squad will be attached to an infantry company. Most engineer manual labor tasks (for example, preparing fighting positions) will have to be completed by infantry units with reinforcing engineer heavy-equipment support and technical supervision.

On offensive missions in support of an infantry platoon, engineers may be required to use explosives to destroy fortifications and strongpoints that cannot be reduced with the maneuver unit's organic assets, locate and/or remove mines that may hamper the unit's movement, and conduct breaching operations.

On defensive missions in support of an infantry platoon, engineers may be required to construct complex obstacle systems and/or assist in the preparation of defensive positions and strongpoints.

## Mortars
Mortars are the most responsive indirect fires available to infantry commanders and leaders. Their mission is to provide close and immediate fire support to the maneuver units. Mortars are well suited for combat in urban areas because of their high rate of fire, steep angle of fall, and short minimum range. Platoon leaders and FOs must plan mortar support with the fire support element as part of the total fire support plan.

## Field Artillery
During urban combat, field artillery (FA) provides direct support, general support, and general support reinforcing to infantry units. In addition to indirect-fire support, FA units are well suited to using their guns in direct-fire mode in urban operations. Employing artillery in the direct-fire mode to destroy fortifications should be considered, especially when assaulting well-prepared enemy positions. However, restrictive fire support coordination measures, such as restrictive fire areas or no-fire areas, may be imposed to protect civilians and critical installations.

## Attack Helicopters
Infantry units may receive support by a variety of attack helicopters, including (but not limited to) the AH-64A, AH-64D, OH-58D, and MH-6. Attack helicopters can provide area fire to suppress targets and precision fire to destroy specific targets or breach structures. Attack helicopters provide real-time reconnaissance information through direct viewing of the AO.

# 9

# Combat Support and Combat Service Support

Combat support is any external support provided by the battalion antitank (AT) and mortar platoons, field artillery (FA), close air support (CAS), air defense artillery (ADA), military intelligence (MI), and combat engineers.

## INDIRECT FIRE
Normally the company plans most of the indirect fires and assigns specific responsibilities to platoons. The platoon is limited by its ability to observe and initiate fires.

### Field Artillery
FA can provide indirect fires to suppress, neutralize, or destroy enemy targets. Because it can mass fire quickly, FA produces more devastating effects on targets than mortars do.

### Mortars
Mortars are organic to the battalion and the company and at times may be attached to or in direct support of platoons. They provide responsive fire against closer and smaller targets. Mortars can be used to do the following:
- Attack infantry in the open.
- Attack infantry in positions without overhead cover (using variable time fuses) or with light overhead cover (using delay fuses).
- Suppress enemy positions and armored vehicles.
- Obscure the enemy's vision (using white phosphorus).
- Engage the enemy on reverse slopes and in gullies, ditches, built-up areas, and other defilade areas.
- Provide continuous battlefield illumination.

- Provide obscuring smoke (smoke on the enemy positions) or screening smoke (smoke between the enemy and friendly units).
- Mark enemy locations for direct fire or CAS.

## DIRECT FIRE

Direct-fire support can be provided by tanks, antitank weapons (TOW, Dragon/Javelin, MK19), and attack helicopters. Leaders can direct tank or antitank and MK19 fires by radio, by phone, or face-to-face. They can identify the target location by TRP or tracer fire, or give the direction, description, and range. Another technique uses the gun barrel or heavy antitank missile (TOW) launcher with the clock method as a baseline for direction—for example, "Enemy tank, 10 o'clock, 1,200 meters." The gun barrel is at 12 o'clock when pointing directly forward from the vehicle or launcher and at 6 o'clock when pointing directly to the rear.

### Attack Helicopters

Attack helicopters are mainly antiarmor weapons, but they do have antipersonnel ability with rockets. Aeroscouts usually arrive ahead of the attack aircraft and set up communication with the ground force.

### Close Air Support

The US Air Force provides CAS on a preplanned or immediate-need basis. A forward air controller (FAC, TACP, JTAC, or CCT), on the ground or in the air, acts as a link between the ground force and the aircraft. Friendly positions must always be marked during close air strikes. Smoke grenades, flares, signal mirrors, strobe lights, vehicle lights, and thermal sources are commonly used as markers.

## AIR DEFENSE ARTILLERY

Divisional air defense weapons may support and be positioned with infantry units. All ADA fires are controlled by orders and procedures established by higher headquarters.

## MILITARY INTELLIGENCE

Military intelligence should be giving constant updates to the ground commander based off of signal intelligence, human intelligence, ISR aircraft, and intelligence from SSE conducted during operations. MI battalion assets should be attached to or support infantry units.

## COMBAT ENGINEERS

Engineers are a valuable asset, and higher commanders determine their priority. Engineers can help the infantry prepare obstacles or positions by providing technical advice or the skills to do work beyond the ability of infantry units.

## COMBAT SERVICE SUPPORT AT THE PLATOON LEVEL
CSS operations at the platoon level are a vital part of infantry operations. They consist of logistical, personnel, and health service functions. CSS is integrated into the tactical planning process from the starting phases of operations. Well-planned and well-executed CSS is a large part of mission accomplishment and the success of combat operations. Like CS, CSS is a combat multiplier. Soldiers well supplied with food, water, ammunition, shelter, and medical care are more successful in accomplishing their missions than those who are not.

At platoon level, the platoon sergeant is the key CSS operator. He consolidates information and needs from the squad leaders, requests support from the executive officer (XO) or first sergeant, and assigns responsibilities to squads.

### Individual Responsibilities for CSS
There are many specific individual responsibilities within the platoon's CSS chain.

*Platoon Sergeant.* As the platoon's main CSS operator, the PSG executes the platoon's logistical plan based on platoon and company SOPs. His CSS duties include:

- Participating in CSS rehearsals at the company level and integrating CSS into the platoon's maneuver rehearsals.
- Receiving, consolidating, and forwarding all administrative, personnel, and casualty reports to the first sergeant as directed or in accordance with unit SOP.
- Obtaining supplies, equipment (except Class VIII), and mail from the supply sergeant and ensuring proper distribution.
- Supervising evacuation of casualties, enemy prisoners of war (EPWs), and damaged equipment.
- Maintaining the platoon's manning roster.

*Squad Leader.* Each squad leader's CSS duties include:

- Ensuring soldiers perform proper maintenance on all assigned equipment.
- Compiling personnel and logistics reports for the platoon and submitting them to the PSG as directed or in accordance with unit SOP.
- Obtaining supplies, equipment (except Class VIII), and mail from the PSG and ensuring proper distribution.

*Platoon Medic.* The platoon medic is detached from the battalion medical platoon and attached to the rifle platoon to provide emergency medical treatment (EMT) for sick, injured, or wounded platoon personnel, including treatment of trauma, opening an airway, starting intravenous fluids, controlling hemorrhage, preventing or treating for shock, splinting fractures or suspected fractures, and providing pain relief. The EMT performed by the platoon medic is under the supervision of the battalion surgeon or physician's assistant (PA).

The platoon medic is also responsible for:
- Triaging injured, wounded, or ill friendly and enemy personnel for priority of treatment.
- Conducting sick call screening for the platoon.
- Evacuating sick, injured, or wounded personnel under the direction of the PSG.
- Assisting in the training of the platoon's combat lifesavers in enhanced first aid procedures.
- Requisitioning Class VIII supplies from the battalion aid station (BAS) for the platoon according to the tactical SOP (TSOP).
- Recommending locations for platoon CCPs.
- Providing guidance to the platoon's combat lifesavers as required.

**Resupply Operations**

Platoon resupply is mainly a "push" system. The platoon receives a standard package of supplies based on past usage factors and planning estimates. Whatever supply technique is directed, leaders must ensure security. This involves security at the resupply point and rotating personnel to ensure continuous manning of crew-served weapons and OPs, leader availability, and unit preparedness in case of enemy attack. Platoons use backhauling to remove residue, casualties, damaged equipment, or excess ammunition to the rear. During each resupply operation, the platoon must plan for backhauling of excess items. Backhauling can be by manpack, vehicles, or aircraft. Effective backhauling lessens the platoon's need to bury, camouflage, or otherwise dispose of unneeded material.

*In-Position or Tailgate Technique.* The company brings forward supplies, equipment, or both to individual fighting positions. This technique is used when an immediate need exists to resupply single classes of supplies during contact or when contact is imminent. It enables leaders to keep squad members in their fighting positions.

*Out-of-Position or Service Station Technique.* To use this technique, soldiers must leave their fighting positions. Selected soldiers move to a company resupply point to the rear of the platoon positions, conduct resupply, and return to their fighting position. This technique is used when contact is not likely and for one or several classes of supplies.

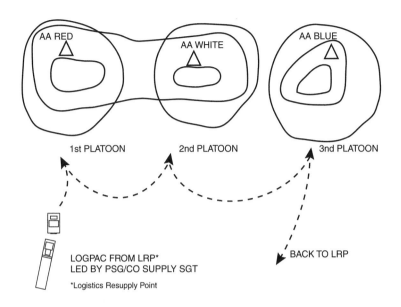

**In-Position or Tailgate Resupply Technique**

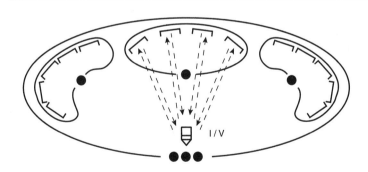

**Out-of-Position or Service Station Resupply Technique**

***Pre-position Technique.*** In this technique, the company pre-positions supplies and equipment along a route to or at a platoon's destination. The company then directs the platoons to the sites. Although this method is often used during defensive operations to position supplies and equipment in subsequent battle positions (fallback positions), it can be equally effective in other operations as a cache.

*Aerial Resupply.* Aerial resupply is often used to get supplies and equipment to the platoon, especially when the routes are determined to be too hazardous for truck resupply. Helicopters are usually more precise than fixed-wing aircraft in delivering supplies and are used to deliver supplies and equipment to LZs; fixed-wing aircraft are used for drop zones (DZs). Fixed-wing aircraft are also used when the distance to the resupply area is out of range of rotary wing aircraft, or when a large resupply is needed (such as 55-gallon drums of fuel). In many cases, air drops are used to resupply troops in remote or nonpermissive areas.

**Personnel Service Support**
The main platoon combat personnel service support functions are strength accounting and casualty reporting. The platoon leader and NCOs are also responsible for handling EPWs and for arranging programs to counter the impact of stress and continuous operations. Platoon leaders coordinate personnel service support provided by the battalion adjutant (S-1), personnel and administration center (PAC), and chaplain through the company headquarters.

*Strength Accounting.* Leaders use battle rosters to keep up-to-date records of their soldiers and to provide reports to the company at specific intervals. During combat, leaders also provide hasty strength reports upon request or when important strength changes occur.

*Killed in Action.* The platoon leader designates a location for the collection of KIAs. All personal effects remain with the body; however, the squad leader removes and safeguards any equipment and issue items. He keeps these until he can turn the items over to the platoon sergeant. The platoon sergeant turns over the KIAs to the first sergeant. As a rule, wounded soldiers take priority in transport to the rear. If KIAs can be transported separately from the wounded, this is preferred.

*Casualty Reporting.* During lulls in the battle, platoons give by-name (roster line number) casualty information to the company. Forms are completed to report KIAs who were not recovered, as well as missing or captured soldiers. A separate form is used to report KIAs who have been recovered and soldiers who have been wounded.

*Handling Enemy Prisoners of War.* EPWs are treated in accordance with international law. They are treated humanely and not physically or mentally abused. If they cannot be evacuated within a reasonable time, they are given food, water, and, if necessary, first aid.

The 5-S procedure reminds soldiers of the basic principles for handling EPWs, which include tagging prisoners and all captured equipment and materiel. The five Ss are search, segregate, silence, safeguard, and speed to the rear.

*Other Services.* Other personnel service support functions include awards, leaves, mail, financial matters, legal assistance, rest and recreation, and other services related to the morale and welfare of soldiers.

**Health Service Support**
Health service support consists of the prevention, treatment, and evacuation of casualties. *Prevention is emphasized;* soldiers can lose their combat effectiveness because of nonhostile injuries or disease. Observing field hygiene and sanitation, preventing weather-related injuries, and considering the soldier's overall condition can cut back on the number of casualties.

*Initial Steps.* When combat begins and casualties occur, the platoon first must provide initial care to those wounded in action (WIA). Casualty evacuation is accomplished through the administration of first aid (self-aid or buddy aid), enhanced first aid (by the combat lifesaver), and EMT (by the trauma specialist or platoon medic). Casualties are cared for at the point of injury or under nearby cover and concealment. During the fight, casualties should remain under cover where they received initial treatment. As soon as the situation allows, squad leaders arrange for casualty evacuation to the platoon CCP.

The platoon normally sets up the CCP in a covered and concealed location to the rear of the platoon position. At the CCP, the platoon medic conducts triage on all casualties, takes steps to stabilize their conditions, and starts the process of moving them to the rear for advanced treatment. Before the platoon evacuates casualties to the CCP or beyond, leaders should remove all key operational items and equipment from each person. This includes signal operating instructions (SOI), maps, position-locating devices, and laser pointers. Every unit should establish an SOP for handling the weapons and ammunition of its WIA.

*Movement.* CASEVAC (casualty evacuation) is the term used to refer to the movement of casualties by air or ground on nonmedical vehicles or aircraft. CASEVAC operations normally involve the initial movement of wounded or injured soldiers to the nearest medical treatment facility. Casualty evacuation operations may also be employed in support of mass casualty operations. While medical evacuation (MEDEVAC) includes the provision of en-route medical care, CASEVAC does not provide any medical care during movement unless medics escort wounded to the rear.

Timely movement of casualties from the battlefield is important. Squad leaders are responsible for casualty evacuation from the battlefield to the platoon CCP. At the CCP, the senior trauma specialist assists the platoon sergeant and first sergeant in arranging evacuation by ground or air ambulance or by nonstandard means. From the platoon area, casualties are normally evacuated to the company CCP and then back to the battalion aid station (BAS).

The company first sergeant, along with the platoon sergeant, is normally responsible for movement of the casualties from the platoon and company CCP. The unit SOP should address this activity, including the marking of casualties during limited-visibility operations. Once the casualties are collected, evaluated, and treated, they are prioritized for evacuation back to the company CCP. Upon their arrival, the above process is repeated while awaiting their evacuation back to the BAS or to other medical facilities.

When the company is widely dispersed, the casualties may be evacuated directly from the platoon CCP by vehicle or helicopter if they are able to fly. Coordination is made for additional transportation assets as necessary. The senior military person present determines whether to request medical evacuation and assigns precedence. Casualties will be picked up as soon as possible, consistent with available resources and pending missions. The following are categories of precedence and the criteria used in their assignment:

- *Priority I—Urgent*: Assigned to emergency cases that should be evacuated as soon as possible and within a maximum of two hours in order to save life, limb, or eyesight; to prevent complications of serious illness; or to avoid permanent disability.
- *Priority IA—Urgent—Surgery*: Assigned to patients who must receive far forward surgical intervention to save their lives and to stabilize them for further evacuation.
- *Priority II—Priority*: Assigned to sick and wounded personnel requiring prompt medical care. Used when the individual should be evacuated within four hours or his medical condition could deteriorate to such a degree that he will become an URGENT precedence, whose requirements for special treatment are not available locally, or who will suffer unnecessary pain or disability.
- *Priority III—Routine*: Assigned to sick and wounded personnel requiring evacuation but whose condition is not expected to deteriorate significantly. The sick and wounded in this category should be evacuated within twenty-four hours.
- *Priority IV—Convenience*: Assigned to patients for whom evacuation by medical vehicle is a matter of medical convenience rather than necessity.

## ARMORED VEHICLE SUPPORT
Based on the considerations of the METT-TC analysis and the operational ROE, a situation may arise that requires the attachment of tanks. The

following are considerations for task-organizing mechanized assets, such as armored vehicles and tanks, and (SBCT) units with infantry platoons.

## Maneuver

Maneuver by the infantry is enhanced by support from the armored vehicles. The infantry assists the heavy forces by infiltrating to clear obstacles or key enemy positions and to disrupt the enemy's defense. It provides security for the armored vehicles by detecting and suppressing or destroying enemy AT weapons. It designates targets and spots the impact of fires for tanks, Bradley fighting vehicles (BFVs), or Stryker mobile gun system (MGS) vehicles.

Mechanized forces support the infantry by moving with it along an axis of advance and providing a protected, fast-moving assault weapons system. They suppress fire from and destroy enemy weapons, bunkers, and tanks by fire and maneuver. They also provide transport when the enemy situation permits. Armored vehicles should never be maneuvered individually. The smallest maneuver level for armor is a section (two vehicles).

## Command and Control

The platoon leader is responsible for incorporating elements in direct support into his $C^2$ functions. Tanks and mechanized infantry must work closely at platoon level. In most operations in which they work together, infantrymen must establish direct communication with individual vehicles to ensure quick and accurate response to directions given. Infantrymen and vehicle crews must know how to communicate by radio, telephone, and visual signals. During the planning phase of an operation, infantry and armor leaders must allocate sufficient time for the conduct of detailed brief-backs and rehearsals.

## Weapon Systems Considerations

The infantry leader must be knowledgeable of the capabilities, limitations, dangers, and effects of the armor weapon systems in support of his missions. The figure below shows the difference in the capabilities of the BFV and the M1A1/A2 tank with regard to fields of fire on urban terrain. Note that the BFV can engage a target 9 to 10 stories high at 20 meters, whereas an M1A1/A2 tank requires 90 meters.

*Bradley Fighting Vehicles.* The primary role of the BFV in most environments is to provide suppressive fires, breach exterior walls, destroy enemy fortifications, and provide shock to the enemy. The vehicle's armor-piercing rounds can penetrate concrete up to 16 inches thick and can easily penetrate brick structures. It is highly effective against earthen- and sandbag-reinforced structures. The BFV can elevate its 25mm gun to about +60 degrees and

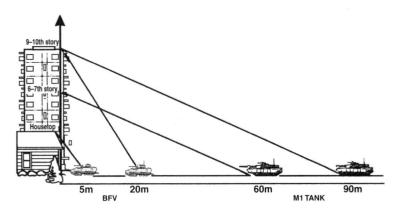

**Fields of Fire in Urban Terrain**

depress the gun to about -10 degrees. The crew has limited visibility to the sides and rear and no visibility to the top when buttoned up. The BFV can be outfitted with an external phone hookup for communications with accompanying infantry. The 25mm gun, firing armor-piercing (AP), high-explosive (HE), and even target practice—tracer (TP-T) rounds, can be used effectively against enemy-occupied buildings and fortifications.

*M1-Series Tanks.* Normally, the primary ammunition for the main gun in the urban and restricted terrain environments is the high-explosive anti-tank (HEAT) round. It is the most effective against masonry and will penetrate all but the thickest reinforced concrete. A HEAT round will create a hole in masonry or concrete large enough for a man to fit through, but will not cut the reinforcing steel bars. HEAT is also effective against earthen- and sandbag-reinforced strongpoints, most bunkers, and fighting positions. Multipurpose antitank (MPAT) rounds will penetrate masonry and concrete but are less effective than HEAT rounds against heavier structures. Sabot ammunition has limited use against nonvehicular targets, and its discarding petals endanger accompanying infantry. Sabot petals create a hazard area extending 70 meters on either side of the gun target line for a distance of 1 kilometer. The external M2 heavy barrel (HB) .50-cal. MG can elevate to +36 degrees; however, to fire the .50-cal. on the M1A2 Abrams, the tank commander must be exposed to enemy fire.

*Mobile Gun System Vehicle.* The thermal sights on the MGS vehicle can detect enemy activity through darkness and smoke, conditions that may limit even the best-equipped infantry. The MGS vehicle can deliver devastating fires; is fully protected against antipersonnel mines, fragments, and small arms; and has excellent mobility along unblocked routes. The MGS vehicle projects a psychological presence, an aura of invulnerability that aids friendly forces in deterring violence. Mounted patrols by MGS vehicles can monitor large areas of a city while making their presence known to the entire populace, both friendly and unfriendly. The mobile, protected firepower of MGS vehicles can also add security to resupply convoys. The MGS vehicle's smoke-generation capability can aid in extracting wounded personnel and in other small-unit actions.

Crewmen in MGS vehicles have poor all-around vision through their vision blocks and are easily blinded by smoke or dust. MGS vehicle gunners cannot easily identify enemy targets unless the commander exposes himself to fire by opening his hatch or other infantrymen direct the gunner to the target. Heavy fires from MGS vehicles can cause unwanted collateral damage and can destabilize basic structures.

***Infantry Carrier Vehicle (ICV) Striker.*** The ICV can provide protection to the infantry by negating the effects of enemy small-arms weapons, either by driving soldiers up to a building or by acting as a shield while the infantry moves behind it along a street or in restricted terrain. ICVs can resupply units quickly and with more ammunition than by foot. Because of their armor protection, ICVs can be used to conduct CASEVAC under fire. If buttoned up, crewmen in ICVs have poor all-around vision through their vision blocks and are easily blinded by smoke or dust. The ICV has only a local defense weapon system mounted. Once the infantry has dismounted and is not supporting the vehicle, its firepower is diminished. The ICV is vulnerable to most weapons systems other than small arms and is particularly vulnerable to AT weapons.

### Infantry Riding on Armored Vehicles

An additional maneuver consideration for a light/mechanized or mechanized/light operation is the decision of whether to move infantrymen on tanks. This mode of transportation can be difficult but is not impossible. It does, in fact, afford some significant advantages. The mounted infantry can provide additional security for the company. When the team conducts a halt or must execute a breach or other tactical tasks, infantry assets are readily available to provide support and security.

The commander must weigh the potential dangers of carrying tank-mounted infantrymen against the advantages of mobility and security they can provide. Some of the safety considerations involved in mounting infantry on tanks are:

1. When mounting an armored vehicle, soldiers must always approach the vehicle from the front to get permission from the vehicle

commander to mount. They then mount the side of the vehicle away from the coaxial machine gun and in view of the driver.

2. If the vehicle has a stabilization system, squad leaders ensure it is off before giving the okay for the vehicle to move.

3. The infantry must dismount as soon as possible when tanks come under fire or when targets appear that require the tank gunner to traverse the turret quickly to fire.

4. All soldiers must be alert for obstacles that can cause the tank to turn suddenly and for trees that can knock riders off the tank.

5. The M1 tank is not designed to carry riders easily. Riders must not move to the rear deck, as engine operating temperatures make this area unsafe for them. Other tank safety measures include the following:

   • One infantry squad can ride on the turret. Soldiers must mount in such a way that their legs cannot become entangled between the turret and the hull by an unexpected turret movement. Rope may be used as a field-expedient infantry rail to provide secure handholds.

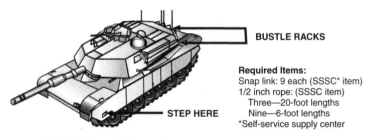

**BUSTLE RACKS**

**Required Items:**
Snap link: 9 each (SSSC* item)
1/2 inch rope: (SSSC item)
Three—20-foot lengths
Nine—6-foot lengths
*Self-service supply center

**STEP HERE**

**NOTE:** Soldiers sit facing out. Personal gear is carried in company trains.

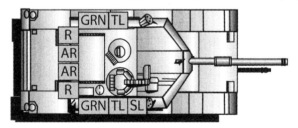

**Mounting and Riding on an M-1 Tank**

- Everyone must be to the rear of the smoke grenade launchers. This automatically keeps soldiers clear of the coaxial machine gun and laser range finder.
- Infantry must always be prepared for sudden turret movement.
- Leaders should caution soldiers about sitting on the turret blowout panels, because 250 pounds of pressure will prevent the panels from working properly. If there is an explosion in the ammunition rack, these panels blow outward to lessen the blast effect in the crew compartment.
- If enemy contact is made, the tank should stop in a covered and concealed position and allow the infantry time to dismount and move away from the tank. This action needs to be practiced before movement.
- The infantry should not ride with anything more than their battle gear. Personal gear should be transported elsewhere.

# PART TWO

# Soldier Combat Skills

# 10

# Call for and Adjust Fire

A call for fire is a concise message prepared by an observer (a person needing indirect-fire support). A soldier or a forward observer (FO) can prepare and request a call for fire but must plan targets and follow proper call-for-fire procedures (see coordination checklists, pages 24 and 28–29) in order to receive immediate fire support. Send a call for fire quickly but clearly enough that it can be understood, recorded, and read back to the observer without error.

**PRINCIPLES: FORWARD OBSERVER EXERCISE**
FOs must continually select or prearrange targets in support of the commander's intent.
- Consider what the commander wants to do.
- Plan early and continuously.
- Exploit all available targeting assets.
- Use all available lethal and non-lethal fire support means.
- Use the lowest echelon able to furnish effective support.
- Observe all fires.
- Use the most effective fire support available.
- Provide adequate fire support.
- Avoid unnecessary duplication.
- Provide for safety, friendly forces, and installations.
- Provide for flexibility.
- Furnish the type of fire support requested.
- Consider the airspace.
- Provide rapid and effective coordination.
- Keep all fire support informed.

## FIRE SUPPORT TASKS FOR ALL OPERATIONS
The unit providing fire support should be able to accomplish the following tasks:
- Locate targets.
- Integrate all available assets.
- Destroy, neutralize, or suppress all enemy fire systems (direct or indirect).
- Provide illumination and smoke.
- Prepare for future operations.
- Provide positive clearance of fires.

## OFFENSIVE OPERATIONS
Offensive operations are additional tasks the fire support units must complete during offense.
- Support the movement to contact or chance contact.
- Soften enemy defenses with short, violent preparations.
- Provide support during attack by attacking high-payoff targets.
- Plan for deep and flanking fires.
- Plan for fires during consolidation.
- Provide counter fires.

| FIELD ARTILLERY | | | | | |
|---|---|---|---|---|---|
| Weapon | Max. Range (Meters) | Min. Range (Meters) | Max. Rate | Burst Radius | Rate of Fire (Minute) |
| 105mm Howitzer M102 Towed | | | | | |
| 105mm Howitzer M119 Towed | | | | | |
| 155mm Howitzer M198 Towed | | | | | |
| 155mm Howitzer M110A2/A3 SP | | | | | |
| 203mm Howitzer M110A2 SP | | | | | |

## NAVAL GUN

| Weapon | Full Charge | Reduced Charge | Max Rate (Min.) | Sustained Rate (Minute) |
|---|---|---|---|---|
| 5 in / 38 | | | | |
| 5 in / 54 | | | | |
| 16 in / 50 | | | | |

*Note:* If the target is within 600 meters of friendly troops, it is important to include the term "danger close" in the "Method of Engagement" section of the call for fire. This applies for both mortars and field artillery. To adjust naval gunfire from guns of 5 inches or smaller, use "danger close" when the target is within 750 meters, or within 1,000 meters for guns larger than 5 inches.

The FO should use the creeping method of adjustment *only* for a danger close mission. He makes his range changes by creeping the rounds to the target, using corrections of no more than 100 meters.

## MORTARS

| Weapon | Ammunition Available | Max. Range (Meters) | Min. Range (Meters) | Max. Rate (per Min.) | Burst Radius | Sustained Rate of Fire (Minute) |
|---|---|---|---|---|---|---|
| 60mm | | | | | | |
| 81mm | | | | | | |
| 107mm | | | | | | |
| 120mm | | | | | | |

## TARGET OVERLAY

A complete fire support overlay must include the following:
  Unit and official capacity of person making overlay
  Date the overlay was prepared
  Map sheet/number
  Effective period of overlay (from when to when)
  Priority targets
  ORP grid/location
  Call signs and frequencies (primary and alternate)
  Routes (primary and alternate)
  Phase lines and checkpoints used by the patrol
  Index marks to position the overlay on the map (grid reference marks)
  Objective
  Target symbols (description and grid)

A *sterile overlay* is a security measure in case of enemy capture and must include target symbols and index marks to position the overlay on the map.

---

### TARGET OVERLAY SYMBOLS

| Target Type | Symbol | Notes |
|---|---|---|
| Point target | | Less than 200 meters in length and width |
| Linear target | | More than 200 meters but less than 600 meters long |
| Circular target | | Undisclosed area and desired radius |

## DANGER CLOSE

Danger close refers to the minimum safe distance from the blast radius:
  Mortars = 600 meters
  Artillery = 600 meters
  Naval guns:
    5 inches or smaller = 750 meters
    Over 5 inches = 1,000 meters
    16 inches = 2,000 meters

## AIRCRAFT CHART—MINIMUM SAFE DISTANCE
## TO EXPLODING ORDNANCE (BOMBS)

| Weapon/Munition | Protected Troops | Unprotected Troops |
|---|---|---|
| Bomb—1,000 lb. | 240 meters | 1,000 meters |
| Bomb—750 lb. low drag | 195 meters | 750 meters |
| Bomb—750 lb. high drag | 150 meters | 750 meters |
| Bomb—500 lb. low drag | 220 meters | 500 meters |
| Bomb—500 lb. high drag | 145 meters | 500 meters |
| Bomb—500 lb. | 145 meters | 500 meters |
| CBU (clamshell only) | 1,000 meters | 1,000 meters |
| Rockets | 220 meters | 220 meters |
| Napalm | 115 meters | 115 meters |

## ELEMENTS AND SEQUENCE OF CALL FOR FIRE
**Observer's Identification/Call Sign**
*Warning Order*
  Adjust fire
  Fire for effect
  Suppress
  Immediate fire suppression
  Size of element to fire for effect (when the observer does not specify
    what size, the battalion fire direction center will decide)
*Method of Target Location*
  Polar plot
  Shift from a known point (give TRP)
  Grid
*Location of Target*
  Grid coordinate: six-digit for large area, eight-digit for smaller, ten-
    digit for point
  Shift from a known point:
    Send observer target (OT) direction:
      Mils (nearest 10); Degrees; Cardinal direction; Send lateral
        shift (right/left, nearest 10 meters); Send range shift
        (add/drop, nearest 100 meters); Send vertical shift
        (up/down)—use only if over 35 meters (nearest 5)
    Polar Plot:
      Send direction (nearest 10 mils); Send distance (nearest 100
        meters); Send vertical shift (nearest 5 meters)

*Description of the Target*
Type
Activity
Number
Degree of protection
Size and shape (length, width, or radius)
*Method of Engagement*
Type of adjustment (when the observer does not request a specific
type, area fire is issued):
Area fire (moving target); Precision fire (point target)
*Danger Close*
When friendly troops are within:
600 meters for mortars; 600 meters for artillery; 750 meters for
naval guns; 1,000 meters for naval guns greater than 5 inches;
2,000 meters for 16-inch naval guns (ICM or controlled
variable time)
*Mark*
Used to orient observer or to indicate targets
*Trajectory*
Low-angle (standard)
High-angle (mortars or if requested)
*Ammunition*
HE quick will be used unless specified by the observer:
Projectile (HE, illum, ICM, smoke, etc.); Fuse (quick, time, etc.);
Volume of fire (observer can request specific number of
rounds)
*Distribution*
100-meter sheaf (standard)
Converged sheaf (small, hard targets)
Special sheaf (any length, width, or altitude)
Open sheaf (separate bursts)
Parallel sheaf (linear targets)
*Method of Fire Control*
*Method of fire*—specific guns and a specific interval between rounds. Nor-
mal adjust fire is one gun used with a five-second interval between rounds
*Method of control*:
"At my command, fire" remains in effect until observer announces,
"Cancel at my command"
"Cannot observe"—observer can't see the target
"Time on target"—observer tells FDC when rounds should impact

"Continuous illumination"—calculated by FDC unless observer indicates interval between rounds in seconds

"Coordinated illumination"—observer may order the interval between illum and HE shells

"Cease loading"—indicates suspension of loading rounds

"Check firing"—immediate halt in firing

"Continuous fire"—load and fire as fast as possible

"Repeat"—fire another round with or without adjustments

***Authentication***

Challenge and reply

***Message to Observer***

Battery(ies) to fire for effect

Adjusting battery

Changes to the initial call for fire

Number of rounds (per tube) to be fired for effect

Target numbers

Additional information:

Time of flight; Probable error in range (normally 38 meters or greater); Angle T (500 mils or greater)

Correction of errors—if the FDC makes an error when reading back the fire support data, announce "Correction" and re-transmit the correct data in its entirety.

## CALL-FOR-FIRE TRANSMISSIONS

A soldier or FO must determine the best method—grid mission, polar mission, or shift from a known point—for sending a call-for-fire transmission.

## Grid Mission

In a grid mission, the observer sends the target location as a six-digit grid. Before the first adjusting rounds are fired, the FDC must know the direction from the observer's location. The observer sends observer-target (OT) direction (to the nearest 10 mils) from his position to the target. OT is the direction in mils from the observer to the target.

| GRID MISSION | |
|---|---|
| **Observer** | **Fire Support Unit** |
| "A66 this is Z33, adjust fire, over." | "Z33 this is A66, adjust fire, out." |
| "Grid AA12345678, direction 0530, over." | "Grid AA12345678, direction 0530, out." |

| GRID MISSION | |
|---|---|
| **Observer** | **Fire Support Unit** |
| "Infantry platoon in the open, over." | "Infantry platoon in the open, out." |
| "Shot, out." | "Shot, over." |
| "Splash, over." | "Splash, out." |
| "End of mission, 10 casualties, platoon dispersed, over." | "End of mission, 10 casualties, platoon dispersed, out." |

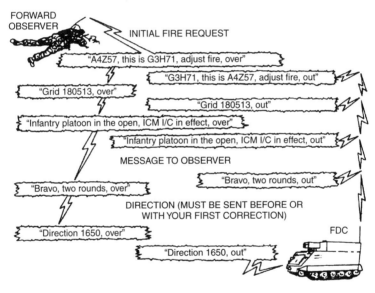

**Grid Request**

**Polar Mission**

For a polar mission, the observer sends a direction, distance, and an up or down measurement (vertical shift) to the target. The word "polar" in the warning order alerts the FDC that the target will be located with respect to the observer's position, which must be known by the FDC. A vertical shift tells the FDC how far in meters the target is located above or below the observer's location.

| POLAR MISSION | |
|---|---|
| **Observer** | **Fire Support Unit** |
| Fire for effect, polar, over | Fire for effect, polar, out |
| Direction 4520, distance 2300, down 35, over | Direction 4520, distance 2300, down 35, out |
| Infantry company in the open, over | Infantry company in the open, out |
| 3 rounds target, over | 3 rounds target, out |

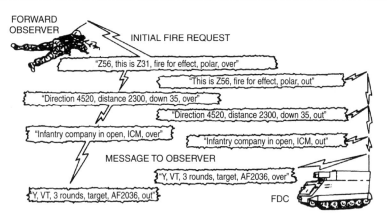

**Polar Request**

### Shift from a Known Point

In a shift from a known point mission, the point or target from which the shift will be made is sent in the warning order. Both the observer and the FDC must know the point. The observer sends a target/registration point number, an OT direction, a right or left correction (lateral shift), an add or drop correction to the nearest 100 meters (range shift), and an up or down correction (vertical shift) from the known point to the target. Normally, the OT direction is sent in mils, but the FDC can accept degrees or cardinal direction if that is all the observer can send. The lateral shift is how far left or right the target is from the known point. The range shift is how much farther (add) or closer (drop) the target is from the known point. The vertical shift is how much the target is above (up) or below (down) the altitude of the known point, to the nearest 5 meters (the vertical shift is ignored unless it exceeds 30 meters).

| SHIFT FROM A KNOWN POINT | |
| --- | --- |
| **Observer** | **Fire Support Unit** |
| "A66 this is Z33, adjust fire, shift BB1001, over." | "Z33 this is A66, adjust fire, shift BB1001, out." |
| "Direction 2420, right 300, add 400, over." | "Direction 2420, right 300, add 400, out." |
| "Two armored vehicles at POL site, over." | "Two armored vehicles at POL site, out." |
| "Authenticate Juliet November, over." | "I authenticate Tango, out." |
| "Shot, out." | "Shot, over." |
| "Splash, over." | "Splash, out." |
| "End of mission, 2 vehicles destroyed, over." | "End of mission, 2 vehicles destroyed, out." |

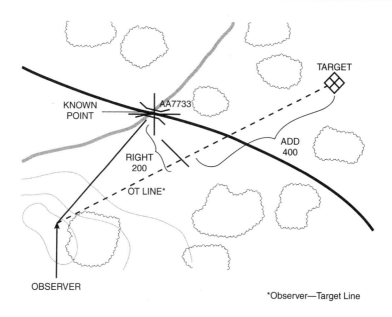

**Lateral and Range Shifts From a Known Point**

## ADJUSTING FIRE

To adjust fire onto a target, use the *bracketing* method of adjustment. Spot each round when it impacts as over or short, right or left of the target. When the first range spotting is observed, make a range correction that would result in a range spotting in the opposite direction. For example, if the first round is short, add enough range to get an *over* on the next round.

Use the following guide to establish a bracket:

| Round Impact from Target | Add or drop + or - |
|---|---|
| Over 400 meters | 800 meters + or - |
| 200–400 | 400 meters + or - |
| 100–200 meters | 200 meters + or - |
| Less than 100 meters | 100 meters |

1. To find deviation, measure the horizontal angle in mils, using either fingers or the reticle pattern in the binoculars. Estimate the range to the target and divide by 1,000. This is the observer target (OT) factor. If the OT distance is 1,000 meters or greater, the OT factor is expressed to the nearest whole number. If the OT distance is less than 1,000 meters, the OT factor is expressed to the nearest tenth. For example, 800 = 0.8. Multiplying the OT factor by the deviation measured in mils produces deviation in meters.

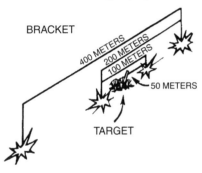

**Successive Bracketing**

**Fingers Pattern**

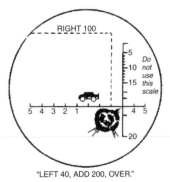

"LEFT 40, ADD 200, OVER."

**Reticle Pattern**

For example, if we measure the round 100 mils right of the target and estimate the range to be 2,200 meters, the OT factor is 2. For adjustment purposes, we express the OT factor to the nearest whole number. Example: 1.1 would be 1; 1.8 would be 2; 2.5 would be 2. Multiplying the angle (100 mils) by the OT factor (2), we get the deviation in meters (200 meters right).

    2. Transmit corrections to the FDC in meters. The initial correction should bracket the target in range. Deviation correction should be made to keep the rounds on the observer target line. The accompanying figure shows the impact of the initial round. Since the round is beyond the target, you must drop. You estimate that the round is 250 meters beyond the target. Therefore, a 400-meter drop will give you a bracket. The round impacted 50 mils left of the target. With an OT factor of 2, the round impacted 100 meters left. Your correction to the FDC is "Right 100, drop 400, over."

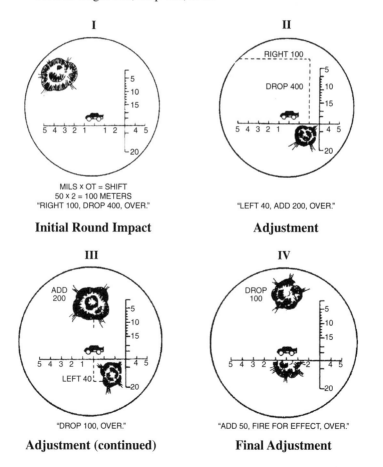

**I**

MILS x OT = SHIFT
50 x 2 = 100 METERS
"RIGHT 100, DROP 400, OVER."

**Initial Round Impact**

**II**

"LEFT 40, ADD 200, OVER."

**Adjustment**

**III**

"DROP 100, OVER."

**Adjustment (continued)**

**IV**

"ADD 50, FIRE FOR EFFECT, OVER."

**Final Adjustment**

3. Continue splitting the range bracket until a 100-meter bracket is split or a range correct spotting is observed, maintaining deviation on line.
4. Initiate fire for effect. When a 100-meter bracket is split or a range correct spotting is made, the fire-for-effect phase is entered, and the call is "Fire for effect."
5. Observe the results of fire for effect and report the results. When the smoke clears, tell the FDC what the results are. Such things as the number of casualties, damaged equipment, stalled tracks, and so forth are important.

## LESSONS LEARNED DURING OPERATION ENDURING FREEDOM

The following text comes from a series of small infantry unit After Action Reviews on indirect-fire support in Afghanistan.

### Mortars at Company and Battalion Level

Despite the desire to go in light, mortars are essential for mountain warfare. Mortars were used to destroy visible targets at long ranges, immediate target engagement, and to cover the abundance of dead space. Mortar platoon members in some units carried 5 rounds per person and every soldier carried 2 rounds. Since the mortars were not static, but had to move positions (sometimes rapidly) several leaders remarked that it worked well in their situation to not have everyone drop off all their rounds at the mortar position. In other words, if the rounds were immediately brought to the mortar position, when they moved it would have been impossible to relocate them with the tubes.

Prior to departure, work out with the artillery three or four easily recognizable target reference points (TRPs). Arrange to communicate directly with the artillery to get rapid action on requests for smoke (for orientation) and supporting fire.

### From a Company First Sergeant

I recommend all squad leaders and platoon leaders carry binoculars with the mil reticule. Countless times team leaders and squad leaders had the opportunity to call in mortars and the binoculars are needed. More importantly is that leaders and soldiers know how to use them. Contrary to popular belief it's not the platoon leader who's going to call it in, it's the soldier in the position who will. Range estimation is probably the most important or critical thing you do. If you close on your estimation you'll get the target. We all carried in 2 mortar rounds apiece and that was more than enough. We took a mix of everything; the only thing we used was WP [white phosphorus] and HE [high-explosive]. All together our company took in at least 120 rounds.

# 11

# Camouflage, Concealment, and Decoys

Camouflage, concealment, and decoys (CCD) all involve the use of materials and techniques to hide, blend, disguise, decoy, or disrupt the appearance of military targets and/or their backgrounds. CCD helps prevent an enemy from detecting or identifying friendly troops, equipment, activities, or installations. Properly designed CCD techniques take advantage of the immediate environment and natural and artificial materials. Good CCD is an action that makes soldiers, equipment, and units difficult to locate.

*Each soldier* is responsible for camouflaging himself, his equipment, and his position. CCD reduces the probability of an enemy placing aimed fire on a soldier. The soldier uses natural and artificial materials for CCD. Natural CCD includes defilade, grass, bushes, trees, and shadows. Artificial CCD for soldiers includes battle dress uniforms (BDUs), lightweight camouflage nets, skin paint, and natural materials removed from their original positions. To be effective, artificial CCD must blend with the natural background.

*Noise, movement, and light discipline* all contribute to individual CCD. Effective noise discipline muffles and eliminates sounds made by soldiers and their equipment. Movement discipline minimizes movement within and between positions and limits movement to routes that cannot be readily observed by the enemy. Light discipline controls the use of lights at night, such as not smoking in the open or not walking around with a lit flashlight.

*Dispersal*, the spreading of soldiers and equipment over a wide area, is a key individual survival technique. It creates a smaller target mass for enemy sensors and weapon systems. Dispersal, therefore, not only reduces casualties and losses in the event of an attack but also makes enemy detection efforts more difficult.

Camouflage

## CCD CONSIDERATIONS
Soldiers should consider the following when practicing CCD.

### Movement
Movement draws attention, whether it involves vehicles on the road or individuals walking around. The naked eye—as well as infrared and radar sensors—can detect movement. Soldiers should minimize movement while they are in the open. They should remember that darkness does not prevent observation by an enemy equipped with modern sensors. When movement is necessary, slow, smooth movement attracts less attention than quick, irregular movement.

### Shape
The soldier should use CCD materials to break up the shapes, outlines, and shadows of positions and equipment, as all three are revealing. Since shadows can visually mask objects, soldiers should stay in shadows whenever possible, especially when moving. When conducting operations close to the enemy, disguise or distort the shape of the helmet and the human body with artificial camouflage materials, as these forms are easily recognized by the enemy at close range.

## Shine and Light

Pay particular attention to gloss and shine, which can also attract attention and are caused by light reflecting from smooth or polished surfaces, such as mess kits, mirrors, eyeglasses, watch crystals, windshields, and starched uniforms. Plastic map cases, dust goggles worn on top of the helmet, and clear plastic garbage bags also reflect light almost as well as windshields and mirrors. Cover or remove these items from exposed areas.

Vehicle headlights, taillights, and safety reflectors reflect not only light but also laser energy used in weapon systems. Cover this equipment when the vehicle is not in operation. Red filters on vehicle dome lights and flashlights, while designed to protect the soldier's night vision, are extremely sensitive to detection by night vision devices. A tank's red dome light, reflecting off the walls and out through the sight and vision blocks, can be seen from as far away as 4 kilometers with a starlight scope.

Flashlights with red lenses, as well as cigarettes and pipes, are equally observable. To reduce the chances of detection, soldiers should replace red with blue-green filters and practice strict light discipline. Soldiers should also use measures to prevent shine at night—moonlight and starlight can be reflected as easily as sunlight.

## Color

The contrast of skin, uniforms, and equipment with the background helps the enemy detect opposing forces. Individual CCD should blend with the surroundings; at a minimum, objects must not contrast with the background. Therefore, the proper camouflage technique is to blend colors with the background or to hide objects with contrasting colors.

**Colors Used in CCD**

## CCD EMPLOYMENT
Before applying CCD to themselves, their equipment, and their positions, soldiers should study the nearby terrain and vegetation. Their reconnaissance should incorporate an analysis of the CCD considerations listed above. They then choose the CCD materials that best blend with the area. When moving from one area to another, they change CCD as required. What works well in one location may draw fire in another.

### Skin
Exposed skin, even very dark skin, reflects light. CCD paint sticks cover these oils and provide blending with the background. Avoid using oils or insect repellent to soften the paint stick because doing so defeats the purpose by making the skin shiny. Soldiers applying CCD paint should work in pairs and help each other. Self-application may leave gaps, such as behind the ears. Paint high, shiny areas (forehead, cheekbones, nose, ears, and chin) a dark color. Paint low, shadowed areas a light color. Paint the exposed skin on the back of the neck, arms, and hands with an irregular pattern. When CCD paint sticks are not available, use field expedients such as burnt cork, bark, charcoal, lampblack, or mud. Mud contains bacteria, so consider it a last priority for field-expedient paint.

### Uniform
ACUs and MultiCam have a CCD pattern but can require additional camouflage, especially when operating very close to the enemy. Soldiers should attach leaves, grass, small branches, or pieces of lightweight camouflage screening system (LCSS) to their uniforms and helmets. These items assist in distorting the shape of the soldier and in blending colors with the natural background. The ACU provides visual as well as near-infrared (NIR) CCD. Do not starch ACUs; doing so counters the infrared properties of the dyes. Replace excessively faded and worn ACUs, because they lose their CCD effectiveness as they wear.

### Equipment
Soldiers should inspect their personal equipment to ensure that shiny items are covered or removed. Take corrective action on items that rattle or make other noises when moved or worn. Soldiers assigned equipment such as vehicles or generators should be knowledgeable of their appropriate CCD techniques.

**Individual Fighting Position**

While building a fighting position, soldiers should camouflage it and carefully dispose of the earth spoil. They must also remember that too much CCD material applied to a position can actually disclose it. Soldiers should obtain CCD materials from a dispersed area to avoid drawing attention to the position because of the stripped area around it.

Camouflage the position as it is built. To avoid disclosing a fighting position, soldiers should observe the following guidelines:

- Do not leave shiny or light-colored objects exposed.
- Do not remove shirts while in the open.
- Do not use fires.
- Do not leave tracks and other signs of movement.
- When aircraft fly overhead, refrain from looking up, as one of the most obvious features on aerial photographs is the upturned faces of soldiers.

When CCD is complete, inspect the position from the enemy's viewpoint. Check CCD periodically to ensure it stays natural looking and conceals the position. When CCD materials become ineffective, change or improve them.

# 12

# Land Navigation
# and Map Reading

## GPS

Global positioning systems (GPS) use radio signals from satellites to determine highly accurate locations and the time of the user. The GPS has become the standard for navigation on today's battlefield. The accuracy and speed with which soldiers can determine their own positions and those of other friendlies and enemies has substantially increased survival. However, the GPS is not a replacement for the fundamental skills of map and compass reading.

There are many types of GPSs available to the soldier, and an intimate knowledge of its use is paramount to successful operations. The GPS receivers come in several configurations, including hand-held, vehicular-mounted, aircraft-mounted, and watercraft-mounted models. During the train-up phase prior to deployment, all soldiers should train and rehearse with a GPS.

Take care to set up the GPS correctly prior to use. It will have a variety of setup options, and it is important that the screens reflect the theater SOP for calling for aircraft, fire support, etc. Some assets will use latitude and longitude, whereas others will use the military grid system. Training and use will show you how to set up the individual menu screens for optimum use and performance.

## COMPASS

Compasses are the fundamental tool used when moving in an outdoor world where there is no other way to find directions. The lensatic compass is the most common and simplest instrument for measuring direction. It consists of the following major parts:

- The *cover* protects the floating dial. It contains a sighting wire and two luminous sighting slots or dots used for night navigation.

- The *base* or body of the compass contains a thumb loop and moving parts that include the floating dial, which is mounted on a pivot and rotates freely when the compass is held level. Printed on the dial in luminous figures are an arrow and the letters "E" and "W." The arrow always points to magnetic north, and the letters rest at east (90 degrees) and west (270 degrees). There are two scales, the outer denoting mils and the inner (normally in red) denoting degrees. Encasing the floating dial is a glass containing a fixed, black index line.
- The *bezel ring* is a ratchet device that clicks when turned. It will make 120 clicks when rotated fully; each click is equal to 3 degrees. A short, luminous line used in conjunction with the north-seeking arrow is contained in the glass face of the bezel ring.
- The *lens* is used to read the dial. It contains the rear-sight slot used in conjunction with the front sight for sighting on objects. The rear sight must be opened more than 45 degrees to allow the dial to float freely.

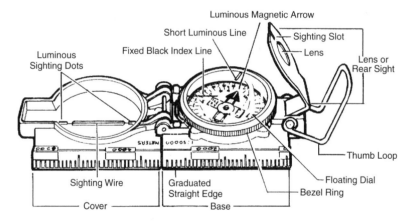

**Lensatic Compass**

**Handling the Compass**

The compass is a delicate instrument and should be closed and kept in its case when not being used. Metal objects and electricity can affect the performance of a compass. Nonmagnetic metals and alloys do not affect it. To ensure its proper functioning, observe these suggested safe distances:

| | |
|---|---|
| High-tension power lines | 55 meters |
| Field gun, truck, or tank | 18 meters |
| Telegraph/telephone wires or barbed wire | 10 meters |
| Machine gun | 2 meters |
| Steel helmet or rifle | 0.5 meter |

## Using the Compass

The compass must always be held level and firm when sighting on an object. Some of the techniques are as follows:

*Centerhold.* Open the compass to its fullest so that the cover forms a straight edge with the base. Place your thumb through the thumb loop, form a steady base with your third and fourth fingers, and extend your index finger along the side of the compass. Place the thumb of the other hand between the lens (rear sight) and the bezel ring; extend the index finger along the other side of the compass and the remaining fingers around the fingers of the other hand. Pull your elbows in firmly to your sides—this places the compass between your chin and belt. To measure an azimuth, simply turn your entire body toward the object, pointing the compass cover directly at the object. Then look down and read the azimuth from beneath the fixed, black index line.

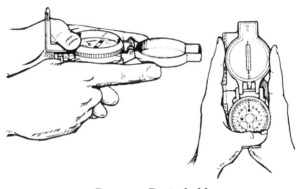

**Compass Centerhold**

*Compass-to-Cheek.* Open the cover of the compass containing the sighting wire to a vertical position and fold the rear sight slightly forward. Look through the rear-sight slot and align the front-sight hairline with the desired object in the distance. Then glance down at the dial through the eye lens to read the azimuth.

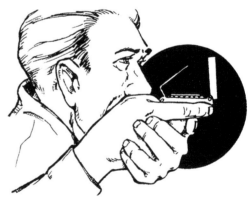

**Compass-to-Cheek**

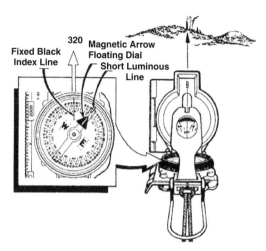

**Presetting a Compass**

## Presetting a Compass and Following an Azimuth

*In Daylight or with a Light Source.* Hold the compass level in the palm of your hand. Rotate it until the desired azimuth falls under the fixed, black index line. Turn the bezel ring until the luminous line is aligned with the north-seeking arrow. The compass is now preset.

To follow the azimuth, use the centerhold technique and turn your body until the north-seeking arrow is aligned with the luminous line. Then proceed forward in the direction of the front cover's sighting wire, which is aligned with the fixed, black index line.

*In Darkness or Limited Visibility.* Set the azimuth by the click method (each click equals a 3-degree interval). Rotate the bezel ring until the luminous line is over the fixed, black index line. Find the desired azimuth and divide it by three. The result is the number of clicks that you have to rotate the bezel ring. If the desired azimuth is smaller than 180 degrees, the number of clicks on the bezel ring should be counted in a counterclockwise direction. If the desired azimuth is larger than 180 degrees, subtract the number of degrees from 360 degrees and divide by three to obtain the number of clicks. Count them in a clockwise direction. For example, if the desired azimuth is 330 degrees, then 360 - 330 = 30 divided by 3 = 10 clicks clockwise.

With the compass preset, use the centerhold technique and rotate your body until the north-seeking arrow is aligned with the luminous line on the bezel. Then proceed forward in the direction of the front cover's luminous dots, which are aligned with the fixed, black index line.

**Offset**

A deliberate offset is a planned magnetic deviation to the right or left of an azimuth to an objective. It is used when the objective is located along or in the vicinity of a linear feature such as a road or stream. Because of errors in reading the compass or map, you may reach the linear feature without knowing whether the objective lies to the right or left. A deliberate offset by a known number of degrees in a known direction compensates for possible errors and ensures that upon reaching the linear feature you will know whether to go left or right.

**Orienting Compass and Map**

Place the compass on the map so that the cover of the compass is pointing toward the top of the map. Align the sighting wire or the straight edge of the compass over a north-south grid line, and rotate the map and compass together until the north arrow of the compass points in the same direction and number of degrees as shown in the current, updated grid-magnetic angle.

**FIELD EXPEDIENT METHODS—USING THE SUN AND STARS**

When a compass is not available, different techniques should be used to determine the four cardinal directions.

**Shadow-Tip Method**

This simple and accurate method of finding direction by the sun consists of four basic steps:

*Step 1.* Place a stick or branch into the ground at a level spot where a distinctive shadow will be cast. Mark the shadow tip with a stone, twig, or other means. This first shadow mark is always the west direction.

*Step 2.* Wait ten to fifteen minutes until the shadow tip moves a few inches. Mark the new position of the shadow tip in the same way as the first.

*Step 3.* Draw a straight line through the two marks to obtain an approximate east-west line.

*Step 4.* Standing with the first mark (west) to your left, the other directions are simple: north is to the front, east is to the right, and south is behind you.

A line drawn perpendicular to the east-west line at any point is the approximate north-south line. If you are uncertain which direction is east and which is west, observe this simple rule—the first shadow-tip mark is always in the west direction, everywhere on earth.

The shadow-tip method can also be used as a shadow clock to find the approximate time of day (see the figure). Move the stick to the intersection of the east-west line and the north-south line, and set it vertically in the

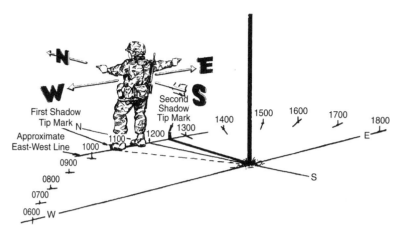

**Shadow-Tip Method to Find Direction and Time**

ground. The west part of the east-west line indicates 0600 hours and the east part is 1800 hours, anywhere on earth, because the basic rule always applies.

The north-south line now becomes the noon line. The shadow of the stick is an hour hand in the shadow clock, and with it you can estimate the time using the noon and 6 o'clock lines as your guides. Depending on your location and the season, the shadow may move either clockwise or counter-clockwise, but this does not alter your manner of reading the shadow clock.

The shadow clock is not a timepiece in the ordinary sense. It makes every day twelve unequal hours long, and always reads 0600 hours at sunrise and 1800 hours at sunset. The shadow clock time is closest to conventional clock time at midday, but the spacing of the other hours compared with conventional time varies somewhat with the locality and the date. However, it does provide a satisfactory means of telling time in the absence of properly set watches.

The shadow-tip system is not intended for use in polar regions, which the Department of Defense defines as being above 60 degrees latitude in either hemisphere.

**Watch Method**

A watch can be used to determine approximate true north and true south. In the north temperate zone only, the hour hand is pointed toward the sun. A south line can be found midway between the hour hand and 1200 hours, standard time. If daylight saving time is in effect, the north-south line is found between the hour hand and 1300 hours. If there is any doubt as to which end of the line is north, remember that the sun is in the east before noon and in the west after noon.

A watch may also be used to determine direction in the south temperate zone, but the method is different. The 1200-hour dial is pointed toward the sun, and the north line is halfway between 1200 hours and the hour hand. If on daylight saving time, the north line lies midway between the hour hand and 1300 hours.

The watch method can be in error, especially in the lower latitudes, and may cause circling. To avoid this, make a shadow clock and set your watch to the time indicated. After traveling for an hour, take another shadow-clock reading. Reset your watch if necessary.

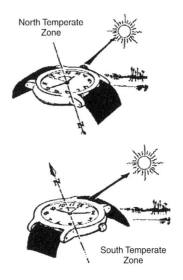

North Temperate Zone

South Temperate Zone

**Watch Method**

## Star Method

Fewer than sixty of approximately five thousand stars visible to the eye are used by navigators. The stars we see when we look up at the night sky are not evenly scattered across the whole sky; they are grouped in constellations. Which constellations we see depends on where we are, the time of the year, and the time of the night. The night sky changes with the seasons because the earth revolves around the sun, and it also changes from hour to hour because the rotation of the earth makes some constellations seem to travel in a circle. But the North Star, also known as the Polar Star or Polaris, is in almost exactly the same place in the sky every night, all night long.

The North Star is less than 1 degree off true north and does not move because the axis of the earth is pointed toward it. It is the last star in the handle of the Little Dipper. Two stars in the Big Dipper are a help in finding the North Star; they are called the Pointers, and an imaginary line drawn through them five times their distance points to the North Star. There are many stars brighter than the North Star, but none is more important. However, the North Star can be seen only in the Northern Hemisphere, so it cannot serve as a guide south of the equator. The farther north you go, the higher the North Star is in the sky; above latitude 70 degrees, it is too high in the sky to be useful.

When navigating using the stars as guides, you must know the different constellation shapes and their locations throughout the world. Depending on the star selected for navigation, azimuth checks may be necessary. A star near the north horizon serves for about a half hour. When moving south,

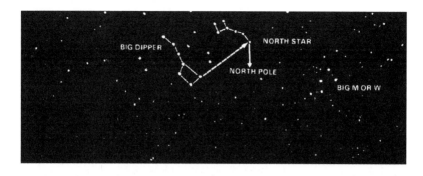

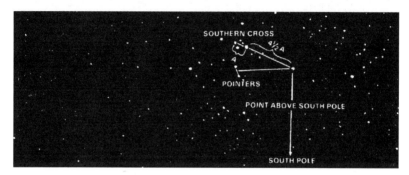

**Determining Direction by the North Star and Southern Cross**

azimuth checks should be made every fifteen minutes. When traveling east or west, the difficulty of staying on azimuth is more likely caused by the star climbing too high in the sky or disappearing below the horizon than by the star changing direction angle. When this happens, it is necessary to choose another guide star.

The Southern Cross is the main constellation used as a guide south of the equator, and the general directions above for using north and south stars are reversed.

## MAP READING
Being in the right place at the right time is essential on the battlefield, so map-reading and land-navigation skills are important for every soldier.

### Military Grid System
A military grid system is a network of squares formed by north-south and east-west grid lines placed on a map. The distance between grid lines represents 1,000 or 10,000 meters, depending on the scale of the map. A grid system enables the map reader to locate a point on a map quickly and accurately.

A grid line is identified by a specific number printed in the margin directly opposite the line it indicates. Any point on a map can be identified by coordinates. Following are rules for reading grid coordinates:

1. Large, bold-faced numbers in the margin label each grid line.
2. Starting at the lower left-hand corner of the map, read right and up.
3. Write the coordinates as a continuous series of numbers. The first half of the total number of the digits represents the "right" reading; the last half represents the "up" reading.

Following are examples using a map with 1,000-meter grid squares:

- *Location of a point within a 1,000-meter grid square.* Use this method to designate an object that is easily identifiable within a large area. Identify the grid square by using the numbers of the two grid lines intersecting at the lower left-hand corner, e.g., 9176.

- *Location of a point within 100 meters.* Use the appropriate corner of a coordinate scale that breaks the 1,000-meter square into 10 equal parts along each side (100-meter segments are indicated by longer lines on the coordinate scale). Place the coordinate scale along the east-west grid at the lower left-hand corner of the grid square, then slide it eastward to the center of the object. Location is expressed as a six-digit coordinate. The third digit is the longer line nearest grid line 91, and

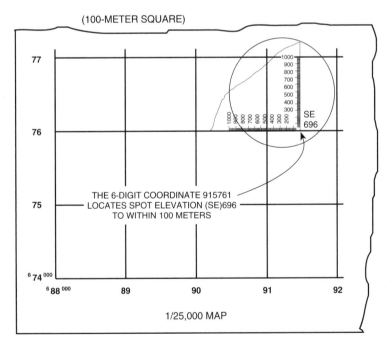

**The Six-Digit Coordinate**

the sixth digit is the longer line nearest the spot elevation (SE), e.g., 915761.

- *Location of a point within 10 meters.* The short lines divide 100-meter segments into 20-meter segments. To read to the nearest 10 meters, interpolate along the scale. The coordinate will be an eight-digit coordinate, e.g., 91547614.

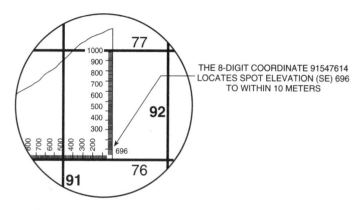

THE 8-DIGIT COORDINATE 91547614
LOCATES SPOT ELEVATION (SE) 696
TO WITHIN 10 METERS

**The Eight-Digit Coordinate**

## Scale

Scale is defined as the fixed relationship between map distance (MD) and the corresponding ground distance (GD). It is expressed as a representative fraction (RF):

$$RF = \frac{MD}{GD}$$

The RF appears in the margin of the map as 1/25,000 or 1:25,000, each of which means that 1 unit of measure on the map represents 25,000 similar units of measure on the ground.

The graphic scale is printed in the margin as a special ruler and is used to measure ground distances on a map. Military maps normally have three graphic scales, expressed in miles, meters, and yards.

## Direction

Direction is defined as an imaginary straight line on the map or ground and is expressed as an azimuth.

*Azimuth.* An azimuth is a horizontal angle measured clockwise from a north baseline. All directions originate from the center of an imaginary circle called the azimuth circle. This circle is divided into 360 equal units of measurement, called degrees. The degrees are numbered in a clockwise direction, with east at 90 degrees, south at 180 degrees, west at 270 degrees, and north at 360 or 0 degrees. Distance has no effect on azimuth.

**Back Azimuth.** The back azimuth of a line differs from its azimuth by exactly 180 degrees. The rules for determining back azimuth are as follows:
- If the azimuth is less than 180 degrees, the back azimuth is the value of the azimuth plus 180.
- If the azimuth is more than 180 degrees, the back azimuth is the value of the azimuth minus 180.
- If the azimuth is 180 degrees, the back azimuth is 0 degrees or 360 degrees.

**Measuring Azimuths on a Map.** Map azimuths are measured with a protractor. The issue protractor (MR-1) is graduated in two scales—0 to 180 degrees, and 180 to 360 degrees—to represent the complete azimuth circle.

To read a map azimuth between any two points:
- Draw a line connecting the two points.
- Place the index at the point from which you are measuring, ensuring that the baseline of the protractor is on or parallel to a north-south grid line.
- Read the azimuth at the point where the line intersects the scale.

To plot an azimuth on a map:
- Place the protractor on the map with the index at the initial point and baseline parallel to a north-south grid line.
- Place a dot on the map at the desired azimuth reading.
- Remove the protractor; connect the initial point and the dot with a line.

**Base Direction.** There are three base directions: true north, grid north, and magnetic north.
1. *True north.* Direction to the north pole. The symbol is a star.
2. *Grid north.* Direction of the north-south grid lines. The symbol is GN.
3. *Magnetic north.* Direction in which the magnetic arrow of a compass points. The symbol is a half arrow.

The angular relationships among these three directions are shown by a declination diagram in the margin of a map.

### Grid-Magnetic Angle

To understand the grid-magnetic (G-M) angle, you must know the meaning of azimuth. Map readers are concerned with two base directions: grid north, from which we read grid azimuths (protractor and map), and magnetic north, from which we read magnetic azimuths (compass and ground).

*Grid azimuth* is a horizontal angle measured clockwise from grid north.

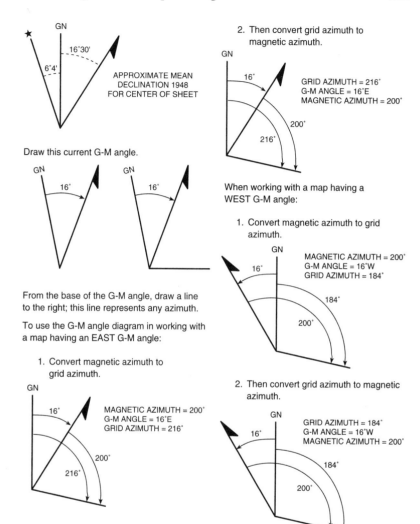

GN

16°30'

6°4'

APPROXIMATE MEAN
DECLINATION 1948
FOR CENTER OF SHEET

Draw this current G-M angle.

GN            GN

16°          16°

From the base of the G-M angle, draw a line
to the right; this line represents any azimuth.

To use the G-M angle diagram in working with
a map having an EAST G-M angle:

1. Convert magnetic azimuth to
   grid azimuth.

GN

16°

MAGNETIC AZIMUTH = 200°
G-M ANGLE = 16°E
GRID AZIMUTH = 216°

200°

216°

2. Then convert grid azimuth to
   magnetic azimuth.

GN

16°

GRID AZIMUTH = 216°
G-M ANGLE = 16°E
MAGNETIC AZIMUTH = 200°

200°

216°

When working with a map having a
WEST G-M angle:

1. Convert magnetic azimuth to grid
   azimuth.

GN

16°

MAGNETIC AZIMUTH = 200°
G-M ANGLE = 16°W
GRID AZIMUTH = 184°

184°

200°

2. Then convert grid azimuth to magnetic
   azimuth.

GN

16°

GRID AZIMUTH = 184°
G-M ANGLE = 16°W
MAGNETIC AZIMUTH = 200°

184°

200°

## Converting Between Grid and Magnetic Azimuth

*Magnetic azimuth* is a horizontal angle measured clockwise from magnetic north.

*G-M angle* is the angular difference between grid north and magnetic north, measured from grid north.

To use a grid azimuth in the field with a compass, you must first change it to a magnetic azimuth. To plot a magnetic azimuth on a map, you must first change it to a grid azimuth. To make either of these changes, you must use a G-M angle diagram as shown in the diagram. You should construct and use the G-M angle diagram each time conversion of azimuths is required. As a time-saving procedure when working frequently with the same map, construct a G-M angle conversion table on the margin. The following is an example, using a map having a G-M angle of 16 degrees east:

For conversion of:

Magnetic azimuth to grid azimuth:    Add 16 degrees

Grid azimuth to magnetic azimuth:    Subtract 16 degrees

*Intersection.* Distant or inaccessible objects can be located on a map by intersecting lines from two known points. For example, a magnetic azimuth from a known observation post (OP) to a distant point is converted to a grid azimuth and drawn on the map. Another magnetic azimuth from another OP to the same distant point is converted to a grid azimuth and drawn on the same map. The intersection of the two lines on the map is the location of the known point.

*Resection.* The resection method lets you locate your position on a map. Take magnetic azimuths to two distant points on the ground that can be identified on the map. Change these azimuths to back azimuths, convert to grid azimuths, and draw the converted azimuths from the known points on the map. Your location is where these two lines intersect. To verify and make a final determination of your position, compare ground features with those shown on the map.

*Modified Resection.* Modified resection is a method of locating your position on a map when you are on a road, stream, or other linear feature identified on the map. Take a magnetic azimuth to a distant point that can be identified both on the ground and on the map. Change this to a back azimuth and convert to a grid azimuth. Draw this converted azimuth on the map from the known point. Your position is where the azimuth line on the map crosses or intersects the linear feature.

**Elevation and Relief (Contour Lines)**
On a standard topographical map, contour lines are the most common method of showing relief and elevation. A contour line represents an imaginary line on the ground, above or below sea level. All points on the contour line are at the same elevation. The elevation represented by contour lines is the vertical distance above or below sea level. The three types of contour lines used on a standard topographic map are as follows:
  • *Index.* Starting at zero elevation or mean sea level, every fifth contour line is a heavier line. These are known as index contour lines.

Normally, each index contour line is numbered at some point. This number is the elevation of that line.

- *Intermediate.* The contour lines falling between the index contour lines are called intermediate contour lines. These lines are finer and do not have their elevations given. There are normally four intermediate contour lines between index contour lines.

- *Supplementary.* These contour lines resemble dashes. They show changes in elevation of at least one-half the contour interval. These lines are normally found where there is very little change in elevation, such as on fairly level terrain.

***Contour Interval.*** Before the elevation of any point on the map can be determined, you must know the contour interval for the map you are using. The contour interval measurement given in the marginal information of the map is the vertical distance between adjacent contour lines. To determine the elevation of a point on the map you must:

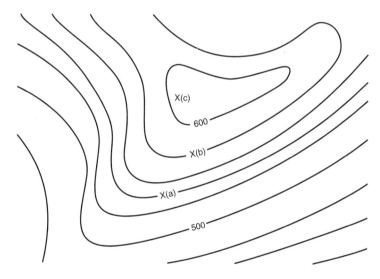

**Points on Contour Lines**

1. Determine the contour interval and the unit of measure used for your map (in the marginal data): for example, feet, meters, or yards.
2. Find the numbered index contour line nearest the point of which you are trying to determine the elevation.
3. Determine if you are going from lower elevation to higher, or vice versa. In the figure, point (a) is between the index contour lines. The

lower index contour line is numbered 500, which means any point on that line is at an elevation of 500 meters above mean sea level. The upper index contour line is numbered 600, or 600 meters. Going from the lower to the upper index contour line shows an increase in elevation.

4. Determine the exact elevation of point (a), start at the index contour line numbered 500 and count the number of intermediate contour lines to point (a). Locate point (a) on the second intermediate contour line above the 500-meter index contour line. The contour interval is 20 meters (see figure on the previous page), thus each one of the intermediate contour lines crossed to get to point (a) adds 20 meters to the 500-meter index contour line. The elevation of point (a) is 540 meters; the elevation has increased.

5. Determine the elevation of point (b). Go to the nearest index contour line. In this case, it is the upper index contour line numbered 600. Locate point (b) on the intermediate contour line immediately below the 600-meter index contour line. Below means downhill or a lower elevation. Therefore, point (b) is located at an elevation of 580 meters.

6. Determine the elevation to a hilltop point (c). Add one-half the contour interval to the elevation of the last contour line. In this example, the last contour line before the hilltop is an index contour line numbered 600. Add one-half the contour interval, 10 meters, to the index contour line. The elevation of the hilltop would be 610 meters.

*Slope.* Depending on the military mission, soldiers may need to determine not only the height of a hill but also the degree of the hill's slope. The slope is the rate of rise or fall of a terrain feature. The speed at which equipment or personnel can move is affected by the slope of the ground or terrain feature. This slope can be determined from the map by studying the contour line. The closer the contour lines, the steeper the slope; the farther apart the contour lines, the gentler the slope.

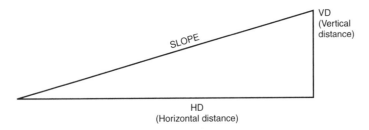

**Slope Diagram**

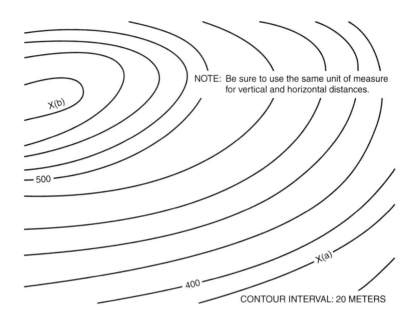

NOTE: Be sure to use the same unit of measure for vertical and horizontal distances.

CONTOUR INTERVAL: 20 METERS

**Contour Line Around a Slope**

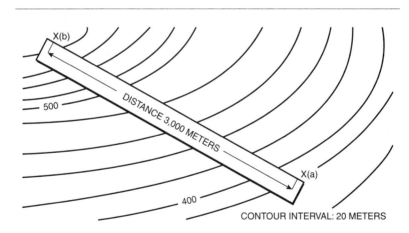

CONTOUR INTERVAL: 20 METERS

**Measuring Horizontal Distance**

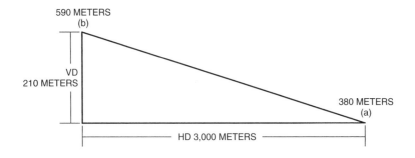

VD = b − a = 210 METERS
HD = 3,000 METERS

$$\% \ \text{SLOPE} = \frac{\text{VD} \times 100}{\text{HD}} \ \text{or} \ \frac{(\text{VD}) \ 210 \times 100}{(\text{HD}) \ 3,000} = \frac{21,000}{3,000} = 7\%$$

Multiply the distance by 100. Divide the total by the
horizontal distance. The result is the percentage of slope.

### Percentage of Slope in Meters

*Percentage of Slope.* The speed at which personnel and equipment can
move up or down a hill is affected by the slope of the ground and the limitations of the equipment. It is often necessary to have a more exact way of
describing a slope.

- Slope may be expressed in several ways, but all depend upon the
  comparison of vertical distance (VD) to horizontal distance (HD).
  Before we can determine the percentage of a slope, we must know the
  VD of the slope. The VD is determined by subtracting the lowest
  point of the slope from the highest point. Use the contour lines to
  determine the highest and lowest point of the slope.
- To determine the percentage of the slope in meters between points (a)
  and (b), determine the elevation of point (b) (590 meters). Then determine the elevation of point (a) (380 meters). Determine the vertical
  distance between the two points by subtracting the elevation of point
  (a) from the elevation of point (b). The difference (210 meters) is the
  VD between points (a) and (b). Then measure the HD between the
  two points on the map. After the horizontal distance has been determined, compute the percentage of the slope by using the formula
  shown in the illustration.

## TERRAIN FEATURES

All terrain features are derived from a complex landmass known as a mountain or ridgeline. The term ridgeline is not interchangeable with the term ridge. A *ridgeline* is a line of high ground, usually with changes in elevation along its top and low ground on all sides, from which a total of ten natural or manmade terrain features are classified.

**Ridgeline**

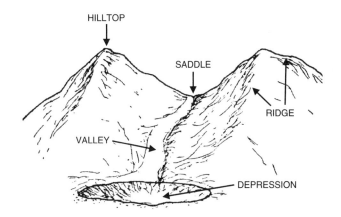

**Terrain Features**

# Hilltop

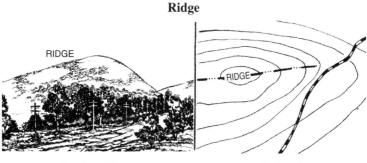

(On Map)
Last closed contour.

(On Ground)
When you are located on a hilltop,
the ground slopes down in all directions.

# Ridge

(On Ground)
When you are located on a ridge,
the ground slopes down in three
directions and up in one direction.

(On Map)
U- or V-shaped contours with the base
of the U or V pointing away from
higher ground.

# Saddle

(On Map)
Hourglass or figure eight–
shaped contours.

(On Ground)
When you are located in a saddle,
there is higher ground in two directions
and lower ground in two directions.

**Primary Terrain Features**

## Valley

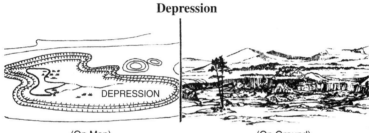

| (On Ground) | (On Map) |
|---|---|
| Reasonably level ground bordered on side by higher ground. Generally has maneuver room and may contain streams. | Contour lines form U. Lines tend to parallel stream before crossing. Contour lines crossing a stream always point uphill. |

## Depression

| (On Map) | (On Ground) |
|---|---|
| Indicated by depression contours. | Low point or hole in the ground with high ground on all sides. |

## Draw

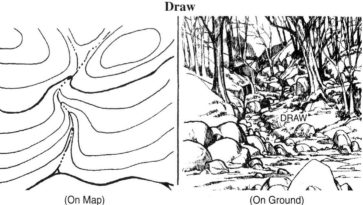

| (On Map) | (On Ground) |
|---|---|
| Contour lines are V-shaped with the point of the V toward the head of the draw (high ground). | Like a valley, but normally has less developed stream course. No level ground and little or no maneuver room. Ground slopes upward on the sides and toward the head of the draw. |

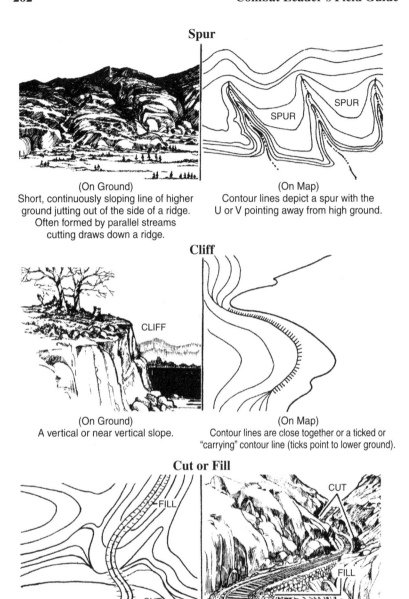

## Spur

(On Ground)
Short, continuously sloping line of higher ground jutting out of the side of a ridge. Often formed by parallel streams cutting draws down a ridge.

(On Map)
Contour lines depict a spur with the U or V pointing away from high ground.

## Cliff

(On Ground)
A vertical or near vertical slope.

(On Map)
Contour lines are close together or a ticked or "carrying" contour line (ticks point to lower ground).

## Cut or Fill

Cuts are manmade features resulting from cutting through high ground, usually to form a level bed for a road or railroad track. Fills are manmade features resulting from filling a low area, usually to form a level bed for a road or railroad track.

## GROUND NAVIGATION

Ground navigation is movement between two points in which an individual, using terrain features as guides, knows both his map and ground location throughout the movement. Before you can navigate on the ground you first must determine your location on the map and on the ground by using the following procedure:

1. Orient the map to the north.
2. Inspect the surrounding area or ground to determine all distinct terrain features.
3. On the map, look for an area having the same types of features in the same relative positions as those observed on the ground. Through comparing the map to the ground and using a process of elimination, isolate the terrain feature on which you are located.
4. Confirm this terrain feature by assuring that the direction to, distance from, and difference in elevation from all adjacent terrain features are identical on the map and on the ground.
5. Determine your exact location on the isolated terrain feature by a detailed analysis of all the immediate terrain features.

Ground navigation demands a thorough knowledge of terrain features as they appear on both the map and on the ground. Since terrain features are used as guides during movement, compass use is minimal. Two basic rules must always be applied:

1. Begin from a known location on both the map and the ground.
2. Then orient the map to the ground and keep it oriented throughout the movement.

With the basic rules established, the following steps outline the ground (land) navigation procedure:

**Step 1.** Through a map study of the terrain, determine the most practical route to your destination and select terrain features along this route to guide your movement.

**Step 2.** Determine the general direction of movement.

**Step 3.** Begin movement, considering the horizontal and vertical distances between terrain features along the route.

**Step 4.** Confirm your location at selected terrain features (checkpoints) along the route.

**Step 5.** Upon arrival at the final destination, confirm your location by a detailed comparative analysis between the ground position and the plotted map position.

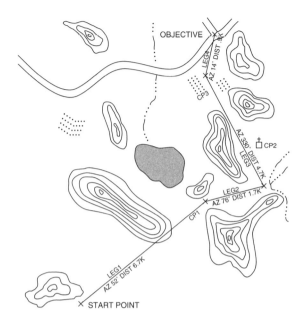

NOTE: All azimuths in this figure are grid.

## Mounted Movement

**Mounted Navigation**

With the addition of more combat vehicles to the Army, your chances of having to navigate while mounted are increasing. The major difference between navigating while mounted and while dismounted is the speed at which you travel. When moving mounted, it is important to designate a navigator who makes sure that the correct distance and direction are followed and recorded, beginning with the leg from the start point to the first prominent feature and then to subsequent easily identifiable features on the ground. The navigator prepares a log to record azimuths and distances for each leg of the movement. During movement, the navigator must face in the direction of travel to keep his map oriented and to identify terrain features.

Mounted navigation with a compass requires determination of the amount of deviation caused by the vehicle. This can be done in the following manner:

1. The navigator dismounts and moves 50 meters in front of the vehicle.
2. The navigator determines an azimuth from his position to a fixed object at least 50 meters to his front.

3. The driver moves the vehicle forward, keeping it centered on the navigator, and stops as close to him as safely possible.
4. The navigator then gets back into the vehicle and measures the azimuth to the fixed object from the vehicle. The vehicle's engine must be running. The difference between the two azimuths is the deviation. The deviation is logged and added to or subtracted from the azimuth to be followed. This procedure should be followed for any change of direction of 10 degrees or more.

Be aware that distance measured on a vehicle's odometer during mounted movement may be greater than that measured on the map, since the map measurements do not take into consideration the rise and fall of the land.

## FOLDING A MAP
Use the following steps to fold a map:
1. Lay the map flat, face up, north at the top. Fold it in half, turning the bottom edge up to the top.
2. Crease the map into three equal parts parallel to the center fold just made.
3. Open the map completely, face up. Turn it so east is at the top.
4. Repeat the folding procedures of steps 1 and 2.

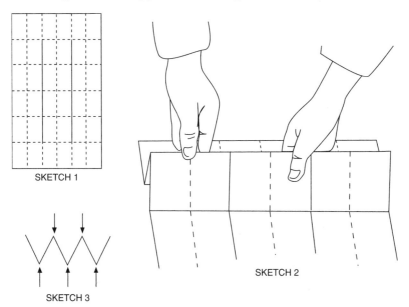

SKETCH 1

SKETCH 2

SKETCH 3

**Folding a Map Sheet**

5. Open the map again, face up, placing north at the top. With a sharp blade, neatly cut the map as shown in sketch 1, along heavy lines.
6. Grasp as in sketch 2, drawing paper up at the crease. Fold over toward the top edge.
7. Repeat step 6 with the second crease from the bottom, folding to meet the top edge of the map. Fold up the remaining flap. The edge view of the map should look like sketch 3.
8. From the center **V**, open the map to the center section without unfolding the remainder. Turn the map so east is at the top.
9. Follow the same creasing and folding procedures as in steps 6 and 7.
10. Again open the map at the center **V** without unfolding the rest, exposing the center section.
11. Without unfolding the map, carefully glue or tape together the eight places where the edges you have cut come together.
12. You now have three sections, each of which may be used like a book map. You can fold the entire map so that only the desired "book" is exposed for use.

# 13

# Fighting Positions

The defensive plan normally will require building fighting positions. Fighting positions protect soldiers. They provide *cover* from direct and indirect fires, and *concealment* through proper positioning and camouflage.

## PRINCIPLES
Leaders follow three basic principles to effectively and efficiently prepare fighting positions:
1. Site positions to best engage the enemy.
2. Prepare positions by stages.
3. Inspect all positions.

### Site Positions to Best Engage the Enemy
The most important aspect of a fighting position is that it be tactically well positioned. Leaders must be able to look at the terrain and quickly identify the best locations for fighting positions that allow:
- Soldiers to engage the intended enemy element within their assigned sectors of fire.
- Soldiers to fire out to the maximum effective range of their weapons with maximum grazing fire and minimal dead space.
- Grenadiers to be placed in positions to cover dead space.

Additionally, leaders site fighting positions to provide mutually supporting, interlocking fires so they can cover the platoon's sector from multiple positions. When possible, they site positions behind natural cover and in easily camouflaged locations. The enemy must not be able to identify the position until it is too late and he has been effectively engaged.

### Prepare Positions by Stages
Leaders and soldiers prepare fighting positions based on the situation. Soldiers prepare fighting positions every time the platoon makes an extended halt. Usually half of the platoon digs in or conducts various priorities of work

while the other half maintains security. Soldiers prepare positions in stages, and a leader inspects the position at each stage before the soldiers move to the next.

**Stage 1.** The leader checks fields of fire from the prone position. For a stage 1 position, the soldiers:

- Emplace sector stakes.
- Stake the primary sector.
- Position a grazing-fire log or sandbag between the sector stakes.
- Place the aiming stake(s), if required, to allow limited-visibility engagement of a specific target.
- Scoop out elbow holes.
- Trace the outline of the position on the ground.
- Clear the fields of fire for both the primary and secondary sectors of fire.
- Ensure the leader inspects the position before they move to stage 2.

**Stage 2.** Soldiers prepare retaining walls for the parapets. They ensure the following:

- There is a minimum distance (equal to the width of one helmet) from the edge of the hole to the beginning of the front, flank, and rear cover.
- The cover to the front consists of sandbags (or logs), two to three high, and for a two-soldier position, about the length of two M203 rifles (about 7 feet).
- The cover to the flanks is the same height, but only one M203 rifle length (about 3.5 feet).
- The cover to the rear is one sandbag high and one M203 long (about 3.5 feet).
- If logs are used, they must be held firmly in place with strong stakes.
- The leader inspects the retaining wall before they begin stage 3.

**Stage 3.** Soldiers dig the position and throw dirt forward of the parapet retaining walls and pack it down hard. They should:

- Dig the position armpit (of the tallest soldier) deep.
- Fill the parapets in order of front, flanks, and rear.
- Camouflage the parapets and the entire position.
- Dig grenade sumps and slope the floor toward them.
- Dig storage areas for two rucksacks into the rear wall if needed.
- Ensure the leader inspects the work.

**Stage 4.** Soldiers prepare the overhead cover. They must:

- Always provide solid support for overhead cover. They build the support with 4- to 6-inch logs on top of each other running the full length of the front and rear cover.

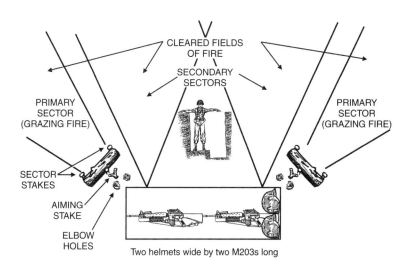

CLEARED FIELDS
OF FIRE

SECONDARY
SECTORS

PRIMARY
SECTOR
(GRAZING FIRE)

PRIMARY
SECTOR
(GRAZING FIRE)

SECTOR
STAKES

AIMING
STAKE

ELBOW
HOLES

Two helmets wide by two M203s long

**Stage 1**

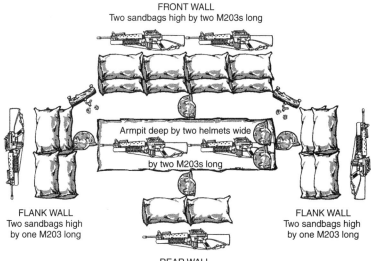

FRONT WALL
Two sandbags high by two M203s long

Armpit deep by two helmets wide

by two M203s long

FLANK WALL
Two sandbags high
by one M203 long

FLANK WALL
Two sandbags high
by one M203 long

REAR WALL
One sandbag high by one M203 long

KEVLAR HELMET (1 FT)

M203 (3.5 FT)

**Stage 2**

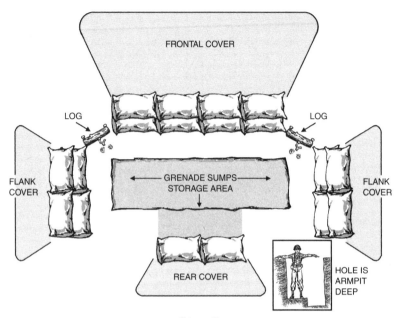

**Stage 3**

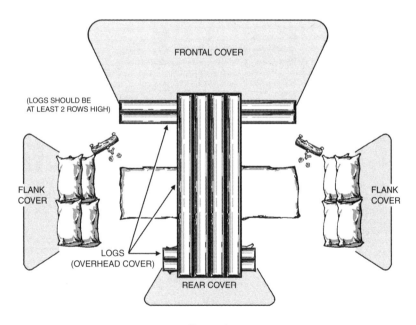

**Stage 4**

- Place five or six logs 4 to 6 inches in diameter and two M203s long (about 7 feet) over the center of the position, resting them on the overhead cover support, not on the sandbags.
- Place waterproofing (plastic bags, ponchos) on top of these logs.
- Put a minimum of 18 inches of packed dirt or sandbags on top of the logs.
- Camouflage the overhead cover and the bottom of the position.
- Ensure the leader inspects the position.

## Inspect All Positions
Leaders must ensure their soldiers build fighting positions that are both effective and safe. An improperly sited position cannot be used and an improperly constructed position is a danger to its occupants. Leaders should inspect the progress of the fighting position at each stage in its preparation.

## TYPES OF FIGHTING POSITIONS
There are many different types of fighting positions. The number of personnel, types of weapons, time available, and terrain are the main factors that dictate the position that will be used.

## Hasty Fighting Position
Soldiers use a hasty fighting position when there is little or no time to prepare. They locate it behind whatever cover is available. It should give frontal protection from direct fire while allowing fire to the front and obliquely. A hasty position may consist simply of a rucksack placed beside a tree or large

**Hasty Fighting Position**

rock. For protection from indirect fire, a hasty fighting position should be in a small depression or hole at least 18 inches deep. The term "hasty position" does not mean that there is no digging. In only a few minutes, a prone shelter can be scraped out or dug to provide some protection. This type of position is well suited for ambushes or for protection of overwatching elements during raids and attacks. Hasty positions can also be the first step in the construction of more elaborate positions.

**One-Soldier Fighting Position**
Positions that contain a single soldier are the least desirable, but they are useful in some situations. One-soldier positions may be required to cover exceptionally wide frontages. They should never be positioned out of sight of adjacent positions. The one-soldier fighting position should allow the soldier to fire to the front or to the oblique from behind frontal cover.

**One-Soldier Fighting Position**

**Two-Soldier Fighting Position**
A two-soldier fighting position can be prepared in close terrain and used where grazing fire and mutual support extend no farther than to an adjacent position. It can be used to cover dead space just in front of the position. One or both ends of the hole are extended around the sides of the frontal cover. Changing a hole this way allows both soldiers to see better and have greater sectors of fire to the front. Also, during rest or eating periods, one soldier can watch the entire sector while the other sleeps or eats. If they receive fire from the front, they can move back to gain the protection of the frontal cover. By moving 1 meter, the soldiers can continue to find and hit targets to the front during lulls in enemy fire. This type of position requires more digging and is harder to camouflage. It is also a better target for enemy hand grenades.

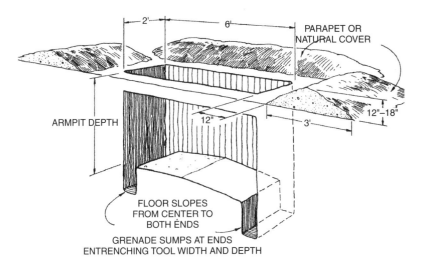

**Cutaway View of Two-Soldier Position**

**Steep Terrain Position**

### Positions on Steep Terrain

On a steep slope, a soldier in a hole behind frontal cover cannot shoot attackers without standing up and exposing himself. To overcome this, the hole is dug and firing ports are dug out at each end of the hole. The ground between the firing ports then serves as frontal cover for the position.

### Three-Soldier Fighting Position

A three-soldier position has several advantages over the other positions. There is a leader in each position, which makes command and control easier.

It also supports continuous, secure operations better than other positions. One soldier can provide security; one can do priority work; and one can rest, eat, or perform maintenance. It allows the platoon to maintain combat power and security without shifting personnel or leaving positions unmanned. Lastly, it provides 360-degree observation and fire.

The leader must consider the following with three-person positions:

- Either the distance between positions must be increased or the size of the squad's sector reduced. The choice depends mainly on visibility and fields of fire.

- Because the squad leader is in a fighting position that will most likely be engaged during the battle, he cannot exert personal control over the other two positions. The squad leader keeps control over the battle by:

    Clearly communicating plans and intent to his squad, including control measures and fire plans

    Using prearranged signals such as flares, whistles, or tracers

    Positioning key weapons in his fighting position

    Placing his fighting position so that it covers key or decisive terrain

    Placing his fighting position where his team might be able to act as a reserve

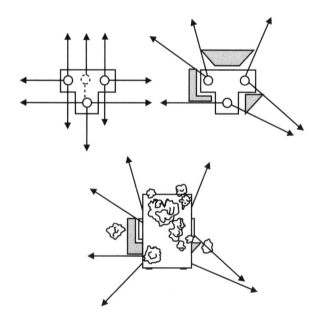

**Three-soldier T-position**

The three-soldier emplacement is the **T**-position. This basic design can be changed by adding or deleting berms, changing the orientation of the **T**, or shifting the position of the third soldier to form an **L** instead of a **T**. Berms, camouflage, and overhead cover are similar to other fighting positions.

## MACHINE-GUN POSITIONS

The primary sector of fire is usually situated obliquely so that the gun can fire across the platoon's front. The tripod is used on the side with the primary sector of fire, and the bipod legs are used on the side with the secondary sector. When changing from primary to secondary sectors, the machine gun is moved but the tripod is left in place. Dig a trench for the bipod legs in the secondary sector. After the platoon leader positions the gun and assigns sectors of fire, mark the position of the tripod legs and the limits of the sector of fire. Then trace the outline of the hole and the frontal cover.

The gun is lowered by digging down the firing platforms where the gun will be placed. The platforms must not be so low that the gun cannot be traversed across the sector of fire. Lowering the gun reduces the profile of the gunner when he is shooting and reduces the height of the frontal cover needed. Dig the firing platform first, to lessen the gunner's exposure in case firing is required before the position is completed.

After the firing platforms have been dug, dig the hole, placing the dirt first where frontal cover is needed. The hole is dug deep enough to provide protection and still let the gunner shoot, usually about armpit deep. When the frontal cover is high and thick enough, the rest of the dirt is used to build the flank and rear cover. Three trench-shaped grenade sumps are dug at various points so that grenades can be kicked into them. Overhead cover is constructed following the steps of stage 4.

*Note*: If only a primary sector of fire is given, dig only half the position.

**Machine-Gun Position Preparation**

**Machine-Gun Position (continued)**

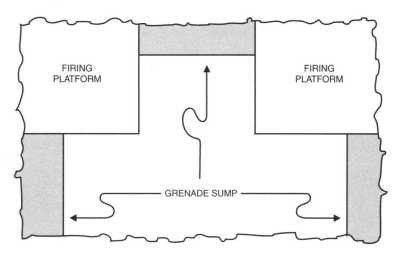

**Machine-Gun Position (continued)**

## JAVELIN POSITION

The Javelin can be employed from initial or completed positions. However, some changes are required:

    1. The gunner must keep the weapon at least 6 inches above the ground to allow room for the stabilizing fins to unfold. The hole is only waist deep to allow the gunner to move while tracking a target. Because the

Javelin gunner must be above ground level, the frontal cover should be high enough to hide his head and, if possible, the backblast of the Javelin. A hole is dug in front of the position for the bipod legs.

2. When the Javelin can be fired in one direction only, the position is adjusted to provide cover and concealment from all other directions, and the Javelin should be fired to the oblique. This protects the position from frontal fire and allows engagement of the target from the flank. Both ends of the launcher must extend out over the edges of the hole.

3. Overhead cover must be built on the flanks. Cover must be large enough for the gunner, the tracker, and the missiles. Overhead cover that allows fire from underneath can be built if the backblast area is clear but must be well camouflaged.

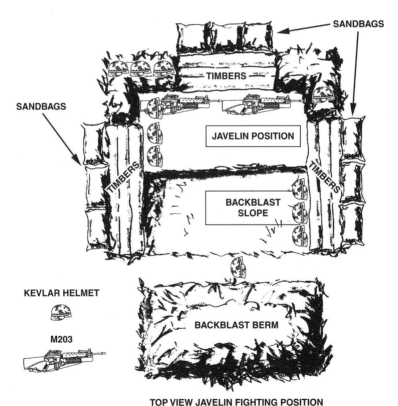

**TOP VIEW JAVELIN FIGHTING POSITION**

**Standard Javelin Position**

**Javelin in an Individual Fighting Position**

4. The Javelin is an important weapon and easy to detect; therefore, selection and preparation of alternate positions have a high priority. When preparing an alternate position, the gunner should select and improve a covered route to it so he can move to the position under fire.

**Flush Position.** The flush position is a hasty position that does not provide overhead protection for the Javelin gunner during firing. The position is basically a hole dug to approximately armpit depth. Overhead cover can be prepared either to the center or the flanks of the position.

**Flush Fighting Position**

## AT4 POSITION

The AT4 can be fired from infantry fighting positions. If the AT4 is to be fired from a two-soldier position, the gunner must ensure the other soldier is not in the backblast area. The soldier should assume the basic standing position, but instead of stepping forward, he leans against the back wall of the fighting position. He should ensure that the rear of the weapon extends beyond the rear of the fighting position.

## MORTAR POSITIONS

The standard dug-in mortar position has three stages of construction:

1. Mortar pit.
2. Personnel shelters.
3. Ammunition bunker.

A dug-in position for 81mm or 60mm mortars is the same as for 4.2-inch mortars, with only slight changes in dimensions. The standard mortar position should be constructed on reasonably flat ground. It can be constructed totally below, partially above, or completely above ground, depending on the time and material available and the composition of the ground.

**Stage 1.** After the general location is selected, the exact baseplate position is marked, and construction of the mortar pit is begun.

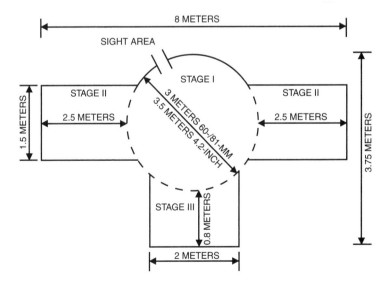

**Mortar Position**
**Three stages of construction: (1) mortar pit;**
**(2) personnel shelters; (3) ammunition bunker**

**Stage 2.** As soon as the mortar pit is completed, and as time allows, personnel shelters with overhead cover are constructed. Firing ports should be built into the personnel shelter and positioned as determined by assigned sectors of fire. There should be a blast barrier at least two sandbags thick separating the personnel shelters from the mortar pit.

**Stage 3.** If time and resources permit, ammunition bunkers are constructed. Each bunker is divided into four sections, one for each type of ammunition: white phosphorus (WP), illumination, final protective fire (FPF), and high-explosive (HE).

Camouflaging the position is done in conjunction with construction through all stages.

## VEHICLE POSITIONS

The deliberate position is constructed in four parts: hull defilade, concealed access ramp or route, hide location, and turret defilade. The access ramp from the hide location to the hull defilade usually provides turret defilade for a vehicle at some point on the ramp. This location is marked to allow the driver to drive to it during daylight and darkness.

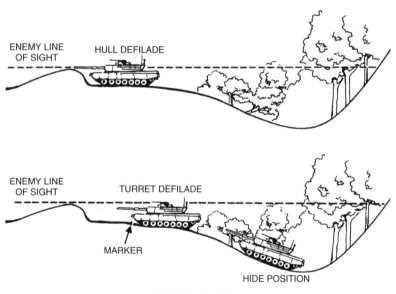

**Vehicle Position**

# 14

# First Aid

It is important for combat leaders to understand that on today's battlefield, first aid begins with the wounded soldier aiding themselves—self-aid should precede buddy aid if at all possible. Buddy aid is not beneficial if soldiers do not begin treating themselves first. Training in skills such as the self-application of tourniquets and hemorrhage control should be mandatory for all soldiers in any unit.

All soldiers should carry individual first aid kits (IFAK) in a predetermined area according to unit SOP and be well versed in all the contents inside the kits. IFAKs should be carried in an area that the wearer can reach in order to administer self-aid and buddy aid. The kit should not be in a location that hinders any movement needed for fighting. Further, all unit members should have training in the medical kit that is carried by the unit medic in case they have to access it themselves during an emergency.

All care should be based on the acronym MARCH—Massive bleeding, Airway, Respirations, Circulation, and Head. The science behind MARCH recognizes a particularly important principle: performing the *correct intervention* at the *correct time* in the continuum of tactical care. A medically correct intervention performed at the *wrong time* in combat may lead to *further casualties*.

## DEATH IN COMBAT
The following are the leading causes of death in combat:

| | |
|---|---|
| 31 percent | Penetrating head trauma |
| 25 percent | Surgically uncorrectable torso trauma |
| 10 percent | Potentially correctable surgical trauma |
| 9 percent | Exsanguination from extremity wounds |
| 7 percent | Mutilating blast trauma |
| 5 percent | Tension pneumothorax |
| 1 percent | Airway problems |

2 percent              Died of wounds after evacuation to an MTF, mostly
                       from infections and complications of shock
*Note*: Over 2,500 soldiers died in Vietnam because of hemorrhage
(bleeding) from extremity wounds (to the arm or leg), even though the soldiers had no other serious injuries.

## Preventable Causes of Combat Death
Preventable causes of combat death include the following. Data is extrapo-
lated from Vietnam to present-day Iraq and Afghanistan.

60 percent             Hemorrhage from extremity wounds
33 percent             Tension pneumothorax
 6 percent             Airway obstruction, e.g. maxillofacial trauma

## COMBAT LIFESAVERS AND TACTICAL COMBAT CASUALTY CARE*
Combat lifesavers (CLS) and tactical combat casualty care (TCCC) training
and providers have proven to be, beyond any doubt, instrumental in dramatically increasing survivability amongst deployed troops during tactical operations (point of wounding). As a leader, ensuring that your unit is properly
trained prior to deployment in both disciplines dramatically increases your
potential for mission success and survivability of those in your charge.
TCCC was developed to bridge the gap between civilian protocol and necessary intervention for individuals and military units deployed in tactical
environments.

Historically, blunt trauma (primarily motor vehicle accidents) is the
major cause of death in the civilian arena. Most medical procedures and
interventions designed for use on the civilian population were based on this,
hence the ABCs (airway, breathing, and circulation) of the civilian first aid
algorithm. In the civilian emergency medical services (EMS) field, medical
personnel are not allowed to assess the patient's airway, breathing, and circulation until the scene is declared "safe." This status is usually determined
by local law enforcement or fire personnel and based on safety parameters
that do not apply in a tactical environment among combat troops.

By comparison, in the tactical and combat arenas the wounding patterns
and causes of death are noticeably and dynamically different. The TCCC
mnemonic MARCH that guides tactical medical care was developed and
implemented specifically to address the leading preventable causes of death
that have been extensively documented throughout military operations, from
Mogadishu to the current actions in the Middle East and Southeast Asia.

---

*Text on CLS and combat casualty care procedures in the field written by Raffaele
Di Giorgio, TCCC.

Differences between civilian and combat trauma include the causes, setting, individuals caring for the casualties, and evacuation time (typically much longer in a combat setting). Under TCCC, tactical medicine is divided into three stages:

1. *Care under fire.* Battlefield care in the "hot zone" while under hostile fire, with only a small aid bag for equipment.
2. *Tactical field care.* Therapy provided once the casualty and unit are out of direct hostile fire, now in the "warm zone"; care is limited to equipment carried into the field.
3. *Casualty evacuation care (CASEVAC).* Treatment provided during evacuation from the immediate scene; care includes a much wider range of equipment and interventions.

It is important to remember that CLS are primarily shooters; *they are not junior medics.* They should be trained to provide lifesaving care as the tactical situation permits, in accordance with TCCC recommendations and guidelines. As leaders, you know what the most common causes of preventable death are and should train all members in your unit to treat these conditions. CLS training and tasks include:

- Rapid casualty assessments.
- Controlling hemorrhages.
- Treating penetrating chest trauma.
- Maintaining the airway.
- Initiating saline locks.
- Packaging casualties for transport.
- Initiating FMC.
- Initiating nine-line MEDEVAC requests.

**Performance Steps**
CLS should follow the following steps in order:
*Step 1. Collect all applicable information needed for MEDEVAC request.*

Determine the grid coordinates for the pickup site
Obtain radio frequency, call sign, and suffix
Obtain the number of patients and precedence
Determine the type of special equipment required
Determine the number and type (litter or ambulatory) of patients
Determine the security of the pickup site
Determine how the pickup site will be marked
Determine patient nationality and status

Obtain pickup site NBC contamination information (normally
   obtained from the senior person or medic). *Note*: Only included
   when contamination exists.
**Step 2. Record the gathered MEDEVAC information using the
authorized brevity codes.**
   *Note*: MEDEVAC information must be encrypted, unless transmitted
over secure communication systems (see step 3b).
   • *Line 1*: Location of pickup site.
   • *Line 2*: Radio frequency, call sign, and suffix.
   • *Line 3*: Number of patients by precedence.
   • *Line 4*: Special equipment required.
   • *Line 5*: Number of patients by type.
   • *Line 6*: Security of pickup site.
   • *Line 7*: Method of marking pickup site.
   • *Line 8*: Patient nationality and status.
   • *Line 9*: NBC contamination.
**Step 3. Transmit the MEDEVAC request.**
   a.) Contact the unit that controls the evacuation assets:
      Make proper contact with the intended receiver.
      Use effective call sign and frequency assignments from the SOI.
      Give the following in the clear: "I have a MEDEVAC request."
         Wait one to three seconds for a response. If no response, repeat
         the statement.
   b.) Transmit the MEDEVAC information in the proper sequence:
      State all line item numbers in clear text.
      The call sign and suffix (if needed) in line 2 may be transmitted
         in the clear.
   *Note*: Line numbers 1–5 must always be transmitted during the initial
contact with the evacuation unit. Lines 6–9 may be transmitted while the aircraft or vehicle is en route.
      Follow the procedure provided in the explanation column of the
         MEDEVAC request format to transmit other required information.
      Pronounce letters and numbers in accordance with appropriate radio
         telephone procedure.
      Take no longer than twenty-five seconds to transmit.
      End the transmission by stating "over."
      Keep the radio on and listen for additional instructions or contact from
         the evacuation unit.

## STANDARD NINE-LINE MEDEVAC REQUEST

*Note*: Lines 1–5 will be given when requesting MEDEVAC. Lines 6–9 can be given when A/C is en route to HLZ/PZ.

- *Line 1.* Six-digit grid coordinate of the pickup site
- *Line 2.* Radio frequency, call sign, and suffix of the requesting unit (encrypted or plain)
- *Line 3.* Number of patients by precedence:
  Urgent—loss of life, limb, or eyesight within two hours
  Urgent surgical—needs surgery to save life within two hours
  Priority—loss of life, limb, or eyesight within four hours
  Routine—evacuate within twenty-four hours (sick or wounded)
  Convenience—for medical convenience only
- *Line 4.* Special equipment needed:
  None
  Hoist (250 feet of usable cable)
  Jungle/forest penetrator
  Semi-rigid litter
  Stokes litter (basket type)
- *Line 5.* Number of patients by type:
  Litter patients
  Ambulatory patients
- *Line 6.* Broken into two situations (war and peace):
  Wartime situation (pick one):
      No enemy troops in the area; Possible enemy troops in the area; Enemy in the area (approach with caution); Enemy troops in the area (armed escort required)
  Peacetime situation (patient information):
      Vital signs; Gunshot, shrapnel, etc.; Broken bones; Illness
- *Line 7.* Method of marking the pickup site
- *Line 8.* Patient nationality and status:
  US military
  US civilian
  Non-US military
  Non-US civilian
- *Line 9.* Broken into two situations (war and peace):
  Wartime: NBC contamination—absorbed radiation dose (RADS) of units in area/hour or type of agent used/know at PZ
  Peacetime: description of the terrain around PZ to aid the pilot in locating site

Above all, *stay calm.* You are in charge—direct others to accomplish the mission.

# TACTICAL COMBAT CASUALTY CARE (TCCC)®
# MIST REPORT

**STABLE**
**UNSTABLE**

**PATIENT:** ______________________ **LAST 4:** __________

**MALE/FEMALE AGE:** _____ **FRIENDLY/ENEMY/UNKNOWN/K-9**

**DATE** (mm/dd/yy): __________ **ONSET/TIME:** __________

## MECHANISM *(circle all that apply)*

| | | |
|---|---|---|
| **BLAST:** Artillery \| Grenade \| IED \| Land-Mine \| RPG | | |
| **BLUNT:** Fall, MVA | **BURN:** 1st \| 2nd \| 3rd | **RAD \| BIO \| CHEM** |
| **PENETRATING:** Frag \| GSW \| Knife \| Crush | | **OTHER:** __________ |

## INJURY

**D** Deform/Discolor
**C** Contusion
**A** Amputation
**P** Penetration
**B** Burn
**T** Tenderness
**L** Laceration
**S** Swelling

TBSA: _____%

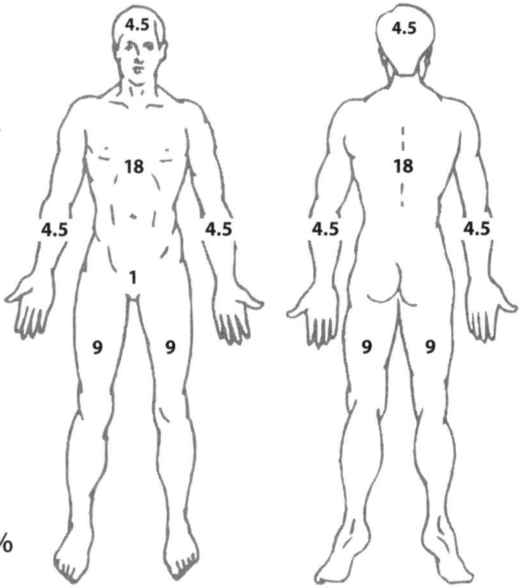
4.5
18
4.5
4.5
1
9
9
4.5
18
4.5
4.5
9
9

**MEDIC:** __________

Tactical Combat Casualty Care (TCCC)® www.ustccc.com

# SYMPTOMS  **RADIAL:** YES | NO     **CAROTIDS:** YES | NO

**MENTALLY ALERT:** YES | NO --- **CONTROLLED:** YES | NO
**AIRWAY:** INTACT | OBSTRUCTED --- **CORRECTED:** YES | NO
**BREATHING:** NORMAL | LABORED --- **CORRECTED:** YES | NO
**PAIN:** HEAD | NECK | CHEST | ABDOMEN | PELVIS | BACK | EXTREMITY

| TIME | | | | |
|------|--|--|--|--|
| AVPU | | | | |
| PULSE | | | | |
| RESP | | | | |
| SPO2 | % | % | % | % |
| BP | | | | |

# TREATMENT                **TQ Time:** _____

**TOURNIQUET ( #      )  ARM:** R | L    **LEG:** R | L
EXTREMITY | JUNCTIONAL | PRESSURE | HEMOSTATIC
WOUNDPACK | SPLINTING | NPA | KING | ENDOTUBE | CRIC | CROC

**CHEST SEAL ( #      )** NEEDLED | CHESTTUBE
IV | IO        NS | HEX        500 ml | 1000 ml | 1500 ml

**PAIN:** FENTANYL _____ time _____ dose _____ route

MORPHINE _____ time _____ dose _____ route

KETAMINE _____ time _____ dose _____ route

**ABX:** INVANZ | AVELOX _____ time _____ dose _____ route

**TXA:** _____ time _____ dose _____ route

**OTHER:**
COMBAT PILL PACK | EYE SHIELD (R/L) | SPLINT | HYPOTHERMIA PREVENTION

_____ drug _____ time _____ dose _____ route

_____ drug _____ time _____ dose _____ route

**Tactical Combat Casualty Care (TCCC)®**        www.ustccc.com

# ⑨ LINE MEDEVAC REQUEST

**LINE 1. Location of the Pick-Up Site (GRID)**

**LINE 2. Radio Frequency | Call Sign | Suffix**

**LINE 3. Number of Patients (by Precedence):**

| | A - Urgent | | C - Priority | | E - Convenience |
|---|---|---|---|---|---|
| _____ | | _____ | | _____ | |
| _____ | B - Urgent Surgical | _____ | D - Routine | | |

**LINE 4. Special Equipment Required:**

A - None        C - Extraction Equipment
B - Hoist        D - Ventilator

**LINE 5. Number of Patients (by Type):**

_____ A - Litter     _____ B - Ambulatroy

**LINE 6. Security at Pick-Up Site:**

N - No enemy troops in area
P - Possible enemy troops in area (approach with caution)
E - Enemy troops in area (approach with caution)
X - Enemy troops in area (armed escort required)
*NOTE: In peacetime - number and types of wounds, injuries, and illnesses*

**LINE 7. Method of Marking Pick-Up Site:**

A - Panels            C - Smoke Signal        E - Other
B - Pyrotechnic Signal    D - None

**LINE 8. Patient Nationality and Status:**

A - US Military      C - Non-US Military     E - EPW
B - US Civilian      D - Non-US Civilian

**LINE 9. NBC Contamination:**

N - Nuclear        B - Biological        C - Chemical
*NOTE: In peacetime - terrain description of pick-up site*

*Lines 1 through 5 must always be transmitted during the initial contact with the evacuation unit. Lines 6 through 9 may be transmitted while the aircraft or vehicle is en route, along with the MIST Report.*

**Tactical Combat Casualty Care (TCCC)®**
www.ustccc.com

# TACTICAL COMBAT CASUALTY CARE (TCCC)®
# REFERENCE CARD
### 10/28/13 Guidelines

## BASIC MANAGEMENT PLAN FOR CARE UNDER FIRE

◆ Return fire and take cover.

◆ Direct or expect casualty to remain engaged as a combatant if appropriate.

◆ Direct casualty to move to cover and apply self-aid if able.

◆ Try to keep the casualty from sustaining additional wounds.

◆ Casualties should be extricated from burning vehicles or buildings and moved to places of relative safety. Do what is necessary to stop the burning process.

◆ Airway management is generally best deferred until the Tactical Field Care phase.

◆ Stop life-threatening external hemorrhage if tactically feasible:
- Direct casualty to control hemorrhage by self-aid if able.
- Use a tourniquet for hemorrhage that is anatomically amenable to tourniquet application.
- Apply the tourniquet proximal to the bleeding site, over the uniform, tighten, and move the casualty to cover.

## BASIC MANAGEMENT PLAN FOR TACTICAL FIELD CARE

◆ Casualties with an altered mental status should be disarmed immediately.

◆ Airway Management

a. Unconscious casualty without airway obstruction:
- Chin lift or jaw thrust maneuver
- Nasopharyngeal airway
- Place casualty in the recovery position

b. Casualty with airway obstruction or impending airway obstruction:
- Chin lift or jaw thrust maneuver
- Nasopharyngeal airway
- Allow casualty to assume any position that best protects the airway; to include sitting up
- Place unconscious casualty in the recovery position

**Tactical Combat Casualty Care (TCCC)®**
www.ustccc.com

## COMBAT INJURIES
The following are essential tasks for tactical combat casualty care in the field.

### Tourniquets
Understand the difference between mild, moderate, and severe bleeding. Know how to identify external severe bleeding (arterial bleeding).
*   Direct the casualty to control hemorrhage by self-aid if possible.
*   Use a tourniquet that you have had previous training on and that is properly sized to fit the extremity.
*   Apply the tourniquet proximal to the bleeding, over the uniform.
*   Tighten the tourniquet until bleeding has ceased, then move the casualty to cover. You may need to add an additional tourniquet above the first tourniquet to control bleeding.

*Note*: Do not place the tourniquet directly over the knee or elbow, holster, or cargo pocket containing items. Tourniquets should not be used if the wound is located in the neck, abdomen, groin, or armpit.

### Wounded Carry Techniques
There are several different carries for injured soldiers. The conditions, manpower, and tactical situation dictate which you should use.
*   One-person drag, with or without line.
*   Two-person drag, with or without line.
*   Hawes carry—the wounded soldier wraps his arms around your neck from behind; lean forward to pick up and carry him.
*   Fireman's carry—the wounded soldier is carried over your shoulder.

### C-Spine Stabilization
Penetrating head and neck injuries do not require C-spine stabilization, as the spinal cord is either already compromised or is in less danger than normally caused by blunt trauma.

Injuries from blunt trauma, such as motor vehicle accidents, fast roping injuries, or falls greater than the height of the individual, may require C-spine stabilization.

*Note*: Apply stabilization only if the danger of hostile fire does not constitute a greater threat.

### Level of Consciousness
When possible, determine the casualty's level of consciousness using the AVPU system:
*   A—casualty is *alert* and knows who he is, the date, where he is, etc.

- V—the casualty is not alert, but does respond to *verbal* commands.
- P—the casualty responds to *pain* but not to verbal commands.
- U—the casualty is *unresponsive* (unconscious).

Ask questions that require more than a "yes" or "no" answer. Examples of questions include: "What is your name?" "What is the date?" and "Where are we?" Recheck the casualty's level of consciousness about every fifteen minutes to determine if his condition has changed.

**Airways**

Assess and secure the casualty's airway. If the casualty is conscious, able to speak, and not in respiratory distress, no airway intervention is needed.

If the casualty is unconscious, perform the following:

- Use a *head-tilt/chin-lift or jaw thrust* to open the airway. The head-tilt/chin-lift method is the normal way to open the casualty's airway. Use the jaw thrust method if you suspect the casualty has suffered a spinal injury.
- Check the casualty for breathing. While maintaining the casualty's airway (head-tilt/chin-lift or jaw thrust), place your ear over the casualty's mouth and nose with your face toward the casualty's chest. Look for the rise and fall of the casualty's chest and abdomen. Listen for sounds of breathing. Feel for his breath on the side of your face. If breathing is not present, begin rescue breathing.
- If the casualty is breathing on his own, use a nasopharyngeal airway (NPA) to maintain the airway.
- If the casualty has no additional injuries, roll the casualty into the recovery position (on his side). This allows accumulated blood and mucus to drain from the mouth instead of choking him.

**Head-Tilt/Chin-Lift Method**

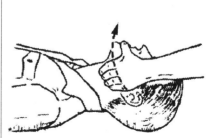

**Thrust Method**

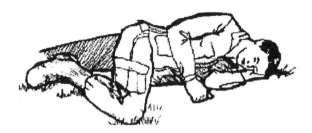

**Unconscious Casualty Placed in the Recovery Position**

*Nasopharyngeal Airway.* The nasopharyngeal airway (NPA) is used to maintain the airway when the casualty is breathing on his own. It is well tolerated by conscious patients.
- Lube before inserting.
- Insert at a 90-degree angle to the face, not along the axis of the nose.
- If the patient gags, withdraw slightly.
- Tape in place.

*Note*: Avoid the use of oral pharyngeal airways on a conscious patient as they are easily dislodged and cause the casualty to gag.

## Chest

Assess and treat the casualty for chest injuries:
- Expose the chest and check for equal rise and fall. Remove the minimum of clothing required to expose and treat injuries. Protect the casualty from the environment (heat and cold) as much as possible.
- Examine the chest for wounds. Check for both entrance and exit (sucking chest) wounds.
- Immediately seal any penetrating injuries to the chest with airtight material. Sealing the wound keeps air from entering. If air can freely enter through the wound, the casualty's lung may collapse. Use a three-sided seal (one side of airtight material left untaped), which prevents air from entering but allows trapped air to escape. You can also use an approved manufactured chest seal.
- Monitor the casualty. Watch carefully for progressive severe respiratory distress (breathing becomes more labored and faster). If respiration becomes progressively worse, assume tension pneumothorax (see next section).

*Caution*: Only perform needle chest decompression (see next section) on a casualty with a penetrating (sucking) chest wound.

If the casualty has been treated for an open chest wound, position or transport him with the affected (injured) side down, if possible. The body pressure acts to "splint" the affected side.

*Open Pneumothorax.* All open and/or sucking chest wounds should be treated immediately. The first course of treatment should be a vented (three-sided) chest seal, or a non-vented chest seal if a vented one is not available. If neither of these is available, substitute any material that will not allow air to flow through it, such as petroleum gauze or the wrapper, or latex gloves.

If the casualty develops increasing respiratory distress, hypotension and a tension pneumothorax should be suspected. Treat by burping or removing the dressing.

If there is no relief of symptoms, follow the steps below to perform a needle decompression:

1. Locate and secure a 14-gauge catheter.
2. If not already done, remove any outer clothing and expose the chest area completely.
3. The needle should enter at the second intercostal space in the mid-clavicular line, two to three fingers' width below the collarbone and in line above the nipple on the same side of the chest as the injury.

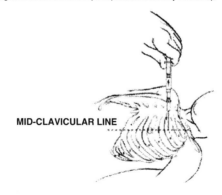

Locating the second intercostal space (wound on casualty's left side).

Locating the mid-clavicular line (wound on casualty's left side).

4. Needle entry should be at a 90-degree angle directly over the third rib. You can touch the third rib and then slide the needle upward and over.
5. Once in place, remove the needle, leaving the catheter, and continue to monitor the casualty.
6. A lateral approach from the side and under the arm may be faster and safer given body-armor configuration and the ability to reassess. This would be performed at the intercostal space at the axillary (mid-side) line. Use the same technique as you would for the second intercostal space.

## HEAT INJURIES

Heat injuries are disabling to varying degrees and can be fatal. They occur when water and salt lost in sweat are not replaced. Heat injuries are especially liable to occur in individuals who are not acclimatized (accustomed) to the heat, are overweight, have fevers (sunburn, infection, or reaction to immunizations), or are already dehydrated (have insufficient water in their bodies) because of diarrhea, alcohol consumption, or simply not having drunk enough water.

### Sweating

The evaporation of sweat is the only way the body can cool itself when the temperature is above 95 degrees Fahrenheit. Evaporation is less efficient and more water intake is required in the humid jungle than in the dry desert. Soldiers working hard in the heat can lose and need to replace more than 3 gallons of water and salt.

*Water.* It's best to replace water as it is lost—soldiers should drink when thirsty. There is no benefit in withholding water until later. It is impossible to train soldiers to get by on less water than the amount required to replace that lost in sweat. Water requirements can be reduced only if sweating is reduced by working during the cooler hours of evening, night, and early morning.

*Salt.* Extra salt is required when soldiers are sweating heavily. Salt tablets should not be used to prevent heat injury, however. Usually eating field rations or liberal salting of the garrison diet provides enough salt to replace what is lost.

### Heat Cramps

Heat cramps are cramps of stomach, arm, or leg muscles. They occur when a person sweats a lot and has not consumed extra water.

**Heat Exhaustion**
A victim of heat exhaustion may have a headache and be dizzy, faint, and weak. He has cool, pale (gray), moist (sweaty) skin and loss of appetite. Move him to a shady area or improvise shade and have him lie down. Loosen or remove clothing and boots, pour water on him, and fan him if it is hot. Elevate his legs and have him slowly drink at least one canteen of water. The patient should not participate in further strenuous activity and should be evacuated if symptoms persist.

**Heatstroke**
Heatstroke is a medical emergency and can be fatal if not treated promptly and correctly. It is caused by failure of the body's cooling mechanisms. Inadequate sweating is a factor. The casualty's skin is flushed, hot, and dry. He may experience dizziness, confusion, headaches, seizures, and nausea, and his respiration and pulse may be weak. Cool the casualty immediately by moving him to a shaded area. Remove outer clothing, pour water on him or immerse him in water, and fan him to permit the cooling effect of evaporation. Massage his skin, elevate his legs, and have him slowly drink water. Get him to a medical facility as soon as possible.

**COLD INJURIES**
Cold injuries occur when the body loses heat. They can cause the loss of toes, fingers, feet, ears, and so on.

**Frostbite**
If body heat is lost quickly and the tissues actually freeze, the injury is called frostbite. Frostbite usually affects the face, hands, or feet. There may be no pain. Frostbitten parts of the body become grayish or white and lose feeling. Use the buddy system to watch each other for signs of frostbite.

Treat frostbite by removing the casualty's clothing (boots, gloves, socks) and thawing the area by placing it next to a warm part of his or somebody else's body. Warm (not hot) water may be used. Remove constrictive clothing that interferes with circulation. Do not rewarm by walking, massage, exposure to open fire, cold water, or rubbing with snow. After the part has been warmed, protect it from further injury by covering it lightly with a blanket or dry clothing. Do not use ointments or other medications.

**Trenchfoot (Immersion Foot)**
Trenchfoot or immersion foot resembles frostbite but occurs when the feet are exposed to cold and wet conditions. (See the foot care section below.)

## Prevention of Cold Injuries

Cold injuries can be prevented by proper leadership and by training in conserving body heat.

Leadership—command interest—is essential. Personnel must be taught how to prevent cold injuries. Reduce their exposure to cold, wet, and wind when possible. Rotate individuals and units to warming tents. Provide changes of dry clothing, hot food, and drinks.

Individuals can take the following steps:

- Do not stand in wet positions—build them up with branches and the like.
- Carry extra dry socks and change after marching or standing.
- Remove cold and wet boots and socks before going to sleep.
- Sleep back to back with a buddy to prevent loss of body heat.
- Massage the feet several times daily, especially when changing socks.
- Do not touch bare metal with bare skin.

To dress properly, remember C-O-L-D:

C: Keep *clean*. Dirty clothing has less insulating quality.

O: Avoid *overheating*. Overheating causes sweating, and clothing wet from sweat causes cold injury.

L: Wear *loose* clothing in *layers*. Warm air is trapped between layers and acts as insulation. Tight clothing, boots, and gloves leave no room for a warm air layer or for the exercise of fingers and toes and may act as a tourniquet to shut off circulation.

D: Keep *dry*. Dry clothing retains heat; wet clothing conducts heat away from the body.

## SNAKEBITES

Keep the bitten person quiet and do not let him walk or run. Kill the snake, if possible, and keep it for identification. If the bite is on an extremity, do not elevate the limb; keep it level with the body. If the bite is on an arm or leg, place a constricting band (narrow gauze bandage) one to two finger widths above and below the bite. If the bite is on a hand or foot, place the band above the wrist or ankle.

The band should be tight enough to stop the flow of blood near the skin, but not so tight as to interfere with circulation. It should not have a tourniquet-like effect. Get the casualty to medical treatment as soon as possible.

## FOOT CARE

### Socks

Wash and dry socks daily. Start each day with a fresh pair. After crossing a wet area, dry your feet, put on foot powder, and change socks if the situation permits. Avoid worn or tight-fitting socks. Carry an extra pair in a pack or inside the shirt.

**Blisters**
Wash the area, open and drain the blister, and cover the area with adhesive tape.

**Athlete's Foot**
Keep feet clean and dry. Use foot powder.

# 15

# Combat Intelligence

One of the most important aspects of patrolling operations is the gathering of up-to-date intelligence. This chapter covers the standard method of what information to collect and how to report it.

## REPORTING
All information should be quickly, completely, and accurately reported. Use the SALUTE report format for reporting and recording information:
>     Size (how many enemy?)
>     Activity (what where they doing?)
>     Location (enemy's grid location)
>     Unit/uniform (what where they wearing?)
>     Time (exact time)
>     Equipment (what weapons and equipment?)
>     A vital aspect of the intelligence report are any tactics, techniques, and procedures (TTPs) that the enemy is using in the patrol area.

## FIELD SKETCHES AND PHOTOGRAPHY
When reporting information, include a sketch or photo if possible. Limit the sketch to aspects of military importance, such as targets, objectives, obstacles, sector limits, or troop dispositions and locations. Notes should be annotated to explain the drawing.

Photos likewise need to be annotated if possible. Attach explanations to each photograph, along with the location where the photo was taken.

## ENEMY PRISONERS OF WAR
Captured persons or EPWs should be treated IAW the Geneva Convention and handled by the 5-S rule: search, silence, segregate, safeguard, and speed to the rear.

*Search* EPWs as soon as they are captured. Take their weapons and papers, except for ID cards and protective masks. Give them a written receipt for any personal property and documents taken. When searching an EPW, have one man guard him while another searches the prisoner. The searcher must not get between the guard and the EPW. To search an EPW, have him spread-eagle against a tree or wall, or get him into a push-up position with his knees on the ground.

*Silence* EPWs and do not let them talk to each other. This keeps them from planning escapes and cautioning each other on security. Report anything an EPW says or does.

*Segregate* EPWs into groups by sex and into subgroups such as officers, enlisted, civilians, and political figures. This keeps the leaders from organizing escape efforts.

*Safeguard* EPWs when taking them to the rear. Do not let anyone abuse them. Watch out for escape attempts. Do not let EPWs bunch up, spread out too far, or start diversions.

*Speed* EPWs to the rear. Turn them over to your leader, who will assemble and move them to the rear for questioning by the S-2.

## Objective Questioning
The following is a list of thirteen questions that a leader can use on an objective to begin the process of determining what persons are of interest. These questions should be the first ones you ask:

What is your name?
What is your father's name?
What is your grandfather's name?
What tribe/ethnicity are you?
What are you doing here?
What are the names of the other people here?
What tribe/ethnicity are the other people?
Where are the other people from?
Why are the other people here?
Where are they going?
How long have the other people been here?
Are there any weapons or explosives here?
Where are any insurgent/anticoalition forces?

## Sensitive Site Exploitation
The following is a processing checklist that will aid in the organization of the sensitive site exploitation (SSE) of a target.

| SSE CHECKLIST | | | |
|---|---|---|---|
| Building found | Floor | Room | Area |
| Full name | | | |
| Son of | | | |
| Tribe/ethnicity | | | |
| Height | Weight | Age | Beard—Y/N |
| Scars | Marks | Tattoo | Disfigure |
| Names of relatives present | | | |
| Names of affiliates/friends present | | | |
| Household status | | | |
| Property | Keys | Phone—Y/N | ID card |
| Documents | | | |
| Village status | | | |
| Occupation | | | |
| Phone number(s) | | | |
| Insurgent affiliation | Y/N | What group | What area |
| Affiliated property | | | |
| Government affiliations | Y/N | What group | What area |
| Weapons | Y/N | Type | |

**Identification**
Before evacuating an EPW, attach a tag to him showing the date and time of capture, place, capturing unit, and circumstances. Use the above template to coordinate and track EPWs.

## HANDLING CAPTURED DOCUMENTS AND EQUIPMENT
Enemy documents and equipment are good sources of information. Documents may be official (maps, orders, records, or photos) or personal (letters or diaries).

If such items are not handled properly, the information in them may become outdated. Give them to your leader quickly. Tag each item with information on when and where it was captured. If it was found on a PW, include the PW's name on the tag.

# 16

# Individual Movement and Security

As a member of a fire team you may have to get close to an enemy position using the correct individual tactical fire and movement techniques dictated by METT-TC. All movement needs to be coordinated with other team or squad members in order for each of you to provide cover for one another.

## MOVEMENT SKILLS
Observe the following practices during movement:
- Camouflage yourself and your equipment.
- Tape your dog tags to each other and to the chain to prevent rattling. Tape or pad loose parts of your weapon and equipment so they do not rattle or get snagged. Jump up and down. Listen for rattles.
- Do not carry unnecessary equipment.
- Stop, look, and listen before moving. Be especially alert when birds or animals are alarmed, as this is a sign the enemy may be nearby. Look for your next position before leaving your current one. Look for covered and concealed routes on which to move.
- Change direction from time to time when moving through tall grass.
- Use battlefield noises to conceal your movement noises.
- Cross roads and trails at places that have the most cover and concealment (large culverts, low spots, curves, or bridges).
- Avoid steep slopes and places with loose dirt or stones.
- Avoid cleared, open areas and tops of hills and ridges.

## INDIVIDUAL MOVEMENT TECHNIQUES
After analysis or orders, determine the correct individual movement technique(s) for each individual movement forward.

## Low Crawl

Select the low crawl when the route provides cover or concealment less than 1 foot high, visibility provides the enemy good observation, and speed is not required. The proper way to do the low crawl is (A) to keep your body as flat as possible to the ground. Hold your weapon by grasping the sling at the upper sling swivel, letting the handguard rest on your forearm and the butt of the weapon drag on the ground, thus keeping the muzzle off the ground. Move forward (B) by pushing both arms forward while pulling your right leg forward, and then pull with both arms while pushing with your right leg (C). Continue these push-pull movements until you reach your next position, changing your pushing leg frequently to avoid fatigue.

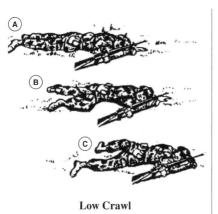

Low Crawl

High Crawl

## High Crawl

Select the high crawl when the route provides cover and concealment, poor visibility reduces enemy observation, and speed is required but the terrain and vegetation are suitable only for the low crawl. The proper way to do the high crawl is to keep your body off the ground while resting your weight on your forearms and lower legs. Cradle your weapon in your arms, keeping its muzzle off the ground. Keep your knees well behind your buttocks so they stay low and move forward by alternately advancing your right elbow and left knee, and left elbow and right knee.

## Rush

Select the rush when you must cross open areas and time is critical. The proper way to do the rush is to move from your firing position by rolling or crawling because the enemy may have your current position identified. Start from the prone position and select your next position by slowly raising your head. Lower your head while drawing your arms into your body, keeping your elbows down, and pulling your right leg forward. Raise your body in one movement by straightening your arms and springing to your feet, stepping off with either foot. Run to the next position, keeping your distance short and trying not to stay up longer than three to five seconds. At your position, plant your feet and fall forward by sliding your right hand down to the heel of the butt of your weapon and break your fall with the butt of your weapon. Roll or crawl to a covered or concealed firing position.

**Rush**

### STEALTH
To move with stealth, use the following procedures:
1. Hold your rifle at port arms (ready position).
2. While stepping, make your footing sure and solid by keeping your body's weight on the leading foot.
3. Raise the moving leg high to clear brush or grass.
4. Gently let the moving foot down toe first, with your body's weight on the rear leg.

5. Lower the heel of the moving foot after the toe is in a solid place.
6. Shift your body's weight and balance to the forward foot before moving the rear foot.
7. Take short steps to help maintain balance.

## NIGHT MOVEMENT

When moving through dense vegetation, avoid making noise. Hold your weapon in one hand and keep the other hand forward, feeling for obstructions.

When going into the prone position:

1. Hold your rifle with one hand and crouch slowly.
2. Feel the ground with your free hand to make sure it is clear of mines, trip wires, or other hazards.
3. Lower your knees one at a time, until your body's weight is on both knees and your free hand.
4. Shift your weight to your free hand and opposite knee.
5. Raise your free leg up and back, and lower it gently to that side.
6. Roll quietly into a prone position.

When crawling at night:

1. Crawl on your hands and knees.
2. Hold your rifle in your firing hand.
3. Use your nonfiring hand to feel for and make clear spots for your hands and knees to move to.
4. Move your hands and knees to those spots and put them down softly.

## FLARES

If you are caught in the light of a ground flare, move quickly out of the lighted area. The enemy knows where the flare is and will be ready to fire into that area. Move well away from the lighted area, and look for other team members. If you hear the firing of an aerial flare while you are moving, hit the ground (behind cover, if possible) while the flare is rising and before it illuminates the area.

The sudden light of a flare may temporarily blind both you and the enemy. To protect your night vision, close one eye while the flare is burning.

If you are caught in the light of an aerial flare and you can easily blend with the background (in a forest), freeze in place until the flare burns out. If caught in the open, immediately crouch low or lie down.

## SECURITY MEASURES

The enemy must not get information about your operations. This means that you and your fellow soldiers must do the following:

• Practice camouflage principles and techniques.

- Practice noise and light discipline.
- Practice field sanitation.
- Use proper radiotelephone procedures.
- Use the challenge and password properly.
- Refrain from taking personal letters or pictures into combat areas.
- Refrain from keeping diaries in combat areas.
- Be careful when discussing military affairs.
- Use only authorized codes.
- Abide by the Code of Conduct.
- Report any soldier or civilian who is believed to be serving or sympathetic with the enemy.
- Report anyone who tries to get information about US operations.
- Destroy all maps or important documents if capture is imminent.

## SURVIVAL

Continuous operations and fast-moving battles increase your chances of becoming separated from your unit. Your mission is to rejoin your unit. Survival is the action of staying alive in the field with limited resources. You must survive when you become separated from your unit, are evading the enemy, or are a prisoner.

### Evasion

Evasion is the action you take to stay out of the hands of the enemy. Your best chance of success is when the escape and evasion (E&E) is preplanned. The planning of E&E is similar to that of an operations order and takes care and time to do properly. This may not be available to the small unit operating in a theater of combat, however. Properly following the coordination checklist will give you the knowledge you will need in order to know where closest friendly forces are and how to link up with them. There are several courses of action you may take:

- Stay in your current position and wait for friendly troops to find you. This may be a good course of action if you are sure that friendly troops will continue to operate in the area, and if there are a lot of enemy units in the area.
- Break out to a friendly area. This may be a good course of action if you know where a friendly area is, and if the enemy is widely dispersed.
- Move farther into enemy territory to temporarily conduct guerrilla-type operations. This is a short-term course of action to be taken only when other courses of action are not feasible. This may be a good course of action when the enemy area is known to be lightly held or when there is a good chance of linking up with friendly guerrillas.

- Combine two or more of the above. For example, you may stay in your current area until the enemy moves out of the area and then break out to a friendly area.

**Enemy**

There may be times when you will have to kill, stun, or capture an enemy soldier without alerting other enemy in the area. At such times, a rifle or pistol makes too much noise; you will need a silent weapon, such as the bayonet, the garotte (a choke wire or cord with handles), or an improvised club.

**RESISTANCE**

The Code of Conduct (found at the front of this book) is an expression of the ideals and principles that traditionally have guided and strengthened American servicemembers. It prescribes the manner in which every soldier of the US Armed Forces must conduct himself when captured or faced with the possibility of capture. You should never surrender of your own free will. Likewise, a leader should never surrender the soldiers under his command while they still have the means to resist. If captured, you must continue to resist in every way you can, remembering the following:

- Make every effort to escape and to help others to escape.
- Do not accept special favors from the enemy.
- Do not give your word not to escape.
- Do nothing that will harm a fellow prisoner.
- Give no information except name, rank, social security number, and date of birth.
- Do not answer any questions other than those concerning your name, rank, social security number, and date of birth.

**ESCAPE**

Escape is the action you take to get away from the enemy if you are captured. The best time for you to escape is right after you are captured. You will probably be in your best physical condition at that time. The following are other reasons for making an early escape:

- Friendly fire or air strikes may cause enough confusion and disorder to provide a chance of escape.
- The first guards you have probably will not be as well trained as guards farther back.
- Some of the first guards may be walking wounded who are distracted by their own condition.
- You know something about the area where you are captured and may know the location of nearby friendly units.

The way you escape depends on what you can think of to fit the situation. The only general rules are to *escape early* and *escape when the enemy is distracted.*

Once you escape, it may not be easy to contact friendly troops, even when you know where they are. You should contact a friendly unit as you would if you were a member of a lost patrol. Time your movement so that you pass through enemy units at night and arrive at a friendly unit at dawn. A good way to make contact is to find a ditch or shallow hole to hide in where you have cover from both friendly and enemy fire. At dawn, attract the attention of the friendly unit by an action such as waving a white cloth, shouting, or showing a panel. When the friendly unit has been alerted, shout who you are and what your situation is, and ask for permission to move toward the unit.

## NIGHT VISION GOGGLES

Units that train individuals in the use of night vision goggles (NVGs) gain an incredible advantage that will allow them to dominate night operations, especially against a lesser-equipped enemy. From the 1960s until recently, the military has gone from Generation I to the very sophisticated Generation IV NVGs. The newer Generation IVs see farther under equal light conditions, provide a clearer picture with greater detail, and make sighting more precise. Some of the older and newer reconnaissance, surveillance, and target acquisition (RSTA) devices or NVGs available today include the following.

### AN/PVS-7A and AN/PVS-7B Night Vision Systems

The AN/PVS-7A and AN/PVS-7B are self-contained night vision systems worn on the head (harnesses differ slightly) or handheld. They provide improved night vision capabilities using available light from the sky and moon. The goggles enable the user to perform normal tasks such as reading, walking, driving, or surveillance during times of darkness. The goggles may be used with or without the standard battle helmet and provide capabilities for all infantry tasks. The 7B version has some improvements over the 7A version. For example, the 7B version has an effective range of 300 meters under optimal conditions while the 7A version has an effective range of 100 meters.

### AN/TAS-5 Dragon Thermal Night Vision Sight

This is a passive thermal imagery system with a range of 1,200 meters.

**AN/PVS-7A/B
Night Vision System**

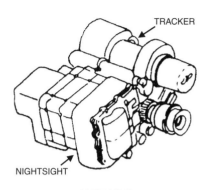

**AN/TAS-5
Dragon Thermal Sight**

**AN/VVS-2
Night Vision Driver's Viewer**

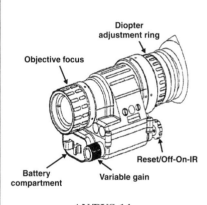

**AN/PVS-14
Monocular NVD**

## AN/VVS-2 Night Vision Driver's Viewer

This image-intensification device is mounted in the Bradley driver's station and has a range in excess of 150 meters. It can observe rounds fired from the 25mm gun and the 7.62mm coaxial machine gun out to greater ranges.

## AN/PVS-14 Monocular NVG

The AN/PVS-14 is either a handheld, helmet-mounted, head-mounted, or weapon-mounted night vision device (NVD) that enables walking, driving, weapon firing, short-range surveillance, map reading, vehicle maintenance, or administering first aid in moonlight and starlight. Each unit allows for vertical adjustment (using head straps), fore and aft adjustment, objective lens focus, and eyepiece focus.

The device is also equipped with an infrared light-emitting source with a variable gain control. It has a magnification of 1× or 3× with an optional magnifier. The AN/PVS-14 amplifies available ambient star, moon, or reflected light to produce an intensified image in the proper perspective.

## AN/PAS-13 Medium/Heavy Weapon Thermal Sight

The AN/PAS-13 (V2) medium weapon thermal sight (MWTS) and the AN/PAS-13 (V3) heavy weapon thermal sight (HWTS) are silent, light-weight, compact, and durable battery-powered infrared-imaging sensors that operate with low battery consumption. The MWTS has a 3.3× magnification and the HWTS has a 10× magnification. When firing your weapon with either WTS, the fundamentals of marksmanship are the same as with each weapon system using the AN/PVS-4, minus certain techniques for the M203 and M2 HB .50-caliber.

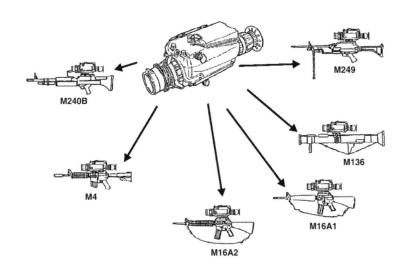

**AN/PAS-13(V2)**
**Medium Weapon Thermal Sight (MWTS)**

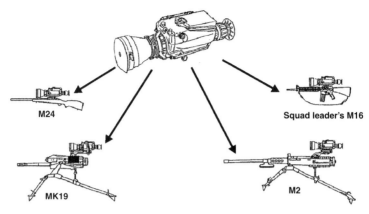

**AN/PAS-13 (V3)**
**Heavy Weapon Thermal Sight (HWTS)**

### AN/TVS-5 NVD

The AN/TVS-5 is a portable, battery-operated electro-optical instrument used for observation and aimed fire of weapons at night. It amplifies reflected light such as moonlight, starlight, and sky glow so that the viewed scene becomes clearly visible to the operator. The only two weapons that use the AN/TVS-5 are the M2 HB .50-caliber machine gun and the MK19 grenade launcher. By using this device, the gunner can observe the area and detect and engage any suitable target. It has a magnification: 5.6× and range of 1,000 to 1,200 meters for vehicle targets (under ideal conditions).

### AN/PVS-10 Night Vision Sniper Scope

The AN/PVS-10 night vision sniper scope, referred to as the sniper night scope (SNS), is an integrated weapon sight that provides both day and night operation in a single sight. The M3A scope is the primary day sight that snipers employ and all sniper marksmanship training is based on this. The scope has an effective range of 800 meters during the day and 600 meters at night.

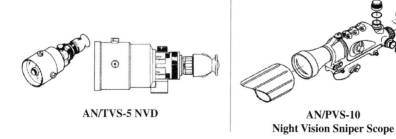

**AN/TVS-5 NVD**

**AN/PVS-10**
**Night Vision Sniper Scope**

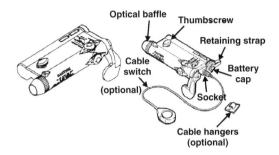

**AN/PAQ-4C**
**Laser Aiming Light**

### AN/PAQ-4C Laser Aiming Light
The AN/PAQ-4C aiming light projects an infrared laser beam that cannot be seen with the eye but can be seen with NVDs. This aiming light works with the AN/PVS-7B/D series goggles and AN/PVS-14. The AN/PAQ-4C mounts on various weapons with mounting brackets and adapters. It has a range of 600 meters or beyond, dependent on the light level and NVD used for observation.

### AN/PEQ-2A Laser Aiming Light
The AN/PEQ-2A is a Class IIIb laser that emits a highly collimated beam of infrared light for precise aiming of the weapon, as well as a separate infrared illumination beam with adjustable focus. Both beams can be zeroed to the weapon and each other, and can be operated individually or in combination. The AN/PEQ-2A is for use in conjunction with NVDs and can be used as either a handheld illuminator/pointer or weapon mounted with included

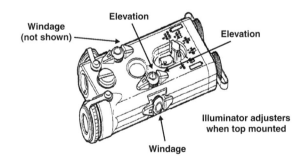

**AN/PEQ-2A**
**Laser Aiming Light**

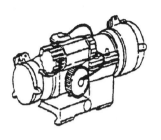
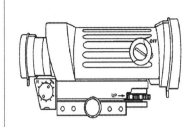

**M68 Close Combat Optic** | **M145 Telescope**

brackets and accessory mounts. In weapon-mounted mode, the AN/PEQ-2A can be used to accurately direct fire as well as to illuminate and designate areas and targets.

### M68 Close Combat Optic

The M68 Close Combat Optic (CCO) sight is a reflex (nontelescopic) sight. It uses a red aiming reference (collimated dot) and is designed for use with both eyes open. At ranges beyond 50 meters, the red dot remains fixed on the target no matter what angle is used, and the gunner fires at the target. No centering is required. The best ranges fall between close combat and 300 meters.

### M145 Telescope

The M145 telescope is a fixed 3.4×, 28mm optical sight designed to engage targets accurately out to 1,200 meters. The optical sight weighs 24 ounces, is extremely rugged, has excellent vision in low light levels, and provides for rapid target acquisition. The M145 straight telescope mounts directly to the mounting rail on the M249 and M240B machine guns.

# 17

# Nuclear, Biological, and Chemical (NBC) Warfare

NBC weapons can cause casualties, destroy or disable equipment, restrict the use of terrain, and disrupt operations. The infantry platoon must be prepared to operate on an NBC-contaminated battlefield without degradation of the platoon's overall effectiveness.

## CHEMICAL AGENTS
Chemical agents can cover large areas and may be delivered as a liquid, vapor, or aerosol. They can be disseminated by artillery, mortars, rockets, missiles, aircraft spray, bombs, land mines, and covert means. The following table provides the characteristics of and treatment for exposure to chemical agents.

## BIOLOGICAL AGENTS
Protective measures against biological attack include up-to-date immunizations, good hygiene, area sanitation, physical conditioning, and water purification. Toxins and pathogens are the two types of biological agents. *Toxins* are poisonous substances produced from living organisms. They can be synthesized (artificially produced) and can mirror the symptoms of nerve agents. They are destroyed by the sun after about eight to twelve hours. *Pathogens* are infectious agents such as bacteria, viruses, and rickettsiae that cause disease in man and animals. Pathogens have a delayed reaction (incubation from one to twenty-one days) and can multiply and overcome natural defenses. When used in vectors (disease-infected insects), they can circumvent protective clothing and prolong hazards.

## CHARACTERISTICS OF CHEMICAL AGENTS

| AGENT | Nerve | Blood | Blister | Choking |
|---|---|---|---|---|
| PROTECTION | Mask and BDO* | Mask and BDO* | Mask | Mask |
| DETECTION | M8A1, M256A1, chemical agent monitor (CAM), M8 and M9 paper | M256A1, CAM, M8 and M9 paper | M256A1 | Odor (freshly mowed hay) |
| SYMPTOMS | Difficult breathing, drooling, nausea, vomiting, convulsions, and blurred vision | Burning eyes, stinging skin, irritated nose | Convulsions and coma | Coughing, nausea, choking, headache, and tight chest |
| EFFECTS | Incapacitates | Blisters skin, damages respiratory tract | Incapacitates | Floods and damages lungs |
| FIRST AID | Mark 1 nerve agent antidote kit (NAAK) | As for 2nd and 3rd degree burns | None | Keep warm and avoid movement |
| DECON | M291 and flush eyes with water | M291 and flush eyes with water | None | None |

*Battle Dress Overgarment

## NUCLEAR WEAPONS

Soldiers should also know the effects of nuclear explosions—even accidental ones—and how to protect themselves from the effects of nuclear detonations. The three principal effects of a nuclear weapon detonation are blast, radiation, and electromagnetic pulse. *Blast* is the high-pressure shock wave that crushes structures and causes missiling damage. *Thermal radiation* is the intense heat and extremely bright light that cause burns, temporary blindness, and dazzle. *Nuclear radiation* is energy released from the detonation that produces fallout in the forms of initial and residual radiation, both of which can cause casualties. An *electromagnetic pulse* is the surge of electrical power that occurs within seconds of a nuclear detonation and damages electrical components in equipment (radios, radar, computers, and vehicles) and weapons systems (TOWs and Javelins).

Cover and or shielding offers the best protection from the immediate effects of a nuclear attack. This includes cover in fighting positions, culverts, and ditches. Soldiers should cover exposed skin and stay down until the blast wave passes and debris stops falling. Immediately after a nuclear attack, the platoon leader should begin continuous monitoring for radiation using the AN/VDR-2 radiacmeter.

## TENETS OF NBC DEFENSE
### Contamination Avoidance

Avoidance allows commanders to shield soldiers and units, thus shaping the battlefield. It involves both active and passive measures. Active measures include detection, reconnaissance, alarms and signals, warning and reporting, marking, and contamination control. Passive measures include training, camouflage, concealment, hardening positions, and dispersion.

NBC reconnaissance is the detection, identification, reporting, and marking of NBC hazards. It consists of search, survey, surveillance, and sampling operations.

### Protection Against Contamination

Techniques that work for avoidance also work for protection (for example, shielding soldiers and units and shaping the battlefield). Other activities that comprise protection involve sealing or hardening positions, protecting soldiers, assuming mission-oriented protective posture (MOPP), reacting to attack, and using collective protection. Individual protective items include the protective mask, battle dress overgarments (BDOs), green vinyl overboots, and gloves. Higher level commanders establish the minimum level of protection; subordinate units may only increase this level as necessary.

| MOPP Level Equipment | MOPP READY | MOPP 0 (ZERO) | MOPP 1 | MOPP 2 | MOPP 3 | MOPP 4 | Command (mask only) |
|---|---|---|---|---|---|---|---|
| Mask | Carried | Carried | Carried | Carried | Worn[1] | Worn | Worn |
| Overgarment | Ready[3] | Available[4] | Worn[1] | Worn[1] | Worn[1] | Worn | |
| Vinyl overboots | Ready[3] | Available[4] | Available[4] | Worn | Worn | Worn | |
| Gloves | Ready[3] | Available[4] | Available[4] | Available[4] | Available[4] | Worn | |
| Helmet protective cover | Ready[3] | Available[4] | Available[4] | Worn | Worn | Worn | |
| Chemical protective undergarment 2 | Ready[3] | Available[4] | Worn[2] | Worn[2] | Worn[2] | Worn[2] | |

[1]In hot weather, coat or hood can be left open for ventilation.
[2]The chemical protective undergarment is worn under the BDU (this primarily applies to armor vehicle crewmen and special operations forces).
[3]These items must be available to the soldier within two hours, with a second set available within six hours.
[4]These items must be positioned within arm's reach of the soldier.

**MOPP LEVELS**

318 Combat Leader's Field Guide

## Individual Protective Gear

Currently, most active-duty military units have the joint service lightweight integrated suit technology (JSLIST) as a replacement for the old chemical protective suit or BDOs. When combined with the chemical protective mask, the JSLIST provides protection against chemical and biological agents, radioactive fallout particles, and battlefield contaminants. The JSLIST chemical protective overgarment is currently qualified by the military to meet the requirements for protection from chemical warfare agents for up to 6 launderings, 45 days of wear, 120 calendar days after removal from the factory-sealed bag, or 24 hours after contamination, whichever comes first.

A complete chemical warfare protective ensemble includes the following components:

- Mask.
- Chemical protective overgarment.
- Chemical protective gloves.
- Chemical protective overboots (compatible with the JSLIST chemical protective overgarment).

During Operation Iraqi Freedom, the lighter nature of the JSLIST allowed the soldiers to operate in temperatures approaching 100 degrees Fahrenheit with only minimal degradation. This was a significant improvement over the BDO. However, the JSLIST proved to be not as durable as the BDO under the strenuous field conditions. Infantry soldiers easily tore many suits as they went about their day-to-day activities. It is recommended to be more careful and to have extra suits on hand.

## DECONTAMINATION

Contamination forces units into protective equipment that degrades performance of individual and collective tasks. Decontamination restores combat power and reduces casualties that may result from exposure, thus allowing commanders to sustain combat operations.

### Principles of Decontamination

Use the four principles of decontamination when planning decon operations:

1. Decon as soon as possible.
2. Decon only what is necessary.
3. Decon as far forward as possible (METT-TC dependent).
4. Decon by priority.

### Levels of Decontamination

The three levels of decontamination are immediate, operational, and thorough.

## COMPARISON DATA FOR DECONTAMINATION LEVELS

| Level | Technique | Best Start Time | Responsibility | Advantages |
|---|---|---|---|---|
| Immediate | Skin decon | Within 1 minute of contamination | Individual | Prevents agents from penetrating* |
| | Personal wipedown | Within 15 minutes | Individual or Crew | |
| | Operator spraydown | Within 30 minutes | | |
| Operational | MOPP gear exchange** | Optimal within 6 hours, but no later than 24 hours | Contaminated Unit | Temporary relief from MOPP4 |
| | Vehicle washdown*** | | | Limit agent spread |
| Thorough | Detailed equipment decon (DED) | When mission allows/reconstitution | Decon PLT | Long-term MOPP reduction with minimal risk |
| | Detailed troop decon (DTD) | | Unit | |

*The techniques become less effective the longer they are delayed.
**Performance degradation and risk assessment must be considered when exceeding 6 hours. See FM 3-7 for information on BDO risk assessment.
***Vehicle washdown is most effective if started within one hour.

1. *Immediate.* Immediate decontamination requires minimal planning. It is a basic soldier survival skill and is performed in accordance with the current soldier manual. Personal wipedown removes contamination from individual equipment using the M291.
2. *Operational.* Operational decontamination involves MOPP gear exchange and vehicle spraydown. MOPP gear exchange should be performed within six hours of being contaminated when thorough decon cannot be performed.
3. *Thorough.* Thorough decontamination involves detailed troop decontamination (DTD) and detailed equipment decontamination (DED). Thorough decontamination is normally conducted by company-size elements as part of restoration or during breaks in combat operations. These operations require support from a chemical decontamination platoon.

**Decontamination Planning Considerations**
Leaders should include the following when planning for decontamination:
- Plan decon sites throughout the width and depth of the sector.
- Tie decon sites to the scheme of maneuver and template NBC strikes.
- Apply the principles of decontamination.
- Plan for contaminated routes.
- Plan for logistics and resupply of MOPP, mask parts, water, and decon supplies.
- Plan for medical concerns, including treatment and evacuation of contaminated casualties.
- Maintain site security.

**MARKING CONTAMINATION**
When contamination is found, it must be marked to prevent other soldiers from being exposed, and then reported. The only exception to marking an area is if the marking would help the enemy avoid contamination; however, the contaminated area must still be reported. When marking an area, place the markers facing away from the contamination. Markers are placed at roads, trails, and other likely points of entry.

**PASSING ALARMS AND SIGNALS**
The vocal alarm for any chemical or biological hazard or attack is the word "gas." The person giving the alarm stops breathing, masks, and shouts "Gas!" as loudly as possible. Everyone hearing this immediately masks and passes the alarm.

The first person to hear or see the M8 automatic chemical alarm sound or flash also stops breathing, masks, and yells "Gas!"

NBC MARKERS

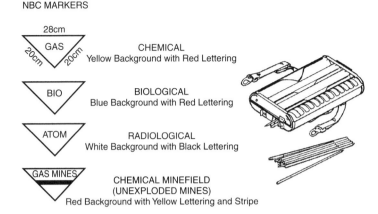

28cm

GAS — CHEMICAL
Yellow Background with Red Lettering

BIO — BIOLOGICAL
Blue Background with Red Lettering

ATOM — RADIOLOGICAL
White Background with Black Lettering

GAS MINES — CHEMICAL MINEFIELD
(UNEXPLODED MINES)
Red Background with Yellow Lettering and Stripe

FRONT SURFACE OF
MARKER FACES AWAY
FROM CONTAMINATION

### NBC Contamination Marking Set

The all-clear signal is given by word of mouth through the chain of command. The signal is given by leaders after testing for contamination proves negative.

## TREATMENT OF CHEMICAL CASUALTIES

Following the all-clear signal, soldiers check for casualties, give first aid, identify the agent, send reports to higher headquarters, request permission to move, schedule decontamination operations, and mark the area to warn friendly soldiers.

### Antidote Treatment, Nerve Agent, Auto-Injector

The ATNAA is a nerve agent antidote device that will be used by the Armed Forces in the treatment of nerve agent poisoning. It is a multichambered device consisting of three components: the auto-injector tube, a spring-activated needle, and a safety cap. The device is packaged in a chemically hardened pouch.

**ANTIDOTE TREATMENT,
NERVE AGENT, AUTO-INJECTOR**
For Use In Nerve Agent Poisoning Only
ATROPINE INJECTION 2.5 MG, PRALIDOXIME CHLORIDE INJECTION 600MG

### Antidote Treatment, Nerve Agent,
### Auto-injector (ATNAA)

**First Aid for Chemical Casualties**
Soldiers must be able to treat themselves and each other after exposure to dangerous chemicals.

*Self-Aid.* If you experience most or all of the mild symptoms of nerve agent poisoning, immediately hold your breath. *Do not inhale.* Put on your protective mask and administer one ATNAA injection into your lateral thigh muscle or buttocks. It will take ten to fifteen minutes for the antidote to take effect. If you are able to ambulate and know who and where you are, you will not need a second ATNAA injection.

*Warning*: Giving yourself a second ATNAA injection may create a nerve agent antidote overdose, which could result in incapacitation. If symptoms of nerve agent poisoning are not relieved after administering one ATNAA injection, seek someone else to check your symptoms. A buddy must administer the second and third sets of injections, if needed.

*Buddy Aid.* If you encounter a servicemember suffering from severe signs of nerve agent poisoning, mask the casualty if necessary. Do not fasten the hood. Administer three ATNAAs in rapid succession. Follow administration procedures outlined below.

*Combat Lifesaver Procedures.* The combat lifesaver (CLS) must check to verify if the individual has received three ATNAAs. If not, the CLS performs first aid as described for buddy aid above. If the individual has received the initial three ATNAAs, then the CLS may administer additional atropine injections at approximately fifteen-minute intervals until atropinization is achieved (heart rate above 90 beats per minute, reduced bronchial secretions, and reduced salivations). Administer additional atropine at intervals of thirty minutes to four hours to maintain atropinization or until the casualty is placed under the care of medical personnel. Check the heart rate by carefully lifting the casualty's mask hood and feeling for a pulse at the carotid artery. Request medical assistance as soon as the tactical situation permits.

*Trauma Specialist/Medics.* When a casualty has received three ATNAAs but atropinization has not been achieved, administer additional atropine at approximately fifteen-minute intervals until atropinization is achieved. Administer additional atropine at intervals of thirty minutes to four hours to maintain atropinization or until the casualty is evacuated to a medical treatment facility (MTF). Check the heart rate by lifting the casualty's mask hood and feeling for a pulse at the carotid artery. Provide assisted ventilation for severely poisoned casualties if equipment is available. Monitor the patient for development of heat stress.

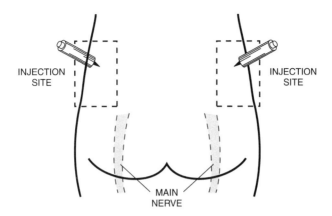

**Antidote Buttocks Injection Site**

*Administering Nerve Agent Antidotes.* The injection site for administering the ATNAA is normally in the outer thigh muscle. The thigh injection site is the area about a hand's width above the knee to a hand's width below the hip joint. It is important that the injections be given into a large muscle area. If the individual is thinly built, then the injections should be administered into the upper outer quarter (quadrant) of the buttocks to avoid injury to the thigh bone (see figures).

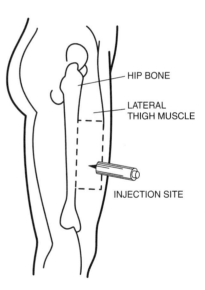

**Thigh Injection Site**

# 18

# Radio Sets, Procedures, and Field Antennas

Radios, the most common means of military communication, are particularly suited for use when you are on the move. Small handheld or backpack radios that communicate for only short distances are found at squad and platoon levels. As the need grows to talk over greater distances and to more units, the size and complexity of radios increase.

From brigade level to the squad level, the Army primarily uses FM (frequency modulating) single-channel radios as its primary means of communication. The FM radio has a range of approximately 35 to 40 kilometers, which covers a brigade/battalion maneuver area. FM radio transmissions are normally line-of-sight (LOS), so large terrain features can block transmission.

## ENVIRONMENT

Factors that affect the range of radios are weather, terrain, power, antenna, and the location of the radio. Manmade objects such as bridges and buildings may affect radio transmission. Interference may also come from power lines, electrical generators, other radio stations, and enemy jamming. You can correct many of the causes of poor radio communications by using common sense. For example, make sure you are not trying to communicate from under a steel bridge.

## RULES FOR RADIO USE

Observe the following rules for radio use:
- Listen before transmitting.
- Avoid excessive radio checks.
- Make messages clear and concise. If possible, write them out before transmitting.

- Speak clearly, slowly, and in natural phrases, enunciating each word. If the receiving operator must write, allow time for writing.
- Always assume the enemy is listening.
- If jammed, notify higher headquarters by established procedures.
- Maintain whip antennas in a vertical position.
- Make sure the radio is turned off before starting a vehicle.

## PROWORDS

Common prowords are those words that are used on a regular basis while conducting radio operations. Prowords are not interchangeable, as the meanings are specific and clear to the receiver. An example is "Say again" versus "Repeat." "Say again" means to repeat the last transmission, while "Repeat" means to fire the last artillery fire mission again. The following are frequently used prowords:

**All after**—I refer to the entire message that follows . . .

**All before**—I refer to the entire message that precedes . . .

**Break**—I now separate the text from other parts of the message.

**Correction**—There is an error in this transmission. Transmission will continue with the last word correctly transmitted.

**Groups**—This message contains the number of groups indicated by the numeral following.

**I say again**—I am repeating transmission or part indicated.

**I spell**—I shall spell the next word phonetically.

**Message**—A message that requires recording is about to follow (transmitted immediately after the call). *Note*: This proword is not used on nets primarily employed for conveying messages. It is intended for use when messages are passed on tactical or reporting net.

**More to follow**—Transmitting station has additional traffic for the receiving station.

**Out**—This is the end of my transmission to you and no answer is required or expected.

**Over**—This is the end of my transmission to you and a response is necessary. Go ahead: transmit.

**Radio check**—What is my signal strength and readability, i.e. how do you hear me?

**Roger**—I have received your last transmission satisfactorily, radio check is loud and clear.

**Say again**—Repeat all of your last transmission. Followed by identification data means "repeat—(portion indicated)."

**This is**—This transmission is from the station whose designator immediately follows.

**Time**—That which immediately follows is the time or date-time group of the message.
**Wait**—I must pause for a few seconds.
**Wait-out**—I must pause longer than a few seconds.
**Wilco**—I have received your transmission, understand it, and will comply, to be used only by the addressee. *Note*: Since the meaning of "Roger" is included in that of WILCO, the two prowords are never used together.
**Word after**—I refer to the word of the message that follows.
**Word before**—I refer to the word of the message that precedes.

## SECURITY
Radio is one of the least secure means of communicating. Each time you talk, your voice travels in all directions. The enemy can listen to your transmissions to get information about you and your unit, or to locate your position to destroy you with artillery fire. Communications security keeps unauthorized persons from gaining information of value from radio and telephone transmissions. It includes the following:

• Using authentication to make sure that the other communicating station is a friendly one.
• Using only approved codes.
• Designating periods when all radios are turned off.
• Restricting the use of radio transmitters and monitoring radio receivers.
• Operating radios on low power.
• Enforcing net discipline and radiotelephone procedure (all stations must use authorized prosigns and prowords and must transmit official traffic only).
• Using radio sites with hills or other shields between them and the enemy.
• Using directional antennas when feasible.

## RADIO SETS AND RECEIVER-TRANSMITTERS
### SINCGARS Ground Combat Net Radio
The bulk of US Army Active and Reserve Component forces are likely to be supplied with one or more versions of the single-channel ground and airborne radio (SINCGARS). The older versions are the Receiver-Transmitter (RT) 1523A/B models. The newer versions are the SIP (Systems Improvement Program) ground combat radio RT-1523C/D models and the even newer SINCGARS ASIP (Advanced Systems Improvement Program) ground combat radio or RT-1523E model. These RT-1523A–D radio systems look very

much alike, but the newer version has better technology for electronic warfare and better data transfer rates.

The newer SINCGARS ASIP is a user-owned-and-operated solid-state frequency modulated (FM) combat net radio (CNR). It operates in the 30.000 to 87.975 MHz frequency range in the single-channel (SC) or frequency-hopping (FH) mode. The ASIP replaces the RT-1523A and RT-1523B model SINCGARS. The ASIP is compatible with the older SINCGARS and with NATO forces in SC, squelch-off mode. It provides electronic warfare (EW) protection and a reduced electromagnetic signature in the FH mode. Maintenance procedures are the same for the older SINCGARS radio. The SINC-GARS has eight preset channels in SC mode and six for FH mode. The cue and manual frequencies are included in the eight single-channel frequencies. It is designed for secure voice and data communications and is an antijam radio. The individual components are interchangeable from one radio to the next.

As mentioned above, the primary component of the SINCGARS is the receiver-transmitter or RT-1523 Series A through E. The RT-1523 series and necessary additional components make up either a dismounted or a mounted configuration. The radio appearance of the RT-1523 Series A–D is basically the same (see figure). The front panels and keyboards for the RT-1523 Series differ depending on the versions (see figures).

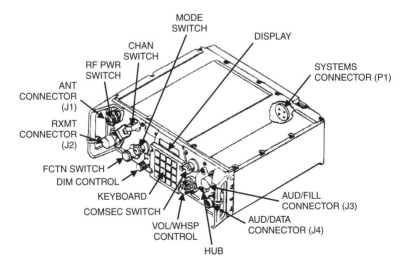

**Receiver-Transmitter (RT-1523A–D Series)**

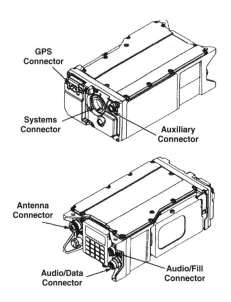

**RT-1523E Series ASIP Model**

**RT-1523C/D FRONT PANEL**

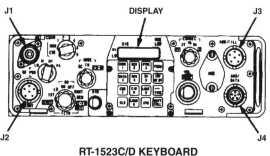

**RT-1523C/D KEYBOARD**

**RT-1523C/D Series
SIP Front Panel and Keyboard**

RT-1523A/B FRONT PANEL

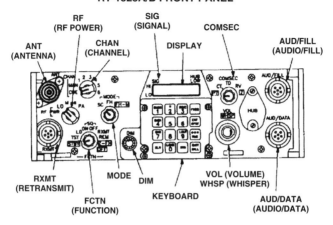

RT-1523A/B KEYBOARD

RT-1523A/B Series
Front Panel and Keyboard

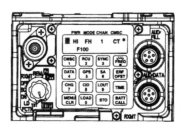

RT-1523E Front Panel

## GENERAL CHARACTERISTICS AND CAPABILITIES
### SINCGARS

| | |
|---|---|
| Operating Voltage: | Manpack: 13.5 volts from primary battery. |
| | Vehicular: 27.5 volts from vehicular battery. |
| Frequency Range: | 30 MHz to 87.975 MHz. |
| Number of Operating Frequencies: | 2320. |
| Channel Spacing: | 25 kHz. |
| Frequency Stability: | Plus or minus 5 parts per million. |
| Frequency Offset Ability (SC): | Plus or minus 5 and 10 kHz. |
| Type of Modulation: | FM. |
| Audio Response Capability: | 300–3000 Hz. |
| Types of Operation: | Push-to-talk (PTT) and release to receive. |
| | Retransmit: automatic. |
| | Remote: push-to-talk, release to receive. |
| | Data: automatic via data device. |
| Modes of Operation: | Voice: SC and FH. |
| | Retransmit: SC to SC, SC to FH, FH to FH. |
| | Digital data: SC, FH. |
| | Remote: with AN/GRA-39, CM, or RCU. |
| | Plain-text or cipher text. |
| Tuning: | Electronic SC frequency entered manually by using keyboard. Up to eight SC channels and six FH channels can be loaded and later selected using CHAN (channel) switch. |

*Components.* A few components make up the basic radio sets. This simplifies the radio's installation, its tailoring for specific missions, and the maintenance support system. The RT-1523 is the main component of all radio sets. The components make the two primary radio configurations: *dismounted configuration* and *vehicle-mounted configuration.*

### Dismounted Configuration (Manpack Radios)
The term "manpack" is the common name for the soldier-carried AN/PRC-119A/D/F. The "A/D/F" indicates this is an ICOM (Integrated COMSEC [communications security]) radio. "Dismount" is the term used to indicate that the equivalent of a manpack radio is included within the components of selected vehicular radios. Once assembled, there is no difference between a radio referred to as manpack and one called dismount.

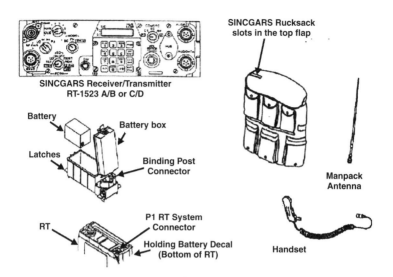

SINCGARS Rucksack
slots in the top flap

SINCGARS Receiver/Transmitter
RT-1523 A/B or C/D

Battery

Battery box

Latches

Binding Post
Connector

Manpack
Antenna

RT

P1 RT System
Connector

Holding Battery Decal
(Bottom of RT)

Handset

**AN/PRC 119A/D/F**
**SINCGARS Manpack System**

### General Information for Manpack Components

* *Antenna, manpack radio*: may be AS-3683/PRC or AS-4266/PRC
  (long antenna).
* *Receiver-Transmitter (RT)*: may be RT-1523 Series.
* *Handset*: H-250/U or new Handheld Remote Control Radio Device
  (HRCRD) (C-12493/U).
* *Battery Box*: may be CY-8523A/B (CY-8523C is used with the
  HRCRD). Not required for ASIP RT.
* *Battery, main power*: may be Battery, Nonrechargeable, BA-5590/U;
  Battery, Rechargeable, BB-590/U; or Battery, Rechargeable, BB-
  390/U.
* *Carrying Case*.

### Vehicular Radios (Mounted Configuration)

There are six configurations of vehicular radios:
1. Short-Range (SR) Radio (AN/VRC-87A/D/F[*])
2. Short-Range Radio with Dismount (AN/VRC-88A/D/F)
3. Long-Range (LR) Radio (AN/VRC-90A/D/F)
4. Short-Range/Long-Range Radio (AN/VRC-89A/D/F)

---

[*]The "A/D/F" in SINCGARS radio nomenclature means that these are ICOM
(secure) radios. The "C" in radio nomenclature indicates Single Radio Mount (SRM)
radios. The components that are used in all vehicular radio configurations are shown
in the graphic.

5. Short-Range/Long-Range Radio with Dismount (AN/VRC-91A/D/F)

6. Long-Range/Long-Range Radio (AN/VRC-92A/D/F)

Common components are the key to tailoring the radio sets for specific missions. The components included in the radio set determine its capabilities. The number of RTs and amplifiers, an installation kit, and a backpack determine the model. The RT is the basic building block for all mounted radio configurations.

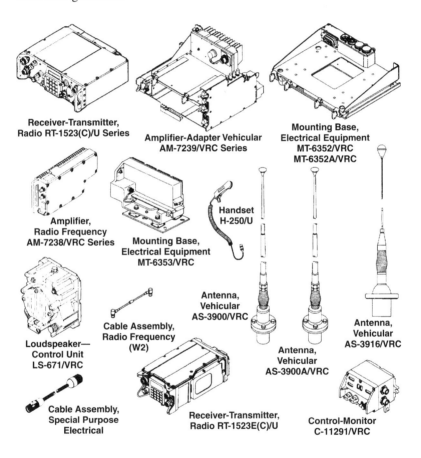

**SINCGARS Vehicle-Mounted
Radio Components**

*Mounted Configurations*

- *Short-Range (SR) Radio Components (AN/VRC-87A/D/F)*: Consists of RT-1523/A/B/C/D/E, Mounting Base (MB) (MT-6352/A), Vehicular Amplifier Adapter (VAA) (AM-7239/A/B/C/D/E), Vehicular Antenna (AS-3900/3916), Handset (HS) (H-250), Loudspeaker (LS) (LS-671), Cable (W4) that connects RT to VAA, Antenna Cable (CG-3856), Loudspeaker Cable (CX-13292), and Power Cable.

- *Short-Range Radio with Dismount (SR-D) Components (AN/VRC-88A/D/F)*: Same as Short-Range Radio, plus Dismount (Manpack) Radio.

- *Long-Range (LR) Radio Components (AN/VRC-90A/D/F)*: Consists of RT-1523/A/B/C/D/E, Mounting Base (MB) (MT-6352/A), Vehicular Amplifier Adapter (VAA) (AM-7239/A/B/C/D/E), Vehicular Antenna (AS-3900/3916), Handset (HS) (H-250), Loudspeaker (LS) (LS-671), Power Amplifier (PA) (AM-7238/A/B), Cable (W2) that connects RT ANT to PA, Cable (W4) that connects RT to VAA, Antenna Cable (CG-3856), Loudspeaker Cable (CX-13292), and Power Cable.

- *Short-Range/Long-Range Radio Components (AN/VRC-89A/D/F)*: Consists of two RT-1523/A/B/C/D/E), Mounting Base (MB) (MT-6352/A), Vehicular Amplifier Adapter (VAA) (AM-7239/A/B/C/D/E), Vehicular Antenna (AS-3900/3916), two Handsets (HS) (H-250), two

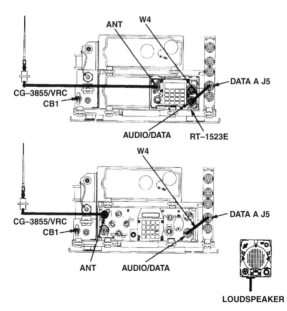

**AN/VRC-87A/D/F**

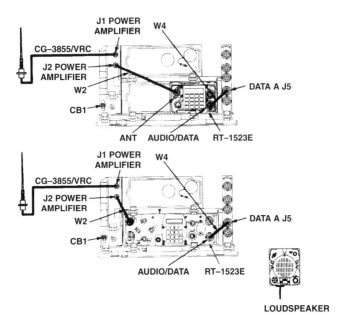

**AN/VRC-88A/D/F**

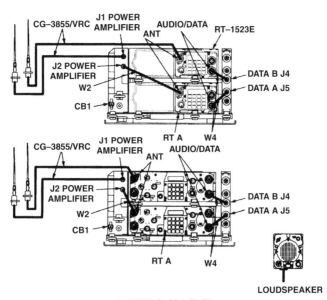

**AN/VRC-89A/D/F**

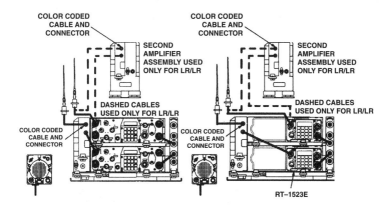

**AN/VRC-92A/D/F**

Loudspeakers (LS) (LS-671), Power Amplifier (PA) (AM-7238/A/B), Cable (W2) that connects RT ANT to PA, two Cables (W4) that connect RTs to VAA, two Antenna Cables (CG-3856), two Loudspeaker Cables (CX-13292), and Power Cable.

- *Short-Range/Long-Range Radio with Dismount Components (AN/VRC-91A/D/F)*: Same as Short-Range/Long-Range Radio, plus Dismount (Manpack) Radio.

- *Long-Range/Long-Range Radio Components (AN/VRC-92A/D/F)*: Consists of 2 RT-1523/A/B/C/D/E), Mounting Base (MB) (MT-6352/A), Vehicular Amplifier Adapter (VAA) (AM-7239/A/B/C/D/E), Vehicular Antenna (AS-3900/3916), 2 Handsets (HS) (H-250), two Loudspeakers (LS) (LS-671), two Power Amplifiers (PA) (AM-7238/A/B), Power Amplifier Mount (PA Mt) (MT-6353), Cable (W2) that connects RT ANT to PA, two Cables (W4) that connect RTs to VAA, three Cables (CG-3856)—one connects PA to antenna (5') (two are in installation kit), Cable (CX-13291) that connects RT-B PA Mt to VAA, Cable (CX-13298) that connects RT-A to RT-B for RXMT, Cable (CX-13303) that connects RT-B PA Mt to MB, and two Loudspeaker Cables (CX-13292).

**Planning Ranges**

The ranges shown in the accompanying chart are based on line-of-sight and are average for normal conditions. Range depends on location, sighting, weather, and surrounding noise level, among other factors. Use of OE-254 antenna increases range for both voice and data transmissions. Enemy jamming and mutual interference conditions degrade these ranges. In data transmissions, using a lower baud rate will increase range.

**VOICE TRANSMISSION MAXIMUM PLANNING RANGES:**

| TYPE RADIO | RF SWITCH POSITION | PLANNING RANGES |
|---|---|---|
| Manpack/Vehicular | LO (low)<br>M (medium)<br>HI (high) | 200 M – 400 M<br>400 M – 5 KM<br>5 KM – 10 KM |
| Vehicular Only | PA (power amplifier) | 10 KM – 40 KM |

**DATA TRANSMISSION MAXIMUM PLANNING RANGES:**

| TYPE RADIO | BAUD RATE USED | RF SWITCH POSITION | PLANNING RANGES |
|---|---|---|---|
| Manpack/Vehicular<br>(Short Range) | 600 – 4800 BPS<br>16,000 BPS (16 KBPS) | HI (high)<br>HI (high) | 3 KM – 5 KM<br>1 KM – 3 KM |
| Vehicular<br>(Long Range) | 600 – 2400 BPS<br>4800 BPS<br>16,000 BPS (16 KBPS) | PA (power amp)<br>PA (power amp)<br>PA (power amp) | 5 KM – 25 KM<br>5 KM – 22 KM<br>3 KM – 10 KM |

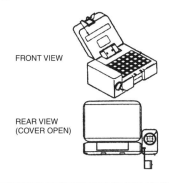

FRONT VIEW

REAR VIEW
(COVER OPEN)

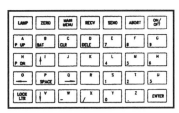

ANCD KEYPAD

**AN-CYZ-10 Automated Net Control Device (ANCD)**

## Loading Frequencies

The procedure for loading single channel (SC) frequencies requires setting the proper switches, pressing the correct number keys for the frequency you wish to load, and storing the load in RT permanent memory by pressing the STO (storage) button. Loading secure frequencies requires special COMSEC devices that transmit the proper "FILL" data to the radio, including frequencies, FH data, secure transmission data, and other necessary information. The current device is called an AN/CYZ-10. The AN/CYZ-10 automated net control device (ANCD) is a handheld device capable of receiving, storing, and transferring data between ANCDs, or between ANCD and a SINCGARS or ASIP radio. The primary application for this device is to fill the ASIP with FH data, time, communications security (COMSEC), and loadset information. Correct operating instructions may be obtained from various technical manuals and the unit signal officer.

**Key Operator Tasks**
Many tasks are needed to become completely proficient with the SINC-GARS and they would fill a good portion of this guide. However, two important and basic operator tasks follow:

1. **Select RT Preparation Settings from MENU.** The tasks listed below are necessary to get the radio in operation.

| | | |
|---|---|---|
| a. Set RT Volume | 1. Press MENU | Press MENU to display VOL level |
| | 2. Press Digit (1–9) for VOL | Display reads WHSP if 0 selected |
| | Setting (0) for Whisper Mode | |
| b. Set RT Channel | 1. Press MENU (until CHAN) | Display reads (1–6), (Q) for CUE, (M) for Manual |
| | 2. Press Digit (1–6) for Channel desired: (0) for MAN, (7) for CUE | |
| c. Set RT Power | 1. Press MENU (until PWR) | Display reads (LO, M, HI, PA) |
| | 2. Press CHG for desired PWR setting | |
| d. Set RT Mode | 1. Press MENU (until MODE) | Display reads (SC, FH, FHM) |
| | 2. Press CHG for desired MODE | |
| e. Set COMSEC | 1. Press MENU (until CMSC) | Display reads (PT, CT, TD, RV) |
| | 2. Press CHG for desired CMSC setting | |
| f. Set Backlight | 1. Place RT in SQ ON | Backlight lights (4 settings Low to High, then OFF) |
| | 2. Press FREQ/Backlight | |
| | 3. Press CHG until desired setting | |

Default settings are: VOL (5), CHAN (1), PWR (LO), MODE (FH), COMSEC (CT).

2. **Load Single-Channel (SC) Frequency into ASIP Radio.** The ASIP operator is required to perform this task in preparation for the employment of single channel communications, use of the CUE (key the radio), and ERF (electronic remote fill) methods of late net entry, and for single channel frequency updates. The operator determines the required frequencies from the ANCD or another source. These frequencies are then loaded into the radio by use of the receiver-transmitter (RT) keyboard. The steps are:

| | | |
|---|---|---|
| a. Prepare to perform task | 1. Obtain proper freq from ANCD | (Load CUE freq only if directed)* |
| b. Load SC freq | 2. Set RT controls:** | RT display shows "GOOD" |
| | COMSEC to PT | (or see unit maintainer) |
| | Mode to SC | |
| | FCTN to Z-FH, TST, and then to LD | |
| | CHAN to MAN, CUE, or 1–6 | |
| c. Store SC freq | 1. Press: [FREQ] | Display shows [00000] or [30000] |
| | 2. Press: [CLR] | Display shows [_____] |
| | 3. Enter 5-digits SC freq | Display shows SC [XXXXX] |
| d. Prepare to communicate | Press STO (within 7 sec) | Display blinks once (data is stored) |
| e. Set COMSEC | 1. Repeat: Step b-1 for each freq needed | (As directed by NCS or unit SOP) |
| | 2. Set: FCTN to SQ ON complete | Loading of SC freq is complete |

*Only NCS and Alt NCS will load a CUE frequency.
**RT settings for ASIP are set via MENU.

## FIELD EXPEDIENT ANTENNAS

Expedient antennas are temporary antennas designed and constructed by the user to increase the range of tactical radio sets. Antennas that are components of tactical radio sets are, for the most part, vertical antennas, resulting in the signal radiating equally in all directions. Expedient antennas increase the operating range of a given radio set, providing increased efficiency through the use of an antenna specifically designed for the operating frequency in use, elevation of the antenna above the ground, or concentration of the radiated signal along a given direction. Field expedient antennas are easily constructed from field wire using poles or trees for support. Whatever antenna is used, remember that the most important considerations are site location and the radio set location. Before deciding to construct a field expedient antenna, other considerations or operating hints that may improve communications are as follows:

- Use a headset to receive weak signals.
- Speak slowly and distinctly, directly into the microphone or handset.
- Use an RC-292 antenna, if available.
- Use continuous wave (CW) in place of voice for increased range on AM radios.

Steel wires should be clipped off, leaving only the copper wires. The copper wires are twisted together and placed into the center hole of the auxiliary antenna connector or the antenna connector. Make sure the wires do not touch any other part of the radio set.

If the whip antenna of your radio becomes damaged, try a piece of communication wire tied to a broomstick or a tree limb. Insert the end of the wire in the antenna connector. If you hold the stick or limb in a vertical position, you should be able to communicate. It will not be as effective as with the whip antenna, but it is better than no antenna at all.

### Vertical Antennas

Vertical field expedient antennas improve radio set performance by virtue of height above the ground. The most effective height above the ground is equal to one-half the wavelength of the operating frequency in meters. Elevation above this height requires ground plane elements.

*Improvised Whip Antenna.* Whip antennas may break during use, with no replacement readily available. If this should happen, it is possible to improvise a satisfactory replacement by using telephone cable WD-1/TT or lashing the broken antenna pieces together.

*Patrol Antenna.* The patrol antenna is used primarily with FM radios. It can be used extensively in heavily wooded areas with the portable radio sets to increase line-of-sight communications. Antenna performance increases with height above the ground up to 13 meters.

| | |
|---|---|
| Length in meters | $1/2$-wavelength of operating frequency |
| Height | Variable (lead-in not over 13 meters) |
| Radiation | 360 degrees |

### Field Expedient RC-292 Antenna

The field expedient 292 antenna is used with FM radios. It is used in place of the RC-292 when such an antenna is not available. Principal parts consist of:

- 65 feet of gutted 550 cord.
- Five insulators (see note 1 on page 341).

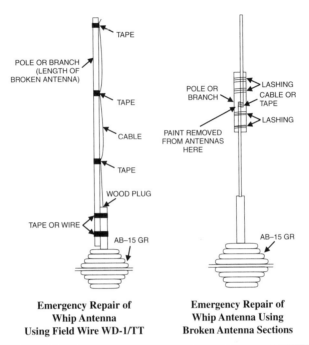

**Emergency Repair of Whip Antenna Using Field Wire WD-1/TT**

**Emergency Repair of Whip Antenna Using Broken Antenna Sections**

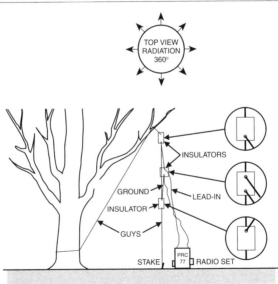

**Patrol Antenna**

To determine length of antenna in meters, divide 142.5 by your operating frequency.
Example: constant = 142.5 divided by op. freq. 45.0 = 3.17 meters.
Or, constant = 468 divided by op. freq. 45.0 = 10.4 feet.

- Four 6.5-foot lengths of antenna elements (16-gauge copper wire, see note 2 below).
- Three 1-foot-long gutted 550 cord (see note 3 below).
- 50 feet of coax cable (RG-58 or RH-174).
- Solderless BNC connector (see note 4 below).

*Notes:*
1. Insulators should be made of a semiflexible plastic (i.e. spoons, flashlight lenses, etc.).
2. Use wire from GRA-50 dipole antenna for the radiator element.
3. The 550 cord end is tied in a loop to create a slip knot to put ends of sticks through during execution.
4. Once coax is connected, use electrical tape to secure and cover bare wires.

**Field Expedient RC–292 Antenna**

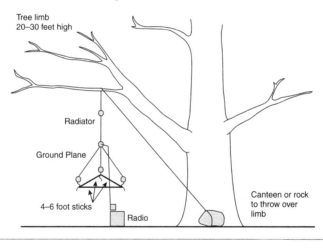

**Construction:**

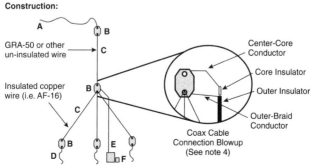

**Blowup of Field Expedient RC-292 Antenna**

## Horizontal Antennas

When the situation does not require mobility and the antenna group RC-292 is not available, you can get greater distance by using the long-wire horizontal antenna. The physical length in meters of one wavelength for a given operating frequency can be computed as follows:

$$\text{length (meters)} = \frac{285}{\text{operating frequency (MHz)}}$$

All horizontal antennas described here are fed by connecting the receiver-transmitter to one end of the antenna.

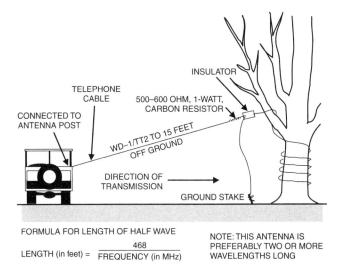

FORMULA FOR LENGTH OF HALF WAVE

$$\text{LENGTH (in feet)} = \frac{468}{\text{FREQUENCY (in MHz)}}$$

NOTE: THIS ANTENNA IS PREFERABLY TWO OR MORE WAVELENGTHS LONG

**Horizontal Antenna for Use with AM and FM Radios**

## Long-Wire Antenna

The long-wire antenna is used with both AM and FM radios to increase the range. It is normally used in open terrain where installation can be accomplished with ease.

| | |
|---|---|
| Length | 5 or 7 wavelengths of operating frequency |
| Height | 3 meters |
| Range | Up to 2 to 3 times the operating range of set |
| Resistor | 400–700 ohms |
| Radiation | Without resistor—from both ends |
| | With resistor—off resistor end only |

**Long-Wire Antenna**

## Vertical Half-Rhombic Antenna

The vertical half-rhombic antenna has the advantage of being smaller in physical size than the horizontal antenna and requires only one pole for construction. It can be made directional with the use of a resistor. The principal disadvantage is that if the angle between the antenna wire and surface of the earth is too small, the signal will be radiated at an upward angle that may be above the intended receiver. A typical vertical half-rhombic antenna consists of 100 feet of field wire WD-1/TT, erected over a single 30-foot support base. One leg of the antenna terminates at the resistor; the other end is connected from the insulator to the radio by a 5-foot lead-in wire.

| | |
|---|---|
| Length | 2 wavelengths of operating frequency, with a 5-foot lead-in |
| Height | 20 meters |
| Range | Up to 2 to 3 times operating range of set |
| Resistor | 400–700 ohms |
| Radiation | Without resistor—equally off both ends |
| | With resistor—off resistor end only |

*Note*: A counterpoise is used as an additional ground in everyday climates. It is placed on top of the ground and installed from one ground stake to the other, and then to the battery case clip. If the counterpoise is not used, the ground lead-in is connected from the ground stake to the battery case clip. The insulators and the resistor are installed approximately knee high.

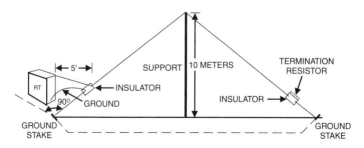

**Vertical Half-Rhombic Antenna**

# Appendix A

# Rules of Engagement and Use of Deadly Force in Combat Zones

*By David G. Bolgiano*

This section is different from the rest of this manual because it is both impractical and unwise to write a "checklist" for when or how to use deadly force. One cannot write a linear "cheat sheet" for ROE and the Use of Force. Checklists are fine for packing lists, TTPs, quick reaction drills, and most other combat preparatory topics. They are *very* bad for comprehending and training on the topic of deadly force encounters. That is why ROE and Escalation of Force (EOF) cards provide poor tactical guidance.

Please take the time to read this appendix and understand the dynamics of such encounters and ways to train to the fight. It is important to be wary of any ROE or EOF card that uses legally and tactically incorrect language like: "Only use deadly force as a last resort," "Do not shoot unless someone is pointing or shooting a weapon at you," or "Do not shoot at fleeing hostile actors." All of these examples are from prior real-world ROE cards—such language breeds confusion and unnecessary hesitation and has no basis in the law. They are attempts to cover up poor training and preparation. They demonstrate a lack of trust that must be assiduously avoided at all cost. Most of these have been properly removed from use, but you may still find similar language, so be forewarned. Nevertheless, because of their ubiquity and the expectation that units be provided with an ROE or EOF card, a good and legally supportable example is set forth below. Also, in the event of an investigation of yourself or a member of your unit as the result of a Use of Force situation, there are simple post-incident guidelines to follow.

## HOW TO RESPOND WHEN INVESTIGATED

For those who may be the subject or target of a use of force investigation: Do not be intimidated by AR 15-6 investigators, Army CID, or *anyone* else. If you use deadly force in the line of duty, follow these guidelines.

**1. Avail yourself of switched-on legal counsel *before* making a statement, especially a sworn statement.** The right to counsel is not only for

**Use of Force, including Deadly Force, may be used in the following situations:**

During Combat Operations

If applicable, against a person or group that has been "Declared Hostile." Such persons or groups will be identified in separate and classified rules or briefed by your chain of command. Positive Identification (PID) is needed before engaging a target that has been Declared Hostile. Rules of proportionality and all Laws of War apply.

Both During Combat Operations and All Other Times

You may use reasonable force while conducting authorized missions, official duties or to meet lawful objectives or mission requirements.

Unit commanders always retain the inherent right and obligation to exercise unit self defense in response to a hostile act or demonstrated hostile intent. Unit self-defense includes the defense of other DoD forces in the vicinity.

You may exercise self-defense in response to a hostile act or hostile intent, unless lawfully directed otherwise by their unit commander to enhance unit self-defense.

The Use of Force does not apply solely to firearms and deadly force confrontations but all applications of force.

All uses of force used should be objectively reasonable as defined on the Reverse Side of this Card. When feasible and circumstances permit, a threatening force should be warned and given the opportunity to withdraw or cease threatening actions, as appropriate and consistent with the lawful objectives or mission requirements.

## REASONABLE USE OF FORCE DEFINED AND EXPLAINED

The use of force must be objectively reasonable in intensity, duration, and magnitude based upon the totality of the circumstances to counter the threat.

**Use of Force, including Deadly Force**

The legal standard of "reasonableness" does not lend itself to a precise definition or application; however, the principle of objective reasonableness can be simplified to establish the basis of reasonableness in use of force. One must perceive the person proposing the action or threat is capable of performing the action. The subject must be in a position to carry out the act or threat.

\*\*\*\*\*\*\*\*\*\*\*\*\*\*\*\*\*\*\*\*\*\*\*\*\*\*\*\*\*\*\*\*\*\*\*\*\*\*\*\*\*\*\*\*\*\*\*\*\*\*\*\*\*\*\*\*

**"If any Soldier, Sailor, Airman or Marine assigned to your unit uses force in self-defense or defense of innocent others, they will not be judged in the clear vision of 20-20 hindsight but rather by how a reasonable person would act under situations that are tense, uncertain and rapidly evolving."**

It is the responsibility of leaders at every level to train all personnel in their command on how to identify and respond to imminent threats and acts.

\*\*\*\*\*\*\*\*\*\*\*\*\*\*\*\*\*\*\*\*\*\*\*\*\*\*\*\*\*\*\*\*\*\*\*\*\*\*\*\*\*\*\*\*\*\*\*\*\*\*\*\*\*\*\*\*

Citation - CJCSI 3121.01B, Enclosure L (June 2005) - Inherent Right of Self-Defense. Applies when an individual reasonably believes they are in immediate danger of death or serious bodily harm. Deadly force is also authorized when individuals reasonably believe that a person poses an immediate threat of death or serious bodily harm to DoD forces. Unit self-defense includes the defense of other DoD forces in the vicinity.

- Defense of Others. When an officer/sentry reasonably believes others are in immediate danger of death or serious bodily harm, deadly force is authorized in defense of non-DoD persons in the vicinity, when directly related to the assigned mission.

**Sample Use of Force Card**

criminals: It is a right guaranteed for all Americans. It is perfectly reasonable to provide a quick situational report (SitRep) to your chain of command. They have a need to know enemy tactics and a need to provide higher head-quarters with situational awareness on the incident. It is not reasonable, however, to question and obtain sworn statements from a soldier at two in the morning, thirty minutes post-incident. There are a number of reasons why this is true. Suppose at an entry control point (ECP) to a sensitive facility a soldier uses deadly force on a bulkily clad civilian-dressed female who fails to heed repeated warnings to halt. In a personal-borne improvised explosive device (PBIED) suicide bomber environment, such force may be perfectly reasonable. Suppose, however, that post-incident it is discovered that the bulkily clad civilian was merely a disoriented pregnant female seeking medical attention. A soldier, feeling guilty for an otherwise lawful use of force, may make self-incriminating, factually incorrect statements. The human mind, after a deadly force encounter, is often encumbered with intrusive thoughts, elation, guilt, and multiple compressed, inaccurate memories. For these reasons alone, it is provident to wait at least twenty-four hours before making a statement.

**2. Understand the pre-assaultive behaviors of the enemy and seek assistance when asked to articulate them.** A switched-on attorney can help articulate these in a sworn statement. Also, it is not enough to say, "I was in fear for my life." A coward may be in fear unwarrantedly, while a fool may never be in fear.

**3. Do not succumb to the arguments of investigators that imply, "If you don't have anything to hide, why not make a statement?"** This is a bullying tactic that should be saved for criminals, not warriors. Moreover, if the law gives a privilege such as the right to remain silent to criminals, it certainly owes the same deference to the fine Americans making life-or-death decisions in the line of duty. And in the end, so long as you act reasonably, all will end well. The law, for the foreseeable future, is on your side. Interestingly enough, by policy, federal law enforcement agencies will not allow their agents who are involved in line-of-duty shootings to make a statement for at least twenty-four hours post-incident, and then only after the agent has had an opportunity to decompress and speak with a counsel, psychologist, or chaplain if he chooses. Tactical leaders should provide the same courtesies to warriors who make decisions in situations that are often more tense and dangerous than those facing law enforcement.

## UNDERSTANDING THE RELATIONSHIP
## BETWEEN LAW AND TACTICS

The Law of War is the body of law, both codified and common, that concerns itself with the acceptable conduct of war. It addresses both *jus ad bellum*, the justifications for engaging in war, and *jus in bello*, acceptable wartime actions or conduct. Some of the central principles underlying the laws of war are that war should be limited to achieving the defined political goals that started the war; war should not include unnecessary destruction; and war should be ended as quickly as possible.

Oftentimes, America's warriors are placed into situations where the demands of *jus ad bellum* and *jus in bello* become unclear. Counterinsurgency (COIN) doctrine, at the strategic level, may call for the use of minimum force. For instance, commanders at the operational and strategic levels may decide to use a squad of infantry to clear a village instead of using indirect fire against a target within that village. This decision to use strategic "minimum force" should in no way limit the tactical decision to use force when confronted by a hostile actor. This misunderstanding and misapplication of a strategic concept at the tactical level has created a wrong impression as to what is the proper legal standard to apply when confronted by dangerous actors at the tactical level.

Since soldiers, sailors, airmen, and marines on the ground at the tip of the spear have little say in how they will be deployed, it is *very* important that they understand their authorities and responsibilities concerning the use of force. Too often, warriors are advised, "You can't shoot unless you have positive identification or PID!" This is misleading and legally incorrect, for when you use force in self-defense, the identity of the person posing an imminent threat is irrelevant at the time force is applied. This is because you do not have time to ascertain PID. As explained below, PID is *only* relevant when targeting an individual or group that has been declared hostile pursuant to the Rules of Engagement.

Killing another without lawful authority constitutes murder, manslaughter, or negligent homicide. This applies in the military, too. There are several manners by which a military member can lawfully employ deadly force, such as defense of certain classified facilities or property, but the most relevant and prevalent two are discussed here:

1. When engaging a target that has been declared hostile by competent authority under your ROE.
2. When in response to a demonstrated hostile intent or hostile act (intended to inflict death or serious bodily injury to self or friendly forces).

Against a declared hostile, once PID is established, then there is no legal obligation to detain, capture, or otherwise take less intrusive means in engaging that target. A soldier could walk into a barracks room filled with sleeping enemy combatants who have been declared hostile and shoot them. There is no legal obligation to wake them, capture them, or make it a fair fight. Similarly, if a tactical operations center can lawfully drop a 2,000-pound laser-guided bomb on that barracks room, then a lone soldier should be able to kill them with his M-4. However, when some judge advocates and commanders review these close-in killing situations, they become squeamish and mistakenly analyze them under a self-defense methodology as set forth below.

In matters of individual or unit self-defense, as spelled out in the unclassified portions of the Standing Rules of Engagement (SROE) and Standing Rules for the Use of Force (SRUF) for US Forces, servicemembers possess an *inherent* right of self-defense predicated solely on a reasonable response to a demonstrated hostile intent or hostile act (intended to inflict death or serious bodily injury to self or friendly forces). In self-defense situations, PID is irrelevant, as it matters little if the threat is a hardcore member of al Qaeda or a crazed pizza deliveryman, and proportionality is rarely an issue. Soldiers need to understand that they can use reasonable force to quell such a threat until that threat is over: the number of rounds fired is irrelevant. One shoots until the threat is over.

Apart from conflicts where America's national leadership has declared a force or group to be "hostile" or designated them as "enemy combatants," soldiers, sailors, airmen, and marines will always be responding to a hostile act or demonstrated hostile intent much as police officers do on a daily basis in the United States. Moreover, even when a group like al Qaeda has been declared hostile, they don't wear al Qaeda T-shirts or distinctive uniforms, so you are nearly always responding in a self-defense mode because the bad guys attack first. Accordingly your servicemembers need to be educated on threat identification or else they risk getting shot in the face before even recognizing that a threat exists.

Most leaders—even many infantry officers—are not very skilled in the martial arts of close personal violence and gun fighting. Quite simply, they are not gun guys. They fear the primary tool in their soldiers' toolkits—the individual weapon—as a necessary evil that should only be handled or taken out of the box when on actual combat operations. The wise tactical leader will take the time to train his warriors to be both intimate and proficient with their sidearm.

For whatever reasons, we have shifted from a nation that respected and relied on firearms to one that views weapons as either intrinsically evil or, at best, instruments to be feared. This has resulted in a military population that needs to be indoctrinated into the gun culture. Weapons don't "accidentally discharge" or shoot themselves. They fire only when a trigger finger or other object is inserted into the trigger-housing group. Skilled handling of a weapon requires repetitive, good practice. It is also a perishable skill. A clearing barrel is not the first time a soldier should be faced with the task of clearing a weapon in a crowded area.

If one were to ask the average soldier, sailor, airman, or marine how often he used a computer keyboard in the performance of his duty or privately, the answer would be on a near-daily basis. Consequently, such an individual would be intimate with the functioning of that keyboard, never needing to look to find the space bar or shift key. On the other hand, if one were to ask the *average* soldier, sailor, airman, or marine to manipulate the selector switch on his M-4 or M-9 weapon, most would have to look to do so. This is because the military, except for select units, does not encourage intimacy with the servicemember's individual weapon. Instead, the military focuses upon "weapons qualification" and safety. Qualification courses, while fine for demonstrating a soldier's ability to use the weapon to actually hit a stationary target that is not firing back, lend very little utility to a soldier's ability to fight and win in combat. They are merely a liability reducer, not a lifesaver. Qualification is *not* training, and training is *not* qualification. This is a subtle yet key distinction that leaders must grasp. Moreover, there is precious little instruction given to the average soldier on how to identify and react to an imminent threat of death or serious bodily injury.

ROE and EOF cards should not be used as a substitute for quality tactical training that incorporates situational training exercises and stress inducers. Additionally, the linear flowchart guidance provided by such cards may look good at a commander's PowerPoint morning briefing, but they provide horrific legal and tactical guidance for a soldier at the tip of the spear.

The practical problem with such linear-based thinking is that at the tactical level it fails to account for simple physics. If a vehicle is approaching a checkpoint at a mere 30 miles per hour, that speed translates into 44 feet per second. So, if a soldier perceives that a vehicle a block away is a potential threat, he will only have a few seconds to observe, discern, decide what action to take, and then act. Additionally, it is impossible to provide a "checklist" that tells a warrior when he can and cannot shoot. The tactical situations whereby force in self-defense is authorized constantly change. This is why situational training exercises (STXs) are so critically important.

Effective STXs should provide an overview of the law *and* the tactical dynamics of deadly force encounters: action versus reaction, emotional intensity (the psycho-physiological reactions of humans under high-stress tactical environments), and wound ballistics. Combat should not be the first time that warriors viscerally experience these phenomena. It is important, therefore, to use non-lethal training aids like Simunitions or Ultimate Training Munitions in situational training exercises. It is also important to drill with judgment-based targets on live-fire ranges.

Such force-on-force training creates a level of "stress inoculation" against some of the more deadly aspects of fear and stress-induced physiological and psychological effects. Students should be forced to rely upon near-instantaneous judgment, which can only be honed by exposure to a variety of complex situations requiring immediate detection, decision, and reaction. Increased understanding of tactical threats cultivates judgment through the fluid integration of decision-making and tactical concerns. Very simply, confidence in Use of Force authority and skill leads to operator competence and increases the likelihood of killing more bad guys and *potentially* fewer civilians.

Soldiers are not born with an ability to discern between friend and foe. Many lessons learned from law enforcement concerning threat identification must be incorporated into the military's training regimen. The first lesson is a psychological one: Human beings rarely, if ever, expect something bad to happen to them. It is always the *other* guy who gets into a car accident, the *other* family's home that is burglarized, and always the *other* convoys that get hit by the IED. If you were expecting to get into a gunfight, wouldn't you bring something bigger than a pistol or rifle? It is almost a universal reaction of surprise that greets most warriors and cops when they become involved in a deadly force encounter, even when responding to armed holdup calls and calls where, intellectually, the officers should have known a violent encounter was likely.

Also, Hollywood and television give a false impression on how bullets work. In the movies, a bad guy is blown through a window when struck by one round. Reality is something quite different. Consider the following account of a civil affairs soldier who was an Arkansas cop in his civilian life. He relates his ordeal of confronting two violent, armed robbers at a convenience store.

Rolling into the store parking lot, he saw two armed men running out the front door. His first reaction was one of surprise. As he got out of his car, he was surprised a second time: The two men did not flee. Instead, they charged at him with their weapons blazing. The officer's first reaction was one of incredulity: Bad guys were supposed to run when confronted by the police. He quickly recovered his wits, retreated to the back of his vehicle, and then went into his training mode: front site on target/trigger press. He quickly and successfully hit both subjects multiple times. Again, to his surprise, only one subject went down immediately, while the second subject hurdled over his downed partner and continued to charge. The officer quickly performed a combat reload (without hesitation and without thinking) and put more rounds into the second bad guy, hitting him with a fatal T shot to the brain. [The fatal T describes that area of the face between the two eyes and the tip of the nose. If you mark this area on a two dimensional target, it creates a "T" shape: hence, the "fatal T."] That subject was DRT (dead right there), with his automatic pistol empty and slide locked to the rear. The officer then shifted his attention back to the first, downed subject, who—unbelievably to the officer, having hit him with multiple rounds—was trying to push himself up off the ground to continue the attack. It took more rounds from the officer to finally finish the job of addressing that threat. This event profoundly shook the officer, but he reports that it was the fact that he was twice-surprised during the event that impacted him most.

This same type of surprise occurs in urban combat settings with surprising frequency, so training soldiers on this type of law enforcement example can only help soldiers learn what to expect and how to react. The first time they see a subject survive multiple hits should not be in a life-and-death combat setting. If they are stuck on a "qualification" mentality, they will never survive combat.

In addition, we are not born preprogrammed with much in the way of threat recognition. For instance, most reasonable adults, without training, would not recognize that an opponent who was "blading" his body into a pre-assaultive stance or balling his fists was showing signals of imminent attack. Neither prudence nor the law requires the law enforcement officer take the first punch in such a situation. In other words, the law does not require an officer to gamble with his life, nor is the Constitution a suicide pact. Similarly, members of the Armed Forces do not give up their inherent, God-given right to self-defense. In fact, the chairman of the Joint Chiefs of Staff's Standing Rules of Engagement (SROE) recognizes this inherent right (CJCSI 3121.01B, 13 June 2005). A mission may require a squad to charge an enemy machine-gun emplacement, but the rules on how to do so should *never* require an American to get shot at first!

Nevertheless, before an individual can lawfully use deadly force in
self-defense or defense of innocent
others, he must be confronted with an
individual or group that has demonstrated the hostile intent, ability, and
opportunity to inflict death or griev-
ous bodily injury upon himself or
innocent others. The law enforcement
model used to instruct on this concept
is called the Threat Triangle.

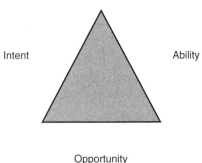

Intent                                           Ability

Opportunity

We do not need to teach our soldiers, sailors, airmen, and marines clair-
voyant skills to divine hostile intent. In fact, a suspect's subjective intent,
legally and tactically, is not at all relevant. An insane person, or someone
highly intoxicated on drugs or alcohol, may possess very little ability to for-
mulate subjective hostile intent. Or as FBI Supervisory Special Agent John
C. Hall, one of America's foremost experts on the law of Use of Force, is
fond of quoting, "Very little mentation is required for deadly action. A rat-
tlesnake is deadly but could not form the mental state required for conviction
of murder."

Rather, at a minimum, we should be training our warriors on threat
recognition as we train our cops, especially when sending them into uncertain environments where the threats are not wearing enemy uniforms. We
should train them to recognize hostile acts and objective hostile intent.

Individuals (other than when striking from a hidden ambush position)
generally do not initiate a violent act without first exhibiting certain pre-
assaultive behaviors (or "clues," as they say in law enforcement settings).
Perhaps the most prevalent pre-assaultive behavior threat indicator is verbal
noncompliance. If a uniformed, armed police officer (or soldier) is pointing
a weapon and yelling "Freeze" or "Halt," compliance is required. Most reasonable people, regardless of whether the verbal warning is in a foreign language, will find it prudent to follow such direction. An individual should not
be surprised if he is shot after openly disobeying a cop or soldier who is
pointing a weapon and ordering him to freeze or halt.

Under certain circumstances, such as when a suspect ignores a command to "Drop the knife" or "Keep your hands where I can see them," the
verbal noncompliance might be an immediate precursor to deadly force.
Under those circumstances, at the very minimum, the verbal noncompliance
of a subject should place the officer or soldier in a heightened state of alertness and awareness that something may be awry. This is especially important at entry control points (ECPs) and traffic control points (TCPs), where

the screening of many innocent persons and noncombatants might be interspersed with the quick, violent assault of an adversary.

More than any other part of the human body, the hands of a suspect are constantly a concern for most prudent law enforcement officers. The hands will most likely access the weapon or initiate the assault upon the suspect's intended victim. That is why verbal noncompliance by a potentially armed suspect to a command "Show me your hands" must be viewed as a sign of demonstrated hostile intent or imminent hostile act. Under such circumstances, persons on patrol or guard duty would be foolhardy to wait to see a weapon before taking immediate action. The same holds true in combat settings, yet very few soldiers are ever taught this lifesaving fact. Many judge advocates and commanders *wrongly* instruct their warriors to wait until a threat actually points or fires his weapon before deadly force is authorized. Never accept such nonsense if written into a tactical directive or ROE: Take the time to educate your judge advocates or superiors on the tactical realities of such situations. They are oftentimes acting out of simple ignorance or "cutting and pasting" old ROE card information that is wrong.

More than one suspect or assailant dramatically increases the danger to a soldier or law enforcement officer. Despite Hollywood movies showing cops (or martial arts experts) fending off two, three, or more attackers, the advantage a group has over an individual is high and the odds are not in favor of the individual, no matter how skilled a fighter he may be. This is true even though the officer or soldier may possess the only firearm on the scene. In addition to the sheer physical advantage multiple assailants possess over the individual, multiple assailants are also a danger because of a tunnel vision dynamic that comes into play. In other words, a soldier may be so distracted by an "obvious" bad guy (either an actual or feigned threat), that he will exclude or not focus on other possible threats within the group until it is too late.

Again, soldiers are often faced with this dilemma at TCPs and ECPs. That is why it is critical that there be sufficient personnel present, hopefully in an overwatch position with a clear field of fire, to attenuate this problem. But when out on patrol or conducting peace-enforcing missions, soldiers may not have that luxury. They need to be trained on threat identification and recognize that a hostile crowd—even if apparently unarmed—can still present a very serious threat. If the mission allows, it may be prudent for the patrol to quickly exfiltrate an area to avoid a potentially ugly and uneven situation. But the soldiers have to first be trained on recognizing the problem before seeking solutions.

Previously used tactics, techniques, and procedures (TTPs) of the enemy can be a huge building block in the development of assessing hostile intent. If the enemy has been known to use an injured civilian as a ruse to stop a convoy or divert the attention of a patrol, should that situation arise again, the patrol would be wise to go into "condition yellow" quickly; in other words be switched on and wary of attack.

Lastly, so long as it is efficiently and accurately pumped down to the lowest tactical levels, theater-specific intelligence can also be used as a building block to divine intent. The law does not require the soldier to be positive, only reasonable. Accordingly, tactical leaders have an ethical and moral responsibility to train those in their charge on both threat identification and proficient weapons handling. Those properly trained will be more likely to engage the enemy and less likely to kill noncombatants or friendly forces.

# Appendix B

# Armored Vehicle Recognition

In the recent past, armored vehicle identification was usually just a matter of distinguishing between vehicles manufactured by Warsaw Pact nations and those manufactured by NATO nations. However, even in those days it was sometimes difficult to tell the difference between vehicles on a simple friend-or-foe basis. In 2003 and 2004, several former Warsaw Pact nations joined NATO, bringing former Warsaw Pact equipment with them. In addition, changes in international relations have made it more likely that we will meet a third world nation's troops, as experienced in our operations in Iraq and Afghanistan. Most third world nations do not manufacture their own combat vehicles, but instead buy them from other countries. As a result, many of them have vehicles from nearly every manufacturing nation in the world.

As a result, one of the best ways to identify armored vehicles is to compare the observed vehicle characteristics with four known vehicle attributes or characteristics. Most, but not all armored vehicles have all four characteristic areas:

1. *Track and suspension system.* Many tanks can be recognized by their track and suspension systems unless grass, dirt, terrain, dust, or other factors are obscuring the tracks. To identify the track and suspension system, check to see whether it has support or return rollers.
   - Most former Warsaw Pact vehicles have a flat (Christie) suspension system, without support or return rollers, without torsion bars, and unevenly spaced road wheels.
   - Most NATO vehicles have a suspended track, support or return rollers, torsion bars, shock absorbers, and evenly spaced road wheels.

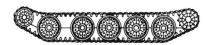

2. *Turret.* Most turrets can be grouped into three categories:
   - Big, bulky turrets—older models.
   - Well-sloped turrets—newer models.
   - Streamlined turrets—newer models.
3. *Main gun.* Armament varies from machine guns to large cannons. In turreted vehicles, normally the heaviest armament is in the turret. Look for the main gun, the main gun bore evacuator, and its relative location on the main gun.

Types of main guns include:
   - Smooth main gun, without bore evacuator or blast deflector.
   - Main gun with bore evacuator.
   - Main gun with bore evacuator and muzzle brake or blast deflector.

Types of muzzles include:
   - Single-baffle.
   - Double-baffle.
   - Multibaffled.
4. *Cupolas.* The cupola is a small, turretlike projection normally on top of the turret. It is used by the vehicle commander and usually mounts a machine gun.

Studying these various characteristics will assist you in remembering unique attributes about various armored vehicles and ultimately allow you to identify most vehicles by nomenclature. The following pages contain common NATO and former Warsaw Pact armored vehicles.

## NATO ARMORED VEHICLES
### Chieftain—British

Large, shallow turret with long, sloping front
Long gun tube with bore evacuator in center
High, flat engine decks
6 road wheels with skirting plates covering support rollers

**Centurion—British**
>   Large square turret
>   Bore evacuator $^2/_3$ down from muzzle
>   6 road wheels with skirting plates covering support rollers

**Challenger—British**
>   Center-mounted turret and fighting compartment
>   6 road wheels (space between third and fourth); 4 return rollers
>   5 smoke dischargers, each side of main gun
>   Steel skirting covering upper track

**MCV 80—British**
>   High rear deck
>   Small, shallow turret
>   Flat engine decks
>   6 road wheels

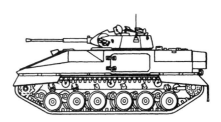

**AMX30—French**
>   Large, squat turret
>   Long gun tube, no bore evacuator
>   Flat engine decks
>   5 road wheels with support rollers

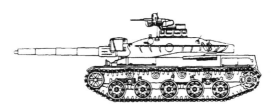

## AMX10—French

    Large cupola set to the left
    Long, thin gun (20mm)
    Flat hull with long, sloping front plate
    5 road wheels with support rollers

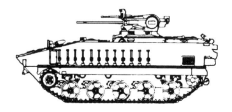

## Leopard—German

    Large, rounded flat turret
    Bore evacuator $2/3$ from muzzle
    Long, sloping-sided hull with horizontal exhaust louvres at rear
    7 road wheels with support rollers

## Leopard II—German

    Large, square turret
    7 evenly spaced road wheels
    Bore evacuator $2/3$ from muzzle
    Grenade launchers on rear side of turret
    Jagged track skirting

### Marder—German

Small turret placed centrally on hull
Gun mounted on turret
Long hull with inward-sloping sides, domed cupola at rear
6 road wheels with support rollers

### M60—United States

High rear deck and prominent cupola
Tortoiseshell-shaped turret
6 road wheels with 3 support rollers

### M60A1—United States[*]

Wedge-shaped turret
Bore evacuator $2/3$ down from muzzle, no blast deflector
6 road wheels with support rollers

---

[*]Drawing from Alan K. Russell, *Modern Battle Tanks and Support Vehicles* (Greenhill Books, London, and Stackpole Books, Mechanicsburg, PA).

## M60A3—United States
Wedge-shaped turret
Large thermal sleeve $^2/_3$ down from muzzle
Thermal sight and laser range finder mounted at body end of gun (not
 shown)
6 road wheels with 3 support rollers

## M113—United States
.50-cal MG, pintle mounted
Rectangular, box-shaped hull
Track—5 road wheels, no support rollers

## M109A61—United States
Self-propelled howitzer with long gun tube
7 evenly spaced road wheels
Large, boxy turret mounted rear of center

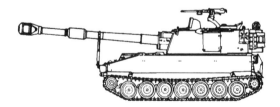

### M1 Abrams—United States
Low and boxy
Low turret—no cupola
7 road wheels covered with skirt

### M2 Bradley—United States
High profile
Distinctive turret in center with tow launcher on left side
6 road wheels, space between third and fourth road wheel
Skirt over road wheels

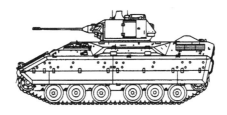

### FORMER WARSAW PACT VEHICLES
### PT 76
Cone-shaped turret set well forward
Short gun with evacuator at center, muzzle brake at end
Wide, long, square hull
Narrow back, 6 road wheels, no support rollers

**T54/55**

Dome-shaped turret mounted over third road wheel
Long gun with bore evacuator at muzzle
Sloped, low-silhouetted hull
5 road wheels with gap between first and second
No support rollers
Infrared searchlight for gun

**T62**

Smooth, round (pear-shaped) turret
Long gun with evacuator $^1/_3$ down from muzzle
Flat engine deck
5 road wheels, with large gaps between third, fourth, and fifth; no
   support rollers

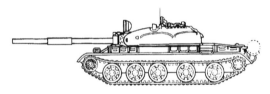

**T64**

Turret centrally mounted on chassis
Support rollers and 6 road wheels
Glacis has 4 steel ribs and **V**-shaped splash guard
Infrared searchlight mounted to left of the main armament
125mm main gun with midtube bore evacuator

## T72

    Turret centrally mounted on chassis
    Support rollers and 6 road wheels
    **V**-shaped mud deflector on front slope
    Infrared searchlight mounted to left of gun tube

## T80

    Rounded turret mounted midway on tank
    Single snorkel mounted on left side of turret
    Long gun with bore evacuator $^1/_3$ distance from muzzle
    6 evenly spaced road wheels with 3 support rollers
    Sharply sloped upper glacis with **V**-shaped splash guard

## T-10

    Turret round, well forward, well sloped
    Long gun tube, bore evacuator near end of muzzle break
    Narrow hull; wide splash guard
    7 road wheels, 3 support rollers

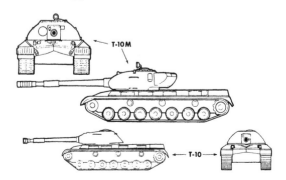

## ZSU 23-4

    Shallow and square-sided turret
    4 antiaircraft guns
    Square-sided hull
    6 road wheels, no support rollers

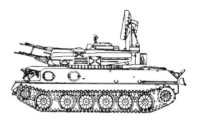

## BMD

    Same turret and armament as
       BMP (see below)
    Driver's hatch centered below
       main gun
    5 road wheels, 4 support rollers
    Found with airborne units

## BMP

    Circular, cone-shaped turret
    Short gun with missile mounted above
    Low, wide hull
    6 road wheels with support rollers

## BTR 60P

    May have small turret
    Machine gun toward front
    Large, boatlike hull with sharp, square nose
    Wheeled—4 large wheels each side

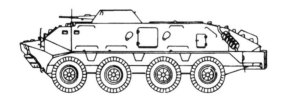

## BRDM

No turret

Armament may vary from pintle-mounted machine gun to antitank
  missiles

Long, sloping hood and raised troop compartment

4 wheels

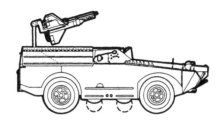

## BRDM-2

Small, cone-shaped turret, centered on hull

Machine gun mounted in turret

Square-shaped hull with distinct undercut at nose

Wheeled—2 each side

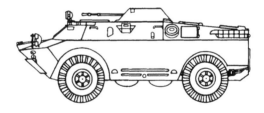

## SAU 122

PT-76–type chassis with 7 road
  wheels

Turret location is rear of center

Infrared searchlight top left of
  turret

Double-baffle muzzle brake and
  bore evacuator

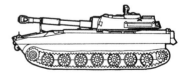

# Appendix C

# Operational Graphics

Operational graphics (map symbols) depict control measures and friendly and enemy units and equipment. These symbols are normally written on graphical overlays, which fit to the individual map scale, to help leaders better identify the battle plan and the placement of units and equipment applicable to the battle.

## RULES
Operational graphics depict both the operational and support roles of the battle and have certain rules.

### Control Measures
All control measures (obstacles, locations, routes, and lines)—friendly, enemy, neutral, or factional—are drawn using the color green.

All other friendly graphic control measures are shown in black. Enemy graphic control measures are shown in red. If red is not available, they are drawn in black with a double line or the abbreviation "ENY" placed in at least two locations to avoid confusion. If colors are used to show friendly or enemy (hostile factions), they must be shown on the overlay in a legend describing what each color means.

| Affiliation | Hand-Drawn | Computer-Generated |
|---|---|---|
| Friend, Assumed Friend | Blue | Cyan |
| Unknown, Pending | Yellow | Yellow |
| Neutral | Green | Green |
| Enemy, Suspect, Joker, Faker | Red | Red |

**Unit Symbol Color Defaults**

366

## Unit and Equipment Symbols

Unit and equipment symbols are composed of three components: a frame (geometric border), fill, and icon. *Frames* are geometric shapes used to display affiliation. The basic affiliation categories are friendly, unknown, neutral, and enemy. The unknown unit frame shape is normally used only for aircraft and ships. The frame shape for suspected friendly, enemy, or neutral is used for ground units not positively identified. The basic frame shapes for units, installations, activities, and logistics sites are shown in the following figure.

| | Friendly Ground Units | Friendly Sea/Air | Unknown Sea/Air | Neutral | Enemy Units |
|---|---|---|---|---|---|
| Surface | | | | | |
| Subsurface | | | | | |
| In-flight | | | | | |

**Unit Installation and Site Symbol Frames**

*Fill* refers to the area within the frame. If color is used in a symbol, it indicates affiliation. Generally, black is used for the frame, icon, and modifiers when symbols are displayed on a light background. White is used for these elements when they are displayed on a dark background. A color fill can be used if an icon is displayed within the area of the frame. The figure on the previous page shows the color defaults for affiliation used for hand-drawn and computer-generated symbols.

The *icon* is a "role indicator" that shows the warfighting function the unit performs either on the ground, in the air, or at sea. An example is the crossed rifles, which represent an infantry unit.

# UNIT SIZE

| Squad/crew | Smallest unit/UK section | • |
| --- | --- | --- |
| Section or unit larger than a squad but smaller than a platoon | Unit larger than a US squad/UK section but smaller than a platoon equivalent | •• |
| Platoon or detachment | Platoon/troop equivalent | ••• |
| Company, battery, or troop | Company/battery/squadron equivalent | &#124; |
| Battalion or squadron | Battalion equivalent | &#124;&#124; |
| Group or regiment | Regiment/group equivalent | &#124;&#124;&#124; |
| Brigade | Brigade equivalent | X |
| Division | Division | XX |
| Corps | Corps | XXX |
| Army | Army | XXXX |
| Army group or front | Army group/front | XXXXX |
| Special size indicator for a nonorganic or temporary grouping | Battalion task force | &#124;&#124;&#124; |
|  | Company team | &#124;&#124; |

## UNIT TYPE

| | |
|---|---|
| Adjutant General (personnel services and administration) | AG |
| Aerial observation | Air Force (surveillance)    Army |
| Airborne (normally associated with another branch symbol) | |
| Air cavalry | |
| Air defense | |
| Amphibious | |
| Amphibious engineer | |
| Antiarmor | |
| Armor | |
| Armored cavalry | |
| Army aviation                Rotary wing | |
| Fixed wing | |
| Attack helicopter | |
| Bridging | |

## UNIT TYPE *(Continued)*

| | |
|---|---|
| Cavalry or reconnaissance | |
| Chemical (NBC) | |
| Chemical (NBC decontamination) | DECON |
| Chemical (NBC reconnaissance) | |
| Chemical (smoke generator) | SMOKE |
| Civil affairs (US only) | CA |
| Data processing unit | DPU |
| Dental | D |
| Engineer | |
| Electronic warfare | EW |
| Field artillery | ● |
| Finance/pay | |
| Infantry | |
| Light | LT |

## UNIT TYPE *(Continued)*

| | | |
|---|---|---|
| | Mechanized<br><br>APC | |
| | BIFV (mounted) | |
| | BIFV (dismounted) | |
| | Motorized | |
| Maintenance | | |
| Medical | | |
| Military intelligence<br>(at corps and below, insert is CEWI) | | MI |
| Military police | | MP |
| Motorized | | |
| Mountain | | |
| Ordnance | | |
| Petroleum supply | | |
| Psychological operations | | |
| Quartermaster | | |

## UNIT TYPE *(Continued)*

| | |
|---|---|
| Ranger | RGR |
| Rocket artillery | |
| Service | SVC |
| Signal/communications | |
| Sound ranging | |
| Special forces | SF |
| Supply | |
| Supply and maintenance | |
| Supply and transportation | |
| Support | SPT |
| Surface-to-air missile | |
| Surface-to-surface missile | |
| Transportation | |
| Unmanned air reconnaissance (RPV, etc.) | |

# WEAPONS AND EQUIPMENT

Select the appropriate weapon symbol.

|                           |              |
|---------------------------|--------------|
| (light automatic weapon)  | (gun)        |

Add horizontal bars (one for medium or two for heavy) to denote the size.

|                          |             |
|--------------------------|-------------|
| (medium machine gun)     | (heavy gun) |

If a weapon has a high trajectory, a ○ is placed at the base of the shaft.
If a weapon has a flat trajectory, a ⌒ is placed at the base of the shaft.

|                  |                      |
|------------------|----------------------|
| (medium mortar)  | (light antitank gun) |

If the weapon is primarily for air defense, a ⌂ is placed at the base of the shaft.

|                        |                   |
|------------------------|-------------------|
| (air defense missile)  | (air defense gun) |

If the weapon is rocket launched, a ⌃ is placed at the head of the shaft. If a weapon is also a tracked, self-propelled vehicle, a ⬭ is placed below the weapon symbol.

|                    |                                                 |
|--------------------|-------------------------------------------------|
| (rocket launcher)  | (tracked, self-propelled medium howitzer)       |

## WEAPONS AND EQUIPMENT *(Continued)*

| | LIGHT | MEDIUM | HEAVY |
|---|---|---|---|
| Air defense gun | | | |
| Antitank gun | | | |
| Antitank missile, self-propelled | | | |
| Antitank rocket launcher | | | |
| Flamethrower | portable | vehicular | |
| Gun in air defense role, self-propelled | | | |
| Gun in antitank role | | | |
| Howitzer | | | |
| Machine gun/automatic weapon | | | |
| Mortar | | | |
| Multibarrel rocket launcher | | | |
| Surface-to-air missile | | | |
| Surface-to-surface missile | | | |

# VEHICLES

| | |
|---|---|
| Armored personnel carrier (APC) | |
| Armored engineer vehicle | |
| Armored vehicle launch bridge (AVLB) | |
| Bradley infantry fighting vehicle (BIFV) | |
| Cavalry fighting vehicle (CFV) | |
| Tank | LIGHT MEDIUM HEAVY |

# LOCATIONS

| | |
|---|---|
| A solid line symbol represents a present or actual location. | |
| A broken line symbol indicates a future or projected location. | |
| Basic symbols other than the headquarters symbol may be placed on a staff that is extended or bent as required. The end of the staff indicated the precise location. | |

## POINTS

| | OWN | ENEMY |
|---|---|---|
| General or unspecified point (Exact location is the tip at the bottom of the symbol) | | |
| Coordinating point (Exact location is the center of the symbol) | ⊗ | ⊗ |
| Contact point | | |
| Start point | SP | SP |
| Release point | RP | RP |
| Strongpoint (May be combined with unit size symbol) | SP 6  SP 5 | SP 2 |
| Checkpoint | 8 | |
| Linkup point | 8 | |
| Passage point | PP 8 | |
| Point of departure | PD | |
| Pop-up point | PUP | |
| Rally point | RALLY | |
| Rendezvous point (Letter in circle appears in alphabetical sequence for number of points required) | A  RDVU | |

# LINES

| Front lines | Own present | |
| | Own planned | |
| | Enemy present | |
| | Enemy anticipated or suspect | |
| General tactical boundary | Own present | —— X X —— |
| | Own planned | – – – – -X X- – – – |
| | Enemy present | EN —— III —— E N —— |
| | Enemy anticipated or suspect | – E N – –III– – E N – |
| Obstacle line (Tips point toward the enemy) | | |
| Fortified line | | |

# ROUTES

| | |
|---|---|
| Attack<br>General symbol for main attack—double arrowhead | |
| General symbol for other than main attack—single arrowhead | |
| Double arrowhead for direction of main attack and axis of advance for the main attack | |
| Single arrowhead for supporting direction of attack and supporting axis of advance | |
| Axis of advance<br><br>Actual | ALPHA |
| Proposed with date and time effective | RED EFF 040530Z NOV |
| Axis of advance for unit designated to conduct main attack | TF 2-7 |
| Bypass<br><br>Bypass easy | |
| Bypass difficult | |
| Bypass impossible | |
| Direction of attack<br><br>Direction of attack is shown graphically as an arrow extending from the line of departure. The arrow is not normally labeled. | LD    X<br>OBJ RED<br>LD    X |
| Follow and support mission | |

## OBSTACLES

| | |
|---|---|
| Abatis | |
| Booby trap | |
| Nonexplosive antitank | |
| Trip wire | |
| Wire | |
| Point<br>Planned abatis reinforced with antipersonnel mines | |
| Executed or fired demolition reinforced with antitank mines | |
| Booby-trapped nonexplosive anititank obstacle with target serial number | |
| Linear<br>Antitank ditch<br>(A rectangle need not be used when the obstacle is drawn to scale on the overlay. Teeth point toward the enemy.) | Under preparation   Completed |
| Unspecified | |
| Wire<br>(enemy under preparation) | |
| Minefields<br>  Indicators<br>    Antipersonnel mine | |
| Antitank mine | |

## OBSTACLES *(Continued)*

| | |
|---|---|
| Antitank mine with antihandling device | |
| Mine cluster | |
| Mine, type unspecified | O |
| Conventional<br>A planned minefield consisting of<br>unspecified mines | |
| A completed minefield consisting of<br>unspecified mines | |
| Scatterable minefield<br>(DTGs used for self-destruct mines) | S<br>DTG |
| Conventional row mining<br>(outline drawn to scale) | |
| Nuisance<br>Nuisance minefield | |
| Phony<br>Phony minefield | |
| Protective<br>Protective minefield | |
| Antitank ditch reinforced with antitank mines | |
| Tactical<br>Tactical minefield of scatterable antitank<br>mines, effective till 101200Z | 101200Z |
| Completed antitank minefield<br>(drawn away from the location and<br>connected by a vector) | |

# FIRE PLANNING

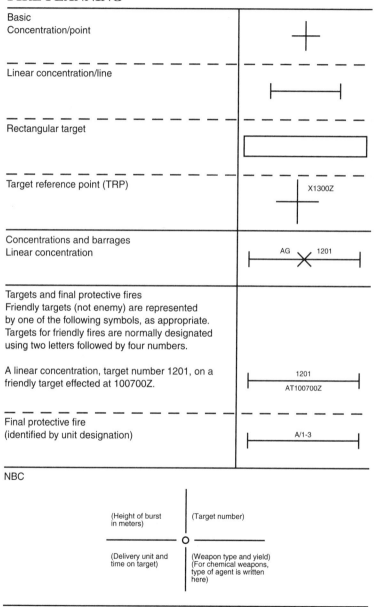

Basic
Concentration/point

Linear concentration/line

Rectangular target

Target reference point (TRP)

X1300Z

Concentrations and barrages
Linear concentration

AG 1201

Targets and final protective fires
Friendly targets (not enemy) are represented
by one of the following symbols, as appropriate.
Targets for friendly fires are normally designated
using two letters followed by four numbers.

A linear concentration, target number 1201, on a
friendly target effected at 100700Z.

1201
AT100700Z

Final protective fire
(identified by unit designation)

A/1-3

NBC

(Height of burst
in meters)

(Target number)

(Delivery unit and
time on target)

(Weapon type and yield)
(For chemical weapons,
type of agent is written
here)

# Appendix D

# Minefields and Minefield Recording

Mines are one of the most effective tank and personnel killers on the battlefield. Minefields that an infantry platoon or squad most commonly emplace are the hasty protective, point, and phony.

US policy regarding the use and employment of antipersonnel land mines (APLs) outlined in this guide is subject to the *Convention on Certain Conventional Weapons* and executive orders. Current US policy limits the use of non-self-destructing APLs to (1) defending the US and its allies from armed aggression across the Korean demilitarized zone and (2) training personnel engaged in demining and countermine operations. The use of the M18A1 Claymore in the command-detonation mode is not restricted under international law or executive order. Note, however, that some countries employ antihandling devices (AHDs) on antipersonnel (AP) mines, but US forces are not authorized to employ AHDs on any type of AP mine.

## HASTY PROTECTIVE MINEFIELD
In the defense, platoons and squads lay hasty protective minefields to supplement weapons, prevent surprise, and give early warning of enemy advance. A platoon can install hasty protective minefields, but only with permission from the company commander. Hasty protective minefields are reported to the company commander and recorded on DA Form 1355-1-R, Hasty Protective Row Minefield Record.

The leader puts the minefield across likely avenues of approach, within range of and covered by his organic weapons. If time permits, the mines should be buried to increase effectiveness, but they may be laid on top of the ground in a random pattern. The minefield should be recorded before the mines are armed. The leader installing the minefield should warn adjacent platoons and tell the company commander of the minefield's location. When the platoon leaves the area (except when forced to withdraw by the enemy),

382

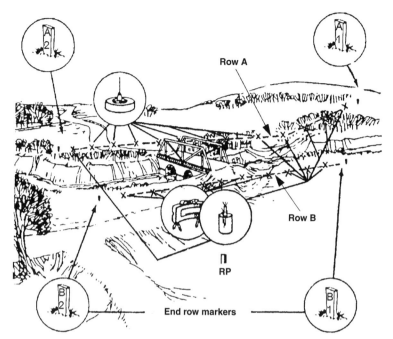

Row A

Row B

RP

End row markers

**Antipersonnel and Antitank Mines
in a Hasty Protective Minefield**

it must remove the minefield or transfer responsibility for the minefield to the relieving platoon leader.

Only metallic mines are used in hasty protective minefields. Booby traps are not used because they delay removal of the mines. The employing platoon must make sure that the minefield can be kept under observation and covered by fire at all times. The following example describes how to lay a hasty protective minefield.

After requesting and receiving permission to lay the minefield, the platoon leader and squad leaders reconnoiter to determine exactly where to place the mines. The leaders determine a need to use antitank mines to block enemy vehicles at the bridge and the ford. The leaders also decide that antipersonnel mines are needed to protect the antitank mines and to cover the likely avenues of approach of enemy infantry.

While the soldiers are placing the mines, the platoon leader finds an easily identifiable reference point (a concrete post) in front of the platoon's position. The platoon leader records the minefield using a reference point. The row of mines closest to the enemy is designated A; the succeeding rows are

B, C, and so on. The ends of a row are shown by two markers. They are labeled with the letter of the row and number 1 for the right end of the row or number 2 for the left end of the row. The rows are numbered from right to left, facing the enemy. The marker can be a steel picket or a wooden stake with a nail or can attached so that it can be found with a metallic mine detector.

From the base reference point (the concrete post), the platoon leader measures the magnetic azimuth in degrees and paces the distance to a point between fifteen and twenty-five paces to the right of the first mine on the friendly side of the minefield. This point, B-1, marks the beginning of the second row. The platoon leader places a marker at B-1 and records the azimuth and distance from the concrete post to B-1 on DA Form 1355-1-R.

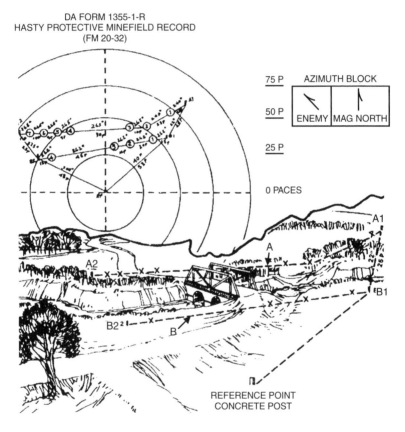

**Marking and Recording Minefield**

Next, from B-1 the platoon leader measures the azimuth and distance to a point fifteen to twenty-five paces from the first mine in row A. He places a marker at this point and records it as A-1. The platoon leader then measures the distance and azimuth from A-1 to the first mine in row A and records the location of the mine. He then measures the distance and azimuth from the first mine to the second, and so on until all mine locations have been recorded as shown. The platoon leader gives each mine a number to identify it in the tabular block of DA Form 1355-1-R. When the last mine location in row A is recorded, the platoon leader measures an azimuth and distance from the last mine to another arbitrary point between fifteen and twenty-five paces beyond the last mine. He places a marker here and calls it A-2. The platoon leader follows the same procedure with row B.

When the platoon leader finishes recording and marking the rows, he measures the distance and azimuth from the reference point to B-2 to A-2, and records them. *Note*: If antitank mines are being used, it is recommended that they be used at the A-2/B-2 markers, because their large size facilitates retrieval.

The platoon leader now ties in the reference point with a permanent landmark that he found on the map. He measures the distance and azimuth from this landmark to the reference point. The landmark might be used to help others locate the minefield should it be abandoned. Finally, he completes the form by filling in the tabular and identification blocks.

While the platoon leader is tying in the landmark, the soldiers arm the mines nearest the enemy first (row A). The platoon leader reports that the minefield is completed and keeps DA Form 1355-1-R. If the minefield is transferred to another platoon, the gaining platoon leader signs and dates the "Mines Transferred" block and accepts the form from the previous leader. When the minefield is removed, the form is destroyed. If the minefield is left unattended or abandoned unexpectedly, the form must be forwarded to the company commander. The company commander forwards it to the battalion to be transferred to more permanent records.

When retrieving the mines, the soldiers start at the reference point and move to B-1, using the azimuth and distances as recorded. They then move from B-1 to the first mine in row B. However, if B-1 is destroyed, they move from the reference point to B-2 using that azimuth and distance. They will have to shoot the back azimuth from B-2 to the last mine. The stakes at A-1, B-1, A-2, and B-2 are necessary because it is safer to find a stake when traversing long distances than to find a live mine. Some rules to remember:

- Measurements are in meters.
- The minimum distance between rows of antitank (AT) mines is 8 meters.

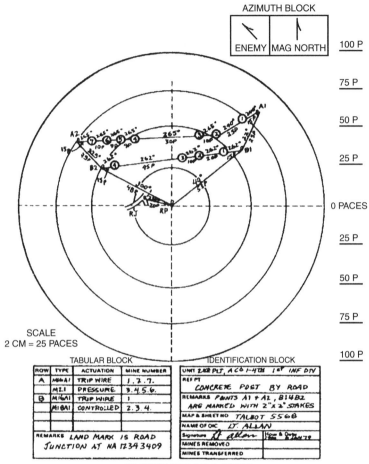

DA FORM 1355-1-R, 1 JULY 75,
REPLACES DA FORM 1335-7, 1 MAR 68, WHICH IS OBSOLETE

### Hasty Protective Minefield Record

- *In Korea only*, the minimum distance between any row and a row containing AP mines is 15 meters.
- The distance between the start row marker and the first mine in a row is the mine spacing for that row.
- Start and end row markers are permanent markers and must be made of detectable material.
- The spacing between mines is at least 4 meters to prevent sympathetic detonation. There is no maximum distance between mines within the row.

- The minefield must be fenced on all sides if M18A1 AP mines are employed and the minefield will be in place for more than seventy-two hours.
- The minefield has at least one landmark that is located to the rear, never to the extreme side or front.
- AHDs, nonmetallic mines, or low-metallic mines are not used.

## POINT MINEFIELDS

Point minefields disorganize enemy forces and hinder their use of key areas. Point minefields are of irregular size and shape and include all types of anti-tank and antipersonnel mines and antihandling devices. They should be used to add to the effect of existing and reinforcing obstacles, or to rapidly block an enemy counterattack along a flank avenue of approach.

## PHONY MINEFIELDS

Phony minefields, used to degrade enemy mobility and preserve friendly mobility, simulate live minefields and deceive the enemy. They are used when lack of time, personnel, or material prevents the use of actual mines. Phony minefields may be used as gaps in live minefields. To be effective, a phony minefield must look like a live minefield, which is accomplished by either burying metallic objects or making the ground look as though objects are buried.

# Appendix E

# Platoon and Squad Organization

All infantry platoons and units acting as infantry use the same basic doctrinal principles in combat, but some differences exist between organizations. Most units operate from a modified table of organization and equipment (MTOE) based on their organization, mission, and location. Rifle platoons are organized as light infantry, mechanized infantry, infantry, air assault infantry, airborne infantry, or Ranger infantry. The importance of organizing units for combat cannot be overemphasized. All military units, regardless of classification as combat arms, combat support, or combat service support, should have a fighting organization. The enemy doesn't care what your specialty is; if you are a cook, mechanic, or other noninfantry element, you need to have a fighting battle roster for those times when you will need to defend yourself. The war in Iraq and the war on terrorism in Afghanistan and around the world have proven to us that there is no safe military occupational duty specialty. Every unit needs to have the minimum ability to fight and defend itself as a collective fighting force.

The most common organization is that of the light infantry platoon, and it is the easiest to duplicate with soldiers who are not used to being infantry. It consists of three rifle squads and a platoon headquarters with two machine-gun teams (if available). Each machine-gun team has a gunner and an assistant gunner. The antiarmor weapons are distributed evenly throughout the squads and are usually assigned to more seasoned soldiers.

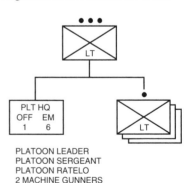

PLT HQ
OFF    EM
1        6

PLATOON LEADER
PLATOON SERGEANT
PLATOON RATELO
2 MACHINE GUNNERS
2 ASSISTANT MACHINE GUNNERS

**Light Infantry Platoon
Organization**

388

The most common rifle squad has nine soldiers and fights as two rifle teams. The squad has one squad leader, two rifle team leaders, and (if weapons are available) two automatic riflemen (M249 SAW), two riflemen (M16), and two grenadiers (M203).

## ORGANIZING FOR COMBAT

In order to organize your unit as a fighting infantry platoon or fighting force, you have to take a look at and analyze your personnel and equipment. Organize your force based on the number of personnel you have. If you only have thirteen people, you might consider just replicating a large infantry squad with three fire teams (you can also have two larger fire teams) or one infantry squad with a machine gunner and an antiarmor specialist.

Additionally, you have to look at your available weapons and determine who is best at using machine guns or antiarmor weapons if you have them available. Often soldiers are assigned more than one weapon, such as an M16 rifle while also responsible for a crew-served machine gun mounted on

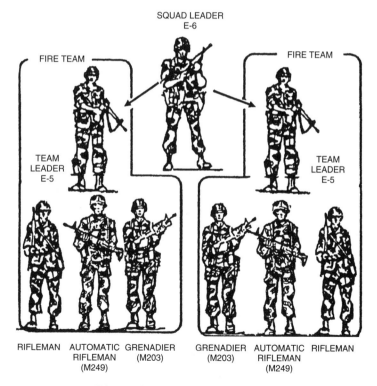

SQUAD LEADER
E-6

FIRE TEAM         FIRE TEAM

TEAM LEADER E-5         TEAM LEADER E-5

RIFLEMAN   AUTOMATIC RIFLEMAN (M249)   GRENADIER (M203)     GRENADIER (M203)   AUTOMATIC RIFLEMAN (M249)   RIFLEMAN

**Light Infantry Squad Organization**

the vehicle. Assign someone the duties of machine gunner in the event your element has to dismount and fight. There is no right or wrong way to organize your element; just ensure your personnel know their assigned duties and their assigned weapon system(s). When time presents itself, conduct the necessary individual and unit training that is most critical to your survival in the event you get into a firefight.

**Duties and Responsibilities**

The *rifle squad leader* is responsible for the squad. He is a tactical leader and leads by example. He controls his squad's movement, rate, and distribution of fire. He controls two fire teams in the offense; selects each fighting position in the defense; and gives the commands and signals to commence, cease, and shift fires. He briefs the squad on orders, trains the squad, manages the squad's administrative and logistical needs, is responsible for accountability and maintenance of personnel and equipment, and keeps the squad fit to fight.

The *team leader* controls the movement and fires of the fire team. He assists the squad leader in tactical control of the squad and in training team members on individual and collective tasks and battle drills. The team leader sends reports as requested to the squad leader when his team makes contact. The team leader controls fire and distribution for his team by designating and marking targets.

The *grenadier* is equipped with an M203 weapon system consisting of an M4/M16 rifle and an attached 40mm grenade launcher. The M203 allows him to fire high-explosive rounds to suppress and destroy enemy infantry and lightly armored vehicles. He also can employ smoke to screen and cover his squad's movement, fire, and maneuver. During night and adverse weather conditions, the grenadier also may employ illumination rounds to increase his squad's visibility and mark enemy or friendly positions. The grenadier provides the fire team with an indirect-fire capability out to 350 meters.

The *automatic rifleman*'s primary weapon is the M249 squad automatic weapon (SAW). Each infantry squad has two automatic weapons. The M249 provides the squad with a high volume of sustained long-range suppressive and lethal fires far beyond the range of the M16/M4 rifle. The gunner employs the SAW to suppress enemy infantry and bunkers, to destroy enemy automatic rifle and antitank (AT) teams, and to enable other teams and squads to maneuver. If a unit does not have a SAW, the next best thing is to designate the automatic riflemen in the squad and have them use the burst mode on their rifles to accomplish rapid fire.

The *rifleman* is armed with an M4 or M16A2 5.56mm rifle. He is employed at the direction of the team leader.

The *antiarmor specialist* is equipped with the Javelin AT missile system, M47 Dragon, or even the M136 AT-4. The available AT weapon system destroys enemy armor threats that may impede the platoon's or unit's progress, or it can be employed to destroy other targets of opportunity. The Javelin provides the squads, platoon, and company with a lethal, fire-and-forget, man-portable, top-attack antiarmor capability to defeat enemy main battle tanks during day, night, and adverse weather conditions at ranges up to 2,000 meters.

The *machine-gun crew* consists of three personnel: the gunner, assistant gunner, and ammunition handler. The gunner is the senior member of the crew and responsible for putting the gun in and out of action. The assistant gunner supports and replaces the gunner in his absence. The ammunition handler carries the spare barrel and additional ammunition for the machine gun and provides local security for the machine-gun crew with his assigned rifle.

# Appendix F

# Organic and
# Supporting Weapons

**ORGANIC WEAPONS**

Organic weapons are those assigned to the platoon over which the platoon leader has direct control. Every leader must know how to employ these weapons effectively in all tactical situations. Additionally, the infantry platoon routinely uses antiarmor weapons, hand grenades, and mines. The following tables outline some of the key organic weapon systems available to the modern infantry platoon.

## WEAPON CAPABILITIES PLANNING REFERENCE

| | | NON-US WEAPONS | US WEAPONS |
|---|---|---|---|
| ASSAULT RIFLES | | AK47/AKM Rifle | M4 Carbine |
| | Caliber | 7.62x39mm | 5.56x45mm |
| | Max. eff. range | 500m | 500m area |
| SNIPER RIFLES | | SVD Sniper Rifle | M14/M24 Sniper Rifle |
| | Caliber | 7.62x54R mm | 7.62x51mm |
| | Max. eff. range | 1,000m area | 900m area |
| MACHINE GUNS | | RPK Machine Gun | M249 SAW Machine Gun |
| | Caliber | 7.62x39mm | 5.56x45mm |
| | Max. eff. range | 800m area | 600m area |
| MACHINE GUNS | | PKM Machine Gun | M240/MAG58 Machine Gun |
| | Caliber | 7.62x54R mm | 7.62x51mm |
| | Max. eff. range | 1,000m area | 1,100m area |
| MACHINE GUNS | | DShKM Machine Gun | M2 BMG Machine Gun |
| | Caliber | 12.7x108mm | .50 BMG (12.7x99mm) |
| | Max. eff. Range | 2,000m area | 1,830m |
| ROCKET LAUNCHERS | | RPG-7 | M136 AT4 |
| | Caliber | 40mm tube w/85mm HEAT head | 84mm |
| | Max. eff. range | 500m | 300m |
| | Max. lethal range | 900m self-destruct | 2,100m |
| | Penetration Capabilities | Sandbags—90 in. Concrete, reinforced—18 in. Homogenous steel—10–12 in. Earthen bunker—60 in. | Homogenous steel—15 in. |

| WEAPON CAPABILITIES | M9 Pistol | M16A2 | M249 MG | M203 | M4 |
|---|---|---|---|---|---|
| WEIGHT (lbs) | 2.6 | 8.7 | 15.5 | 11 | 7.5 |
| LENGTH (in) | 8.5 | 39 | 41.1 | 39 | 29.75 closed; 35 open |
| MAXIMUM RANGE (m) | 1,800 | 3,600 | 3,600 | 400 | 3,600 |
| ARMING RANGE (m) | N/A | N/A | N/A | 14 | N/A |
| MINIMUM SAFE RANGE (m) | N/A | N/A | N/A | 31 | N/A |

**RATE OF FIRE**
(rounds per minute)

| | M9 Pistol | M16A2 | M249 MG | M203 | M4 |
|---|---|---|---|---|---|
| CYCLIC (rpm) | N/A | 700–800 | 800 | N/A | 700–900 |
| RAPID (m) | N/A | N/A | 200* | 35 | N/A |
| SUSTAINED | 60 | 16 | 85 | 35 | 12/15 |

**EFFECTIVE RANGE**

| | M9 Pistol | M16A2 | M249 MG | M203 | M4 |
|---|---|---|---|---|---|
| AREA (m) | N/A | 800 | 800 | 350 | 600 |
| POINT | 50 | 580 | 600 | 160 | 500 |
| MOVING (m) | N/A | 200 | N/A | N/A | N/A |

**AMMUNITION**

| | M9 Pistol | M16A2 | M249 MG | M203 | M4 |
|---|---|---|---|---|---|
| TYPE | BALL | BALL, TRACER, DUMMY, PRACTICE, and BLANK | BALL, TRACER, DUMMY, PRACTICE, and BLANK | HE,WP, CS, ILLUM, TP, and BUCKSHOT | |
| EXAMPLE LOAD (rds) | 30 | 210 | 600 | | |

* With barrel change

**M870 ARMY SHOTGUN**

| | |
|---|---|
| LENGTH OF SHOTGUN | 39 INCHES, APPROXIMATELY |
| LENGTH OF BARREL | 20 INCHES |
| MAGAZINE CAPACITY—ROUNDS | 4 |
| SHELL (GAUGE) | 12 |
| AMMUNITION | 12 GAUGE, 2 3/4 INCH 00 BUCK, MILITARY RD |
| SAFETY | CROSSBOLT TYPE |
| FORE-END | PLAIN BEAVER-TAIL STYLE |

## Organic Weapons

| TECHNICAL SPECIFICATIONS | M72 LAW | M136 AT4 | JAVELIN |
|---|---|---|---|
| WEIGHT (lbs) | 5.1 | 14.8 | 49.5 |
| LENGTH (in) | 24/36 | 40 | 47.2 |
| MAXIMUM RANGE (m) | 1,000 | 2,100 | 2,500 |
| ARMING RANGE (m) | 10 | 10 | 65 |
| MINIMUM SAFE RANGE (m) | 10 | 30 | 65 |
| **EFFECTIVE RANGE** | | | |
| STATIONARY(m) | 200 | 300 | 2,000 |
| MOVING (m) | 165 | 300 | 2,000 |
| BACKBLAST(m) | 50 | 60 | 25 at 60 degree angle |

## Antiarmor Weapons

| GRENADE SPECIFICATIONS | FRAGMENTARY | WP | THERMITE | CONCUSS |
|---|---|---|---|---|
| WEIGHT (oz) | 14 | 27 | 32 | 15.6 |
| RANGE (m) | 35 | 30 | 25 | 40 |
| (Thrown by average soldier) | | | | |
| PACKING (box) | 30 | N/A | 16 | 20 |
| BURST RADIUS (m) | 15 | 35 60-sec. burn | 40-sec. burn | 2 |

| MINE SPECIFICATIONS | M21 ANTITANK | M18A1 AP (Claymore) | M14 AP Toe Popper* | M16A1 AP Bouncing Betty* |
|---|---|---|---|---|
| WEIGHT (lbs) | 18 | 3.5 | 3.6 | 3.5 |
| PACKING (box) | 4 mines 4 fuses | 6 mines with accessories | 90 mines 90 detonators | 4 fuses, trip wire |
| BURST RADIUS (m) | N/A | 100 (eff); 250 (max) | 1 individual | 30 |

*U.S. policy regarding the use and employment of this mine is subject to the Convention on Certain Conventional Weapons and Executive Orders. Current U.S. policy limits the use of non-self-destructing mines to (1) defending the U.S. and its allies from armed aggression across the Korean demilitarized zone and (2) training personnel engaged in demining and countermine operations. The use of the M18A1 Claymore in the command-detonation mode is not restricted under law of Executive Order.

## Hand Grenades and Mines

## SUPPORTING WEAPONS

Supporting weapons provide the platoon and squad leaders with additional firepower. Leaders must know how to effectively integrate the fires of these weapons with the fires of their organic weapons. The following tables outline some of the key supporting weapon systems available to the modern infantry platoon:

| SPECIFICATIONS | M2 (.50 CAL) MG | MK 19 | M202 FLASH | M3 RAAWS |
|---|---|---|---|---|
| WEIGHT (lbs) | 84 | 72.5 | 26.7 | 22 |
| LENGTH (in) | 65.1 | 43.1 | 34.7 | 42.6 |
| MAXIMUM RANGE (m) | 6,767 | 2,200 | N/A | |
| ARMING RANGE (m) | N/A | 15 to 30 | N/A | |
| MINIMUM SAFE RANGE (m) | N/A | 28 | 20 | 50 (HEAT) |
| | | | | 500 (illum) |
| | | | | 250 (HE) |
| | | | | 50 (SMOKE) |
| | | | | 50 (TNG) |
| **RATE OF FIRE** | | | | |
| CYCLIC (rpm) | 500 | 375 | N/A | |
| RAPID (rpm) | 40* | 60 | N/A | |
| SUSTAINED (rpm) | 40* | 40 | N/A | 6 |
| **EFFECTIVE RANGE** | | | | |
| AREA (m) | 1,830 | 2,200 | 750 | 200–1,300 |
| POINT (m) | 1,200 | 1,500 | 200 | |
| STATIONARY (m) | N/A | N/A | N/A | 700 (HEAT) |
| MOVING (m) | N/A | N/A | N/A | 250 |
| BACKBLAST (m) | | | 50 | 60 |
| BURST RADIUS (m) | | 30 | 20 | |
| **AMMUNITION** | | | | |
| TYPE | BALL, AP, TRACER, API, API-T, INCEN, and BLANK | HEDP, HE | FLAME | HEAT, ILLUM, HE, HEDP, SMOKE, TP, and TNG |

*\* with barrel change*

**Supporting Weapons**

| WEAPON | AMMUNITION MODEL | TYPE | (meters) MIN RANGE | MAX RANGE | RATE OF FIRE |
|---|---|---|---|---|---|
| M224 | M720/M888 | HE | 70 | 3,490* | 30 rounds per minute |
| 60-mm | M722 | WP | 70 | 3,490 | for 4 minutes**, then |
|  | M721 | ILLUM | 200 | 3,490 | 20 rounds per minute, |
|  | M302A1 | WP | 33 | 1,630 | sustained. |
|  | M83A3 | ILLUM | 725 | 931 |  |
|  | M49A4 | HE | 44 | 1,930 |  |
|  |  |  |  |  |  |
| M252 | M821 | HE | 83 | 5,608 | 30 rounds per minute |
| 81-mm | M889 | HE | 83 | 5,608 | for 2 minutes, then |
|  | M819 | RP | 300 | 4,875 | 15 rounds per minute, |
|  | M853 | ILLUM | 300 | 5,100 | sustained. |
|  |  |  |  |  |  |
| M120 | M57 | HE | 200 | 7,200 | 16 rounds per minute |
| 120-mm | M68 | WP | 200 | 7,200 | for 1 minute, then |
|  | M91 | ILLUM | 200 | 7,100 | 4 rounds per minute, |
|  | M933 | HE | 200 | 7,200 | sustained. |
|  | M934 | HE | 200 | 7,200 |  |
|  | M929 | WP | 200 | 7,200 |  |
|  | M930 | ILLUM | 400 | 6,900 |  |

*Bipod mounted, charge 4 (maximum range handheld is 1,340 meters).
**Charge 2 and over, 30 rounds per minute can be sustained with charge 0 or 1.

## Mortars

|  | M119 | M198 | M109A6 |
|---|---|---|---|
| CALIBER | 105-mm | 155-mm | 155-mm |
| MAXIMUM RANGE (for HE) (m) | 14,000 | 24,000 | 24,000 |
| PLANNING RANGE (m) | 11,500 | 14,600 | 14,600 |
| MINIMUM RANGE (m) | DIRECT FIRE | DIRECT FIRE | DIRECT FIRE |
| DANGER CLOSE RANGE (m) at Planning Range | 600 | 600 | 600 |
| **RATE OF FIRE** | | | |
| MAXIMUM (rpm) | 6 rpm for 3 min. | 4 rpm for 3 min. | 4 rpm for 3 min. |
| SUSTAINED (rpm) | 3 | 2 | 1 |
| **PROJECTILE** | | | |
| TYPE | HE, M760, ILLUM, HEP-T, APICM, CHEM, RAP | HE, WP, ILLUM, SMK, CHEM, NUC, RAP, FASCAM, CPHD, AP/DPICM | HE, WP, ILLUM, SMK, CHEM, NUC, RAP, FASCAM, CPHD, AP/DPICM |
| **FUSES** | | | |
| TYPE | PD, VT, MTSQ, CP, MT, DLY | PD, VT, CP, MT, MTSQ, DLY | PD, VT, CP, MT, MTSQ, DLY |

**LEGEND:**

AP — Armor Piercing
APICM — Antipersonnel Improved Conventional Munitions
CHEM — Chemical
CP — Concrete Piercing
CPHD — Copperhead
DLY — Delay
DPICM — Dual Purpose Improved Conventional Munitions
FASCAM — Family of Scatterable Mines
HE — High Explosive
HEP-T — High-Explosive Plastic Tracer
ILLUM — Illumination

MIN — Minute
MO — Multioption—VT, PD, DLY
MT — Mechanical Time
MTSQ — Mechanical Time Super Quick
NUC — Nuclear
PD — Point Detonating
RAP — Rocket Assisted Projectile
RD — Round
RP — Red Phosphorus
RPM — Rounds per Minute
SMK — Smoke
TIME — Adjustable Time Delay
VT — Variable Time
WP — White Phosphorus

**Field Artillery**

# G

# Body Armor Levels

All armor has a shelf life of approximately five years, but less if it is:
- Exposed to UV sunlight.
- Exposed to excessive heat (over 100 degrees).
- Exposed to dirt.
- Dropped, which will crack the ceramic plates.
- Exposed to general abuse.

## NATIONAL INSTITUTE OF JUSTICE (NIJ) RATINGS FOR BODY ARMOR

### Level IIA (Lower Velocity 9mm, .40 S&W)

This armor protects against 9mm Full-Metal-Jacketed Round-Nose (FMJ RN) bullets with nominal masses of 8 grams (124 grain) impacting at a minimum velocity of 332 m/s (1090 ft/s) or less and .40 S&W caliber Full-Metal-Jacketed (FMJ) bullets with nominal masses of 11.7 grams (180 grains) impacting at a minimum velocity of 312 m/s (1025 ft/s) or less. It also provides protection against Level I threats. Level IIA body armor is well suited for full-time use by police departments, particularly those seeking protection for their officers from lower velocity .40 S&W and 9mm ammunition.

### Level II (Higher Velocity 9mm, .357 Magnum)

This armor protects against .357 Magnum jacketed soft-point bullets with nominal masses of 10.2 grams (158 grain) impacting at a velocity of 425 m/s (1,395 ft/s) or less and against 9mm full-jacketed bullets with nominal velocities of 358 m/s (1,175 ft/s). It also protects against most other factory loads in caliber .357 Magnum and 9mm, as well as the Level I and IIA threats. Level II body armor is heavier and bulkier than either Levels I or IIA. It is worn full time by officers seeking protection against higher-velocity .357 Magnum and 9mm ammunition.

## Level IIIA (High Velocity .44 Magnum, Submachine Gun 9mm)
This armor protects against .44 Magnum, Semi-Jacketed Hollow-Point (SJHP) bullets with nominal masses of 15.55 gram (240 grain) impacting at a velocity of 426 m/s (1,400 ft/s) or less and against 9mm full-metal-jacketed bullets with nominal masses of 8 grams (124 grain) impacting at a velocity of 426 m/s (1,400 ft/s) or less. It also provides protection against most handgun threats, as well as the Level I, IIA, and II threats. Level IIIA body armor provides the highest level of protection currently available from concealable body armor and is generally suitable for routine wear in many situations. However, departments located in hot, humid climates may need to evaluate the use of Level IIIA armor carefully.

## Level III (High-powered Rifle)
This armor, normally of hard or semi-rigid construction, protects against 7.62mm FMJ bullets (US military designation M80) with nominal masses of 9.7 grams (150 grain) impacting at a velocity of 838 m/s (2,750 ft/s) or less. It also provides protection against threats such as .223 Remington (5.56x45mm FMJ), .30 Carbine FMJ, and 12-gauge rifled slug, as well as Level I through IIIA threats. Level III body armor is clearly intended only for tactical situations when the threat warrants such protection, such as barricade confrontations involving sporting rifles.

## Level IV (Armor-piercing Rifle)
This armor protects against .30-06-caliber armor-piercing bullets (US military designation AP-M2) with nominal masses of 10.8 grams (166 grain) impacting at a velocity of 868 m/s (2,850 ft/s) or less. It also provides at least single-hit protection against the Level I through III threats.

Level IV body armor provides the highest level of protection currently available. Because this armor is intended to resist "armor piercing" bullets, it often uses ceramic materials. Such materials are brittle in nature and may provide only single-shot protection since the ceramic tends to break up when struck. As with Level III armor, Level IV armor is clearly intended only for tactical situations when the threat warrants such protection.

# Appendix H

# Acronyms and Abbreviations

| | |
|---|---|
| AA | assembly area; avenue of approach |
| AAR | After Action Report |
| A/C | aircraft |
| ACE | ammo, casualties, and equipment report |
| ACL | allowable cargo load |
| ACP | air space control plan |
| AD | accidental discharge |
| ADA | air defense artillery |
| AFO | advance force operations |
| AG | adjutant general |
| AGL | above ground level |
| AH | attack helicopter |
| ALICE | all-purpose lightweight individual carrying equipment |
| ALT | alternate |
| AMC | at my command |
| ANCD | automated net control device |
| ANGLE T | greater than 90-degree angle to target from guns |
| AO | area of operation |
| AOR | area of responsibility |
| AP | armor-piercing |
| APC | armored personnel carrier |
| APERS | antipersonnel |
| API | armor-piercing incendiary |
| API-T | armor-piercing incendiary-tracer |
| APL | antipersonnel land mine |
| AR | automatic rifle |
| ARF | air reaction force |
| ASL | assistant squad leader; above sea level |
| AT | antitank |
| ATL | assistant team leader |
| ATGM | antitank guided missile |
| AVLB | armored vehicle launch bridge |

| | |
|---|---|
| BANG | explosives |
| BANGER | flash bang grenade |
| BAS | battalion aid station |
| BCS | battery computer system |
| BD | battle drill |
| BDU | battle dress uniform |
| BFV | Bradley fighting vehicle |
| BIFV | Bradley infantry fighting vehicle |
| BINOS | binoculars |
| BIP | blow in place kit |
| BIT | battlefield interrogation team |
| BLUE ON BLUE | friendly units firing on each other |
| BMNT | begin morning nautical twilight |
| BMP | a Soviet infantry fighting vehicle |
| BOS | battlefield operating system |
| BP | battle position; blocking position |
| BPT | be prepared to |
| BRDM | a Soviet vehicle used by reconnaissance units |
| BTR | a Soviet wheeled vehicle |
| $C^2$ | command and control |
| C4 | command, control, communication, and casualties |
| CAS | close air support |
| CASEVAC | casualty evacuation |
| CCD | camouflage, concealment, and decoys |
| CCIR | commander's critical intelligence guidance requirements |
| CCP | casualty collection point |
| CCT | combat control team (combat air controller) |
| CEWI | combat electronics warfare and intelligence |
| CFV | cavalry fighting vehicle |
| CGIS | Coast Guard Investigative Service (US Coast Guard) |
| CH | cargo helicopter |
| CI | counterintelligence |
| CID | Criminal Investigation Division (US Army) |
| CLASS I–X | see pages 412–13 |
| CLU | command launch unit |
| CN | counternarcotics |
| CNR | combat net radio |
| CO | commanding officer |
| COA | course of action |
| COC | chain of command |
| COMSEC | communication security |
| CONT | contingency |
| CP | command post |
| CRYPTO | electric encryption keys used in radios |
| CS | combat support |
| CSS | combat service support |

| | |
|---|---|
| CQB | close quarter battle |
| CT | counterterrorism; common task |
| CTR | close-target reconnaissance |
| CW | continuous wave |
| DANGER CLOSE | minimum safe distance from blast radius |
| DEA | Drug Enforcement Administration |
| DED | detailed equipment decontamination |
| DEMO | demolitions/explosives |
| DET CORD | detonation cord |
| DEW | directed-energy weapon |
| DF | direction finder |
| DH | defense HUMINT (human intelligence) |
| DIA | Defense Intelligence Agency |
| DLIC | detachment left in contact |
| DSS | Diplomatic Security Service |
| DTD | detailed troop decontamination |
| DTG | date-time group |
| DZ | drop zone |
| EA | engagement area; each |
| ECAS | emergency close air support |
| E&E | escape and evade |
| EENT | ending evening nautical twilight |
| EF | enemy forces |
| EKIA | enemy killed in action |
| EMP | electromagnetic pulse |
| EOD | explosive ordnance disposal |
| EPW | enemy prisoner of war |
| ERP | en-route rally point |
| EVAC | evacuation |
| EW | electronic warfare |
| EXFIL | exfiltration |
| EZ | extraction zone |
| FA | field artillery |
| FAC | forward air controller |
| FBI | Federal Bureau of Investigation |
| FDC | fire direction center |
| FDO | fire direction officer |
| FEBA | forward edge of battle area |
| FF | friendly forces |
| FFE | fire for effect |
| FFU | friendly forward unit |
| FH | frequency hopping |
| FIRES | mission-supporting direct or indirect fire |
| FIST | fire support team |
| FLIR | forward-looking infrared |
| FLOT | forward line of own troops |

| FM | frequency modulation; field manual |
|---|---|
| FO | forward observer |
| FOB | forward operating base |
| FPF | final protective fire |
| FPL | final protective line |
| FPS | feet per second |
| FRAG | fragmentation grenade |
| FRAGO | fragmentary order |
| FREQ | frequency for radio |
| FRIES | fast rope infiltration exfiltration system |
| FSO | fire support officer |
| GAF | ground assault force |
| GD | ground distance |
| GL | grenade launcher; grid line |
| G-M | grid-magnetic |
| GOTWA | five-point contingency plan (going, others, time, what, actions on contact) |
| GPS | global positioning system |
| GRG | grid reference graphic |
| GS | general support |
| GTA | graphic training aid |
| HAF | helicopter assault force |
| HALO | high altitude low opening |
| HE | high-explosive |
| HEAT | high-explosive antitank |
| HEDP | high-explosive, dual-purpose |
| HHC | headquarters and headquarters company |
| H HOUR | start time of operation |
| HHQ | higher headquarters |
| HLZ | helicopter landing zone |
| HMMWV | high-mobility, multipurpose wheeled vehicle |
| HQ | headquarters |
| HR | hostage rescue |
| HUMINT | human intelligence |
| IAD | immediate action drill |
| IAW | in accordance with |
| ICM | improved conventional munition |
| ICOM | integrated communications security; type of radio routinely used by enemy |
| ICV | infantry carrier vehicle |
| IED | improvised explosive device |
| IEDK | individual equipment decontamination kit |
| IFAK | individual first aid kit |
| IFF | identify friendly forces |
| ILLUM | illumination/to light an area |
| INCEN | incendiary |

| | |
|---|---|
| INFIL | infiltration |
| IOT | in order to |
| IP | insertion point; initial point (terrain feature that pilot references once in operational area) |
| IPW | interrogate prisoner of war |
| IR | infrared; intelligence requirement |
| IRP | initial rally point |
| ISR | intelligence, surveillance, and reconnaissance |
| ISU | integrated sight unit |
| IVIS | intervehicular information system |
| IVO | in vicinity of |
| KIA | killed in action |
| KIT | personal gear |
| KM | kilometer |
| LASSO | mark a target with an IR laser (circle pattern) |
| LAW | light antitank weapon |
| LAZ | mark a target with an IR laser |
| LBE | load-bearing equipment |
| LBV | load-bearing vest |
| LC | line of contact |
| LCC | last covered and concealed position |
| LCSS | lightweight camouflage screening system |
| LD | line of departure |
| LD/LC | line of departure/line of contact |
| LDR | leader |
| LMG/COAX | light machine gun/coaxial |
| L/O | liaison officer |
| LOA | limit of advance |
| LOC | location |
| LOGPAC | logistics package |
| LOS | line of sight |
| LOW VIS | operations that use civilian attire/vehicles |
| LP | listening post |
| LP/OP | listening post observation post |
| LT | local time; light; lieutenant |
| LTL | laser (to) target line (azimuth) |
| L/U | linkup |
| LZ | landing zone |
| MAW | medium antitank weapon |
| MAX | maximum |
| MBA | main battle area |
| MBITR | multiband inter-team radio |
| MCS | maneuver control system |
| MD | map distance |
| MDL | mission deployment load |
| MDMP | military decision-making process |

| | |
|---|---|
| MEDEVAC | medical evacuation |
| MEL | maximum engagement line |
| METL | mission essential task list |
| METT-TC | mission, enemy, terrain and weather, troops available, time available, and civilian considerations |
| MG | machine gun |
| MGRS | military grid reference system (map) |
| MGS | mobile gun system |
| MIA | missing in action |
| MIL | milradian (6400 to a circle) |
| MILDOT | equals 3.25 MOA |
| MIN | minimum |
| MOA | minute of angle (1 inch @ 100 meters, 2 inch @ 200); memorandum of agreement |
| MOLLE | modular lightweight load-carrying equipment |
| MOPP | mission-oriented protective posture |
| MOUT | military operations in urban terrain |
| MRE | meal, ready to eat |
| MSL | mean sea level (feet) |
| MSR | main service route |
| MSS | mission support site |
| MTC | movement to contact |
| MTOE | modified table of organization and equipment |
| MTP | mission training plan |
| MVMT | movement |
| MWR | morale, welfare, and relaxation |
| N | north |
| N/A | not applicable |
| NAI | named area of interest |
| NATO | North Atlantic Treaty Organization |
| NBC | nuclear, biological, chemical |
| NCIS | Naval Criminal Investigative Service |
| NCO | noncommissioned officer |
| ND | negligent discharge |
| NEW | net explosive weight |
| NIR | near-infrared |
| NLT | not later than |
| NM | nautical miles |
| NOD | night optical device |
| NVD | night vision devices |
| NVG | night vision goggle |
| OAKOC + Water | obstacles (avenues of approach, key terrain, observation/fields of fire, cover and concealment, and water sources) |
| OBJ | objective |

| | |
|---|---|
| OCOKA | observation, cover and concealment, obstacles, key terrain, avenues of approach |
| OGA | other government agency |
| OH | observation helicopter |
| OP | observation post |
| OPCON | operational control |
| OPLAN | operations plan |
| OPORD | operations order |
| OPSEC | operations security |
| OPSKEDS | operation schedule |
| ORP | objective rally point |
| O/S | offset (used in nine-line CAS) |
| OSI | Office of Security Investigations (US Air Force) |
| OT | observer to target (line) azimuth |
| PAC | personnel and administration center |
| PACE | primary, alternate, contingency, and emergency |
| PAX | persons/passenger |
| PB | patrol base |
| PC | precious cargo |
| PCC | pre-combat check |
| PCI | pre-combat inspection |
| PD | point of departure |
| PDF | principal direction of fire |
| PDSS | pre-deployment site survey |
| PIR | priority of intelligence requirement |
| PJ | parajumper (Air Force trauma medic) |
| PL | phase line; platoon leader |
| PLT | platoon |
| PMCS | preventive maintenance checks and services |
| POC | point of contact |
| POSNAV | position navigation |
| PRI | primary |
| PSG | platoon sergeant |
| PSYOP | psychological operations |
| P/U | pickup (point) |
| PUC | person under control |
| PUP | pop-up point |
| PW | prisoner of war |
| PZ | pickup zone |
| QRF | quick reaction force |
| RAP | rocket-assisted projectile |
| RATELO | radiotelephone operator |
| RD | road; round or ammunition |
| RDF | radio direction finder |
| RDS | ammunition |
| RDVU | rendezvous point |

| | |
|---|---|
| RECON | reconnaissance |
| REDCON | readiness condition |
| RF | representative fraction |
| RFA | restrictive fire area |
| RFL | restrictive fire line |
| RGR | roger; Ranger |
| ROCK DRILL | a rehearsal that takes place in a small area |
| ROE | rules of engagement |
| ROI | rules of interaction |
| ROPE | mark a target with an IR laser (circle pattern)—LASSO; fast rope insertion/infiltration |
| RP | rally point; release point |
| RPG | rocket-propelled grenade |
| RPM | revolutions per minute |
| RPV | remotely piloted vehicle |
| RRP | reentry rally point |
| R&S | reconnaissance and security |
| RS | road space |
| RSTA | reconnaissance, surveillance, and target acquisition |
| RT | receiver-transmitter |
| RTO | radiotelephone operator |
| S- | staff |
| S-1 | administration/personnel |
| S-2 | intelligence |
| S-3 | operations |
| S-4 | supply |
| S-5 | public affairs |
| S-6 | communications |
| S/A | staging area |
| SA | situational awareness |
| SALUTE | size, activity, location, uniform, time, and equipment |
| SASO | stability and support operations |
| SAT | satellite |
| SAT COM | satellite communications |
| SAW | squad automatic weapon |
| SBCT | Stryker brigade combat team |
| SBF | support by fire |
| SC | single-channel |
| SCIF | sensitive compartmented information facility |
| SE | spot elevation |
| SEC | section; second |
| SF | Special Forces, US Army |
| SINCGARS | single-channel ground and airborne radio system |
| SITREP | situation report |
| SL | squad leader |
| SM | signal mirror |

| | |
|---|---|
| S/O | sniper observer |
| SOA | Special Operations area |
| SOF | Special Operations Force |
| SOI | signal operation instructions |
| SOP | standard/standing operating procedure |
| SOSR | suppress, obscure, secure, and reduce |
| SOTAC | Special Operations terminal attack controller |
| SP | start point |
| SPARKLE | marking of target with IR laser |
| SPEED BALL | emergency resupply bundle |
| SPLASH fire | support round hitting target area |
| SPOTREP | spot report |
| SQD | squad |
| SR | special reconnaissance |
| SSE | sensitive site exploitation |
| SSN | social security number |
| TAC-P | tactical air command party |
| TACP | tactical command post |
| TACSOP | tactical SOP |
| T&E | traversing and elevation |
| TERP | interpreter |
| TF | task force |
| TIC | troops in contact |
| TL | team leader; time length |
| TLP | troop leading procedures (eight)—receive mission, issue warning order, make tentative plan, initiate movement, reconnoiter, complete plan, issue complete order, and supervise |
| TM | team; technical manual |
| TNG | training |
| TOE | table(s) of organization and equipment |
| TOT | time on target (objective; aircraft play time) |
| TOW | tube-launched, optically tracked, wire-guided |
| TP | training practice |
| TRP | target reference point |
| TSCIF | tactical/temporary sensitive compartmentalized information facility (forward deployed) |
| TP | tactics, techniques, and procedures |
| TT | time to target |
| UAV | unmanned aerial vehicle |
| UCMJ | Uniform Code of Military Justice |
| UH | utility helicopter |
| UO | urban operations |
| UTM | universal transverse Mercator (grid reference system) |
| VA | vertical angle |
| VDO | vehicle drop-off |

| | |
|---|---|
| VI | vehicle interdiction |
| VIC | vicinity |
| VIP | very important person |
| VS-17 | visual signal (bright orange/violet) panel |
| VT | variable time (fuse) |
| W | with |
| WARNORD | warning order |
| WIA | wounded in action |
| WP | white phosphorus |
| WPN | weapon |
| WRP | weapons reference point |
| XO | executive officer |
| ZULU | military operational standard of time |

## DOCTRINAL TERMS

There are three key doctrinal terms used in intents, mission statements, and concepts of the operation: task, purpose, and operations.

**Task.** A task is an action with clearly defined and measurable components and is completed by an individual or group. These specific actions contribute to the successful completion of the mission or other requirement. Tasks should be definable, measurable, and decisive (achieve the stated purpose).

| **ENEMY** | **TERRAIN** | **FRIENDLY** |
|---|---|---|
| Attack by fire | Clear | Breach |
| Block | Occupy | Cover |
| Bypass | Reconnoiter | Disengage |
| Canalize | Retain | Exfiltrate |
| Contain | Secure | Follow and support |
| Defeat | Seize | Guard |
| Delay | | Infiltrate |
| Demonstrate | | Retire |
| Destroy | | Screen |
| Feint | | Support by fire |
| Fix | | Withdraw |
| Interdict | | |
| Isolate | | |
| Neutralize | | |
| Penetrate | | |
| Pursue | | |
| Recon | | |
| Rupture | | |
| Suppress | | |

**Purpose.** The purpose states the desired or intended result of the operation as it applies to the specific enemy or the desired situation. It is the most important component of the Mission paragraph because it encompasses the "why" of the mission.

| ENEMY | TERRAIN | FRIENDLY |
|---|---|---|
| Allow | Divert | Prevent |
| Cause | Enable | Protect |
| Deceive | Envelope | Support |
| Deny | Influence | Surprise |
| | Open | |

**Operations.** Operations are the actions carried out to achieve the objective of a battle or campaign. Operation types can include:

| ENEMY | TERRAIN | FRIENDLY |
|---|---|---|
| Attack | Counterattack | Defend |
| Movement to contact | Retrograde | Mobility |
| Counter-mobility | Survivability | River |
| Crossing | Breakout | Security |
| Exploitation | | |
| Deception | | |

### ENGLISH SYSTEM OF MEASURE

| 12 inches | = | 1 foot |
|---|---|---|
| 36 inches | = | 1 yard |
| 3 feet | = | 1 yard |
| 1,760 yards | = | 1 mile (statute) |
| 5,280 feet | = | 1 mile (statute) |
| 6,080.4 feet | = | 1 mile (nautical) |
| 63,360 inches | = | 1 mile (statute) |
| 72,963 inches | = | 1 mile (nautical) |

## METRIC TO ENGLISH CONVERSIONS

| | | | | |
|---|---|---|---|---|
| 1 millimeter | = | 0.0393 inches | | |
| 10 millimeters | = | centimeter | = | 0.3937 inches |
| 10 centimeters | = | decimeter | = | 3.937 inches |
| 10 decimeters | = | meter | = | 39.37 inches |
| 1 meter | = | 3.28 feet | | |
| 10 meters | = | decameter | = | 32.81 feet |
| 10 decameter | = | hectometer | = | 328.1 feet |
| 10 hectometers | = | kilometer | = | 0.62 mile |
| 1,000 meters | = | kilometer | = | 0.62 mile |
| 10 kilometers | = | 6.2 miles | | |

## CLASSES I–X

Class I        **Subsistence:** food; gratuitous (free) health and comfort items.

Class II       **Clothing:** individual equipment, tentage, organizational tool sets and kits, hand tools, unclassified maps, administrative and housekeeping supplies and equipment.

Class III      **Petroleum, Oil and Lubricants (POL), package, and bulk:** petroleum, fuels, lubricants, hydraulic and insulating oils, preservatives, liquids and gases, bulk chemical products, coolants, deicer and antifreeze compounds, components and additives of petroleum and chemical products, and coal.

Class IV       **Construction Materials:** including installed equipment and all fortification and barrier materials.

Class V        **Ammunition of All Types:** bombs, explosives, mines, fuses, detonators, pyrotechnics, missiles, rockets, propellants, and associated items.

Class VI       **Personal Demand Items:** health and hygiene products, soaps and toothpaste, writing material, snack food, beverages, cigarettes, batteries, alcohol, and cameras—nonmilitary sale items.

Class VII      **Major End Items:** launchers, tanks, mobile machine shops, and vehicles.

Class VIII     **Medical Material:** (equipment and consumables), including repair parts peculiar to medical equipment.

Class VIIIa   **Medical Consumable Supplies:** not including blood and blood products.

Class VIIIb   **Blood and Blood Components:** whole blood, platelets, plasma, packed red cells, etc.

Class IX            **Repair Parts and Components:** kits, assemblies, and sub-assemblies (repairable or nonrepairable) required for maintenance support of all equipment.

Class X             **Material to Support Nonmilitary Programs:** such as agriculture and economic development (not included in classes I–IX).

Miscellaneous   Water, salvage, and captured material.

# Appendix I

# References

## FIELD MANUALS

| | |
|---|---|
| ATP 3-09.30 | Techniques for Observed Fire, 2 August 2013 |
| ATP 6-02.72 | TAC Radios, Multi-Service Tactics, Techniques, and Procedures For Tactical Radios, 5 January 2013 |
| ATTP 3-21.71 | Mechanized Infantry Platoon and Squad (Bradley), 9 November 2010 |
| FM 3-0 | Operations, 27 February 2008 |
| FM 3-06 | Urban Operations, 26 October 2006 |
| FM 3-7 | NBC Field Handbook, 29 September 1994 |
| FM 3-21.71(FM 7-7J) | Mechanized Infantry Platoon and Squad (Bradley), 20 August 2002 |
| FM 3-21.8 (FM 7-8) Draft | The Infantry Rifle Platoon and Squad, 28 March 2007 |
| FM 3-22.68 | Crew-Served Machine Guns, 5.56mm and 7.62mm; 21 July 2006 |
| FM 3-75 | Ranger Operations, 23 May 2012 |
| FM 3-90 | Tactics, 31 August 2012 |
| FM 3-90.1 (FM 71-1) | Tank and Mechanized Infantry Company Team, December 2002 |
| FM 3-100 | NBC Operations, May 1996 |
| FM 4-25.11 (FM 21-11) | First Aid, 23 December 2002 |
| FM 6-30 | Tactics, Techniques, and Procedures for Observed Fire, 16 July 1991 |
| FM 7-10 | The Infantry Rifle Company, 27 July 2006 |
| FM 7-20 | The Infantry Battalion, 13 December 2006 |
| FM 20-3 | Camouflage, Concealment, and Decoys, 1 November 2010 |
| FM 20-32 | Mine, Countermine Operations, 27 March 2007 |
| FM 21-18 | Foot Marches, 1 June 1990 |
| FM 21-75 | The Warrior Ethos and Soldier Combat Skills, January 2008 |
| FM 22-100/ADP 6-22 | Army Leadership, August 2012 |

**414**

| | |
|---|---|
| FM 101-5-1 | Operational Terms and Graphics, 21 September 2004 |
| GTA 05-08-001 | Survivability Positions, 1 August 1993 |
| GTA 07-06-001 | Fighting Position Construction: Infantry Leader's Reference Card, 1 June 1992 |
| STP 7-11B1-SM-TG | Soldier's Manual and Trainer's Guide, MOS 11B, Infantry, Skill Level 1, June 2004 |
| STP 7-11B24-SM-TG | Soldier's Manual and Trainer's Guide, MOS 11B, Infantry, Skills Level 2, 3, and 4, June 2004 |
| STP 7-11C14-SM-TG | Soldier's Manual and Trainer's Guide, MOS 11C, Indirect Fire Infantryman, Skill Levels 1, 2, 3, and 4, June 2004 |
| STP 21-1-SMCT | Soldier's Manual of Common Tasks, Warrior Skills Level 1, April 2014 |
| STP 21-24-SMCT | Soldier's Manual of Common Tasks, Skill Level 1, August 2003 |
| STP 21-24-SMCT | Soldier's Manual of Common Tasks, Warrior Leader, Skill Level 2, 3, and 4, September 2008 |
| TC 3-21.8 | Infantry Rifle and Mechanized Platoon Collective Task Publication, 19 August 2013 |
| TC 3-21.10 | Infantry Rifle Company Collective Task Publication, 28 June 2012 |
| TM 11-5820-890-10-8 | SINCGARS Ground Combat Net Radio (ICOM), February 1995 |

## HANDBOOKS

Call Handbook No. 03-15    The Radio Telephone Operator (RTO) Handbook, June 2003

*Practical Guide to the Operational Use of the AK-47/AKM/AK74* by Erik Lawrence

*Practical Guide to the Operational Use of the DShK/DShKM* by Erik Lawrence

*Practical Guide to the Operational Use of the PK/PKM* by Erik Lawrence

*Practical Guide to the Operational Use of the RPG-7* by Erik Lawrence

*Practical Guide to the Operational Use of the SVD Dragunov* by Erik Lawrence

*Small Unit Leaders Operational Planning Guide* by Jeff Kirkham and Erik Lawrence

# Index

*Page numbers in italics indicate illustrations, drawings, etc.*

# About the Author

Jeff Kirkham is a master sergeant in the US Army Special Forces. He owns and operates Praetorian Innovations LLC, providing paramilitary training, evaluation, operational planning, and mission oversight in hostile combat environments. Since 2003, he has spent more than 50 months in Iraq and Afghanistan training, advising, and supporting indigenous elite commando units. He is also president of TwistRate, a web-based company dedicated to helping veteran entrepreneurs or "veteranpreneurs" get their inventions prototyped, funded, and sold. He is the author of the *Small Unit Leaders Operational Planning Guide* (Blackheart International, 2012).

# STACKPOLE BOOKS

## Military Professional Reference Library

*Air Force Officer's Guide*

*Airman's Guide*

*Army Dictionary and Desk Reference*

*Army Medical Officer's Guide*

*Army Officer's Guide*

*Career Progression Guide for Soldiers*

*Combat Leader's Field Guide*

*Combat Service Support Guide*

*Enlisted Soldier's Guide*

*Guide to Effective Military Writing*

*Guide to Personal Financial Planning for the Armed Forces*

*Job Search: Marketing Your Military Experience*

*NCO Guide*

*Servicemember's Guide to a College Degree*

*Servicemember's Legal Guide*

*Soldier's Study Guide*

*Today's Military Wife*

*Veteran's Guide to Benefits*